THE ROB

D1757360

ENGLISH ARCHITECTURE
PUBLIC AND PRIVATE

St Paul's Cathedral, Wren's Great Model, interior view looking west.

ENGLISH ARCHITECTURE
PUBLIC AND PRIVATE

———————

ESSAYS FOR KERRY DOWNES

EDITED BY
JOHN BOLD AND EDWARD CHANEY

THE HAMBLEDON PRESS
LONDON   AND   RIO GRANDE

Published by the Hambledon Press 1993

102 Gloucester Avenue, London NW1 8HX (U.K.)

P.O. Box 162, Rio Grande, Ohio 45674 (U.S.A.)

ISBN 1 85285 095 7

A description of this book is available from
the British Library and from the Library of Congress

This book has been published with the assistance
of a grant from the Marc Fitch Fund

Typeset by York House Typographic Ltd
Printed on acid-free paper and bound in Great
Britain by Cambridge University Press

Contents

Preface

Many debts have been incurred in the preparation of this volume. We are especially grateful to all those who have given generously of their time in order to contribute. It is with sorrow that we record our particular thanks to two contributors who died in 1992. Professor Peter Murray and Sir John Summerson both made outstanding contributions to the analysis and understanding of European architecture, placing all the other contributors to this volume in their debt. They brought to architectural history a breadth of vision and range of reference which have set standards for others to follow. We were very grateful to them for answering so promptly and positively this further call on their time in difficult circumstances; we only regret that they were not able to see their essays in print.

The contributions of individuals and institutions are cited in the notes to the essays and in the list of acknowledgements: we thank them all, with particular thanks to the photographic staff of the Royal Commission on the Historical Monuments of England. We also wish to thank Margaret Downes for her discreet encouragement and Professor Eric Fernie for recommending an approach to our publisher. Martin Sheppard, of the Hambledon Press, has shouldered the responsibility of producing yet another volume of essays with very little persuasion and has been unfailingly supportive throughout its preparation. Lastly, we are grateful to the Marc Fitch Fund for providing a grant to set against the costs of the illustrations.

Kerry Downes

Photo: Grahame Mellanby

Introduction

It is a great pleasure to celebrate and pay tribute to the achievement of a scholar and teacher who, after more than thirty years of lucid exposition, remains the preeminent authority on the architecture of the English Baroque. Kerry Downes has not only described and analysed the achievements of Hawksmoor, Vanbrugh and Wren in an apparently inexhaustible flow of publications (which belies the recreational 'procrastination' he claims in *Who's Who*), he has re-defined the way in which others see them. This is a contribution to architectural history of a very high order.

Trained at the Courtauld Institute of Art, Kerry was for eight years Librarian at the Barber Institute of Fine Arts, University of Birmingham, before moving to the University of Reading in 1966. For twenty-five years as Lecturer, Reader and finally Professor of History of Art, he has given generously of his time and knowledge to a succession of students who came to value the judiciousness of his silences as well as the acuity of his comments; the significance of both often dawned only hours after the seminar's end. That same ability to illuminate, quietly and undemonstratively, has distinguished Kerry's twelve years as a Commissioner with the Royal Commission on the Historical Monuments of England, latterly as its senior architectural spokesman.

In the twenty years which elapsed between the first and second editions of Kerry's first major monograph, on the life and work of Nicholas Hawksmoor, public perceptions changed to a degree which the author can scarcely have predicted. This overdue change was due in large measure to his success in setting the record straight so that, to paraphrase his own words, the new taste could be an informed one. All modern scholars must take his pioneering work and his subsequent reconsiderations, listed in our appended bibliography, as their starting point, not only on Hawksmoor but also on Sir Christopher Wren and Sir John Vanbrugh. His presentations, distinguished by sedulous scholarship, clarity of expression and a passion for the built works, have changed fundamentally the way in which these men, the preeminent English architects of the late seventeenth and early eighteenth centuries, are viewed. If we believe that we now understand the building histories of such major monuments as St Paul's Cathedral, Castle Howard and Blenheim Palace, it is because Kerry

Downes has described them for us. He has charted a path, notoriously difficult to establish, which marries the evidence of documents and drawings with the evidence on the ground. Those who have been privileged to accompany Kerry on such surreal expeditions as crawling around the outside of Hawksmoor's Easton Neston in the snow in order to ascertain whether or not it has been refaced, will testify to the undeviating search for observable evidence which has characterised his approach to architectural history. Those who visited his masterly exhibitions on Hawksmoor and Wren at the Whitechapel Art Gallery in 1977 and 1982, or that on St Paul's at the Royal Academy in 1991, will acknowledge that serious scholarship, the expansion of visual awareness and the thrill of discovery are capable of going hand in hand.

Kerry Downes has dealt consistently with the great masters. It is characteristic that he, like Sir John Summerson, should have campaigned for Architecture, represented by Mies van der Rohe, at the notorious Mansion House enquiry. It is characteristic also that in turning from architecture to painting he should have chosen to write authoritatively not on lesser men but on one of the greatest of northern painters, Rubens, whose harmonisation of history, intellect, sensuality and human understanding offers an encapsulation of the baroque style which the author has sought always, both in books and lecture theatres, to define and illuminate.

This collection of essays, by contemporaries, colleagues and former students is presented, with thanks, as a tribute, but also in the hope and expectation that it will encourage its dedicatee to continue his long and fruitful association with the art and architecture of the seventeenth and eighteenth centuries and perhaps beyond.

Some of these essays fall outside the range of Kerry's published work, but not outside his sphere of interests. They range from the late middle ages to the twentieth century; from the towers and spires of Northamptonshire and the European double staircases and classical porticoes which inspired Inigo Jones; through the work of the little-known eighteenth-century architect William Baker and the nineteenth-century church of Avon Dassett in Warwickshire, by Thomas Meyer, to the uncompromisingly modernist work of Wells Coates, Maxwell Fry and Berthold Lubetkin in the 1930s, discussed here in a personal reminiscence.

Taken together, they demonstrate a wide range of approaches to the English architecture of both the public and private realms, from the detailed description of the City of London house of the Member of Parliament John Pollexfen, and the related discussion of the ways in which architects of the seventeenth and eighteenth centuries fulfilled the need of owners for a separation of public and private spaces, to the analysis of administrative chaos in the Victorian metropolis, where the once creative web of authorities eventually proved incapable of working together for the public good.

Many of the essays break new ground. Here for the first time is a full discussion of the extensive architectural patronage of the 10th Earl of Northumberland, with a detailed description of the work carried out at Northumberland House, Petworth and Syon. The patronage of the Earl of Clarendon is also presented, with the publication of letters from his London steward to the steward of his Oxfordshire estates, concerning the rebuilding of Cornbury by Hugh May. Other essays offer new perspectives on buildings and landscapes with which we might have considered ourselves familiar. These include the first detailed survey of Vanbrugh's partially flooded Grand Bridge at Blenheim, as well as new documents which chronicle the role of Charles Bridgeman in reshaping the gardens of, among others, Lumley Castle, Wroxall Manor and Wimpole.

Only one contribution, on a portrait of Stephen Duck, the 'thresher poet' who in a fit of dejection drowned himself in a Reading trout stream, is not directly concerned with architecture. Sir James Thornhill, however, who painted this portrait, was not only the King's Sergeant Painter and the leading English decorative artist of the day, but also a candidate for the Surveyorship of the King's Works, fully capable of designing buildings and thus able, like Jones, Wren and Vanbrugh before him, to demonstrate mastery in more than one profession.

The essays concentrate on the study of the period to which Kerry Downes has contributed so much, discussing not only the buildings, but also the history of the sources and ideas which informed them. For example, the significance for architecture of writers on mathematics, prior to the great age of pattern books, is here reviewed, a matter of particular concern to all who seek to understand the mind and art of Wren, the mathematician who turned to architecture. Three of the essays consider aspects of Wren's work and his legacy: his use of the architectural model, the eighteenth-century derivatives of St Paul's Cathedral and the wartime representations by the great perspectivist Cyril Farey of Wren's masterpiece, when it stood as a symbol of continuity and resistance during the Blitz. Others offer new evidence for attributions to Hawksmoor and Vanbrugh: the barracks at Berwick, the first Ordnance building for which documentary evidence can be advanced to support such an attribution, complemented by a more general study of the building practice of the Board of Ordnance; Sir William Strickland's hunting lodge at Malton, which has features in common with the neighbouring Castle Howard, and a church in Berkshire, once attributed to a ubiquitous and improbably long-lived Inigo Jones.

Jones himself, in company with the Earl and Countess of Arundel, is documented on his formative journey to Naples in 1614, which provided him with *exempla*, hitherto unregarded, for his subsequent architectural practice. The concentration on the Palladian influence in seventeenth- and eighteenth-century England has obscured the debt which architectural travellers owed to others. The sustained interest in the architecture of Sanmicheli, discussed here, was manifested particularly during the era of mid eighteenth-century British neo-classicism when the sculptural and planar qualities of the Pellegrini Chapel were found to provide a more appropriate model than the work of Palladio. The British enthusiasm for Sanmicheli was shared by Sir John Soane who illustrated a number of his buildings in his Royal Academy lectures. The one example of Soane's built work which is discussed in this volume, however, owes rather more to Palladio. This, appropriately for the recipient of these essays, is the elegant yet little known Simeon Monument in the Market Place in Reading, one of the architect's two works in the town closest to his birthplace.

Monuments, as statements, embody both the public and private. By looking at the architecture of the past and seeking to learn from it, as the contributors to this volume have done, we may find profit in considering how the needs of the public and private domains within society may inform an architecture for our times. Such an architecture, balanced, intelligent and humane, building on the best examples from the past, would respect the inherent tension between polarities and seek to achieve harmony rather than to perpetuate opposition.

If Kerry Downes were to retire from research and writing as well as from teaching and administration, he would have done enough already to show how we might benefit from investigating, analysing and understanding historic architecture, and how much that understanding might contribute to our perception of contemporary needs and solutions. It is our hope, however, in presenting this volume, that he will continue to apply the 'strong reason and good fancy', learned from Nicholas Hawksmoor, to many more books and essays of his own.

John Bold   Edward Chaney
London   Oxford

December 1992

Kerry Downes: A Bibliography

BOOKS AND EXHIBITION CATALOGUES

Hawksmoor (A. Zwemmer Ltd., London, 1959; 2nd edition 1979), 298 pp., 46 figs, 165 pls.

Hawksmoor [with J.H.V. Davies], (Arts Council of Great Britain, London, 1962), 40 pp., 8 pls.

English Baroque Architecture (A. Zwemmer Ltd., London, 1966), 136 pp., 68 figs, 578 pls.

Hawksmoor (Thames and Hudson, London, 1969; reprinted 1987), 216 pp., 185 pls.

Christopher Wren (Allen Lanc The Penguin Press, London, 1971), 192 pp., 101 pls.

Vanbrugh (A. Zwemmer Ltd., London, 1977), 292 pp., 20 figs, 160 pls.

Hawksmoor (Whitechapel Art Gallery, London, 1977), 32 pp., 6 pls.

The Georgian Cities of Britain (Phaidon, Oxford, 1979), 64 pp., 45 pls.

Rubens (Jupiter Books, London, 1980), 170pp., 9 figs, 136 pls.

Sir Christopher Wren (Whitechapel Art Gallery, Trefoil Books, London, 1982), 96 pp., 101 pls.

The Architecture of Wren (Granada Publishing, London, 1982; 2nd edition Redhedge, 1988), 140 pp., 21 figs, 169 pls.

Sir John Vanbrugh: A Biography (Sidgwick and Jackson, London, 1987), 560 pp., 22 figs, 40 pls.

Sir Christopher Wren: The Design of St Paul's Cathedral (Trefoil Publications Ltd., London, 1988), 192 pp., 265 pls.

Sir Christopher Wren and the Making of St Paul's [with R. Hyde] (Royal Academy of Arts, London, 1991), 56 pp., 18 pls.

ARTICLES, CONTRIBUTIONS TO ENCYCLOPAEDIAS OF ARCHITECTURE
AND TO VOLUMES ON ARCHITECTURAL HISTORY

'Hawksmoor's Sale Catalogue', *Burlington Magazine*, xcv (1953), pp. 332-35.

'Fuller's "Last Judgement"', *Burlington Magazine*, cii (1960), pp. 451-52.

'A Church with an Obelisk Steeple', *Country Life*, cxxviii (1960), p. 479.

'Two Hawksmoor Drawings', *Burlington Magazine*, ciii (1961), pp. 279-80.

'The Kings Weston Book of Drawings', *Architectural History*, x (1967), pp. 9-88.

'John Evelyn and Architecture: A First Enquiry', in *Concerning Architecture*, ed. J. Summerson (London, 1968), pp. 28-39.

'Three Drawings for Ingestre Hall', in *The Country Seat*, ed. H.M. Colvin and J. Harris (London, 1970), pp. 55-57.

'Wren and Whitehall in 1664', *Burlington Magazine*, cxiii (1971), pp. 89-92.

'The Regata in Venice', in *Tamesis*, ed. E. Chaney (Reading, 1973).

'Whitehall Palace', in *The History of the King's Works*, v, *1660-1782*, ed. H.M. Colvin (London, 1976), pp. 263-304.

'Vanbrugh and the British Style', *The Listener*, xcv (1976), pp. 407-09.

'The Little Colony on Greenwich Hill: Vanbrugh's Field at Blackheath', *Country Life*, clix (1976), pp. 1406-8.

'Vanbrugh, Sir John', in *Who's Who in Architecture*, ed. J.M. Richards (London, 1977).

'England' and 'Holland', in *Baroque and Rococo Architecture and Decoration*, ed. A. Blunt (London, 1978; reissued London, 1982), pp. 148-63.

'Chiswick Villa', *Architectural Review*, clxiv (1978), pp. 225-36.

'The Whitehall Ceiling' [letter], *Burlington Magazine*, cxx (1978), p. 167

'The Evolution of Hawksmoor's Design', in 'Hawksmoor's Christ Church Spitalfields', *Architectural Design*, xlix, 7 (1979), p. 5.

'Jones and Wren at St Paul's' [letter], *Burlington Magazine*, cxxiii (1981), pp. 35-36.

'Hawksmoor, Nicholas', 'Vanbrugh, John' and 'Wren, Christopher', in *Macmillan Encyclopaedia of Architects*, ed. A.K. Placzek (New York, 1982).

'Vanbrugh's Heslington Lady', *Burlington Magazine*, cxxiv (1982), pp. 153-55.

'The Publication of Shaftesbury's "Letter Concerning Design"', *Architectural History*, xxvii (*Design and Practice in British Architecture*) (1984), pp. 519-23.

Introduction to *The Architectural Outsiders*, ed. R. Brown (London, 1985), pp. ix-x.

'Hawksmoor's House at Easton Neston', *Architectural History*, xxx (1987), pp. 50-76.

SELECTED BOOK AND EXHIBITION REVIEWS

'The Amsterdam Town Hall', review of K. Fremantle, *The Baroque Town Hall of Amsterdam*, *Burlington Magazine*, ciii (1961), pp. 437-38.

L. Hall Fowler and E. Baer, *The Fowler Architectural Collection of the Johns Hopkins University*, *Burlington Magazine*, cv (1963), p. 515.

J. Lees-Milne, *Earls of Creation*, *Burlington Magazine*, cvii (1965), pp. 583-84.

'Rubens's "Peace and War" at the National Gallery', review of *Painting in Focus* exhibition, *Burlington Magazine*, cxxi (1979), pp. 397-98.

A. Blunt, *Borromini*, *Burlington Magazine*, cxxi (1979), p. 803.

A. Blunt, *Guide to Baroque Rome*, *Burlington Magazine*, cxxv (1983), p. 40.

W. Kuyper, *Dutch Classicist Architecture*, *Burlington Magazine*, cxxv (1983), pp. 367-68.

S. Tobriner, *The Genesis of Noto: An Eighteenth-Century Sicilian City*, *Burlington Magazine*, cxxvi (1984), pp. 360-61.

'Buildings and How to Look at Them', reviews of architectural exhibitions, *Times Educational Supplement* (11 January 1985), p. 22.

M. Girouard, *Robert Smythson and the Elizabethan Country House*, *Burlington Magazine*, cxxvii (1985), pp. 98-99.

T. Friedman, *James Gibbs*, *Burlington Magazine*, cxxvii (1985), p. 311.

A. Rowan, *Designs for Castles and Country Villas by Robert and James Adam*; and J. and A. Rykwert, *The Brothers Adam*, *Times Literary Supplement* (13 December 1985).

'Arundel's Quartercentenary: A Book and an Exhibition', reviews of D. Howarth, *Lord Arundel and his Circle* and *Thomas Howard, Earl of Arundel: Patronage and Collecting in the Seventeenth Century*, introduction by D. Howarth, Ashmolean Museum Exhibition 1985, *Burlington Magazine*, cxxviii (1986), pp. 161-62.

E. McParland, *James Gandon, Vitruvius Hibernicus*, *Burlington Magazine*, cxxviii (1986), pp. 224-25

J. Harris, *The Design of the English Country House, 1620-1920*, Burlington Magazine, cxxviii (1986), p 441

J. Dixon Hunt, *Garden and Grove: The Italian Renaissance Garden in the English Imagination 1600-1700*, Burlington Magazine, cxxx (1988), pp. 634-35.

H.A. Meek, *Guarino Guarini and his Architecture*, Architectural Review, clxxxiv (1988), p. 12.

J. Harris and G. Higgott, *Inigo Jones: Complete Architectural Drawings*, Times Literary Supplement, (7-13 July 1989).

C. Saumarez Smith, *The Building of Castle Howard*, Times Literary Supplement (30 March-5 April 1990).

H.M. Colvin, *The Canterbury Quadrangle, St John's College, Oxford*; H.M. Colvin and J.S.G. Simmons, *All Souls: An Oxford College and its Buildings*, Society of Architectural Historians *Newsletter*, xlii (1990).

List of Illustrations

Acknowledgements

Original material is reproduced by courtesy of the following:

The British Architectural Library, RIBA 21, 23, 27-31, 41, 43, 46; the Bodleian Library 60, 64-65; the British Library 85-86, 88, 103c; the Trustees of the British Museum 42, 112; the Evelyn Trustees 34; Gloucestershire County Record Office (by courtesy of the owner) 98; the Guildhall Library 130-31; Mr J. Henderson 75-77; Lord Montagu 20; the National Galleries of Scotland 111; the Trustees of the National Maritime Museum 61-62; the National Trust 99, 102, 103a-b, 110; the Duke of Northumberland 32; the Earl of Pembroke and the Wilton House Trustees 87; the Public Record Office 84; the Earl of Scarbrough 100-1; the Trustees of Sir John Soane's Museum 24-25, 44-45, 48, 113; the Dean and Chapter of St Paul's Cathedral frontispiece, 53, 58-59; the Victoria and Albert Museum 80; the Warburg Institute 15; Warwickshire County Record Office 104-5; Wiltshire County Record Office 87; the Provost and Fellows of Worcester College, Oxford 16-19.

Photographs are reproduced by kind permission of the following:

The British Architectural Library, RIBA 28-29, 41, 43, 46; the Conway Library, Courtauld Institute of Art frontispiece, 6-7, 21, 23-25, 27, 30-31, 35, 53, 58-59, 61-62, 88; English Heritage 81; the Controller of Her Majesty's Stationery Office 84; Liverpool City Libraries Archives 52; the Metropolitan Museum of Art, New York 54-56; Dr T. Mowl 76; Stephen Randall Photography 84-86; the Royal Commission on the Historical Monuments of England 8-14, 32-33, 75, 77, 87, 89, 91-92, 94, 115, 117-22; the Warburg Institute 26; the Witt Library, Courtauld Institute of Art 106, 109-10; the University of York (Centre for the Conservation of Historic Parks and Gardens) 100-1.

Abbreviations

BAL	British Architectural Library
BL	British Library
HMC	Historical Manuscripts Commission
OS	Ordnance Survey
PRO	Public Record Office
RCHME	Royal Commission on the Historical Monuments of England
RIBA	Royal Institute of British Architects
VCH	The Victoria County History

1

The Role and Function of the Interior Double Staircase

MARY WHITELEY

Double staircases hold a special fascination; the majority of authors writing on the interior double staircase of the sixteenth century onwards make the different types of stair their main line of study. However no staircase can be judged without considering its relationship to the rest of its building and the role and function for which it was designed.

Interior double staircases are first found as an established feature in Europe as early as the fourteenth century. An example survives in Staffordshire at St Editha church in Tamworth (Fig. 1).[1] In the south-west turret of the west tower, which was added to the church in the fifteenth century, two interlocking spiral staircases climb round a communal newel. The two flights are quite independent having separate entrances and no intercommunication before arriving at the top of the tower. The staircase which is entered from the interior of the church served the rooms with an ecclesiastical role, the ringing chamber, the belfry and the two eastern turrets. The other staircase, approached from the outside, gives access to the tower terrace and at the first level to the room in the north-west turret, via a corridor that bypasses the ringing chamber. The role of the second staircase is not clear, but its function was obviously intended to provide a circulation that was separate from the church.

Many staircases, similar both in type and function to the double newel spiral at Tamworth, were built in western Europe during the late medieval period. The majority that survive or are recorded were in religious establishments: in the Collégiale Saint-Pierre at La Romieu, Gascony (1313-18),[2] in the Collège des Bernardins, Paris (begun 1338);[3] in St Vitus Cathedral, Prague (from

---

* This study lies on the edge of the guidelines for this commemorative book as the majority of examples are on the other side of the Channel; it does, however, cover the subject for which Kerry Downes knows me best – *l'escalier*.

1 C.F. Palmer, *History and Antiquites of the Collegiate Church of Tamworth* (Tamworth and London, 1871), pp. 64-65; H.C. Mitchell, *Tamworth Parish Church* (Welwyn, 1935), pp. 32-33; R. Sherlock, 'St Editha's Church, Tam-

worth', *Archaeological Journal*, cxx (1963), pp. 295-96.

2 Marcel Durliat, 'La Romieu', *Congrès archéologique de France*, cxxviii (1970), pp. 181-93.

3 A. Lenoir, *Statisque monumentale de Paris*, ii (1867), pp. 224-27; H. Sauval, *Histoire et recherches de antiquités de la ville de Paris* (1724; facsimile, Farnborough 1969), i, pp. 435-36; P. Hurtaut and Magny, *Dictionnaire historique de la ville de Paris et ses environs* (Paris, 1779), i, p. 588.

c. 1350);[4] in Bavarian churches at Weissenburg, Wertheim am Main and Regensburg;[5] at All Saints Church, Pontefract (fifteenth century);[6] and at the Prior's Lodge at Wenlock Priory (*c.* 1500).[7] This type of staircase was also used for military and residential architecture: at the château of Saumur (fourteenth century);[8] in the tour Saint-Nicolas at La Rochelle (after 1372);[9] and at the Grand Châtelet, Paris (second half of the fourteenth century).

In five of the staircases it is possible to identify the individual role and function of the separated flights. At Saumur, one flight which originally started on the ground floor provided the access for the guards climbing up to the look-out tower on the roof, the other a much shorter flight beginning only at the first floor linked the two levels of an important lodging. A similar division between the military and residential requirements occurs in the double spiral at the tour Saint-Nicolas, La Rochelle. At the Collège des Bernardins the two flights kept the circulations of the church and the college distinct, one starting in the sacristy served the upper levels of the church, the other provided the night stairs linking the dormitory to the choir. Communication between the two flights could be provided, as occurred in the church at La Romieu where a small corridor curves round the outside of the staircage which enabled the cardinal approaching from his palace to pass from one flight to the other.

The use of double spiral staircases was widespread, especially it seems in religious establishments, for this type is also found in churches in eastern Europe,[10] and in minarets in the Middle East.[11] All the examples of this stairtype share common features, they are small in size and minor in role, but their great advantage was their practicality in providing two separate circulations within a minimum of space.

Double staircases providing the same function were still being built at the beginning of the sixteenth century. Leonardo da Vinci advocates their use in military architecture as a means of preventing the intermingling of different categories of people: 'double stairs, one for the castellan, another one for the mercenaries' (Fig. 2).[12] Leonardo illustrates two types with this function; the doubled newel spiral and the X-type double staircase that consisted of crossed

4 M. Radová-Štiková, 'Steinerne Treppen des 13. bis 16. Jahrhunderts in der Tschechoslowakei', *Scalalogia*, ii (1986), p. 66.
5 Articles in *Scalalogia*, i (1985).
6 N. Pevsner and E. Radcliffe, *The Buildings of England: Yorkshire, The West Riding* (Harmondsworth, 1967), p. 393.
7 N. Pevsner, *The Buildings of England: Shropshire* (Harmondsworth, 1958), pp. 207-11.
8 H. Landais, 'Le château de Saumur', *Congrès archéologique de France*, cxxii (1964), pp. 523-58.
9 J. Mesqui, 'Une double révolution à La Rochelle: la tour Saint-Nicolas', *Bulletin monumental*, cxlviii (1990), pp. 155-90.

10 M. Radová-Štiková, ('Steinerne Treppen ...', p. 66) names double spirals in churches at Sázava, at Milíčin, and at Kutná Hora.
11 The earliest minaret in Afghanistan dates from the second half of the twelfth century, J. Moline, 'The Minaret of Ğām', *Kunst des Orients*, ix (1973/1974), pp. 131-48; Emir Taylan's Mosque in Tripoli, Lebanon (13th-14th century); Manar Khwadjeh 'Alam (14th-15th century), M. Smith, 'The Manars of Isfahan', *Athar-e Iran* (1936), p. 353.
12 C. Pedretti, *A Chronology of Leonardo da Vinci's Architectural Studies after 1500* (Geneva, 1962), p. 36ff; C. Pedretti, *Leonardo Architect* (London, 1986).

straight flights. The survival of literally dozens of this second type in Venice allows their different functions to be identified.[13] In the palaces one flight was used as the main staircase, the other as the service stairs. In the housing blocks built by the confraternities they served two adjoining apartments; the way they were arranged provided each apartment with its own separate entrance from the street, allowing each to have its principal room(s) on an upper floor, one on the first, the other on the second. Their popularity in Venice was no doubt due to their practicality in a city where space was so restricted and privacy a much valued commodity. They differed from their medieval counterparts in being the principal staircase of the house.

Different types of double staircase are found in the architectural sketches made by Leonardo, and by Francesco di Giorgio and the pseudo-Bramantino.[14] One particular design which can be interpreted as consisting of two straight flights divided by a passage, with a returning central flight continuing up (Fig. 3), would have provided alternative options for arriving at the same destination on the first floor. This type of double staircase satisfied the Renaissance desire for symmetry. Important single-flight staircases with a ceremonial role had been built from the fourteenth century,[15] but the idea of introducing symmetrical stairs was significant for the development of the staircase as a monumental feature during the later sixteenth century.

Early examples of large double staircases were built in a group of royal houses in France during the first half of the sixteenth century. They include the famous double spiral at Chambord (late 1520s), and the doubled straight flights at Challuau (1541) and at La Muette (begun 1542) (Fig. 4).[16] All three have a central space or passage between their flights which substantially increased the size of their staircage. At La Muette a conscious intention to make the staircase a more important feature is confirmed in the *devis* for masonry; the staircase was to be made equal in size to the chapel and both flights were to be used for access to the three floors.[17] These three impressive staircases were not, as might be expected, in important residential palaces but in isolated buildings in parks. A tradition, said to have dated from the time of François I

13 G. Gianighian and P. Pavanini, *Dietro i palazzi: tre secoli di architettura minore a Venezia, 1492-1803* (Venice, 1984), pp. 63f, exhibition held at Scuola Grande di San Giovanni Evangelista; M. Whiteley, review of 1984 exhibition, *Bulletin of the Society for Renaissance Studies* (1985), pp. 59-62.

14 J. Guillaume, 'Léonard et l'architecture', *Léonard de Vinci, ingénieur et architecte* (Montreal, 1987), pp. 261-66, exhibition held at Musée des Beaux Arts.

15 M. Whiteley, '*La grande Vis*: Its Development in France from the Mid Fourteenth to the Mid Fifteenth centuries', *L'escalier dans l'archi-*

tecture de la renaissance, proceedings of a conference held at Tours in 1979 (Paris, 1985), pp. 15-20; M. Whiteley, 'Deux escaliers royaux du XIVe siècle; les "grands degrez" du palais de la Cité et la "grande viz" du Louvre', *Bulletin monumental*, cxlvii (1989), pp. 142-54.

16 J. Guillaume, 'Escalier dans l'architecture française de la première moitié du XVIe siècle', *L'escalier dans l'architecture de la Renaissance* (Paris, 1985), p. 38.

17 L. de Laborde, *Comptes des bâtiments du roy (1528-1571)* (Paris, 1877), i, p. 219.

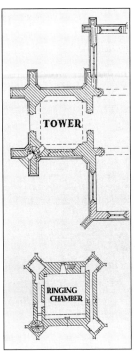

Fig 1. St Editha, Tamworth, plans of west side of church and of first level of west tower.

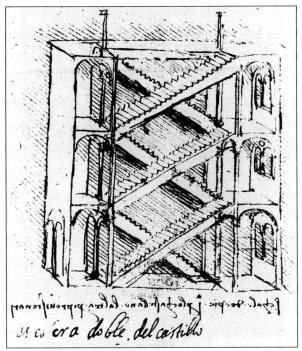

Fig 2. Leonardo da Vinci, design of double 'X' staircase, inscribed 'Scale doppie; una per lo castellano, l'altra per i provisionati'. (*Bibliothèque Nationale, Paris, Codex B 68 V*)

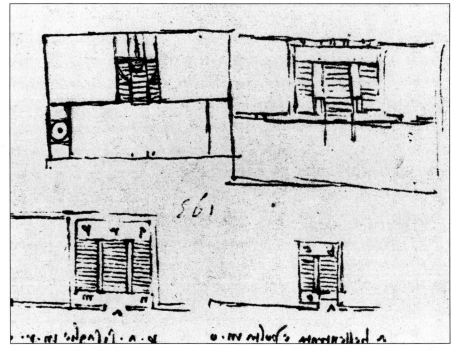

Fig. 3 Leonardo da Vinci, designs of triple-flight staircases. (*Biblioteca Ambrosiana, Milan, Codex Atlanticus 220 v-b*)

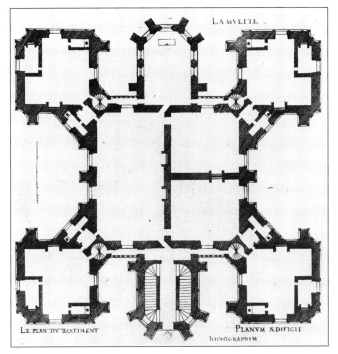

Fig. 4 La Muette, plan after Du Cerceau engraving.

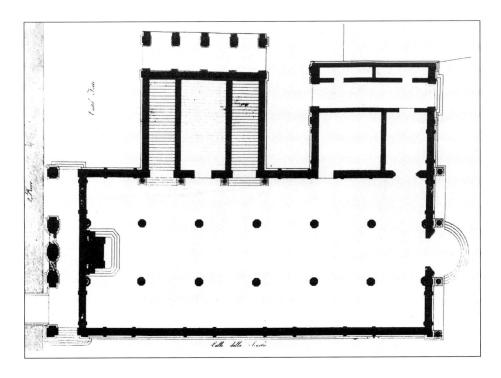

Fig. 5 Scuola di S. Rocco, Venice, plan of ground floor.

Fig. 6 Alcázar, Toledo, the imperial staircase before destruction in 1936.

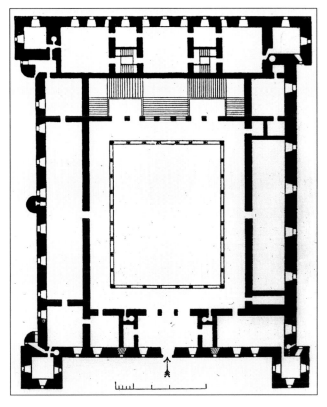

Fig. 7 Alcázar, Toledo, plan of the ground floor.

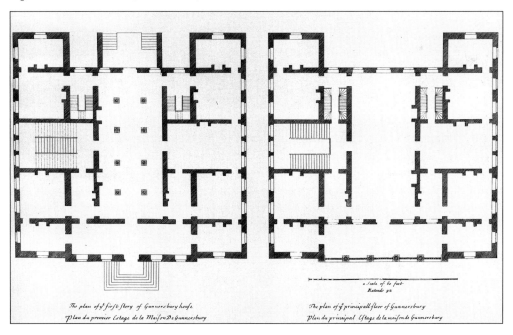

The plan of y.e first story of Gunnersbury house
Plan du premier Estage de la Maison De Gunnersbury

a Scale of 60 feet
Extends 92

The plan of y.e principall floor of Gunnersbury
Plan du principal Estage de la maison de Gunnersbury

Fig. 8 Gunnersbury House, plans of the ground and first floors, from Colen Campbell, *Vitruvius Britannicus*, i (1715).

and first recorded in print in the middle of the nineteenth century, associated the playing of games of hide and seek by children in the double spiral at Chambord,[18] and it is conceivable that the three double staircases were designed with an element of fun. Certainly no other explanation can be given for the extraordinary double newel spiral on the north side of the west front of Rodez Cathedral in southern France (*c.* 1540).[19] Its main function was to link the nave of the church to the terrace at its summit, but climbing this staircase is similar to entering a maze. At each of its seven revolutions, another curving flight projects out from the main staircase to form a connection between the two independent flights, thus providing a continuing choice of changing direction from one flight to the other.

The main trend from the middle of the sixteenth century was the development of the double staircase for its ceremonial role. A large staircase, similar in type to Leonardo's triple flight design, was added to the Scuola Grande di San Rocco (1545) in Venice to link the two large halls (Fig. 5).[20] The lower hall was used amongst other functions to distribute alms to the poor, while the upper hall was reserved for the meetings and religious ceremonies attended by the members of the confraternity. The two vaulted flights that rise out of the lower hall converge to return as a single central wider flight that leads straight without landing or door into the *sala maggiore*. In design as well as in decoration the staircase is conceived as an integral part of the architectural composition and was undoubtedly used for the ceremonial processions that played such an important part in the life of the Venetian confraternities.[21]

The staircase at the Alcázar in Toledo (*c.* 1550), which was destroyed in 1936 but has been rebuilt, is one of a series of monumental double staircases that were designed and built in the Spanish royal palaces during the later sixteenth century (Figs. 6, 7).[22] The staircase, a full imperial in type, became the main focus of the palace, rivalling the great hall in its huge size, its architectural decoration and in its spatial unity. The central first flight directly faced the main entrance so that the visitor immediately on entering the courtyard was invited to ascend. At the first landing the flight divides into two flights which then rise round open wells to lead, not directly into the great hall, but to the upper galleries. This conception of the staircase being treated as an independent architectural theme conforms to the new ideals of staircase design that

18 I am indebted to Dr David Thomson for bringing the mythology of Chambord to my notice.

19 A.F. Blunt, *Art and Architecture in France 1500 to 1700* (London, 1953), pp. 61-62; L. Bousquet, 'La cathédrale de Rodez', *Congrès archéologique de France* (1937), pp. 367, 372.

20 D. Howard, *The Architectural History of Venice* (London, 1980), pp. 133-35; P.L. Sohm, 'The Staircases of the Venetian *Scuole Grandi* and Mauro Coducci', *Architectura*, vii (1978), pp.

125-49.

21 J. Glixon, 'Music and Ceremony at the Scuola Grande di San Giovanni Evangelista: A New Document from the Venetian State Archives', *Crossing the Boundaries, Christian Piety and the Arts in Italian Medieval and Renaissance Confraternities* (Michigan, 1991), pp. 56-87.

22 C. Wilkinson, 'The Escorial and the Invention of the Imperial Staircase', *Art Bulletin*, lvii (1975), pp. 65-90.

were added by Vasari into the 1568 edition of his book.[23] He advised that public staircases should not only be wide, spacious, well-lit and gentle to climb but that every part should have an air of magnificence, since a large number of visitors saw no more of the house beyond the staircase.

The first grand processional staircase to be built in England was added to Bridewell Palace in 1522, nearly 150 years after their introduction in France.[24] Symmetrical staircases were also built in England but never on the same scale or with the same enthusiasm as elsewhere in western Europe. During their travels both Inigo Jones and John Evelyn made observations on the double spiral at Chambord. Jones studied the mechanics, while Evelyn was impressed by 'the extravagancy of the designe'.[25] Large-scale double staircases were designed in the projects for Whitehall Palace,[26] but one of the earliest to be actually executed in England was at Gunnersbury House (late 1650s) (Fig. 8)[27]. It is an imperial staircase with a central flight returning in two, but the spatial design and the decoration are more constrained than in its continental counterparts. English architects generally seem to have favoured large twin staircases in their designs for palaces and country houses that could be placed discreetly on either side or behind the entrance hall without intruding on its space. In *English Baroque Architecture*, Kerry Downes praises two English staircases in particular, the King's and Queen's Stairs built by Hugh May at Windsor Castle (1674-84), but comments that their dramatic lighting, illusionism and real spatial complexity was never surpassed in later English architecture.[28]

A new concern during the late medieval period for making a division between the different functions of a building promoted an improvement in the circulation. The use of the small double newel spiral was a practical solution in that it provided in the minimum of space two distinct circulations that could be flexibly adapted to their separate needs. During the sixteenth century the introduction of new types of double stairs for the principal staircase and the increased importance given to the ceremonial role in public and residential buildings led to the development of the double staircase as a monumental feature. Variations, many of which have great spatial complexity, were built during the Baroque period, yet the double staircase retained the role and function that had been developed during the sixteenth century, that of providing an imposing entrance to the main rooms on the *piano nobile*.

23 *Le vite de' più eccellenti pittori, scultori et architettori* (Milan, 1962), i, p. 92. In the earlier edition of 1550 Vasari merely recommends staircases to be serviceable and unpretentious.

24 S. Thurley, *English Royal Palaces 1450-1550*, (unpublished Ph.D. dissertation, University of London, 1989/90) pp. 101-3.

25 I am grateful to Dr E. Chaney for telling me about Jones's annotation in his copy of Palladio, Book i, p. 64; *The Diary of John Evelyn*, ed. E.S. de Beer (Oxford, 1955), i, p. 91; ii. pp. 139-40.

26 J. Bold, *John Webb: Architectural Theory and Practice in the Seventeenth Century* (Oxford, 1989), pp. 107-25.

27 Ibid., pp. 91-94.

28 K. Downes, *English Baroque Architecture* (London, 1966), pp. 17-20.

2

Northamptonshire Towers and Spires

T.H. COCKE

The towers and spires of Northamptonshire have often been described but rarely studied. Some attention has been given to their morphology; hardly any to their history and stylistic development. The only monograph on them, L.G.H. Lee's *The Church Towers of Northamptonshire* (Rushden, 1946), is avowedly amateur; Pevsner devotes six tightly compressed paragraphs to them in his introduction to the Northamptonshire volume of the *Buildings of England* series.[1] This essay is concerned chiefly with the later periods but must begin with a brief summary of the origins and flowering of the Northamptonshire steeple.

Simple statistics show that the west tower is the dominant form in Northamptonshire. There are some 300 medieval churches in the county, 90 per cent of which have towers at the west end of the nave and approximately a third of these have spires. The remaining 10 per cent have bellcotes or central towers or towers set either north or south of the main body of the church. By contrast of the fifty medieval churches covered by RCHME's survey of south-east Wiltshire only 38 per cent have towers to the west.

Before 1200 there were two types of tower to be found in the county, the centre tower, as at King's Cliffe, and the west tower.[2] The latter was established in its essential form by at least *c.* 1000. While Brixworth can be interpreted as having a westwork, only later adapted to form a conventional tower, and Earl's Barton was apparently associated with secular buildings to the west, Brigstock is a monumental autonomous structure (Fig. 9).

---

* The research upon which this essay is based was conducted during a project for RCHME in 1982/7, recording the physical development of the medieval churches of Northamptonshire. My colleague was Hugh Richmond to whose sensitive understanding of structural logic, not to mention patience and good humour, this essay owes so much. His own detailed analysis of the churches as a whole will be published in due course by RCHME.

1. N. Pevsner, revised B. Cherry, *Northampton-shire* (Harmondsworth, 1973), pp. 33, 39-41.
2. The cruciform early plan of some of the major medieval churches, e.g. Oundle, is no proof of the existence of a central tower. There is no evidence in surviving fabric for the strengthening necessary to carry a tower. Nor would the rectangular plan of the 'crossing' area be suitable for a conventional tower. What appear on plan to be transepts were distinct but subsidiary chapels similar to and perhaps replacing Anglo-Saxon porticus.

Little evidence survives of the development of towers in the twelfth century. A rare dateable example, at Spratton, suggests that the tower was added not more than fifty years after the west front had been built; the sculpted west doorway of *c.* 1150 seems to have been reset in the new tower. This hints that during the twelfth century it was increasingly felt that a major church was somehow lacking without a west tower. Smaller churches would be content with a gable bellcote, such as existed at Faxton until that church's demolition in 1958. As to spires, nothing survives from the twelfth century, although of course there are representations of such constructions, presumably of timber and lead, in seals and manuscripts. We simply do not know whether the masonry spire had yet to be introduced to the country or if there were modest attempts made which have all been replaced or, conceivably, that even timber spires were restricted to cathedrals and great abbeys and only descended to the level of parish churches in the next century.

There is equally no easy explanation of the sudden and simultaneous flowering of the classic design of tower and broach spire in the mid thirteenth century in the north and east of the county (which continues east across Huntingdonshire into Lincolnshire). The availability of stone, the ease of water transport on the rivers Nene, Ouse and Welland, the sheer prosperity and vigour attested by the scale of the buildings themselves, are all relevant but could apply elsewhere in the kingdom.

Close dating of spires is notoriously difficult. Pevsner put Barnack in the early thirteenth century as 'one of the earliest in the country'.[3] Raunds can be dated to *c.* 1250-75 by the elaborate arcading of the tower. Yet at Barnwell St Andrew the detailing includes both lavish Early English dogtooth and Decorated trailing foliage and ballflower.

Another problematic element is the obvious vulnerability of towers and especially spires. More than most parts of a church they will have been repaired and reconstructed. Many have documented rebuildings in the seventeenth and eighteenth centuries, the accuracy of which cannot be certain. We know little of earlier repairs, however extensive. The west tower at Higham Ferrers is sometimes discussed as a closely-dated building, with the Westminster-style reliefs of the porch giving *c.* 1250 as the date of the original construction and the collapse of 1630 and rebuilding in 1631/33 that of the alterations to the fabric and sculpture now visible. Examination of the stonework, however, suggests that there already had been a major reconstruction, especially on the south side and the south-west corner, in the fourteenth century, perhaps when the parapet spire was erected. The efforts made to maintain the Higham Ferrers steeple are a strong demonstration of its continuing importance to the community. The image of an ornate west tower crowned by a tall spire must

3. Pevsner, *Northamptonshire* (1973), p. 33.

Fig. 9 St Andrew, Brigstock.
Fig. 10 St Peter, Oundle.

have been the model for the great steeples of the fifteenth century such as those at Kettering and Rushden.

Another testimony to the enduring power of the image is the survival rate of spires. There have been surprisingly few losses. Amongst major churches the only exception is Rothwell, where the spire and part of the tower collapsed about 1660. When the spire at Great Billing was thrown down by a spectacular lightning strike in April 1759, wrecking much of the nave and leaving a powerful 'sulphureous smell', it was not rebuilt but seventeen years later compensation was made by adding an Elizabethan-style parapet, allegedly reused from the nearby mansion.[4]

By 1350 churches were well supplied with steeples. Even so there continued to be adaptations and alterations. These can be divided into three main categories. The first, to be found in wealthy parishes, was to build a totally new tower immediately west of the existing church, with substantial buttresses on the eastern as well as the western angles. This was an expensive option, not only for the masonry of the new structure but also for the demolition of the previous tower which a church of that status presumably already possessed. On the other hand the sheer size of these late steeples – Oundle is over 200 feet high – necessitated such radical action. These ambitious designs presumably took years to complete. Again at Oundle the details seem to change in style as the tower rises. One characteristic they all share is that broaches to the spire are rejected in favour of a parapet round the top of the tower, behind which is set the spire (Fig. 10).

The second alternative was to retain the existing tower as a base and add a contemporary spire. The most intriguing cases are at Brigstock and Brixworth where the Saxon fabric of the towers was given Gothic crownings, without any stylistic compromise. At Nassington however and perhaps at King's Sutton the exterior faces of the Saxon tower were stripped away and reclothed so that the tower appears to be a new structure. This economical solution may well be true in other cases so far undetected.

There were less conventional possibilities in steeple design in the later middle ages. One was the polygonal tower, with spire or lantern. At Stanwick the octagonal spire is carried on an octagonal tower, apparently of the mid-thirteenth century. This elegant device was not repeated, perhaps indicating that the desired image for a parish required a square tower. Crowning the tower with an octagonal lantern was a device favoured in the late fourteenth century and after, perhaps following the example of the west tower of Ely Cathedral. The most notable examples in the county were at Lowick (Fig. 11) and Fotheringhay. Is it coincidence that in both cases they were erected under

---

4. G. Baker, *The History and Antiquities of the County of Northampton* (London, 1822-1830), i, p. 24.

the auspices not of a wealthy parish but of powerful lords, the Greens of Drayton and the Dukes of York?

There were some quite unusual solutions. At Irthlingborough a new steeple was erected to serve both the existing parish church and the college founded in 1373-92 to the west which spread around the tower. Above a square tower rose a tall, rather spindly octagon. Its enforced demolition in 1886 and rebuilding in 1890 make the details of the original design hard to reconstruct. The steeple at Newnham was originally constructed free-standing over the roadway to the west of the church, with arches to north, south and west. This peculiarity was matched by its internal arrangement, with stairs rising within the east wall to give access to a large chamber, clearly for official or domestic use, not for bells.

Paradoxically it was a humble variant of late medieval tower building which continued the longest. The gable bellcote of the twelfth or thirteenth century was clearly inadequate once churches possessed more than one or two bells. Some small churches now converted the bellcotes into towers by building back into the nave. At Brockhall the mouldings on the arches show that conversion was made in the fifteenth century. At Strixton the story has come full circle; the tower built to replace a bellcote in the fifteenth century was itself removed two centuries later in favour again of a bellcote (Fig. 12). Hannington presented a different problem. The thirteenth-century nave has, thanks to a Gilbertine connection, the unusual plan of two parallel aisles. It seems that a twelfth-century tower was opened up to east and west and the west wall of the body of the church arranged so that the tower straddles it. The west 'porch' seems to have been filled in when the belfry was rebuilt in the fifteenth century to give a more conventional tower-like appearance. This way of converting bellcotes into belfry towers continued far beyond the middle ages, with Furtho being thus adapted *c.* 1620 and Whilton not until 1767.

The religious changes of the Reformation and Dissolution made little impact on the fate of towers. Since they were indisputably the responsibility of the parish, not of the patron or the incumbent, and since the ringing of bells continued whatever the liturgy, they were never at risk. There was certainly a pause in the building of new towers after the construction of Whiston by Anthony Catesby during the very years of the Reformation but this was common to all Elizabethan church work.[5] Some rebuilding went on in the late sixteenth century to judge from the (decayed) inscriptions and shields of arms on the tower of Maidwell. It is surely significant that when the new lay owners of Canons Ashby, the Copes and then the Drydens, converted the Augustinian priory to domestic use, they retained the impressive tower and west front of the monastic church, though they served no function save display.

5. The legend of Anthony Catesby having to sell his flock to finance the tower is belied by the detailing, especially of the west doorway, which suggests the incorporation of earlier work.

Fig. 11 St Peter, Lowick.
Fig. 12 St Romwald, Strixton.

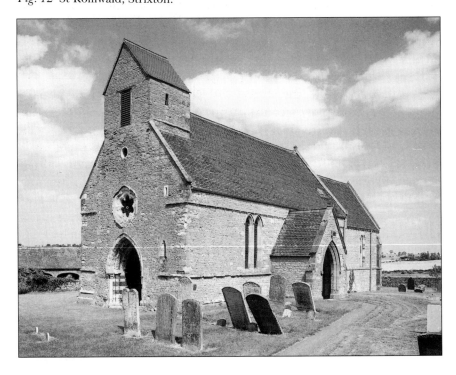

The first half of the seventeenth century saw a lively resurgence in work on steeples.[6] The most notable brand-new tower lies just east of the county at Leighton Bromswold in Huntingdonshire where the Duke of Lennox sponsored a striking design which retained the proportions of a late medieval tower such as that of neighbouring Titchmarsh but adopted openings and pinnacles derived from Inigo Jones's restoration of Old St Paul's Cathedral, London. Apethorpe, built only a few years earlier in 1633, presumably for the Mildmay family, is much less adventurous in its stylistic language (Fig. 13). Its three stages are still entirely Gothic and only betray their date by the simplification of the detailing and the omission of buttresses. The same conservatism is true of Wicken, where Lord Spencer rebuilt the tower in 1617. At nearby Passenham another generous patron, Sir Robert Banastre, completely reconstructed the chancel and furnished and decorated it lavishly, as well as providing a new pulpit in the nave, all in a contemporary style. At the same time the spire and upper parts of the tower were removed and replaced by a belfry with twin lancets of an Early English flavour.[7]

There were many similar rebuildings, probably more than we can now judge. The most bizarre was the dismantling and re-erection of the twelfth-century west tower of St Peter's at Northampton within the westernmost bay of the nave. The rich Romanesque ornament was retained both for the tower arch and a new west doorway. Also in Northampton, the central tower of St Giles, together with the clerestory and north wall of the nave, had to be rebuilt in 1616 following collapse three years earlier.[8] The reconstruction of the spire at Higham Ferrers in 1631/3 is well known; the spire at Guilsborough has an inscription recording its rebuilding in 1618.

After the Civil War the pattern altered to one of routine maintenance with occasional examples of complete rebuilding, usually classical rather than Gothic in style. When All Saints, the largest church in Northampton, was burnt in the disastrous town fire of 1675, the citizens did not follow the example of those at Warwick twenty years later and adopt a reinterpreted but still Gothic style for the rebuilding but conformed to contemporary types of plan and decoration. They converted the former crossing tower into a western tower, but its effect was partly concealed behind a classical portico.

Stoke Doyle is one of the rare examples in the county of the complete replacement of a medieval church. The new design of 1722/5, by Thomas Eayre of Kettering, was smaller and appears to incorporate nothing of its predecessor. The tower still has a traditional outline but is detailed with

6. Interesting comparative material is found in A. Woodger, 'Post-Reformation Mixed Gothic in Huntingdonshire Church Towers and its Campanological Associations', *Archaeological Journal*, cxli (1984), pp. 269-308.

7. J. Bridges, *The History and Antiquities of Northamptonshire* (Oxford, 1791), i, p. 306.

8. RCHME, *An Inventory of the Historical Monuments in the County of Northampton*, v, *Archaeological Sites and Churches in Northampton* (London, 1985), p. 64.

Fig. 13 St Leonard, Apethorpe.

pilasters at the angles, obelisk pinnacles and round-headed openings. Another example, much grander in scale, is Daventry, of 1752/8. The Hiorne brothers derived their design from the London city models by Wren and Gibbs but crowned it with a steeple of 'gouty' outline, with a ribbed spire arising above pedimented clock faces.[9] The Hiornes at the same period replaced the church at Great Houghton in an austere classical style but for the tower, which has a polygonal colonnade linked to a spire by bold volutes. A similar design was adopted in 1807 at Green's Norton where, though the Saxon nave and later chancel were left unmodernised, the belfry and spire were replaced by a classical belfry with angle pilasters and Gibbs surround to the windows, carrying a polygonal spire of medieval outline. A pattern found elsewhere, for example at what is now the cathedral in Derby, where Gibbs completely rebuilt the body of the church but left the medieval tower in its Gothic glory, can be found at Aynho, where the tower was the only survivor of the 1720s rebuilding.

The regular maintenance required by features so exposed to the weather as towers and spires is hard to document. The more accurate the mason, the harder it is to detect his handiwork.[10] It is easier where for lack of money or interest the belfry openings were simplified as at Great Doddington, or where, as at Lamport, a great buttress was boldly added to support the north-west corner. It is tempting to try and correlate the rebuilding of towers with the interest in bells and especially change-ringing which was reaching a peak of popularity at this time. Unfortunately, while Northamptonshire can boast a good number of peals of bells cast during this period, surprisingly few can be associated with a rebuilding of the tower which housed them. At Stoke Doyle and Daventry the new towers received new bells. At Easton Neston however, Sir Hatton Fermor had given a peal of four bells in 1647 which were then recast in 1771 by the 2nd Lord Pomfret, but there is no evidence of the fifteenth-century belfry being taken down or reconstructed to accommodate them on either occasion.

What can be asserted more confidently is that bells contributed to the parish's own pride and sense of worth and therefore made the tower which housed them more significant. Local rhymes mocked a parish which was considered deficient. Well into the nineteenth century and later the ringing of bells was a continuous part of parish life, not only to summon the congregation to worship but to ring knells for the departed, curfews or celebratory peals for great national or local events.[11]

The pride of an eighteenth-century parish in its tower is well demonstrated by the print of Ecton church of 1749, commissioned by the squire, which shows

9. M. Whiffen, *Stuart and Georgian Churches* (London, 1947), p. 43.

10. Examples in the West Country are cited in H.M. Colvin, 'Gothic Survival and Gothick Revival' *Architectural Review*, ciii (1948) pp.

91-98.

11. Thomas North, *The Church Bells of Northamptonshire: Their Inscriptions, Traditions and Peculiar Uses* (Leicester, 1878), pp. 123-57.

Fig. 14 St Mary, Ecton.

the tower as the most prominent element of the church, dwarfing both gentry and grave-diggers standing in the foreground (Fig. 14). The squire, John Palmer, spent generously on the church, though adding little of his own time save the triangular marble slabs, commemorating the Palmer and Whalley families, shaped to fit the arches of the arcade.

Finally, one must not forget the role of the steeple as eye-catcher. At Naseby, where a decayed spire was not returned to its full height till the mid nineteenth century, the stump was capped by struts carrying an ingenious brass ball and weathercock to glitter in the sun. At Horton, close to the great house of the Earls of Halifax, the tower was rebuilt *c.* 1720 by the Earl and crowned by an intricate metal weathervane. Although Northamptonshire cannot repeat the case of Downton in Wiltshire, where Lord Radnor added a whole extra stage to give the tower more prominence in the local landscape, the relationship with the great houses and families of the county should not be ignored.

This essay can only chart the main lines of the development of steeple building in Northamptonshire. Much work remains to be done on individual churches, investigating the timberwork of the tower roofs, floors and bell-frames as well as the masonry. Yet the power of the classic design of monumental west tower and spire, established by 1300 as the dominant type in the county, remains such that parishes have ever since sought to retain and maintain their steeples.

3

Architecture and Mathematical Practice in England, 1550-1650

J.A. BENNETT

> This candle did I light: this lighte haue I kindeled: that learned
> men maie se, to practise their pennes, their eloquence to
> aduaunce, to register their names in the booke of memorie. I
> drew the platte rudelie, whereon thei maie builde . . . [1]

It is appropriate that the first English geometry begins with a building
metaphor. Robert Recorde's *Pathway to Knowledg* of 1551 was one of a group of
vernacular textbooks through which the author sought to establish the basis of
a new area of practical expertise in England, the mathematical arts and
sciences. The movement to advance English mathematics was soon characterised by assumptions of expansion, development, reform and intellectual col-
onisation.[2] The foundations of geometry and arithmetic were deemed
appropriate to a range of practical activities – navigation, surveying, gunnery,
fortification and so on. Each would be reformed, improved and perfected, and
in turn would contribute new prosperity to the commonwealth. The notion of
an expansive reform, effected by importing a common foundation across a
range of crafts and disciplines, lent itself to images of building and rebuilding.
Recorde's very first textbook, his arithmetic of 1542, was titled *The Grounde of
Artes*.[3] The movement's most elaborate didactic schema was an ambitious
representation of the extent of mathematical applicability; it accompanied and
epitomised John Dee's celebrated preface to the first English Euclid of 1570,
and he called it 'the Groundplat of my Mathematicall Praeface'.[4]

The metaphor was appropriate not only because of the 'refounding' dynamic of this mathematical movement, but also on account of its content.

---

1. R. Recorde, *The Pathway to Knowledg* (London,
1551), 'To the gentle reader'.
2 On this movement the best general text is still
E.G.R. Taylor, *The Mathematical Practitioners of
Tudor and Stuart England* (Cambridge, 1954);
for recent comments on its significance, see
J.A. Bennett, 'The Challenge of Practical
Mathematics' in S. Pumfrey et al., *Science,
Culture and Popular Belief in Renaissance Europe*
(Manchester, 1991), pp. 176-90.

3 R. Recorde, *The Grounde of Artes* (London,
1542).
4 J. Dee, 'Iohn Dee his Mathematicall Praeface',
to Euclid, *The Elements of Geometrie*, trans. H.
Billingsley (London, 1570); see also J. Dee,
*The Mathematicall Praeface to the Elements of
Geometrie of Euclid of Megara (1570)*, introduc-
tion by A.G. Debus (New York, 1975). The
'Groundplat' is also reproduced in Taylor,
Mathematical Practitioners.

'Building' or 'architecture' was part of its prospectus. This is immediately clear from Recorde's *Pathway*, where his dedication to Edward VI asserts the primitive necessity of mathematics to all the arts, whose students 'must also before al other arts, taste of the mathematical sciences, specially Arithmetike and Geometry, without which it is not possible to attayn full knowledg in any art'. Building is a ready instance of his claim: through arithmetic and geometry 'not only great things ar wrought touchīg accōptes in al kinds, & in suruaiyng & measuring of lādes, but also al arts depend partly of thē, & building which is most necessary can not be wthout them . . .'[5] Recorde continues in his preface to argue the widespread usefulness of geometry, and building is again a central example: 'Carpenters, Karuers, Joyners, and Masons, doe willingly acknowledge that they can worke nothyng without reason of Geometrie . . .'[6] Recorde represents only the beginning of a practical mathematical tradition, but the inclusion of architecture within the programme of mathematical reform became commonplace.

The significance of these mathematical writers for the history of architecture in England has, in part, been recognised by its historians. An important work by a leading mathematical practitioner – the *Tectonicon* of Leonard Digges, (1556)[7] – is the inaugural book cited in Harris's *British Architectural Books and Writers, 1556-1785*.[8] Indeed this and John Shute's *First and Chief Groundes of Architecture* (1563)[9] are the only original works, in various editions, cited (along with one translated work) for the sixteenth century. The nature of the wider mathematical movement, however, and the extent of its concern with architecture deserve further attention. Here, after all, is the beginning of the printed English architectural literature.

Tectonicon is concerned principally with surveying and the introduction to its practice in England of unfamiliar mathematical techniques and novel instruments. Among the latter are Digges's version of the carpenter's rule, an instrument for relating lengths to areas and volumes of timber. The rule is one reason why we readily recognise the relevance of Digges's book to architecture as we understand it, and he himself announces on the title-page that his work is 'most conducible for Surueyers, Landemeaters, Joyners, Carpenters, and Masons'. The scales of the carpenter's rule, however, might be engraved on instruments with dedicated applications to surveying, just as the rule illustrated by Digges is also a surveying instrument, with sights and angular scales. Instruments of this type, made, for example, by the mathematical instrument-

5   Recorde, *Pathway to Knowledg*, dedication.
6   Ibid., preface.
7   L. Digges, *A Boke Named Tectonicon* (London, 1556).
8   E. Harris, *British Architectural Books and*

Writers, 1556-1785 (Cambridge, 1990), p. 513.
9   J. Shute, *The First and Chief Groundes of Architecture* (London, 1563).

maker Humphrey Cole,[10] illustrate the contemporary professional overlap between surveying and practices we are inclined to classify as architectural.

The title-page of *Tectonicon* announces the intellectual thrust of the book, for it shows the height of a tower being measured by use of a cross-staff. This instrument, which Digges called the 'profitable staff', derived from a measuring instrument of astronomy, had widespread applications in practical mathematics and had been particularly successfully adapted to navigation.[11] A cross-piece sliding on a graduated staff was adjusted to indicate the angle subtended at the eye by two targets – in this case the extremities of the tower. The required distance could be calculated from the measures of the angles subtended at either end of a base-line. Geometrical survey of this kind was a radical departure from straightforward linear measure and, by illustrating the use of the cross-staff on his title-page, Digges was emphasising that geometrical instruments, rather than ropes and poles, should characterise surveying practice. Geometry would reform surveying, just as it would other arts, and the outcome – an assertion typical of books in this genre – was personal success for the practitioner, and political success for his country.[12]

The range of interests and activities of the early practitioners indicates that it was not only in its literature that architecture was linked to other mathematical arts. Evidence can be drawn, for example, from each of John Summerson's 'Three Elizabethan Architects'.[13] Thus Robert Adams was a surveyor and map-maker, an expert in the mathematical art of fortification and a designer of a sundial, in collaboration with Humphrey Cole.[14] Summerson sees Adams as a novelty in England – an expert of the kind who would previously have been introduced from abroad;[15] exactly this point can also be made of Cole. John Symonds was experienced in fortification and owned at least two of the mathematical instruments now being introduced into England by makers such as Cole – 'my Geometricall instrument of wood called Jacobs Staff' (an instrument similar to Digges's profitable staff) and 'my Geometricall square of latten for measuringe of lande'.[16] Robert Stickells, Summerson's third example, was a military and naval engineer.[17]

Publications of the mathematical programme other than the books listed by Harris might be included in the architectural literature of early modern England. Leonard Digges's *Pantometria*, completed and edited by his son

10 G.L'E. Turner, 'Mathematical Instrument-Making in London in the Sixteenth Century', in S. Tyacke (ed.), *English Map-Making, 1500-1600* (London, 1983), pp. 93-106.

11 J.J. Roche, 'The Radius Astronomicus in England', *Annals of Science*, xxxviii (1981), pp. 1-32.

12 On the mathematicians' efforts to reform surveying, see J.A. Bennett, 'Geometry and Surveying in Early-Seventeenth-Century England', *Annals of Science*, xlviii (1991), pp. 345-54.

13 J. Summerson, 'Three Elizabethan Architects', *Bulletin of the John Rylands Library*, xl (1957-58), pp. 202-28.

14 Ibid., pp. 204-8.

15 Ibid., p. 208.

16 Ibid., pp. 209, 223.

17 Ibid., pp. 216-17, 221,227.

Thomas, first appeared in 1571, and was presented as a more advanced account than *Tectonicon*. In keeping with this claim, the material is divided on theoretical grounds into three books, dealing with lines ('*Longimetria*', measuring lengths, heights, etc), areas ('*Planimetria*') and volumes ('*Stereometria*'). The same pretension may explain the references to 'architecture', rather than to the work of carpenters and masons:

> the skilful in Architecture can applye the Stereometria to serue his turne in preordinance and forecasting both of the charges, quantities and proportion of all parcels necessarily appertayning to any kinde of buyldings: so Planimetria maye serue for disposing all manner grounde plattes of Cities, Townes, Fortes, Castles, Pallaces or other edifices.[18]

Other mathematical writers of the sixteenth century, such as William Bourne or Thomas Hood,[19] saw their work as relevant to architecture and, as is well known, the central programmatic text – Dee's *Praeface* – contributed one of the early English analyses of the architect's role. It was fully in keeping with the ambitions of the mathematicians that Dee justified the inclusion of architecture in his scheme of mathematical arts and sciences on the grounds that the architect was a geometer, carefully distinguishing the responsibilities of architect and artificer. Though he cited the authorities of Vitruvius and Alberti, he presented his notion as a contentious novelty in England:

> Architecture, to many may seme not worthy, or not mete, to be reckned among the Artes Mathematicall. The whom, I thinke good, to giue some account of my so doyng. Not worthy, (will they say,) bycause it is but for building, of a house, Pallace, Church, Forte, or such like, grosse workes . . . the Architect procureth, enformeth, & directeth, the Mechanicien, to handworke, & the building actuall, of house, Castell, or Pallace, and is chief Iudge of the same: yet, with his selfe (as chief Master and Architect,) remaineth the Demonstratiue reason and cause, of the Mechaniciens worke: in Lyne, plaine, and Solid . . .[20]

Seven years before Dee's *Praeface*, there was published the book traditionally regarded as the first English architectural text, Shute's *First and Chief Groundes of Architecture*. Its role as the founding text of English architectural literature can be ascribed only with hindsight; in the context of its time it was squarely in the practical mathematical programme. Shute is as clear on this as all the other writers in the genre: architecture, he says

18 L. Digges and T. Digges, *A Geometrical Practise, Named Pantometria* (London, 1571), sigs. Aii-Aii v.

19 W. Bourne, *A Booke Called the Treasure for Traueilers* (London, 1578); T. Hood, *A Copie of the Speache: Made by the Mathematical Lecturer* (London, 1588); T. Hood, *The Vse of the Two Mathematicall Instrumentes, the Crosse Staffe . . . and the Jacobes Staffe* (London, 1590); T. Hood, *The Making and Vse of the Geometricall Instrument called a Sector* (London, 1598).

20 Dee, *Mathematicall Praeface*, sig. d.iij.

hath a natural societie and as it were by a sertaine kinred & affinitie is knit vnto all the Mathematicalles which sciences and knowledges are frendes and a maintayner of diuers rationall artes: so that without a meane acquaintance of vnderstanding in thē neyther paynters, masons, Gold smythes, enbroderers, Caruers, Ioynars, Glassyers, Grauers, in all Manner of metalls and diuers others mōe can obtayne anye worthy praise at all Nowe all these being branches of that forsayd foundatiō, stocke or science shall bring forthe the fruites of it to their great profites, and the Commoditie of the Realme, which cōtinuing and throughlye practised in the same by time shall increase riches, worshippe, and fame.[21]

Such assertions of intellectual foundation – as mathematical science – and of practical worth, might have come from any of the books in the mathematical programme. If Shute's choice of cognate arts seems unusual, it can be echoed in the first geometry, Recorde's *Pathway*:

> Carpenters, Caruers, Joiners and Masons,
> Painters and Limners with suche occupations,
> Broderers, Goldesmithes, if they be cunning,
> Must yelde to Geometrye thankes for their learning.[22]

Shute's printer, Thomas Marshe, maintained an interest in mathematical texts, for he took over Digges's *Tectonicon* from the instrument-maker Thomas Gemini, and printed editions in 1566, 1570, 1578 and 1585, as well as Thomas Digges's *Alae seu scalae mathematicae* (1573).[23] Within the mathematical programme, Shute's specialist architectural book parallels the slightly earlier work on cosmography by William Cuningham. In his dialogue *The Cosmographical Glasse* of 1559 – dedicated to Robert Dudley, son of Shute's patron, John, Duke of Northumberland, who had been executed in 1553 – Cuningham too places his subject among the many linked by their dependence on mathematics. The master begins by insisting that his pupil must have a knowledge of geometry and arithmetic, and instruction can proceed only when the pupil affirms that he has read the textbooks of Robert Recorde, 'For he that wyll couer the roufe of his house, before he haue made the foundation, and buildyd the walles: besyde the losse of his cost, shall be thought scarce a wytty builder'.[24] Indeed the master recommends some more advanced mathematical texts, 'not only for this studies sake whiche you now haue in hande: but for all other artes (which taste of the Mathematicalles) that you shall here after trauell in'.[25]

Other features of Shute's writing that are common to the wider programme are the importance he ascribes to his use of the vernacular, and the sense that

21 Shute, *First and Chief Groundes*, sig. Aij v.
22 Recorde, *Pathway to Knowledg*, preface.
23 A.W. Pollard and G.R. Redgrave, *A Short-Title Catalogue of Books Printed in England, Scotland and Ireland . . . 1475-1640* (London, 1986), i,

pp. 308-9.
24 W. Cuningham, *The Cosmographical Glasse* (London, 1559), pp. 4-5.
25 Ibid., p. 5.

he is introducing to Englishmen skills that have for too long been the monopoly of foreigners.[26] At the same time as Shute was in Italy to experience Renaissance architecture, Dee was in France and the Low Countries to learn mathematics. Shute has also caught the significance attached to mathematical instruments: 'Geometry teacheth vs the order of rules, Compasses, Squiers, Quadrantes, and Iuste waterleueles . . .'[27] His authorities are Euclid and Serlio and, like Dee, he deploys the Vitruvian vision of the architect as a geometrical paragon.[28]

Eileen Harris has noted the links between the treatments of architecture in Shute and Dee, and has agreed with Yates that the target audience was middle-class and artisan, rather than courtly and gentle.[29] All of this is consistent with seeing Shute as a specialist representative of a wider mathematical programme, and it remains to recognise that the books of Digges and Shute, as the acknowledged architectural writers of sixteenth-century England, fall within a wider campaign to advance practical mathematics. Refounding a range of practical arts on geometry and arithmetic was a move to enhance their status: mathematical 'science' was a bold and contentious claim, since the term was more generally associated with natural philosophy. The syllogism, not the geometrical demonstration, was the customary touchstone of science. It is a tension acknowledged by Shute himself:

> Notwithstanding I know well there hath bene a multitude and at this time be very many lerned men who hath (throughe trauaile receiued) the ful perfectiō of the prudent ladye *Scientia*, of whom so depely learned I craue pardon for my rude rashnes . . .[30]

The further aim of the mathematical writers was to demonstrate the practical and political value of the mathematical arts, and thus to advance the status of those who practised the mathematical sciences – not just among the learned, but in the commonwealth.

This context for architectural writing survived into the seventeenth century. Many of the authors listed by Harris were general mathematical practitioners. Richard More, represented by *The Carpenters Rule* of 1602, advised his fellow carpenters to read Digges and the English Euclid and to attend the weekly geometry lecture in Gresham College, now the centre of practical mathematics in England.[31] Thomas Bedwell described himself as engaged in the 'profession of the mathematicalls'.[32] John Speidell was identified in the period as a

26 Shute, *First and Chief Groundes*, sigs. Aij v-Aiij.
27 Ibid., fo. ii v.
28 Ibid., sig. Aiij, fos. ii v-iii v.
29 Harris, *British Architectural Books*, pp. 420-21; F.A. Yates, *Theatre of the World* (London, 1969), p. 40.
30 Shute, *First and Chief Groundes*, sigs. A. ii v-A.iii.
31 R. More. *The Carpenters Rule* (London, 1602), Preface.
32 S. Johnston, 'Mathematical Practitioners and Instruments in Elizabethan England', *Annals of Science*, xlviii (1991), pp. 318-44, see p. 321.

'Practitioner in the Mathematicks, and Professor thereof in London'.[33] Outside the date limits of this study, the links between practical mathematical science and architecture were sustained in the works of, for example, the mathematical instrument-maker John Brown,[34] the general mathematical practitioner and writer William Leybourne,[35] and the mathematician and architect Christopher Wren. Both the seventeenth-century English translations of Vignola were prepared by men prominent in 'the mathematicalls', namely Joseph Moxon and John Leeke.[36]

By looking at less obvious titles, Harris's list for the seventeenth century could readily be extended. The new generation of calculating instruments, such as the rule incorporating logarithmic scales designed by the Gresham Professor of Astronomy, Edmund Gunter, or the logarithmic rule which William Oughtred called his 'circles of proportion', were applied to the same problems of area and volume measurement as those addressed in Digges's *Tectonicon*.[37] Arthur Hopton's surveying text, *Speculum Topographicum* (1611), for example, also covered timber measurement, and had chapters on siting and planning cities and on building country houses.[38] None of this is surprising, given the position architecture continued to occupy in the disciplinary outlook of the mathematical practitioners.

The mathematicians, however, could not keep architecture to themselves. Their robust geometry and their new instruments continued to have applications to building, and the geometrical idiom of classicism reinforced their conviction that architecture fell within their domain. The emergence of an author such as Henry Wotton, however, in 1624 announced that other sensibilities would contribute to the fuller development of the subject in England.[39] The practical mathematical programme, with its forging confidence and ambitious scope, had provided the locus for the genesis of English architectural literature. It was too narrow a base to sustain a discipline that elsewhere in Europe already had a strong literary tradition and a sophisticated aesthetic theory, but it might be worth considering whether these beginnings had any lasting significance for the 'English Baroque', where 'not rules, but works, were supreme'.[40]

33 J. Speidell, *A Geometrical Extraction* (London, 1657), title-page.

34 Harris, *British Architectural Books*, pp. 126-8, 409-10.

35 Ibid., pp. 292-95.

36 Ibid., pp. 458-62.

37 E. Gunter, *The Description and Use of the Sector, the Crosse-Staffe and Other Instruments* (London, 1623), 'The First Booke of the Crosse-Staffe', pp. 31-36, 39-49; W. Oughtred, *The Circles of Proportion and the Horizontall Instrument* (London, 1632), pp. 48-58.

38 A. Hopton, *Speculum Topographicum, or the Topographicall Glasse* (London, 1611), pp. 196-203, 173-77.

39 H. Wotton, *The Elements of Architecture* (London, 1624).

40 K. Downes, *Hawksmoor* (London, 1959), p. 32; see also, K. Downes, *English Baroque Architecture* (London, 1966).

4

Inigo Jones in Naples

EDWARD CHANEY

The farthest south Inigo Jones is known to have travelled was to Naples in March 1614. Together with his patron Lord Arundel (and the latter's wife who joined them there), he stayed in this huge, Spanish-dominated city for two months. Today, the church of S. Paolo Maggiore looks much like any other post-Renaissance Neapolitan church. Prior to the 1688 earthquake which severely damaged it, however, it looked like the Roman temple it essentially was, featuring a magnificent, hexastyle Corinthian portico. Since Palladio had fully discussed and illustrated this, the so-called Temple of Castor and Pollux, in the copy of *I quattro libri* which Jones possessed and carried everywhere with him, Jones had known of this building even before seeing the real thing. From the annotations in his Palladio (now in Worcester College Library, Oxford), we find the former painter and masque-designer and now aspiring architect visited the church-temple at least three times, judging it 'on[e] of the Best things that I have seen'. Towards the end of his stay in Naples, Jones acquired another book which survives at Worcester College, a then recently published history of Naples. This contains a critique of Palladio's account of the temple which is illustrated by a more accurate engraving. This may have encouraged Jones to return yet again to the site prior to returning to Rome where he fully exploited his enhanced understanding of classical building. The giant statuary which had stood on the pediment of the Neapolitan temple and whose 'exellent' remains Jones found lying beneath it, became a favourite feature of his most distinguished buildings for the Stuart Court in London.

Turning to Richard Lassels's *Voyage of Italy* in preparation for a journey from Rome to Naples, the late seventeenth-century Grand Tourist would have read the following account of the Appian Way: 'The frequent passing of *horses* and *mules* (for so many years) upon this cawssey, have made it both so *smooth* and *shyneing*, that when the *Sunn* shines upon it you may see it glitter two miles off,

---

* This essay was delivered as a lecture to the Society of Antiquaries on 11 April 1991. A summary was published in *Rivista: The Journal of the British-Italian Society*, no. 341 (1991), pp. 1-2.

like a sylver highway.'[1] In March 1614, the response of Britain's first classical architect, Inigo Jones, had been more pedantically archaeological. In the 1601 edition of Palladio's *Quattro libri* which he had brought along to help him and his patron, Thomas Howard, 2nd Earl of Arundel, fully appreciate the buildings of Italy, alongside a passage on the Appian Way Jones wrote: 'This waye I obsearued in my voyage to Napels 1614 and yt remains much intyre.'[2] On the verso, next to the plate which illustrates the typical Roman road, with its central paved area for pedestrians, continuous cut-stone borders with regularly placed pedestals for mounting horses, and flanking, sand-covered tracks allocated to the equestrian travellers, Jones commented:

> The Via Appia wch I saw in my Jorney to Napels is as this is but ye horse wais on the sydes are not deserned. The high stones stand upon ye side nigh ye Castrico marked D [B?] I immagin to gett up the esier.[3]

At about the same time, in Palladio's chapter on Roman wall-building, Jones annotated the illustration of *opus reticulatum*: 'In my Jorney to Napels I saw much of this opera ritticulata . . . '[4] On the following page, at the lower left-hand corner of Palladio's illustration of 'Pietre incerte', Jones noted that: 'going to Napels I saw a wall of an Anticke house as this and yt did well.'[5]

Jones had already annotated this woodcut prior to leaving England. As in six other instances, he indicated at the foot of the page that the original drawing for the print belonged to Sir Henry Wotton: 'The drawing of thes wales S^r He Woo: and slyght sciczos of alltertables.' Wotton had returned from his first stint as ambassador to Venice in July 1612, thus nine months before Jones left England with the Arundels. So drastically had Britain's visual culture suffered from its post-Reformation isolation from the Catholic continent, that eight years in Italy had enabled Wotton to emerge as one of our leading connoisseurs of painting and architecture.[6] He was a major patron of Odoardo Fialetti, the

1 R. Lassels, *The Voyage of Italy* (Paris, 1670), ii, p. 262. This passage is not included in the *c.* 1664 manuscript of the *Voyage* in my possession and may therefore have been added posthumously to Lassels's text by fellow priest Simon Wilson who saw the printed *Voyage* through the press; E. Chaney, *The Grand Tour and the Great Rebellion* (Geneva-Turin, 1985), pp. 133-40 and 425-26.

2 A. Palladio, *I quattro libri dell'architettura* (Venice, 1601) (copy in Worcester College Library, Oxford), iii, p. 9. I thank the Provost and Fellows of Worcester College for permission to consult, quote from and photograph this book. I am especially grateful to the former College Librarian, Mrs Lesley Le Claire, and her assistant Lawrence Weeks, for their help and hospitality at all times.

3 Ibid., iii, p. 10.

4 Ibid., i (though running title on this page has 'Quarto'), p. 11.

5 Ibid., i, p. 12.

6 The standard work is still Logan Pearsall Smith, *The Life and Letters of Sir Henry Wotton*, 2 vols. (Oxford, 1907). Jones's references to Wotton were first discussed by W. Grant Keith, 'Inigo Jones as a Collector', *RIBA Journal*, xxxiii (1925), pp. 94-108, and most recently by Gordon Higgott, 'The Architectural Drawings of Inigo Jones: Attribution, Dating and Analysis' (unpublished Ph.D. dissertation, University of London, 1987), p. 226. For Wotton and Fialetti, see my 'Pilgrims to Pictures', *Country Life* (4 October 1990), pp. 146-49, and 'Two Unpublished Letters by Sir Henry Wotton to Vincenzo I Gonzaga, Duke of Mantua', *Journal of Anglo-Italian Studies*, i (1991), pp. 156-59. The 1614 etching (after

artist who published a treatise on drawing which influenced Jones, befriended Edward Norgate and dedicated etchings to Lords Roos and Arundel. In 1608 Wotton was preparing for Lord Salisbury (with Anne of Denmark, Jones's principal patron prior to Prince Henry and Arundel), 'some things about the subject of architecture, [which] shall be within a few days sent you in picture [as] you command'. His scholarly interest in Palladio was to culminate in his highly sophisticated treatise, *The Elements of Architecture* of 1624.[7] Meanwhile it was no doubt he who inspired Thomas Coryate to describe Palladio's buildings with unprecedented thoroughness in his *Crudities*, published, complete with a satirical introductory poem by Inigo Jones, in 1611.[8] Wotton was probably also responsible for Salisbury's son, Viscount Cranborne visiting Vicenza and praising Palladio by name for the first time in English in his 1610 diary account.[9] Most interesting for our purposes, however, is that his collection of Palladio's drawings seems to have been acquired by Jones prior to his departure for Italy. Inspired by Wotton's example, once in the Veneto with Arundel, Jones expanded this collection to more than 250 items.[10]

Jones was to add one further comment to the first page of Palladio's chapter on walls. Highlighted by a pointing hand and in slightly darker ink, between the printed captions beneath the illustration of *opus reticulatum* and his previous annotaton, he wrote:

1614 Baia: 17 January Like wise at y[e] Thearmi at Baia thear ar many wales wth mor courses of Brick and Sum great Bricke amongst for y[e] Romans varied thes things according to thear Cappriccio mingling on[e] wth an other, so yt sheaud well.[11]

This technical point which turns into a quasi-aesthetic one (raising a point Jones was to elaborate in his *Roman Sketchbook* on 20 January 1615) was

Pordenone's *Diana*) which Fialetti dedicated to 'Baron e Cavalier da Rondel' is reproduced in D. Howarth, *Lord Arundel and his Circle* (New Haven and London, 1985), p. 171. Fialetti dedicated the series entitled 'The Sport of Love' to Lord Roos. Four large three-quarter length Fialettis of Doges, probably including the portrait of Leonardo Donato which Wotton gave to Charles I, now hang above the doors in the King's Drawing Room at Kensington Palace. The influence on Jones of Fialetti's illustrated drawing manual, *Tutte le parti del corpo humano* (Venice, 1608), has been argued by John Peacock, most recently in 'Inigo Jones as a Figurative Artist', *Renaissance Bodies* (ed.) L. Gent and N. Llewellyn (London, 1990), pp. 154-79. Jeremy Wood has since drawn attention to sources via which Jones might have known Fialetti indirectly whilst confirming that he used Oliviero Gatti's

set of engravings after Guercino; see J. Wood, 'Inigo Jones, Italian Art and the Practice of Drawing', *Art Bulletin*, lxxiv, 2 (June 1992), pp. 247-70.

7 L.P. Smith, *Life and Letters of Sir Henry Wotton*, p. 412. For the *Elements*, see the facsimile edition by F. Hard (Charlottesville, 1968).

8 See my entry on Coryate, forthcoming in the *Macmillan Dictionary of Art*.

9 Cranborne's Italian diary is published (in French) in *H.M.C. Salisbury MSS*, xxi (1970), pp. 237-49; the references to Palladio are on pp. 242-43. See below, n. 24, for the argument that Jones accompanied Cranborne through France in the previous year.

10 See W. Grant Keith, 'Inigo Jones as a Collector', and J. Harris and G. Higgott, *Inigo Jones: Complete Architectural Drawings* (New York and London, 1989), p. 25.

11 Palladio, i, p. 11.

probably prompted by his visit to the Palatium Imperiale at Baia.[12] Jones is unlikely to have visited this in January 1614 when he was still based in Rome, but very likely to have done so between the beginning of March and May of that year, when, as we shall see, he was based in Naples. For this reason it is almost certain that by '1614 Baia: 17 January', 1615 New Style was intended, and that like several other entries dating from January and February 1615, it was added in London after Jones's return home. Thus it dates from just three days before the related entry in the *Roman Sketchbook*.[13]

Given Jones's importance as Britain's first professional architect and connoisseur of the classical tradition, and Arundel's, as our first great patron and collector of art and antiquities, it is surprising that their formative journey to Naples together has not been studied in more detail.[14] Having left England in order to accompany the newly-wed Princess Elizabeth to Heidelberg, as soon as they had accomplished this duty the Arundels headed surreptitiously for Italy. Arundel himself had briefly visited the Veneto to take the waters near Padua but had returned the previous November, apparently on hearing that his wife threatened to join him for the winter.[15] His journey home was hastened, however, on receiving news of the death of Prince Henry. Now, some seven months later, the Earl and Countess selected three of their most trusted and sophisticated servants to remain part of a scaled-down Grand Touring entourage. These were Arundel's cosmopolitan Catholic cousin, Robert Cansfield, Thomas Coke, a great favourite of Lady Arundel's father, Lord Shrewsbury, and the newly patronless Inigo Jones.[16] On 27 April 1613, ten days after

12 For the complete text of Jones's January 1615 discursion on variety and decorum, see J. Alfred Gotch, *Inigo Jones* (London, 1928), pp. 81-82.

13 Prior to the work of John Newman and Gordon Higgott, these January and February '1614' dates confounded scholars despite Jones's more or less logical return to Old Style dating after his return to England in late 1614. In mid January 1615 he began a period of intense study of his Palladio, both the text itself, his own on-the-spot annotations and his fading memories of specific details; for further instances, see Higgott, 'Architectural Drawings of Inigo Jones', p. 247, n. 17. I am very grateful to both John Newman and Gordon Higgott for commenting on a draft of this essay.

14 The most detailed accounts available are given by M. Hervey, *The Life, Correspondence and Collections of Thomas Howard, Earl of Arundel* (Cambridge, 1921), J.A. Gotch, *Inigo Jones* (London, 1928) and D. Howarth, *Lord Arundel and his Circle* (New Haven and London, 1985).

15 Letter from Carleton in Hervey (p. 67): 'He pretends his going home to be to hinder his

Lady from a winter's journey, who had asked leave of the King to come hither at this time, to prevent her Lord's coming home before his cure was performed'.

16 The size of the entourages of the three peers, Lennox, Arundel and Lisle, delegated to accompany Princess Elizabeth, are given in BL, Add. MS 64875 (Coke Papers), vi, fo. 90. (Formerly at Melbourne Hall, these papers were purchased from the Marquis of Lothian by the BL in 1987). The Earl's servants numbered twenty, his wife's ten. I thank Professor K.J. Höltgen for photocopies of guest lists in Leiden and Germany which show that Cansfield, Coke and Jones (in that order and immediately under Francis Quarles) were part of the large Arundel entourage from the beginning of the continental tour. Thomas Coke had 'long served' the Countess of Arundel's father, Lord Shrewsbury who confessed 'there neither is nor ever was any man towards whom I have or do more love or affect than I do this man'; see Howarth, *Lord Arundel and his Circle*, pp. 16-22, and his unpublished Ph. D. dissertation, 'Lord Arundel as a Patron and Collector, 1604-1646' (Cambridge, 1979), pp. 228-31, though beware his

leaving England, Jones had been granted the reversion of the Surveyorship of the King's Works, making him next in line for the most important architectural position in the country. Though he had been Prince Henry's Surveyor for two years and was now almost forty, he had built very little and was still known less as an architect than as the leading designer of court masques and 'a great traveller'.[17] It was indeed as the latter that Wotton's successor as ambassador to Venice, Sir Dudley Carleton, described Jones on 9 July in a letter to his friend John Chamberlain. Reporting on the arrival of two gentlemen who had been with the Arundels and Princess Elizabeth in Germany, Carleton writes:

> They tell us my lord of Arundel and his lady, whom they left with the duke of Lennox at Strasburg, will return through France home without passing any further, but I rather believe they were so told to be rid of their companies, and the more because I hear my lord had taken Inigo Jones into his train, who will be of best use to him (by reason of his language and experience) in these parts.[18]

Even as he wrote, Jones and Arundel had left Basle and were crossing the Alps via the St Gothard Pass. They arrived in Milan on 11 July and described it as 'soe hott, as without danger, wee can not (they say) stirr, till some rayne fall'. In the event, however, they stayed little more than a week (just long enough to have celebrated Jones's fortieth birthday there), for, offended by the Spanish Governor's lack of respect for their presence, the Arundels suddenly left Milan, and via Parma reached Padua on 20 July.[19] Basing themselves in a villa two miles outside Padua, they spent the rest of the summer here and in Venice, where they were lavishly entertained by the Doge and Senate. On 13 September Arundel wrote to Sir Robert Cotton from Padua, asking him to 'pick

confusion, following J. I. Whalley in *Apollo*, xciv (1971), pp. 184-91, between the Earl of Exeter and his son, William Cecil, 3rd Lord Burleigh, the Catholic traveller and connoisseur who suggested Shrewsbury might use Coke in the acquisition of works of art in Italy. There is more detail in his dissertation where Cansfield, as 'Causfield', is documented as travelling with Burleigh's son, Lord Roos, in 1612 and writing to William Trumbull about plants and Arundel's return from Ireland in 1616 (p. 244, n. 46). It seems likely that it is Cansfield (rather than 'Cannefield') who co-mortgages Arundel House in 1607 (Hervey, *The Life of Arundel*, p. 41).

17 During the royal visit to Oxford in 1605 a contemporary reported that, 'They hired one Mr Jones, a great traveller, who undertooke to further them much, and furnish them with rare Devices, but performed very little to that which was expected'; Gotch, *Inigo Jones*, p. 38.

18 Maurice Lee ed., *Dudley Carleton to John*

Chamberlain, 1603-1624: Jacobean Letters (New Brunswick, NJ, 1972), pp. 144-45.

19 The Viceroy had offended Lord Cranborne and his entourage, arresting one of the latter, just three years earlier; see J. Stoye, *English Travellers Abroad, 1604-1667* (2nd ed., New Haven and London, 1989), p. 85. Isaac Wake writes from Venice: 'To my assured good friend Mr Thomas Coke at Milan', on 20 July (BL, Add. MS 64875, vi, fos. 97r–98v.) For Arundel's indignation, see Hervey, *The Life of Arundel*, pp. 75-77. On 3 August Isaac Wake wrote to Coke saying he will come to Padua to pay his respects if the party postpones coming to Venice any longer (BL, Add. MS 64875, vi, fo. 101). A formal letter from Pietro Martire Martignone dated 18 September pursued Arundel to Padua, explaining away the writer's inability (and that of his daughter) to have 'far la dovuta riverenza et servitu, conforme all'obligo et desiderio mio, . . .' HMC, *Cowper MSS*, i, p. 79.

out some story of my Ancestors' which he could have painted in Venice, adding that Cotton should 'send it in writing and direct unto Mr Richard Willoughby in case I be not here'.[20] On 23 and 24 September, perhaps with one or both Arundels but certainly in the footsteps of his friend Thomas Coryate (who in 1608 had had Willoughby as his guide), Jones made his historic visits to the Villa Capra and the Teatro Olimpico in Vicenza.[21] On 30 September Carleton reported that, after a lavish farewell party given by Gregorio Barbarigo, 'My lord Arundel is gone privately to Florence, having left his lady at a villa hereby towards Cataio'.[22] He wrote back to her from Bologna on 1 October and from Florence on the 5th. Lady Arundel and her entourage followed him to Florence about three weeks later and then discreetly established winter quarters (complete with Italian lessons) in a monastery (delle Grazie) near Siena.[23]

By 2 January 1614 (and here he specifies 'new stille' in his annotation), Jones was in Rome studying large-scale classical remains for the first time since the late summer of 1609 when he had completed a tour of southern France, probably with Lord Cranborne.[24] As one who would continue to design royal

20 Howarth, *Lord Arundel and his Circle*, p. 37.
21 Palladio, ii, p. 64, and *Coryat's Crudities* . . . 2 vols. (Glasgow, 1905), i, p. 299: 'Mr Willoughby a learned student in the University (of Padua)'. When Willoughby died in 1617, Henry Wotton described him as 'an infectious papist'; L.P. Smith, *Life and Letters of Sir Henry Wotton*, ii, p. 114. That Arundel visited the Rotonda and Theatre with Jones seems likely. That later he knew both buildings is clear from the MS 'Remembrances of things worth seeing in Italy' which he wrote for John Evelyn on 25 April 1646; see new ed. by J.M. Robinson for the Roxburghe Club (1987), p. 23.
22 Lee (ed.), *Carleton to Chamberlain*, p. 148. Carleton also describes the farewell party for the Arundels 'made by Signore Barbarigo, where were about 20 of the most principal women'.
23 Ibid., p. 149 and Hervey, *The Life of Arundel*, pp. 80-81. Coke wrote soon after, probably to Lady Kent (who studied Italian): 'Siamo qui in un paese vago e piacevole ed abondante. L'eccell^ma Signora contessa sua sorella sta bene e qui in Siena e ogni di accarezzata e visitata di queste signori per dozzene a volta . . . '. On 14 January 1614, Gilbert, Lord Shrewsbury writes from his house in Broad Street, 'To my very lovyne frend Mr Thomas Coke': 'The last we hard from any of you, was a letter from my Lo: of Arundel to me dated at Sienna the 24 Novem: last wch I receaved but a weeke synce . . . We heare y^t [that] my Lo: of Ar: & my daughter have sent all theyr company to Pysa, except only 3 or 4 y^t are of necessity to be aboute them, to th'end they may better learne y^t language but this other

day y^t Lyttel dapp [?] Italian fellow y^t fested my daughter Grey [the Countess of Kent] before Ascanio came last to her (Antonio they say his is [sic]) toulde my Wyfe, that he hard my daughter hadd put her selfe into a monastery for vj or viij weeks, the better to Learne y^t Language. I doubt not but ther are many other Idle reports as well as this, spredd of you in this Towne, w^ich never cum to o^r eares, but I trust no wyse man will gyve credite to them:' (BL, Add. MS 64875 [Coke Papers vi], fo. 109 r; cf. summary in *HMC, Cowper MSS*, i, p. 80). At this stage, Shrewsbury trusts that the Arundels will return home by midsummer.
24 On the basis of a reference to Jones's arrival in Paris on the eve of Cranborne's tour of southern France I have argued that he was sent by Salisbury to accompany his son. This tour was distinct from Cranborne's visit to the Veneto in the following year; see my review of A.C. Fusco, *Inigo Jones Vitruvius Britannicus* (Rimini, 1985), in the *Burlington Magazine*, cxxx (1988), pp. 633-34. On 3 July 1609, the English ambassador, Sir George Carew, reported to Salisbury that he 'received his M^ties letters of the 19 of the last . . . [on] the 28. of the same . . . At the same time, I also receaved your L^ps. by Mr Jones, for wch I geve your L.^P mine humble thankes' (PRO, MSS, SP 78 [France], 55/122). Previously it had been thought that the payment made to Jones on 16 June 'for carreinge Lres for his Mat's servyce into France' must have dated from after the completion of his journey (as such payments usually were). If both dates are Old

masques until the Civil War, Jones meanwhile maintained an active interest in Italian theatre. Twenty-one years later, the Papal Nuncio in London would suggest that the reason the machines in Jones's Shrovetide masque, *The Temple of Love*, were so 'maraviglie belle' was that 'l'Architetto' had been at Rome 'a tempo che il Principe Peretti fece quella sua festa tanto celebre'. This *festa* is identifiable as the spectacular wedding entertainment, complete with fictive sea and mobile boats laden with singers, given by Sixtus V's nephew on 8 February 1614.[25]

Arundel seems to have been anxious to see Naples after a relatively short stay in Rome. His haste may have been motivated by fear of recall. Like his previous Italian journey, when he reached no further than the Veneto, this 1613-14 journey was also to be concluded by news of a distinguished death, that of Arundel's uncle, the Earl of Northampton. Fortunately, this occurred only after the Arundels had spent almost a year in Italy and even then they did not hasten back, savouring the details of Northampton's generous will in Tuscany.[26] But premature recall may have been feared for another reason, one which would also account for the high degree of secrecy maintained. Although James I had signed his historic peace treaty with Spain ten years previously, there was still considerable concern regarding communication between English Catholics and their co-religionists abroad.[27] So far as the government was concerned, Arundel's father and grandfather had both been Catholic traitors and Arundel himself, though thought relatively well of by James, was not to renounce the family faith for more than a year after his return to England.[28] On 26 May 1613 Arundel's father-in-law, Lord Shrewsbury, was already warning Thomas Coke in the Hague that 'four of our Court Bishops much noted that neither Lord Arundel nor my daughter have at any time been at

Style, this payment seems to have been made in advance, however, a thesis supported by comparison with others of this period; see for example PRO, E 351/543, recording a payment to Mr Andrew Bussey 'for carreigne of lettres for his Majesties service into ffraunce and retornynge back againe wth letters of answere xxx li'. Jones was paid less than half this amount, no return task being specified; cf. G. Higgott, 'Inigo Jones in Provence', *Architectural History*, xxvi (1983), pp. 24-34. Higgott and Harris, *Inigo Jones: Complete Architectural Drawings*, pp. 40-42, have accepted this hypothesis as, implicitly, has Stoye in the revised edition of *English Travellers Abroad*, p. 332, n. 28.

25 Howarth, 'Lord Arundel as a Patron and Collector', pp. 43 and 245. Interestingly, Peretti had visited England in 1612.

26 The news arrived in Siena and was immediately forwarded to Arundel in Rome in a letter dated 4 June 1614 by 'Frate Angelo Ing[se] Cap[no] Ind[o]': 'Jesu+Maria Sta Most Right Honourable Lord, I making something bould to write these fewe lines only to guife your Honour to understand that Sig[r] Ottaviano Perini hath newse out of England that the Earle of Northampton departed this life, and that he hath made your Honour his heare . . . ' (BL, Add. MS 64875, fo. 131r). A letter of 17 August 1614 reveals that Arundel is in Genoa and has received details of Northampton's will. Anthony Tracy sends news and Robert Cansfield is with Arundel, *HMC, Cowper MSS*, i, pp. 86-87.

27 E. Chaney, '"Quo Vadis?": Travel as Education and the Impact of Italy in the 16th Century', *International Currents in Educational Ideas and Practices*, ed. P. Cunningham and C. Brock (History of Education Society, 1988), pp. 26-28.

28 Hervey, *The Life of Arundel*, p. 112.

prayers with her highness since they went hence'.[29] When Arundel returned to England he was investigated by the Calvinist Archbishop of Canterbury and later felt obliged to send a servant abroad to clear his name.[30] The official line is clear enough in Dudley Carleton's anxious report on hearing that the Arundels had arrived in Rome, a city still specifically excluded from the travel licences issued by the Privy Council:

> The common recourse of his Ma[ties] subjects to Rome, notwithstanding their direct inhibitions on their licenses for travaile, to the contrarie, is continued wth th[t] freedom th[t] both the Earle of Arundel and his Lady have spent many days in th[t] place: w[ch] I could not beleeve uppon advertisements from thence, until I had spoken wth some who had seen them there. I heare of no English who did much resort unto them but Toby Mathew and George Gage, neither of any course they took for the purpose than the satisfying of curiosity; yet the quality of their persons being so much above other travellers, I held it my duty to give this advertisement.[31]

Ironically, by the time Carleton was writing this in Venice, Arundel and Inigo Jones had left the Countess and most of their entourage and had established themselves in Spanish-dominated Naples, a fact which Carleton was not to report until the 25 April.[32] It is only in mid May, by which time he prematurely expected them back in the Veneto, that Carleton reveals that Lady Arundel had joined them in Naples, having left most of her servants 'divided betwixt Sienna and Luca'.[33] How horrified Carleton and the British government would have been had they known – as Arundel may have done – that throughout this period, George Gage and his friend Tobie Matthew, the Archbishop of York's convert son whom James eventually knighted, had been preparing for the Catholic priesthood.[34] Already acting as travelling art agent, on the 10 May Matthew wrote from Rome to Thomas Coke in Naples that:

29 *HMC, Cowper MSS*, i, p. 78; see also D. Mathew, *The Jacobean Age* (London, 1938), p. 134. Shrewsbury concludes: 'I have not heard that the King hath heard thereof'.

30 Chaney, 'Quo Vadis?', pp. 27-28. Hervey, *The Life of Arundel*, p. 89, quotes a letter from Chamberlain to Carleton: 'It is whispered abroad that your Don Diego's master [probably Lord Roos] gave very malignant intelligence of the Lord of Arundel's being at Rome, and of his entertainment and conversation there; which being related to the King by the Ar[chbishop?], that had the advertisement, he was put to his answer, and gave very good satisfaction'.

31 Hervey, *The Life of Arundel*, pp. 83-84.

32 Ibid., p. 85.

33 Ibid., pp. 85-86. The reference to the Arun-

del's servants as 'theyre great family' suggests that more were brought with them from Germany than is sometimes thought though Italians would no doubt also have been recruited.

34 Chaney, *The Grand Tour and the Great Rebellion*, pp. 263-67. Especially useful on Matthew is J.P. Feil, 'Sir Tobie Matthew and his Collection of Letters' (unpublished Ph.D. thesis, University of Chicago, 1962). Jones and Matthew were no doubt well acquainted but Howarth's conclusion (*Lord Arundel and his Circle*, p. 100) that they were 'very close as a result of Jones's acting as gaoler to Matthew while he prepared for his banishment' is based on the mistaken assumption that Matthew's guarantor in 1608 was Inigo Jones. It was in fact Edward Jones M.P., for whom see the forthcoming volume of the *History of Parliament*.

if I can recover a little health, I think to go into a villa for the taking of some fresh air. If in the mean time you return[,] this letter will meet with you and also a roll of pictures I have left for Don Roberto [Cansfield].[35]

If, as Matthew clearly anticipated they might, the Arundel party arrived back in Rome by 20 May, it was as well that he had invented an explanation for his failure to appear, for on that day he and Gage were secretly ordained by Cardinal Bellarmine.[36] Ironically, it had been in Naples, where he had gone in defiance of a parental veto against travelling in Italy in general, that Matthew began the path to his notorious conversion. A conversation with Robert Cansfield in the Duomo at Fiesole had encouraged this process as had another with a nephew of Henry Wotton who had witnessed the liquefaction of the blood of San Gennaro.[37]

Jones arrived in Naples by 8 March at the latest.[38] We can assume that Arundel travelled south with him via Gaeta and Capua and thence on the road that John Evelyn was to describe as 'of a huge breadth, swarming with travellers more then ever I remember any of our greatest, & most frequented roads neere London'.[39] That Arundel was accompanied by the minimum of servants and tolerated the maximum of discomfort, we know from the letter he sent back to his wife soon after his arrival:

> Sweet Hart, I can only let y[u] knowe that I have done nothinge for a lodginge, M[r] Wrath mette me the other day, and though I avoided him, he must needes see me, soe as I mean to be knowne to him, and some english heere, that may help me better in my business/[40] all that is heere to be seene you may in a short time dispach, soe as I would wish y[u] to see Rome well, for there are noe more such, I wish yu could have bin there the Settimana Santa, w[ch] I desire much to see (if I can) there. the Soccoloes for women (to my likinge) are much better at Rome than heere [.] in y[r] way hither y[u] shall finde vile Hosteriass, one Mattresse, & one blankette, and neyther any bolster, or any thinge els. in y[r] way hither only Gayetta [Gaeta] (some two miles from mola), is worth y[r] seeinge. there is a rocke w[ch] (they say) clove at Christ his death iust like that

35 *HMC, Cowper MSS*, i, p. 84.
36 J.P. Feil, 'Sir Tobie Matthew', pp. 78-79 and G. Anstruther, *The Seminary Priests*. (Great Wakering, 1975), ii, pp. 120-21. The Arundels were still socialising with George Gage in the 1630s. On the basis of a somewhat cryptic reference in a letter from the painter, Nicholas Herman, to Lionel Cranfield, to Gage as 'the Architect of Tart-halle', Howarth has transferred the traditional attribution of Lady Arundel's house from Nicholas Stone to Gage, Howarth, *Lord Arundel and his Circle*, p. 245, n. 38, but cf. Chaney, *The Grand Tour*, p. 264.
37 A.H. Matthew (ed.), *A True Historical Relation of the Conversion of Sir Tobie Matthew*, (London 1904), pp. 12-15.
38 Palladio, ii, p. 96 (see below).

39 E.S. de Beer (ed.), *The Diary of John Evelyn* (Oxford, 1955), ii, pp. 324-25. It is worth noting here that early seventeenth-century Naples was one of the largest cities in the world with a population of approximately 250,000. It was only in this period that London overtook it in size.
40 A former diplomatic rival of Henry Wotton, John Wrath was effectively British consul in Naples. On Monday 16 March (Old Style) his brother, Sir Robert Wrath died leaving a young wife, daughter of the Earl of Leicester, and month-old baby. On the death of the latter, John inherited his brother's estates; cf. letter from Arundel's mother, BL Add. MS 64875, vi, fo. 128.

of Hierusalem, and, in the Castell, Bourbon his body, to be seene, wch y^u may see, askinge leave as strangers of Florence, to goe see, the Houses (though poore) alonge that shore, are very neate. Mr Coke should doe well, to put all his mony in Pistolles so the[y] be full of wayte, & Roman testony goe well heere too, if y^u send Shovanne [? presumably a servant] before, from Capua y^u may there stay, till wee eyther provide heere, or send a coach thither for y^u, as y^u shall like best, wee are yet at the Fontana de i Serpi, & there he shall eyther heare of us or else at Mr Wrath his lodginge, at the Orso del Oro. Soe I ever rest commendinge us all to God his holy protection.

Y^r most faithful husband
T: Arundell

Naples 14° Marzo
St° Rome 1614
If this letter come to y^r handes, before y^r cominge from Rome I shall be glad, where I wish wee might both have seen the Settimana Santa if it might well be, and after, I might come along with you hither in Easter weeke.[41]

   Whatever Arundel meant by the latter he clearly cannot have meant that he had 'been wonderfully fortunate' in having spent Holy Week in Rome.[42] Easter itself fell on the 30 March. Neither is it likely that he and Jones were in Rome in April when the great column in front of S. Maria Maggiore was raised.[43] Instead, having been joined by Lady Arundel, they seem to have remained in Naples for a full two months, an unusually long time in a city which, when visited at all by the English in this period, tended to be visited for a mere five days, with a total of ten more allowed for the journey to and from Rome.

When Christopher Marlowe's Doctor Faustus flew 'up to Naples, rich Campania', he saw:

41 BL, Add. MSS, 64875 (Coke Papers), vi, fo. 126 r-v. The exterior of the folded letter carried an address to 'Tomaso Cocko, Nobile Inglese in Roma, Racc^ta al Sg Fr^co Ruggieri M^ro dell Poste di Firenza in Roma'. Lassels (who knew Arundel) summarises the story of Bourbon's body from du Bellay's history, (*Voyage of Italy*, [Paris, 1670], ii, p. 264). He says that 'it stands with its *clothes*, *bootes* and *spurrs* on, in a *long boxe* streight up, with this *Spanish Epitaph* over his head . . .'. Arundel later purchased what he thought was a Titian portrait of Charles de Bourbon. It was engraved by Vorsterman; ill. in Howarth, *Lord Arundel and his Circle*, p. 50.

42 As stated by Howarth, ibid., p. 44.

43 Howarth, ibid., p. 49, says that the column in front of S. Maria Maggiore was raised 'while Arundel and Jones were there' and attributes Jones's skill in raising the drums for the columns of St Paul's portico to his having wit-

nessed its construction. What Jones actually writes, alongside the *Quattro libri* illustration of the Temple of Nerva Trajanus (Palladio, iv, p. 24) is 'January ye 5. 1614 whilst I was in Roome the Pillors then stood of this Tempell was Pulled doune by Pau. V: to sett a figur on before St Maria Maiore'. Perhaps Jones encouraged Arundel to attempt to acquire the obelisk of Domitian which Bernini eventually erected in the Piazza Navona, then lying just off the Appian Way in the Circus of Maxentius, 'broken in three peices and neglected untill that the noble Earle of Arondel and Lord Marshal of England offering to buy it, and having given threescore crownes [in] earnest, made the Romans beginn to think it a fine thing, and to stop the transporting of it into England . . .'; Richard Lassels, 'Voyage of Italy' MS of *c*. 1664, quoted in Chaney, *The Grand Tour*, pp. 407-8.

> Buildings fair, and gorgeous to the eye
> Whose streets straight forth, and paved with finest brick,
> Quarter the town in four equivalents;
> There saw we learned Maro's golden tomb,
> The way he cut an English mile in length
> Through a rock of stone in one night's space: [44]

Even within the five-day package recommended by Lassels's *Voyage*, the typical tourist devoted more than half his time to what John Raymond, in an earlier guidebook, called 'the Wonders a little distant from Naples', rather than to the city itself.[45] Prior to the discovery of Pompeii and Herculaneum, this meant the area to the west of the city rather than the now more popular south east. For the aspiring architect, the ruins around the Phlegrean Fields were, however, too ruinous to be very instructive. The brickwork at Baia has been mentioned. Like Fynes Moryson and George Sandys before him, Jones also explored Pozzuoli, and no doubt also the Solfatara and the so-called Sybil's Cave, pausing, prior to entering the extraordinary Grotta di Posillipo, to contemplate the legendary tomb of Virgil (to whose magic Faustus attributed the mile-long tunnel).[46]

In Naples itself the architecture was mainly modern, albeit constructed on the ancient grid-plan referred to by Marlowe. There were the great triumphal arches such as Alfonso of Aragon's entrance to the Castel Nuovo, or Da Maiano's Capuan Gate, through which Arundel and Jones would have entered the city. There was an extraordinary range of churches, from the intriguing Quattrocento Cappella Pontano, with its composite pilasters and high attic, to

---

44 Marlowe, *Doctor Faustus*, III, i.

45 E. Chaney, 'The Grand Tour and Beyond: British and American Travellers in Southern Italy, 1545-1960', *Oxford, China and Italy: Writings in Honour of Sir Harold Acton* ed. E. Chaney and N. Ritchie (London, 1984), pp. 133-60.

46 The best secondary account of contemporary tourists (albeit dealing mainly with Germans who are better documented), is Malcolm Letts, 'Some Sixteenth-Century Travellers in Naples', *English Historical Review*, xxxiii (1918), pp. 176-96. For the French, see G. Labrot, *Un instrument polémique: l'image de Naples au temps du schisme, 1534-1667* (Lille, 1978). The most relevant contemporary guidebook is Giuseppe Mormile, *Descrittione del amenissimo distretto della città di Napoli* (Naples, 1617); see also G.C. Capaccio, *Neapolitanae historiae . . . tomus primus* (1607) and above all, Carlo Celano, *Notitie del bello, dell'antico, e del curioso della città di Napoli*, 10 vols. (Naples, 1692). The best contemporary plan is Alessandro Baratta's of 1627. Fynes Moryson's *Itinerary* (1617) is the most detailed English account though it fails to mention the Temple of Castor and Pollux. George Sandys, *Relation of a Journey begun An: Dom: 1610* (London, 1615), is both less detailed and more derivative. For other relevant literature, see G. Alisio, 'L'immagine della città', *Civiltà del seicento a Napoli* (Naples, 1984), pp. 77-90. That Jones visited Pozzuoli is confirmed by an annotation in his copy of Vitruvius (now at Chatsworth), *I dieci libri dell'architettura* (Venice, 1567), p. 268: 'of this Potsolano wch is a burned sulferous yearth I brought from Pottsioli / 1614'. He also refers to having drawn 'the Temple at Putioli', in his Palladio (iv, p. 31). I thank Gordon Higgott for both these references. Arundel's grandson, Henry Howard, later Duke of Norfolk, built his own Grotta di Posillipo through a hill in his garden at Albury. John Evelyn designed this in 1667 (*Diary*, iii, p. 496). What is presumably the work of Arundel (and Jones?) is visible beneath this spot in Hollar's etching, which dates from 1645; ill. in Howarth, *Lord Arundel and his Circle*, p. 123.

Dosio's still unfinished cloister of the Certosa di San Martino. Jones would have been particularly interested in Domenico Fontana's massive new Palazzo Vicereale, having tried his hand at a similarly monotonous building, Lord Salisbury's New Exchange, as his first known architectural design in 1608.[47]

But, in the words of Raymond's *Mercurio Italico*, 'the onely Antiquity within the city' was the now all but forgotten Temple of Castor and Pollux. When Jones and Raymond saw it, the body of this temple had been incorporated into the church of S. Paolo Maggiore by the distinguished Theatine architect, Fabrizio Grimaldi.[48] Prior to its almost total collapse in the 1688 earthquake, its well-preserved Corinthian portico stood proud of Grimaldi's proto-Baroque building, functioning like those Roman porticoes still to be seen in Assisi and Pola. This had been greatly admired even before the Theatines began their 1580s rebuilding, most notably by the Portuguese-born artist, Francisco d'Ollanda, who in drawing it around 1540 (Fig. 15) deliberately omitted the medieval church which then crouched behind it, but also by Giuliano da Sangallo, who commented upon it in his notebooks.[49] Shortly before Grimaldi began work on the church, Palladio devoted an illustrated chapter of his *Quattro libri* to the temple, omitting in his woodcut the Greek inscription then still visible on the frieze, but sketching a fanciful version of the relief sculpture in the pediment and reinstating the three, by then already absent statues above (Fig. 16).[50] Even before setting out for Italy in 1613, Jones had studied this chapter, adding a translated paraphrase of Palladio's praise for the intertwined acanthus stalks which support the rosette on the abacus, in the margin alongside the relevant illustration (Fig. 17):

47 In a review of the quatercentenary exhibition in the Banqueting House, (*Op. Cit.*, n. 29, Naples, January 1974), Cesare de Seta argued that the Palazzo Vicereale must have influenced Jones's design for the New Exchange but the buildings are only similar in general proportions and while the latter is pre-1613, the former was not complete when Jones was previously in Italy; see also de Seta's 'L'Italia nello specchio del "Grand Tour"', *Storia d'Italia*, annali 5, *Il paesaggio*, ed. C. de Seta (Turin, 1982), pp. 148-51.

48 John Raymond, *Il Mercurio Italico: An Itinerary contayning a Voyage made through Italy in the yeare 1646 and 1647* (London, 1648), p. 141, transcribes the Greek inscription on the frieze, and refers to 'the Frontispiece, or Porch of ancient Pillars . . . as likewise the remnants of their two Statues yet standing'. This account provided the basis for John Evelyn's when he came to write up his '1645' *Diary* account several decades later (ii, pp. 327-28). For Grimaldi, see A. Quattrone, 'P.D. Francesco Grimaldi C.R. architetto', *Regnum Dei*, v

(1949), pp. 25f. For the early history of S. Paolo, see L. Correra, 'Il Tempio dei Dioscuri a Napoli', *Atti della Reale Accademia di Archeologia, Lettere e Belle Arti di Napoli*, xxiii (1905), pt. 2, pp. 214-28; see also C. Celano, *Notitie*, ii, pp. 151-77. There is a brief account in A. Blunt, *Neapolitan Baroque and Rococo Architecture* (London, 1975), pp. 39-41.

49 Correra illustrates d'Ollanda's then unpublished drawing in his 1905 article, 'Il Tempio dei Dioscuri'. The Escorial sketchbook has since been published twice in its entirety, most recently with commentary by Elias Tormo, *Os Desenhos das antigualhas que vio Francisco d'Ollanda, pintor Portugues* (Madrid, 1940), fo. 45v and pp. 199-203. Sangallo's comments are discussed in Cornel von Fabriczy, *Die Handzeichnungen Giuliano da Sangallo* (Stuttgart, 1902), p. 67. Richard Symonds included an annotated sketch of the portico in his 1651 travel notebook; Bodleian Library, MS Rawlinson D. 121, fo. 23 r.

50 Palladio, *I quattro libri*, p. 96.

Fig. 15 Francisco d'Ollanda, The Temple of Castor and Pollux; from E. Tormo, *Os desenhos das antigualhas que vio Francisco d'Ollanda . . .* (Madrid, 1940), fo. 45 v. (*Warburg Institute, London*)

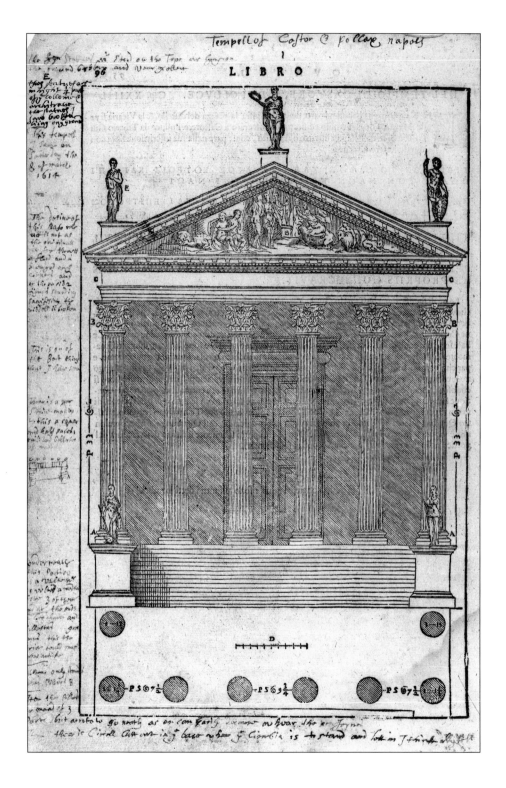

Fig. 16 The Temple of Castor and Pollux, annotated by Inigo Jones in his copy of Palladio's *Quattro libri* (Venice, 1601), iv, p. 96. (*Worcester College, Oxford*)

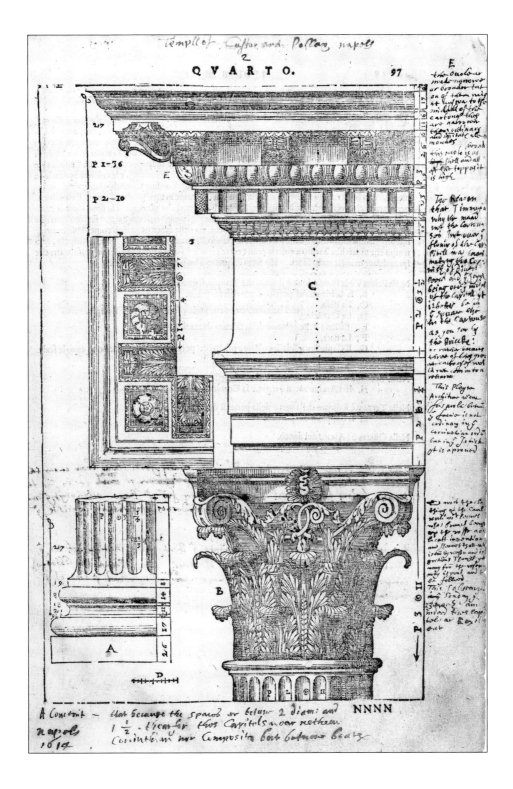

Fig. 17 The Temple of Castor and Pollux, annotated by Inigo Jones in his copy of Palladio's *Quattro libri* (Venice, 1601), iv, p. 97 (*Worcester College, Oxford*)

noat the clothing of the Cauliculi wth leaves whos branch beares up the rosse a delicatt inuention and sheaues thatt w[ch] is doo[n] by reason and is gratious Though y[t] varry fro[m] the useual way is good and to be folloed.[51]

It must have been thrilling for Jones to have seen the capitals themselves soon after his arrival in Naples. Something of his excitement is conveyed in the first of his on-the-spot marginal notes to the left of Palladio's woodcut of the reconstructed temple façade: 'This tempell I sawe on Satterday the 8 of March 1614.'[52] Beneath this we find an early example of Jones's empirical criticism of Palladio: 'The desine of this Baso relevo is not as the orignall is for thear is a flood and a Seagod on ye corners and on the on[e] sid 2 figures standing sacrifising the middell is broken. ' Below this, referring again to the portico as a whole, he added: 'This is on[e] of the Best things that I have seen. '

Jones also observed that: 'Thear is a fine stair made up to this a squar and half pases, rails and ballester of marbell.' He then sketched a miniature plan of this post-Palladian stair. Leaving a space so that what he wrote was roughly in line with what he was describing he continued to document what Palladio had not, revealing that he had discussed the history of the building with one of the Theatine monks attached to the church: 'Underneath this Portico is a Valte w[ch] is volted a medza botte 3 of them and at the ends a Crochura and Pillasters gros / onns this the friar tould mee was anticke. '

The extent of Jones's enthusiasm for the temple is indicated by the fact that a fortnight later he returned to survey it again, this time focusing his attention on those rich columns he had first admired in reproduction. Directly under his pre-1613 paraphrase of Palladio's account of the capitals, he announced: 'This I obsearved Sonday y[e] 23 March and indeed thes capitels are Exelent. '

Carleton's report of the 25 April implies that Arundel must still have been in Naples shortly before he wrote it. We can confirm this thanks to the survival of an elaborately illustrated two-part folio by the Sicilian gentleman-scholar, Don Vincenzo Mirabella e Alagona. Entitled *Dichiarazioni della pianta dell'antiche Siracuse . . .* , it had been published in Naples by Lazzaro Scoriggio only months before Arundel's arrival. On its titlepage are inscribed the price, his name and the date, presumably in new style: 'Napoli Pre[zzo]: Carlini 13 T. Arundell. Aprile 23 1614'.[53] As well as the large, fold-out street plans of Syracuse, detailed topographical text and a first-hand account of Caravaggio's 1608 visit to the 'Ear of Dionysius', this book contains the earliest illustration I know of a Greek Doric temple. Though its columns are no longer baseless and the

---

51 Ibid., iv, p. 97.
52 Ibid., iv, p. 96.
53 Sotheby's, 4 May 1925, lot 135. This sale was ordered by the President and Council of the Royal Society and consisted largely of books donated in 1667 by Arundel's grand- son, Henry Howard, 6th Duke of Norfolk. Many were from Arundel's library, a sizeable number therefore from Pirckheimer's. This item, according to the annotated copy of the sale catalogue in the BL, was sold to W. Leith for £1 10s.

absurdly over-size statues on the pediment look like seventeenth-century nightclub dancers, this was a gallant attempt to depict the Temple of Athene prior to its transformation into Syracuse's cathedral.[54] Perhaps an expedition to Sicily had been envisaged. If so, nothing further is known of one and, like Milton's projected expedition fifteen years later, it must have been abandoned.[55] It was thus left to Isaac Basire and his pupils in December 1648, to become the first British travellers known to have visited Sicily's Doric temples, and to John Breval, almost a century later, to publish the first recognisable engravings of them in the second edition of his *Remarks on Several Parts of Europe* in 1738.[56]

From another publication which Arundel purchased and inscribed during this tour, a catalogue of the Vatican Library now in the Beinecke at Yale, we know that he was back in Rome by 28 May at the latest.[57] Three days later, Jones embarked on his fullest study of a Roman building to date, that of the Pantheon, volunteering with unprecedented confidence opinions not vouchsafed by Palladio.[58]

Dudley Carleton's mid May statement that the Arundels were, 'when I last heard from them, at Naples', is too vague to build upon but as exceptionally 'curious' Grand Tourists, and Catholics to boot, the Earl and Countess may well have postponed their departure long enough to witness what John Raymond described as the 'famous Miracle of the bloud of Santo Gennaro, carryed in procession' on the first Saturday in May.[59] To judge from the autobiographical account of his conversion, Tobie Matthew for one would have encouraged them to stay for this spectacular event. So too, no doubt, would the proselytising Robert Cansfield.[60] That the Arundels were indeed still in Naples at the beginning of May is suggested by yet another surviving purchase, this time by Inigo Jones, of a two-volume history of the city, each of which he carefully

54 Vincenzo Mirabella, *Dichiarazioni della pianta dell'antiche Siracuse* (Naples, 1613), pp. 28-29.

55 For Milton's intended voyage from Naples to Sicily and Greece in 1638/9, see the Columbia edition of his *Works* (New York 1933), viii, pp. 125-26; for a sceptical account of his intentions, however, see Chaney, *Grand Tour*, p. 249 and idem, 'The Visit to Vallombrosa: A Literary Tradition', *Milton in Italy: Contexts, Images, Contradictions*, ed. M. di Cesare (Binghamton, NY, 1991), pp. 113-46.

56 E. Chaney, 'Quo Vadis?', pp. 17-18 and idem, 'British and American Travellers in Sicily', *Blue Guide Sicily*, ed. A. Macadam (London-New York, 1988; revised ed. 1990), pp. 18-38. Prior to Breval, only Bishop Berkeley seems to have appreciated the Sicilian temples for what they were; Chaney, 'Architectural Taste and the Grand Tour: George Berkeley's Evolving Canon', *Journal of Anglo-Italian Studies*, i (1991), pp. 74-91.

57 It is inscribed: '28 di Maggio 1614. Roma. T. Arundell'; see Howarth, *Lord Arundel and his Circle*, p. 230, n. 47. In Siena Arundel acquired a MS Vitruvius, which he inscribed 'Thomae Comite de Arundel emptus Siennae 14 Junii 1614' (now BL, Arundel MS 122).

58 According to the inscription on his drawing of it, now at Chatsworth, Jones sketched the Castel Sant'Angelo the next day, 29 May 1614.

59 Raymond, *Il Mercurio Italico*, p. 141.

60 A. H. Mathew (ed.), *A true historical Relation of the Conversion of Sir Tobie Matthew . . .* (London, 1904), pp. 7-9. A mutual friend of both Jones and Matthew, the then Catholic John Donne, probably visited his exiled Jesuit uncle, Jasper Heywood, in Naples *c*. 1590. Father Heywood died there eight years later; R.C. Bald, *John Donne: A Life* (Oxford, 1986), pp. 45 and 52.

inscribed: 'Napoli 1 Magio 1614: 14 Carlini 2 volls' above his newly-improved italic signature. Probably it was the embarrassed heirs to his heir, John Webb, who obliterated Jones's signature from the title-page of volume one of this work when they sold it together with the rest of his library in the 1670s or '80s. Fortunately, whoever it was forgot to check volume two where Jones had pedantically repeated the entire inscription (Fig. 18). Both volumes are now in Worcester College Library, Oxford, together with almost all his other surviving books, and are of special interest in shedding further light on Jones's response to the Temple of Castor and Pollux.

Giovanni Antonio Summonte's *Historia della città e regno di Napoli*, published in Naples in 1601-2, is a wide-ranging, informative work and carries the kind of illustrations which would have appealed to Jones. But I believe that one illustration would have been especially influential in persuading Jones to purchase the *Historia*. This is a full-page engraving of the Temple of Castor and Pollux, which, though less architecturally sophisticated than Palladio's wood-cut, was considerably more detailed as to the current state of the temple (Fig. 19). It depicts the relief sculpture in the pediment more precisely, and revises the *Quattro libri* in the light of the late sixteenth-century rebuilding of the church, illustrating in particular those additions to the temple which Jones admired: the 'fine stair', with its vaulted entrance beneath (soon to be imitated at the Queen's House), and the great entrance gate, which is clearly visible in the painting of S. Paolo by Antonio Joli, commissioned by John Lord Brudenell in the 1750s as one of a series of topographical views of southern Italy (Fig. 20).[61] I would argue that this gate, and more specifically, Grimaldi's great door to the church itself (Fig. 21), which is only glimpsed through the central columns in Summonte's illustration, influenced Jones in designs he undertook on his return to England. In particular, his unbuilt elevation for the 'Great Door' of the Banqueting House of 1619 (Fig. 22), with its confident broken pediment and identical surround, is surely closer in style to the door of S. Paolo Maggiore than it is to Scamozzi's doors in the Sala di Consiglio in the Doge's Palace, the source usually cited for Jones's design.[62]

After a long discussion of the pediment's Apollonian iconography, based largely on Stefano Vinando's (or Pighius's) *Peregrinatio*,[63] Summonte justly

61 Summonte, *Historia della città a regno di Napoli*, i, ill. facing p. 90. The Joli is now at Beaulieu in the collection of Lord Montagu; see exhibition catalogue, *All'ombra del Vesuvio: Napoli nella veduta europea dal quattrocento all'ottocento* (Naples, 1990), pp. 186 and 400. I thank Lord Montagu for his permission to reproduce the painting here.

62 Cf. Per Palme, *Triumph of Peace: A Study of the Whitehall Banqueting House* (London, 1957), p. 227 and J. Harris, *Catalogue of the Drawings Collection of the Royal Institute of British Archi-*

tects: Inigo Jones and John Webb (Farnborough 1972), p. 13, item 6, fig. 6, citing J. Charlton, *The Banqueting House, Whitehall* (London, 1964).

63 S.W. Pighius, *Hercules prodicius, seu principis inventutis vita et peregrinatio* (Antwerp, 1587), was the major source for Andrea (later François) Schott's *Itinerarii Italiae rerumque Romanorum libri tres* (Antwerp, 1600), the most influential seventeenth-century guidebook to Italy, translated from a later Italian edition into English by Edmund Warcupp in 1660.

Fig. 18 Inigo Jones's signature in Giovanni Antonio Summonte, *Historia della città . . . di Napoli* (Naples, 1601), title-page of volume II. (*Worcester College, Oxford*)

Fig. 19 Giovanni Antonio Summonte, engraving of the Temple of Castor and Pollux, from his *Historia della città . . . di Napoli* (Naples, 1601). (*Worcester College, Oxford*)

Fig. 20 Antonio Joli, *The church of S. Paolo Maggiore, Naples, c.* 1750. (*Beaulieu*)

Fig. 21 Fabrizio Grimaldi, Doorcase of S. Paolo Maggiore, Naples.

Fig. 22 Inigo Jones, the Banqueting House, Whitehall, unexecuted design for the great door, *c.* 1619. (*BAL, RIBA*)

criticises Palladio for the poor quality of his illustration of the sculpture and rather less justly – citing post-Palladian archaeological discoveries – claims the credit for an aspect of his etching which Palladio had in fact already hypothesised, the placing of the free-standing statues on the marble pedestals on the roof:

> And although in his book of architecture, Andrea Palladio illustrated the said columns well, he nevertheless failed to illustrate the figures above [i.e. in the pediment] properly, which are different from the way he has depicted them, but which we have had engraved with great care as anyone who doubts can go and see for themselves.
>
> In excavating the foundations for the rebuilding of this church in 1578, the two marble figures that one [now] sees leaning under the same columns were found, which suggests that they were the statues of Julius Caesar and the Emperor Octavian [Augustus] of those times, and that they would have stood on those marble bases which can be seen above the great cornice [pediment], in the way that we have had them engraved, which due to an earthquake, or for some other reason, fell and were spoiled.[64]

We have demonstrated the extent of Jones's interest in the Temple of Castor and Pollux by documenting three distinct moments when he consulted and annotated Palladio's chapter on the subject: first, prior to setting out for Italy; second, on site on 8 March 1614 shortly after arriving in Naples, and third; a fortnight later when he returned to the temple to study its columns and capitals more closely. I believe that the acquisition of Summonte's *Historia* may have prompted him to return to S. Paolo Maggiore yet again. Jones's criticism of Palladio's depiction of the pedimental sculpture need not have followed his announcement that he first saw the temple 'on Satterday the 8 of March 1614' as closely in time as in its position on the page. It could have been added in May. Moreover, his remarks that 'the desine of this Baso relevo is not as the originall is', and that 'the middell is broken' are remarkably similar to Summonte's 1601 criticisms of Palladio as reinforced by the *Historia's* representation of the 'broken' relief figures in the centre of the pediment in outline. By depicting them in this way Summonte clearly distinguished his version of the damaged or

64 Summonte, *Historia della città e regno d: Napoli*, i, p. 92: 'E se ben' Andrea Palladio nel suo libro de Achitettura [sic], fè essemplare le Colonne sudette, nondimeno le figure di sovra non l'esemplò bene, essendo diverse da quelle che con effetto vi sono, e da noi con gran diligenza fatte scolpire come ciasche-duno che ne dubitasse ne potrebbe far saggio.
   Nel Cavare i fondamenti per la renovatione di questo Tempio l'anno 1578. si trovaron due Busti di marmo, che si veggono appoggiate sotto l'istesse Colonne de quali si fa giuditio che fussero le statue di Giulio Cesare, e di Ottaviano Imperadori di quei tempi, e dovevano stare sopra quelle Basi di Marmo che si scorgono sovra del Cornicione, nel modo che l'habbiamo fatti ivi scolpire le quali per terremoto, o per altro accidente debbero cascare, e rovinare.'

missing central portion of the relief from his corrected depictions of what Jones described as 'a flood', 'a Seagod on ye corners and on the on[e] sid[e] 2 figures sacrifising'. So apparently close a relationship could be the result of independent observation and given that Jones only acquired his copy of Summonte on 1 May, not long before leaving Naples, we might leave it at that. But if Summonte's more precise account of the pedimental relief sculpture may not have prompted Jones to return to the temple a third time, his specifically archaeological information may well have done. Certainly, he annotated the relevant pages of his *Quattro libri* again, even if only back in London. On the top left of page 96 of Book IV, above Palladio's hypothesised statues, he wrote: 'the Statues wch stand on the Tope ar lying on the ground beelow and wear exellent.'

About twenty years later, now the grand old man of English architecture, theatre design and connoisseurship (and incidentally, ex-Member of Parliament), Jones returned for the last time to this page and to the memory of what he had seen in Naples. Squeezed between his enthusiastic remark about the statues and his dated declaration beneath, in darker ink, Jones inscribed the letter 'E' (referring to the one he had also placed to the right of Palladio's left-hand statue), and added: 'thes statues are in hight $\frac{1}{4}$ part of y^e collome and architrave the statues I saw broken liing on y^e ground.'

Jones's consciousness of the relative proportions of temple façade to roof-top sculpture was manifest even in his earliest architectural designs. Three of these, the preliminary side elevation for the Queen's House at Greenwich, the designs for the Prince's Lodging at Newmarket and the first scheme for the Banqueting House, date to within five years of his return from Italy, that is between 1616-19. Jones's fascination with the use of large-scale sculpture surmounting architecture never waned. One has only to think of his 1625 catafalque for James I, his design for a triumphal arch at Temple Bar, and, most spectacularly, his massive Corinthian portico for the west front of St Paul's Cathedral which carried two or three enormous statues though many more had been intended (Fig. 50). It was probably Jones's work on the latter that prompted him to return to Palladio's account of the Neapolitan temple and add this final remark.[65]

It is clear that Jones had been fascinated by the use of monumental sculpture in architecture for several years before his 1613-14 journey to Italy. One of his earliest surviving drawings, dated to around 1608, is for an archway – presumably intended for a masque or entertainment – upon whose pediment he has posed three large statues, if indeed live actors were not intended. A live tableau certainly featured in his 'House of Fame' which was constructed for the *Masque of Queens* in February 1609.[66] Jones's first truly architectural design, for Lord

65 For all these, see now the relevant entries in Harris and Higgott, *Inigo Jones: Complete Architectural Drawings*.

66 Ibid., fig. 3 and S. Orgel and R. Strong, *Inigo*

Jones: The Theatre of the Stuart Court, 2 vols. (London-Berkeley-Los Angeles, 1973), i, p. 130.

Salisbury's New Exchange, also dates from this period and features what would have been three huge classicising statues on pedestals placed just as those in Palladio's engraving of the Temple of Castor and Pollux (and, it has to be said, several other temples as well as Palladian villas). Most prominent of all, in these early designs, would have been the giant trio on the stable building he designed soon after this, perhaps also for Lord Salisbury.[67] Here the statues would have been nearer a third than a quarter the height of the façade. According to the most recent study of this drawing it should be dated several years earlier than hitherto, that is to around 1610. This is approximately the same date given to Jones's earliest marginal comment on the Temple of Castor and Pollux. Already then, perhaps, and certainly later, when Jones thought of monumental sculpture placed on pedestals above a classical pediment, he thought of the Temple of Castor and Pollux in Naples. Like the similarly sculptural 'Palais Tutele' at Bordeaux, which Jones and Cranborne so admired in 1609, this major classical monument deserves to be better remembered, for despite its virtual disappearance, it was once an inspiration to more than one great architect.[68]

67 Harris and Higgot, *Inigo Jones: Complete Architectural Drawings* cat. no. 9.

68 Viewing the extraordinary 'Palais Tutele' (destroyed later in the century) together with the so-called Palais Gallien just outside Bordeaux, Cranborne concluded that they were 'remarques ancien[n]es de la grandeur et magnificence des Romains'; see his travel journal in *HMC Salisbury MSS*, xxi, p. 107. The argument that Jones's presence may have prompted such enthusiasm for architecture on the part of his patron's son and heir (see n. 24 above) is strengthened by his stage design for the first scene of Prince Henry's *Barriers*, 'The Fallen House of Chivalry', in which an almost identical ruined colonnade with arcade above appears in the middle distance on the right. Jones designed this in the winter of 1609 soon after returning from his tour of France. The most vivid pre-Jonesian illustration of Les Tutelles was the fold out woodcut in Elie Vinet, *L'antiquité de Bordeaus* (Bordeaux, 1574), opposite sig. Bv.

5

The Architectural Patronage of Algernon Percy, 10th Earl of Northumberland

JEREMY WOOD

In 1619 a young man, watching the funeral procession of Anne of Denmark, fell to his death from the letter S on the alphabetical balustrade at Northumberland House in the Strand.[1] About twenty-five years later this decorative parapet, old-fashioned, and on one occasion fatal, was swept away during a major rebuilding of the house undertaken by Edward Carter (successor to Inigo Jones as Surveyor of the King's Works) for Algernon Percy, 10th Earl of Northumberland (1602-68). Northumberland was one of the most lavish architectural patrons during the Civil War and Commonwealth, spending upwards of £15,000 during this period,[2] but the extent of his activity has gone unrecognised since little of what he built has survived: Petworth, his house in Sussex, was extensively remodelled for the 6th Duke of Somerset between 1688 and 1693;[3] Syon House in Middlesex was transformed by Robert Adam between 1761 and 1769;[4] and Northumberland House itself was demolished in 1874.[5] Fortunately the Earl's building projects are well documented in the Northumberland household accounts.

* Permission to quote from documents in the Petworth House Archives has been kindly granted by Lord Egremont and Mrs P. Gill, County Archivist for West Sussex. Permission to publish extracts from the papers at Alnwick Castle has been granted by the Trustees of the 10th Duke of Northumberland. Thanks are due to Alison McCann at West Sussex Record Office for help in consulting documents. I am particularly grateful to Clare Tilbury whose comments on an early draft of this essay did much to improve it, and to John Bold for help and advice.

1 G. Gater and W.H. Godfrey, (ed.), *Survey of London*, xviii *The Strand (The Parish of St Martin-in-the Fields, Part II)* (London, 1937), p. 12.
2 The Earl's largest items of expenditure were the remodelling of Northumberland House in the years 1642-49 for £6,570 18s. 0d.; the addition of an exterior staircase there in the years 1655-57 for £1,728 5s. 0d.; and the rebuilding of Syon House in the years 1657 to 1662 for approximately £9,370. These figures are based on the General Household Accounts for the relevant years: Alnwick MSS: Syon House, U.I.6, and Petworth House Archives 5835, 5844, 5853, 5861, 5870, 5882, 5892, 5902, 5912, 5915, 5920, 5939, 5949, 5761; supplemented by the building accounts: Alnwick MSS: Syon House, U.III.2 and U.III.3.
3 See G. Jackson-Stops, 'Petworth and the Proud Duke', *Country Life*, cliii (28 June 1973), pp. 1870-74; and idem, 'The Building of Petworth', *Apollo*, cv, no. 183 (1977), pp. 324-33.
4 See D. Stillman, *The Decorative Work of Robert Adam* (London and New York, 1973), pp. 63-65.
5 See Gater and Godfrey (ed.), *Survey of London: The Strand*, p. 15.

Northumberland succeeded to the title in 1632 and it might be expected, given the favour shown to him by Charles I, that the decade before the King's break with Parliament in 1642 would have provided the Earl with both the means and the ambition to build. He did indeed make improvements to his houses at Petworth and Syon at this time but it was not until the 1640s, and the acquisition of Suffolk (later Northumberland) House, that the Earl decided to undertake large-scale building work, despite the political insecurity of the period. In this decade, when Northumberland sided with Parliament, he became an even more influential figure than in the 1630s, some considering him a potential Lord Protector. This may explain why Northumberland felt able to embark on costly architectural projects, despite the financial difficulties that he experienced from the loan of huge sums of money to Parliament and the disruption of his northern rents.[6] After the execution of Charles I, Northumberland withdrew from public life and increasingly concerned himself with his houses. It can now be shown that proposals by John Webb and Edward Marshall for the rebuilding of Syon were put into execution between 1657 and 1663, and that this project was no less extensive in scope than the work done at the London house in the 1640s.

Petworth House

Petworth had belonged to the Percy family since 1150, but it was not until the 1570s that it became the chief residence of the Earls of Northumberland.[7] The property that the 10th Earl inherited in the 1630s had been enlarged by his father from a simple manor house into one which could accommodate a sizeable household. Major additions had been made by the 9th Earl around 1616-23 when the Great Chamber was enlarged, and the famous quadrangular stables were constructed about a quarter of a mile from the house.[8] Petworth was also extended to the west and the south so that a series of bedrooms could be added to the core of the Hall, Great Chamber, Withdrawing Chamber, Parlour, Chapel and Kitchen.[9] The 9th Earl drew up plans for a large new house in 1615 (while imprisoned in the Tower on a charge amounting to constructive treason),[10] which was to be built on a site to the west of the existing buildings. This two-storey mansion was to be constructed around a courtyard with towers at each corner, as at Syon, and approached along a central axis

6 See S.R. Gardiner, *History of the Great Civil War*, 4 vols. (London, 1893), iii, p. 196.
7 G. Batho, 'The Percies at Petworth, 1574-1632', *Sussex Archaeological Collections*, xcv (1957), p. 2.
8 Ibid., pp. 14-16, 18-19. See also Jackson-

Stops, 'Building of Petworth', p. 325.
9 Batho, 'Percies at Petworth', p. 19.
10 See G.R. Batho, 'The Wizard Earl in the Tower, 1605-1621', *History Today*, vi (1956), pp. 344-51.

through an outer paved court and a square inner walled one.[11] The scheme was never executed.

In 1633/4, soon after his succession to the title, Northumberland paid John Dee, the estate carpenter, for 'makeing a plott of Petworth house & directing Boys for the levelling of ground'.[12] John Dee, assisted by Robert Flood, had originally drawn up the 'computation' of costs of the 9th Earl's scheme for a new house in 1615,[13] and so knew every detail of it. The work that Thomas Boys carried out can be discovered from a series of payments made to him between 1632 and 1637. The largest of these was £550 paid for levelling the ground and constructing 'rampiers' in front of the stables (completed by January 1637),[14] and an additional £250 was paid for levelling the bowling green and two courts before the house (completed by January 1638).[15] 10,736 feet of Purbeck stone costing £126 10s 0d. was laid in the 'rampiers' by William Bondfield in 1637/8.[16] Northumberland therefore initiated large-scale and costly work in the grounds around Petworth in the 1630s, and this seems to have been either an attempt to begin work on his father's ambitious scheme of 1615, or a modification of it.

Northumberland also spent very substantial sums on building work and reparations in the house itself during the years 1632-34, amounting to an expenditure of at least £4,500.[17] The household accounts are surprisingly uninformative about what was carried out, although since £192 18s. 8d. was paid for 'plomers worke', and a further £56 7s. 9d. was spent 'newe couveringe the partt of the howse that was altered this sommer [1633]',[18] it seems likely that changes were made to the upper floors and roof. In 1635 this high level of spending dropped to less than a third of what it had been in the previous year.[19]

11 Batho, 'Percies at Petworth', pp. 22-25. For an important correction concerning the cost of the scheme, see G. Batho, 'Notes and Documents on Petworth House, 1574-1632', *Sussex Archaeological Collections*, xcvi (1958), pp. 111-13. Jackson-Stops, 'Building of Petworth', p. 325, mistakenly followed the smaller estimate given in Batho's previous article, which related to the southern extension of the house.

12 Alnwick MSS: Syon House, U.I.5. The Account of Nicholas Holroyd from 12 January 1632/3 to 12 January 1633/4.

13 See the extract from 'A Booke of Computations of Buildings' in Batho, 'Notes and Documents on Petworth', pp. 113-29.

14 Alnwick MSS: Syon House, U.I.5. The Account of Nicholas Holroyd for the year ending 12 January 1636/7. See also Petworth House Archives, 453, 'Disborsmentts of moneys for the year 1633', fo. 4 r: 'to Thomas Boys for levillinge of the grownd befor the

stables and for making a way in the parke . . . £375 00 00'. Further details of Boys's work can be found in Holroyd's account for the year ending 12 January 1634/5 in the manuscripts at Alnwick (U.I.5).

15 Alnwick MSS: Syon House, U.I.5. The Account of Nicholas Holroyd for the year ending 12 January 1637/8.

16 Ibid. The Account of Nicholas Holroyd for the year ending 12 January 1637/8. An earlier payment for Purbeck stone can be found in Holroyd's account for the period 12 January 1633/4 to 12 January 1634/5; and, in addition, see the account for the year ending 12 January 1636/7.

17 The General Accounts for this period show that £1,020 2s. 5d. was spent in 1632; £1,831 4s. 7d. in 1633; and £1,607 11s. 7d. in 1634; see Alnwick MSS: Syon House, U.I.5.

18 Petworth House Archives, 453, fo. 4 r.

19 Alnwick MSS: Syon House, U.I.5. 'Generall Accompte 1635'.

It is clear that Northumberland decided, on coming into his inheritance, that the house should be improved according to his taste. There was also lavish spending on furnishings. In 1633/4 he spent over £1,000 on tapestries, including a set of the 'Story of Vulcan' which cost £225 and another of the 'Story of David' that cost £120, as well as quantities of 'landscape', 'gardening' and 'flowerpot' hangings.[20] The 'Six Peeces of . . . the Story of David and Goliah' can be traced in one of the later inventories at Petworth.[21] Among many other purchases, four perpetuana beds 'with chayres stooles and ffurniture suteable' were bought for the house in 1634/5, as well as £180 worth of 'chayres of guilt lether' and 'carpettes of turkey woorke'.[22] Payments in 1635/6 establish the date when Northumberland purchased the 'guilte hanginges and 6 carved chaires' (costing £25 5s. 0d.) and 'backstooles of the Italian fashion and guilded leather carpettes' (costing £18),[23] which can be identified with the eighteen *sgabello* chairs now in the Beauty Room and Grand Stairs at Petworth. Nine of these chairs have Percy half-moons painted in the oval cartouches on their backs. The accounts do not, unfortunately, clarify whether the chairs are of Italian origin or were made in England in imitation of continental designs by Francis Cleyn, to whom they have been attributed.[24]

This energetic phase of building and refurnishing at Petworth in the 1630s provides a foretaste of the more comprehensive schemes to be initiated at Northumberland's other houses during the 1640s and 1650s. The expenditure at Petworth, although in excess of £4,500, would not have been enough for a completely new building. In this period Trentham Hall in Staffordshire was built for £6,165 17s. 4d., and Aston Hall in Warwickshire was constructed for Sir Thomas Holte for a similar sum.[25] However, Northumberland is likely to have made substantial changes to Petworth and, as will be shown, this was characteristic of him, since elsewhere he preferred to remodel an existing building rather than start afresh.

Northumberland House

In 1642 Northumberland acquired the mansion then known as Suffolk House through his marriage to Elizabeth Howard, daughter of the 2nd Earl of Suffolk. Northumberland needed a male heir; he also needed to own one of

20 Ibid. The Account of Peter Dodesworth from 12 January 1632/3 to 14 January 1633/4.
21 Alnwick MSS, 107 GC 26, 'An Inventory of the late Right Honourable Jocelin, Earl of Northumberland's Personal Estate as it was at the time of his Decease, the $\frac{21}{31}$ of May 1670', fo. 2 r.
22 Alnwick MSS: Syon House, U.I.5. The Account of Peter Dodesworth from 14 January 1633/4 to 16 January 1634/5.
23 Ibid. The Account of Peter Dodesworth from

16 January 1634/5 to 16 January 1635/6.
24 See G. Jackson-Stops, 'Furniture at Petworth', *Apollo*, cv. no. 183 (1977), p. 358 (as Italian in origin); and idem in *The Treasure Houses of Britain: Five Hundred Years of Private Patronage and Art Collecting*, National Gallery of Art (Washington, DC, 1985), p. 135 (as attributed to Cleyn).
25 See O. Fairclough, *The Grand Old Mansion: The Holtes and their Successors at Aston Hall, 1618-1864* (Birmingham, 1984), pp. 64-65.

the patrician mansions close to Whitehall and situated between the Strand and the River Thames, commensurate with his political and social importance. The house had been built around 1605-9 by Henry Howard, Earl of Northampton.[26] Evidence of the original layout comes from a plan by Robert Smythson inscribed 'The Platforme of my Lord of Northamtons house in London' (Fig. 23),[27] which can thus be dated before 1614 when the house passed to Northampton's nephew, Thomas Howard, Earl of Suffolk. Two more detailed plans by John Thorpe of the ground floor and second floor survive (Figs. 24, 25),[28] but these are confusing to interpret and could contain information about more than one floor on each plan, as well as what may be proposed alterations added by a second hand. The house was three storeys high, surrounded a courtyard, and had four corner towers. A drawing by Wenceslaus Hollar, which depicts it from the river,[29] shows the south front as one storey lower than the other three ranges, and this is confirmed by Thorpe's plan of the second floor (Fig. 25). The house was on a sloping site which dropped down towards the river, and this meant that the *piano nobile* of the south range was entered on the level of the street. This is confirmed by both early plans of the ground floor which do not show any doorways into the garden on this level of the south front. Northumberland's alterations to the house were so radical, however, that these plans are of limited use in recreating its appearance after the rebuilding of the 1640s, and since, unfortunately, none survives from the mid seventeenth century, knowledge of this phase in the history of the house must depend on the very detailed payments for building work found in the household accounts.

Northumberland's architect was Edward Carter who was paid £100 for 'his paines in this worke' in 1649.[30] He was the son of Francis Carter who had been Chief Clerk of the Office of Works from 1614 to 1630.[31] In 1643 Edward Carter became Surveyor of the King's Works after skilfully aggravating Inigo Jones's delinquency in the eyes of the Committee of Revenue.[32] Carter was not unfit for the post, however, since he had acted as Jones's deputy in the restoration of St Paul's, and had been involved with the Earl of Bedford's building scheme in Covent Garden.[33] Some of the craftsmen recruited by Carter to work at Northumberland House were formerly employed by the

26 See Gater and Godfrey (ed.), *Survey of London: The Strand*, pp. 10-11.

27 RIBA, Smythson Collection, I/12. See M. Girouard, (ed.), 'The Smythson Collection of the Royal Institute of British Architects', *Architectural History*, v (1962), p. 32.

28 Sir John Soane Museum, London. See J. Summerson, *The Book of Architecture of John Thorpe*, *Walpole Society*, xl (1966), pp. 108-9.

29 Pepsyian Library, Magdalene College, Cambridge. An engraving of this drawing was made in 1808; it is conveniently reproduced

in H. Hobhouse, *Lost London: A Century of Demolition and Decay* (London, 1971), p. 20.

30 Alnwick MSS: Syon House, U.III.2, 'Mr Scawens Accompte for buildinges and reparacones don at Northumberland house divers yeares ended 1649'.

31 H.M. Colvin, *A Biographical Dictionary of British Architects, 1600-1840* (London, 1978), p. 197.

32 Idem (ed.), *The History of the King's Works*, iii, *1485-1660* (part I) (London, 1975), p. 156.

33 Ibid., pp. 144, 149.

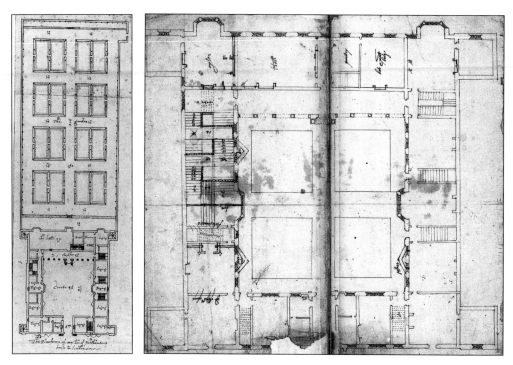

Fig. 23 Robert Smythson, Northampton (later Northumberland) House, London, ground plan (*above left*). (*BAL, RIBA*)

Fig. 24 John Thorpe, Northampton House, ground plan (*above right*). (*Sir John Soane's Museum*)

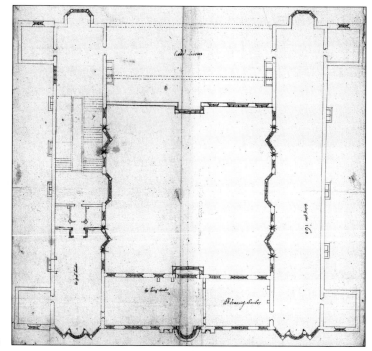

Fig. 25 John Thorpe, Northampton House, second floor plan (*right*). (*Sir John Soane's Museum*)

Fig. 26 G. Grignion after S. Wale, Northumberland House, south front, from R. and J. Dodsley, *London and its Environs* (1761).

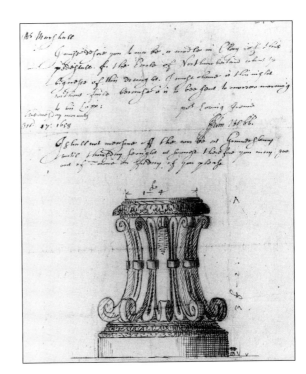

Fig. 27 Letter from John Webb to Edward Marshall with an elevation for a pedestal, 17 October 1658. (*BAL, RIBA*)

Office of Works,[34] and, no doubt, had found little to do after the king's departure from London in 1642. The most notable among them were Thomas Steevens, John Embree, and Zachary Taylor. Steevens, a mason, had been employed at St Paul's around 1640,[35] and was later to work for Northumberland at Syon in 1650-51.[36] Embree, who was Carter's neighbour in Scotland Yard not far from Northumberland House,[37] had been appointed Sergeant Plumber in 1639, and was later to supersede Carter as Surveyor during the Protectorate.[38] Taylor, the carver, had executed a great deal of work in the Queen's Chapel at Somerset House during the mid 1630s, and in the Cross Gallery and the Queen's Cabinet Room there.[39] He had also carved picture frames for the royal collection and pedestals for statues at Greenwich,[40] as well as having worked at St James's and Whitehall. Little is known of his work in the 1640s, although he is documented carving a chair for the Speaker of the House of Commons in 1645/6.[41] It is not easy to detect any particular artistic or political bias behind Northumberland's choice of architect and craftsmen:[42] they were simply the best available in London at the beginning of the Civil War.

Masons and bricklayers were employed (or subcontracted) to take down portions of the south range of the house through to the inner courtyard, of the east range of the house adjacent to the property owned by Sir Henry Vane,[43] and of the west range on the level of the Long Gallery.[44] The rebuilding was therefore concentrated on the southern part of the house towards the garden and river, and also entailed substantial work in the courtyard. The north range which faced the Strand and contained an elaborate Jacobean entrance was left untouched.[45] The new scheme was largely concerned with making the internal

34 J. Bold, *John Webb, Architectural Theory and Practice in the Seventeenth Century* (Oxford, 1989), p. 164. The same point is made in F. Allardyce 'The Patronage of the 9th and 10th Earls of Northumberland: A Comparison' (unpublished M.A. thesis, Courtauld Institute of Art, University of London, 1987), p. 13. This is, to my knowledge, the only previous attempt to assess the 10th Earl of Northumberland as an architectural patron. Only chapter 2, devoted to some aspects of the building work at Northumberland House is relevant here, and Allardyce provides no account of the 10th Earl's building work at Petworth or Syon. Her discussion is largely based on Alnwick MSS: Syon House, U.III.2, and U.III.3. Some differences of opinion with Allardyce are noted below, but corrections have been kept to a minimum.

35 Colvin (ed.), *King's Works*, iii (part I), p. 151.

36 Alnwick MSS: Syon House, U.I.6. The Account of Robert Scawen from 30 March 1649/50 to 25 March 1650/1: 'for laying 553 foote of old purbecke stone'.

37 Colvin (ed.), *King's Works*, iii (part I), p. 158.

38 Ibid., p. 161.

39 H.M. Colvin (ed.), *The History of the King's Works*, iv, *1485-1660*, (part II) (London, 1982), pp. 259, 262, 265, 267, 268.

40 Ibid., pp. 39, 121.

41 Colvin (ed.), *King's Works*, iii (part I), p. 163.

42 Allardyce, 'Patronage', p. 13, suggested that Northumberland employed Carter for political reasons, but since Jones, the obvious alternative, was absent from London at this time, the choice was limited.

43 See Gater and Godfrey (ed.), *Survey of London: The Strand*, pp.18-19.

44 Alnwick MSS: Syon House, U.III.2. Payments to William Andrewes for demolishing brickwork.

45 See Gater and Godfrey (ed.), *Survey of London: The Strand*, p. 16, who also illustrate a drawing of this frontispiece by Vertue (pl. 4). In addition, see the painting by Canaletto at Alnwick Castle, and the related drawing in the Minneapolis Institute of Art, which show the exterior of Northumberland House as it survived around 1752; W.G. Constable, *Canaletto: Giovanni Antonio Canale, 1697-1768*, rev. ed. J.G. Links, 2 vols. (Oxford, 1976), ii, pp. 411-13, 573, nos. 419, 740.

organisation of the rooms more convenient. For example, Thorpe's plan of the original house (Fig. 25) shows that the 'dining chamber' was formerly located on the second floor overlooking the Strand, but in the rebuilding it was moved to the south-east corner away from the noise of the street.[46] Northumberland may well have thought that he had acquired an old-fashioned house in 1642, but the courtyard plan was left undisturbed, and Carter's new south front, which reflected Inigo Jones's work of the previous twenty years, was not balanced by any remodelling of the north front.

Workmen employed by William Andrewes, the bricklayer, took down the upper storeys of the south front, overlooking the gardens, between the end of the Long Gallery at the south-west corner of the building and the end of the new Dining room at the south-east corner.[47] At least part of the two square corner towers must have been retained, although it is clear that their fenestration was completely altered. Some of the existing brickwork in the basement of the south front was left standing since the doorway into the garden, which was at the centre, was given an arched top and strengthened to allow a balcony to be constructed above it.[48] The brickwork of the basement also appears to have been reworked to give arched tops to the eight windows on either side of the central doorway, which was flanked by the Low Hall and the Orange House,[49] and ten new capitals were made by the masons for the 'old pillosters' of the garden front.[50] Workmen employed by Andrewes also took down a partition in the 'Lower tarras which now is ye hall', removed other old brick walls in this part of the house, and demolished '3 little houses next Sir Henry Vanes'.[51]

This extensive rebuilding of the south front also affected the side of this range facing the inner courtyard. Before this, the visitor would have entered the house from the Strand through the elaborate frontispiece, and, on reaching the courtyard, have faced a projecting bay to the south that echoed the main entrance. Smythson's plan (Fig. 23) shows that this bay and its portico marked the doorway into the Hall which then occupied the south-east corner of the building. Thorpe's slightly later plan (Fig. 24) shows some modifications to this, including the removal of an adjacent staircase, but the arrangement survived until Carter divided the Hall with a floor and made it possible to create

---

46 The Dining Room is described as on the side of the building facing Sir Henry Vane's house on two occasions in Alnwick MSS, U.III.2 (see n. 47 below), and as part of the south range in Alnwick MSS, U.III.3.

47 Alnwick MSS: Syon House, U.III.2. 'For making scaffoldes and takeing downe the 2 stories of bricke worke vpon the front next the garden, between the retourne of the long gallery, and the retourne of the Dineing roome next S.' Henry Vanes'.

48 Ibid., 'Turning a bricke arch at the entrance

into the garden to beare the stone iambs of the doreway above and building vp the 2 stories of bricke worke againe'.

49 Ibid., Payment to William Andrewes: 'for workeing the bricke worke of 8 Arches about the windowes in the Low hall, and orange house ix.^{li} v.^{s} x.^{d}'

50 Ibid. Payment to Thomas Steevens: 'for sawing workeing and setting 10 Capitalls vpon the old pillosters on the gardenside being of portland stone at 5.^{s} a peece l.^{s}'

51 Ibid. The cost was £1 7s. 10d.

new suites of rooms in the main levels of the south range. As a result the Hall seems to have been relegated to the basement level, and was henceforth referred to as the 'Low Hall'.[52]

Both Smythson's and Thorpe's plans show that, on either side of this portico in the courtyard, an arcade opened into what Smythson described as the 'cloyster', a covered passage running along the south end of the courtyard. Some elements of the arrangement were retained in Carter's new scheme since the carpenter's accounts contain a payment for 'makeing Centers betweene the Collonmes in the Courte to hold vp the stone worke whilst the walls were taken downe, and made vp againe'.[53] Carter did not fill in the arcading since a description of the courtyard in 1720 refers to it as having 'a Piazza, with Buildings over it, sustained by Stone Pillars'.[54]

Extensive payments for new windows in the courtyard suggest that they were changed to harmonise with the Jonesian style adopted in the south front. New architraves, mouldings and cornices were specified in the accounts, as well as four new brackets provided by Thomas Steevens for £4. The most expensive items of this kind were the cornice of Portland stone, 395 feet in length, which was set around the courtyard at a cost of £125 1s. 8d., and a rail of the same length which ran along a new brick parapet wall at a cost of £105 6s. 8d.[55] Some of the carved work from the earlier building must have been retained, however, since there are payments for 'clensing 4 Cherubines heades and 12 Cartooses [brackets] with frutage and heades vnder the 4 groine windowes in the Courte'.[56]

Workmen under the direction of William Andrewes were employed 'cutting downe parte of the bricke worke next Mr Vanes', that is, on the east side of the building, 'and removeing the stone windowes and the 2 Chimneys that stand in the little roomes by the backstaires'.[57] This cost £7 19s. 9d., and erecting scaffolding, taking down the brick work around the stone windows, and rebuilding the wall 'soe high as the stone railes with 3 tunnells for Chimneys in it' cost a further £10 12s. 2d.[58] The small sums involved suggest that work here was more limited than in the south range.

Part of the side wall of the Long Gallery was also taken down where it joined the leads of the south range, and, in order to raise the height of the building, it

52 See n. 49 above.
53 Alnwick MSS: Syon House, U.III.2. Payment to Richard Veasey.
54 J. Stow, *A Survey of the Cities of London and Westminster . . . written in 1698 . . . Corrected, Improved and very much Enlarged in the Year 1720 . . .* , rev. ed. J. Strype, 2 vols. (London, 1754-55), ii, p. 651.
55 Alnwick MSS: Syon House, U.III.2. 'For stone workeing craneing and setting of 4 Cartooses vnder the Clossett and staires at 20.ˢ a peece iiij.ˡⁱ 'For stone rubbing workeing and

setting 395 foote of Cornish round the Courte, and home to the 2 towers gardenside vnder the parrapett wall of brickes being of portland stone at 6.ˢ-4.ᵈ the foote Cxxv.ˡⁱ xx.ᵈ For stone workeing and setting 395 foote of raile for the Covering of the said parrapett at 5.ˢ-4.ᵈ the foote Cv.ˡⁱ vj.ˢ viij.ᵈ'
56 Ibid. Payment to Thomas Steevens, £2 10s. 0d.
57 Ibid. Payment to William Andrewes.
58 Ibid.

was necessary to remove two chimney stacks and make a new doorway.[59] Thorpe's plan of the earlier building shows that the Long Gallery, 160 feet in length, ran uninterrupted along the length of the west range and was located high up on the top floor of the house (Fig. 25). It had projecting windows looking out to the Strand at the north, and a bay window over the garden and river at the south. The plan shows that there were previously no windows on the west wall, but three 'great windowes' overlooking Angel Court were added by Carter,[60] and this change to the fenestration is confirmed by a payment to Thomas Simson, the joiner, for taking down the wainscot in the Long Gallery 'where ye windowes were wrought vp'.[61] It seems likely that these were given proportions to harmonise with those of the south front. The new windows would have made the room less suited for displaying pictures and better fitted for exercise.[62] However, since Northumberland had been actively collecting paintings for a number of years, a gallery must have been fitted up for their display in the new scheme of decoration.[63]

The changes made in the south-west corner of the house also involved the construction, or enlargement, of a staircase rising from the courtyard to the Long Gallery and from thence giving access to the leaded terrace on the roof of the south range. This staircase is generally described in the accounts as the 'greate staires' or the 'carved staires' to distinguish it from the stairs in the east range which had previously provided the most imposing access to the upper levels of the house, as well as to distinguish it from a new stone staircase that is discussed below. Since the existing 'bricke worke of the staircase that is to rise to the greate gallerie' was taken down 'from the Lower Leades [the roof of the south range] downe to the stone arches [the arcading of the courtyard in the south range]',[64] the new staircase can be located at the south-west corner of the courtyard. The reference to the 'stone arches' suggests that the staircase was entered from, or was close to, the arcade described by Smythson as the 'cloyster'. Both his plan (Fig. 23) and Thorpe's (Fig. 24) show that a staircase

59 Ibid. 'For makeing scaffoldes and takeing downe part of the side wall of the great gallery above the Lower Leades, and workeing it vp againe to the vnder side of the vpp Leades, with the Carriage of 2 stackes of Chimneys that stood vpon the same wall, and makeing another doreway into the new staircase, and workeing vp the window that was in the gallery in the place where the staires riseth, with the brickeworke over the next window on the Courte side, where yᵉ stone freese retournes and knittes viijˡⁱ: vijˢ: vjᵈ:

60 Ibid. Payment to William Andrewes: 'for workeing vp with brickes 3 greate windowes on the west side of yᵉ long gallery towards Angell Courte xlviijˢ: xjᵈ:

61 Ibid. See also the payments to joiners 'for 399

daies worke don in the long gallery xxxvijˡⁱ:

62 See R. Coope, 'The 'Long Gallery': Its Origins, Development, Use and Decoration', *Architectural History*, xxix (1986), pp. 59-63.

63 It appears that Northumberland kept his pictures at York House, next door to Northumberland House, which he rented from the Duchess of Buckingham and the Earl of Antrim from 1640 to 1647. For further discussion see J. Wood, 'Van Dyck and the Earl of Northumberland: Taste and Collecting in Stuart England', *Van Dyck 350: A Symposium*, eds. S. Barnes and A.K. Wheelock, Jr., *Studies in the History of Art*, National Gallery of Art, Washington, DC (forthcoming).

64 Alnwick MSS: Syon House, U.III.2. Payment to William Andrewes. £14 2s. 6d.

going up to the first floor already existed in this part of the original building, but it did not give access to the Long Gallery. It seems that one of the windows of the Long Gallery (presumably overlooking the courtyard) was removed to make a new entrance for the staircase.[65] Richard Veasey, the carpenter, provided the twenty-three wooden steps (rather than the more usual thirty) for 'the staires that rise vp to the greate gallery, and soe vp to the lower Leades', together with twenty-two feet of railing and balustrade, and the flooring of the 'half-paces' (landings).[66] Thorpe's slightly ambiguous plan (Fig. 24) suggests that the stairs had previously risen to a height of twenty or twenty-one treads. However, if these stairs were continued to the level of the Long Gallery they must have blocked off the east window overlooking the gardens.

The importance given to the staircase is shown by its elaborate carved decoration by Zachary Taylor which included '8 Roses on the endes of the postes of the staires', '12 Ionicke heades for the french Tearmes in the Joyners worke', '8 brestes cutt with gold roundes and water leaves', as well as '4 ffestoones cutt with fruitage' and shields bearing the Order of the Garter and the Percy half-moon.[67]

Another new flight of stairs, in this case built of stone and utilitarian in function, was made next to the existing staircase in the east range. It connected the new Dining Room at the south-east corner of the building with the Waiters' Room directly below it in the basement, and the kitchens. Thomas Steevens, the mason, laid 88 feet 10 inches of Kentish stone 'in the new staires leading to the greate kitchen' and paved the 'lower halfe paces' (landings).[68] William Andrewes, the bricklayer, worked up two existing doorcases at the foot of the stone staircase in order to provide access to the kitchen.[69] He also inserted a timber doorcase into the brick wall at the bottom of the old 'great staires' to make an entrance into the Waiters' Room.[70] This older staircase still gave access to the south and north ranges, and was linked to the Carved Stairs by a new series of apartments in the remodelled south range.

The accounts indicate that the new rooms, on two levels, ran from the Dining Room (at the south east of the building) through the Withdrawing Room, the Countess's Bedroom and Closet, the Earl's Bedroom and Closet, and the Lobby, to the carved staircase rising to the Long Gallery (in the west range).[71]

65 See no. 59 above.
66 Alnwick MSS: Syon House, U.III.2. Payments of £7 13s. 4d. for the stairs, £11 for the railing and balustrade, and £2 10s. 0d. for the landings.
67 Ibid. The total payment for all carving by Taylor amounted to £196 14s. 6d.
68 Ibid. 'For stone squareing and laying 88 foot 10 inches of Kentish stepp in the new staires leading to the greate kitchen at 20ᵈ the foote vijˡⁱ viijˢ jᵈ For squareing and laying 65 foote of paveing in the lower halfe paces at 3ᵈ the foote xvjˢ iijᵈ.'
69 Ibid. 'For workeing vp 3 dorecases 2 in the old bricke walles at the foote of the stone stepps made new to goe into the kitchen, and one in the passage at the foote of the backstaires lˢ iijᵈ.'
70 Ibid. 'For setting in a timber dorecase at the feet of yᵉ great staires goeing into the wayters Chamber xxxvijˢ xjᵈ.'
71 Ibid. See the accounts for work done by Zachary Taylor and John Gomersall.

The arrangement of these rooms is uncertain. Two smaller rooms in the square towers at the south-west and north-west corners of the house, opening off the Long Gallery at either end, were also sometimes referred to as closets,[72] but seem to have been decorated in a more simple style than the main sequence of rooms.

The principal rooms in the south range were given visual coherence in their decoration by the same team of craftsmen: Richard Veasey, Thomas Simson, Zachary Taylor and John Gomersall (the painter), working under Carter's direction. A major contribution came from Taylor who was responsible for the carving in these rooms and who, as has been shown, decorated the staircase that provided the main approach to them. The Dining Room was given a new window,[73] and had wainscoting made by Thomas Simson at the high cost of £42 8s. 0d.[74] He also provided '33 Compartementes and sheildes' in the Withdrawing Room, in the 'balcony room' (which must have been in the centre of the south front overlooking the garden), and in the 'bedchamber' (presumably that of the Earl).[75] Simson provided a low wainscot for these rooms which were hung with tapestry.[76] The Withdrawing Room had an existing chimney removed in order to make a door into the Countess's Closet;[77] it was, like the Dining Room and other adjacent rooms richly carved by Zachary Taylor with 'festoones' and 'ffoliage'. The Countess's Closet was obviously next to her bedchamber and was also situated close to the 'new staires',[78] which probably means the Carved Staircase, ensuring a degree of self-containment and direct access. The Earl's Bedchamber and Closet appear to have been more richly decorated than those of his wife (though the accounts may be incomplete), and he had the cornice, wainscot, and shutters supplied by Thomas Simson.[79] The quantities and measurements suggest that the Closet was about half the size of the Bedchamber. The latter contained a black marble chimney-piece made by Thomas Steevens at a cost of £13, the marble itself having been provided by the

72 Ibid. Payment to Thomas Simson: 'for 25 yardes 5 inches of Crest and Batten in the Clossettes at the endes of the gallery at 3ˢ. the yard lxxvˢ. vᵈˢ'

73 Ibid. Payment to William Andrewes: 'for takeing downe the brickeworke about the stone windowes . . . and workeing them in againe with an other window that was placed where the old Chimney of the dining roome stood'.

74 Ibid. 'For wainscotting in the dining roome being 106 yards at 8ˢ. yᵉ yard xlijˡⁱ. viijˢ'

75 Ibid. 'For 99 yardes square measure in the drawing roome, balcony roome, bedchamber, peeres [=piers] over the dores, and vnder the windowes at 12ˢ. p[er] yard lixˡⁱ. ixˢ. iiijᵈ. For 33 Compartementes and sheildes in the 3 roomes at 5ˢ. a peece viijˡⁱ. vˢ'

76 Ibid. 'For 39 yardes ½ of wainscott vnder the

hangings in those roomes at 7ˢ. the yard xiijˡⁱ. xvjˢ. vjᵈˢ'

77 Ibid. Payment to William Andrewes: 'for takeing away the Chimney that did belong to my Ladys Clossett and placeing a dorecase there, to goe out of the withdrawing roome into that Clossett'.

78 Ibid. Payment to Richard Veasey: 'furring and boarding the vpper floore in my Ladys bedchamber next yᵉ new staires and Clossett within the same'.

79 Ibid. 'For 25 yardes of Cornice in his Loꝗꝓˢ Bedchamber at 6ˢ. the yard vijˡⁱ. xˢ. For 34 yardes 2 foot of wainscott in the same roome at 7ˢ. the yard xijˡⁱ. vijᵈ . . . For 13 yardes one foote of Cornice in the Clossett to this bedchambʳ. at 3ˢ. the yard xlˢ. For 20 yardes 5 inches of wainscott at 7ˢ. the yard vijˡⁱ. vjᵈˢ'

Earl.[80] The Lobby, which is described as being near the backstairs, contained a chimney-piece of Portland stone inlaid with black marble made by Henry Stone (one of Nicholas Stone's sons) for £6 10s. 0d.[81] Stone provided a similar chimney-piece for the Waiters' Room on the floor below, and eight far more expensive ones of 'severall sortes of Marbles' at a cost of £200.[82] Their locations are not specified in the accounts and may have been intended for some of the more important rooms in those parts of the house that had not been rebuilt. The Lobby also contained an architrave, frieze and cornice (costing £11 0s. 6d.) as well as a wainscot (costing £22 12s. 9d.) supplied by Simson,[83] and the decorative carving there was executed by Zachary Taylor. The character of Taylor's carving may well have recalled the work that he had carried out at the royal palaces, particularly at St James's, Oatlands, Somerset House, and White-hall in the late 1620s and 1630s, often to designs by Inigo Jones.[84] The plasterwork in these rooms by William Hollins and John Martin seems to have been very simple and no inset paintings are specified for the ceilings,[85] so that the enrichment of these interiors was largely restricted to the carving.

The greatest opportunity for Edward Carter, as architect at Northumberland House, was provided by the rebuilding of the south front, and some idea of its appearance can be gained from a mid eighteenth-century engraving (Fig. 26).[86] It is clear from the accounts that the central section of the south front was 80 feet 6 inches wide (the same width as the inner courtyard),[87] and two storeys high with a basement from which a centrally placed door gave access to the gardens. Each storey contained eight windows.[88] Payments to Richard Veasey, the carpenter, show that the main floor window frames were 11 feet high by 4 feet wide and cost £22, and that the second floor window frames (dimensions

80 Ibid. 'For stone workeing and setting the Marble Chimney peece in his Lo.pps Bed-chamber, the blacke marble of it being my Lordes with the harth paces of black and white Marble new xiijli'

81 Ibid. 'For one Chimney peece of portland stone with some inlayes of blacke marble and a footpace of blacke and white Marble sett vp in the Lobby vjli: xs'

82 Ibid. Seven of these are described as 'sett vp, and one of them reserved for his Lops: owne vse where he shall appointe'.

83 Ibid. 'For 22 yardes 6 inches of Archatrave freese and Cornice in the Lobby at 10s: the yard xjli: vjd. For 64 yardes 5 foote of wainscott in the Lobby at 7s: the yard xxijli: xijs: ixd'

84 See Colvin (ed.), *King's Works*, iv (part II), pp. 39, 121, 145, 216, 249, 259, 262, 263, 265, 267, 268, 334-35.

85 Alnwick MSS: Syon House, U.III.2. 'For 528 yardes ½ of lathed worke in the dineing roome next Sr: Henry Vanes, and in the 4 roomes on that floore next the garden and in the Ceelings and pucones there at 13d: the yard xxviijli: xijs' For the later careers of Hollins and Martin, see G. Beard, *Decorative Plasterwork in Great Britain* (London, 1975), pp. 37, 46, 225, 229.

86 R. and J. Dodsley, *London and its Environs* (London, 1761), v.

87 Alnwich MSS: Syon House, U.III.2. Payment to Thomas Steevens: 'for sawing workeing and setting the lower facia being 80 foote ½ on each side of the dore goeing out of the house at 4s-6d the foote xviijli: ijs: iijd' See Allardyce, 'Patronage', pp. 15-16. Inigo Jones made a note in his copy of the *Quattro libri* that 'The front of Northamton Ho is 162fo - the court is 81fo'; see B. Allsop (ed.), *Inigo Jones on Palladio* (Newcastle upon Tyne, 1970), 3rd flyleaf r.

88 Alnwick MSS: Syon House, U.III.2. See the payments for 'the 8 windowes of the second storie on the garden side being of portland stone at 3s-9d the foote xlvijli: js: ijd'

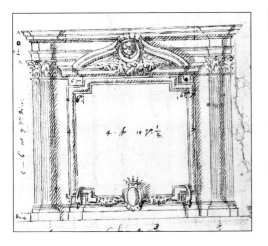

Fig. 28 John Webb, Northumberland House, elevation for an overmantel in the Dining Room, 1657. (*BAL, RIBA*)

Fig. 29 John Webb, Northumberland House, elevation and plan for a chimney-piece and overmantel in the Withdrawing Room, 1660. (*BAL, RIBA*)

Fig. 30 John Webb, Northumberland House, design for a composite capital for the Dining Room, 1657. (*BAL, RIBA*)

Fig. 31 John Webb, Northumberland House, design for a composite capital for the Withdrawing Room. (*BAL, RIBA*)

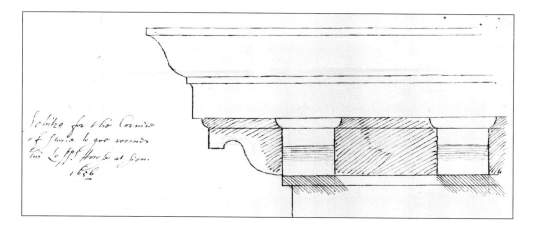

Fig. 32 John Webb, Syon House, London, design for a stone cornice for the exterior, 1656. (*Alnwick Castle*)

Fig. 33 William Capon, *The Courtyard at Syon House*. (*Private Collection*)

unspecified) cost £18. The wooden balcony doors on the main floor, opening above the garden, and the answering doors into the courtyard, were 13 feet high and 5 feet 6 inches wide and cost £5 each.[89] The 'lower door' in the basement, so-called to distinguish it from the balcony door above, was flanked by pilasters 11 feet 6 inches high and 16 inches in diameter which are described as 'standing 3 quarters from the wall'.[90] The doorway was covered by a portico 3 feet 6 inches deep with two pillars of the same height and dimension as the pilasters.[91] Directly above this was a 'purgola' (balcony) on the level of the main floor which contained a door flanked by two pillasters 8 feet 6 inches in height and 13 inches in diameter.[92] The detailed carving, however, was not carried out by Thomas Steevens, who was responsible for most of the stonework on the south front, but by unspecified 'stone carvers'. A reference to '2 Ionicke Capitalls for Collumes in the second storie', and '2 Capitalls for the pillosters in the same storie', confirms that this balcony door had a canopy supported by pillars.[93] A further payment to the stone carvers for 'the 2 Composita Capitalls in the third storie', establishes the use of the Orders on this front. Although little is known of Carter's architectural work, the evidence suggests that this design was a competent exercise in Inigo Jones's manner.

Steevens's accounts provide detailed payments for two other doors in the south front opening onto the terrace, one of these was at the foot of the stairs and had elaborate decorations that included a coat of arms between '2 greate scroles'.[94] The other door is described as leading out of the Hall into the terrace walk and had less ornate carved decoration.[95] These doorways can perhaps be located in the corner towers which had been retained from the old building, and it is here that four new windows 'with Compasse heades standing on the garden side', made by Richard Veasey, should also be placed.[96]

Although the date of 1649 on Robert Scawen's detailed accounts for the building work establish that most of it had been completed by then, payments as late as 1652/3 show that Thomas Simson did new work on the wainscot of the

89 Ibid. 'For 8 greate windowes in the vpper floore next the garden side at 45.ˢ a peece xviij.ˡⁱ For one balcony dorecase with a paire of leaves iiij.ˡⁱ x.ˢ For 8 greate windowes in the first storie 4 foote wide and 11 foote high at 55.ˢ a peece xxij.ˡⁱ For 2 greate balcony cases 5 foote ½ wide and 13 foote high with shutting leaves to them, standing on the first floore, one to the Courte, the other goeing to the garden at 5.ˡⁱ a peece x.ˡⁱ'

90 Ibid. Payment to Thomas Steevens: 'for sawing workeing and setting 2 pillosters in height 11 foote ½ and the diameter 16 inches and standing 3 quarters from the wall with 2 half ballisters at 40.ˢ a peece iiij.ˡⁱ'

91 Ibid. 'For sawing workeing and setting 3 foote ½ of raile and ballister betweene the pillers and pillosters and setting of it into the pillers

and pillosters at 10.ˢ the foote xxxv.ˢ'

92 Ibid. 'For sawing workeing and setting 2 pillosters standing 3 quarters out of the wall being in height 8 foote ½ a peece and the diameter 13 inches at 30.ˢ a peece lx.ˢ'

93 Ibid. The Ionic capitals for the columns cost £3 3s. 0d. and those for the pilasters cost £1 16s. 0d.

94 Ibid. 'For sawing workeing and setting 2 greate scroles in the ffronticepeece of the said dore with the Carving at 4.ˡⁱ a peece viij.ˡⁱ For sawing workeing and setting of a pedistall and shield of Armes betweene the 2 scroles C.ˢ'

95 Ibid. There are also references to further doors 'at each side of the tarras'.

96 Ibid. 'For 4 windowes with Compasse heades standing on the garden side at 25.ˢ a peece C.ˢ'

Long Gallery, and that Thomas Carvell, a carver not mentioned among the
team working on the house in the late 1640s, made '4 dorricke Capitalles, 4
Joynicke Capitalles and 4 peeces of gold roundes' for the same room.[97]

In 1655 it was decided to remedy one of the main defects in Carter's scheme,
the difficulty of reaching the garden from the main floor of the south range.
Edward Marshall, the mason who had recently built the portico at The Vyne to
John Webb's designs, was paid for making 'the greate stone Staires which
leades from the Dyning roome downe to the Tarrace' at a cost of £200.[98] The
size of this staircase is suggested by a payment of £42 for '63 foote of Rayle and
Balister wrought compasse'.[99] The stairs were designed in two flights ascend-
ing on either side to what had previously been the balcony door on the main
floor,[100] and which now gave access from the south front into the garden. John
Evelyn, who visited the house in June 1658, shortly after completion of the
work in 1657, wrote that: 'The new front towards the Gardens, is tollerable,
were it not drown'd by a too massie, & clowdy pair of stayers of stone, without
any neeate Invention'.[101] John Webb's responsibility for this design has become
more likely following the discovery of a payment, dating from 1658/9, 'to
Leonard Gammon by the appointment of Mr Webb for large paper for
draughtes and designes for Syon and Northumberland house for 5 yeares last
past'.[102] Webb had used Marshall as his mason at The Vyne in 1654, and he was
also to employ him on the rebuilding of another of Northumberland's houses,
Syon, that began around 1656-57, and which will be discussed below. There
can be little doubt that in the period 1654-59 Webb was in charge of all the
significant architectural work undertaken for the Earl at London and Syon.

The 'greate stone Staires' were conceived as part of a new design for the
terrace and gardens. In 1657 Marshall was paid for a 'greate Carved Pedistall'
which was transported from Fetter Lane (where his workshops were located)
and for '4 stones provided for the bodies of the round pedistalles';[103] it seems
likely that these were to display sculpture on the terrace. An account for 1656/7
contains a payment to Marshall for taking up the paving 'where the brasse
Statues did lye' and replacing it.[104] Northumberland seems to have decided
that Carter's south front would make a suitable setting for antique statues, and

97 Petworth House Archives, 5848. The
    Account of Robert Scawen from February
    1651/2 to February 1652/3.
98 Alnwick MSS: Syon House, U.III.3. 'Mr Scaw-
    ens Disbursments for Northumberland house
    Gardens [in] the yeares 1655, 1656, and
    [1657]'.
99 Ibid. Payment to Edward Marshall.
100 See Gater and Godfrey (ed.), *Survey of London,
    The Strand*, pp. 12, 16-17; and Bold, *John
    Webb*, p. 164.
101 E.S. de Beer (ed.), *The Diary of John Evelyn*, 6
    vols. (Oxford, 1955), iii, *Kalendarium, 1650-*

    1672, p. 216.
102 Petworth House Archives, 5906. The
    Account of Robert Scawen for the year end-
    ing 7 March 1658/9. Allardyce, 'Patronage', p.
    20, attributed the design of the stairs to
    Marshall.
103 Alnwick MSS: Syon House, U.III.3. The cost
    was £9 for the 'carved' pedistal, and £5 4s. 0d.
    for stone for the 'round pedistalles'.
104 Petworth House Archives, 5886. The
    Account of Robert Scawen for the year end-
    ing 10 January 1656/7. For a full discussion
    see Wood, 'Van Dyck and the Earl of North-
    umberland' (see n. 63 above).

in 1657 he bought five unspecified sculptures and a 'Bacchus' from Emmanuel de Critz,[105] younger son of the Sergeant Painter. In the same year Marshall was paid for 'plinthes vnder the 6 timber pedistalles . . . for carryage of the Statues', and for '2 pedistalles to raise the marble Statues higher'.[106] An account for 1658/9 shows that Northumberland enlarged his collection of antiquities by purchasing ten marble heads, two statues of Bacchus, a 'Young Apollo', and a head of Jupiter from Thomas Beauchamp, Clerk to the Trustees of the Sale of the King's Goods. Five bronze statues, presumably those removed from the terrace by Marshall in 1656, were accepted by Beauchamp at a value of £65 against the cost of the antiquities.[107] A letter from Webb to Marshall concerning a 'pedestall for the Earle of Northumberland', dated 17 October 1658, and including a sketch of the design by Webb (Fig. 27),[108] is likely to be connected with the display of the newly acquired statues. In 1659/60 there are payments to Robert Cleare, the joiner, for making nineteen pedestals, and to Richard Cleare for carving six of these 'inriched with fowleage shieldes and Corronettes, and the vpper mouldings inriched with lace'.[109] The collection did not remain on display for long, however; the statues had formerly been part of the collection of Charles I and Northumberland returned them to the Crown at the Restoration.[110] It is interesting to note that Webb was active in recovering works of art on behalf of Charles II.[111]

Webb also provided some designs for the remodelling of the interiors at Northumberland House, less than ten years after completion of work under Carter's direction. A drawing by Webb survives, dated 1657, for an overmantel in the Dining Room (Fig. 28),[112] and detailed payments confirm that this design was executed.[113] An account for 1657/8 shows that Erasmus Armstrong constructed the wainscot and cornice in this room, and that these were carved

105 Petworth House Archives, 5893. The Account of Orlando Gee for the year ending 31 January 1657/8. 'To Mr de Critz for 5 statues with 4^{li}-10^s-0^d given him by his Lo^{pps} Comand Cvij^{li} to him more for a Statue of Bacchus [30-0-0 *above*] with a pedistall'.

106 Ibid., 5896. The Account of Robert Scawen for the year ending 20 January 1657/8.

107 Ibid., 5903. The Account of Orlando Gee for the year ending 31 January 1658/9. 'To Mr Beaucampe for 10 Marble heades and a figure called a Bacchus 190^{li} whereof allowed for 5 brasse statues 65^{li} soe there was paid him in money Cxxv^{li}. To him more for a statue of a young Apollo, another of a Bachus and a head of Jupiter xxv^{li}.'

108 RIBA, Burlington-Devonshire Drawings, E.5. Allardyce, 'Patronage', p. 21, attempted to redate this letter and identified this pedestal with the one supplied by Marshall in 1657 (see note 103 above).

109 Petworth House Archives, 5915. The Account of Robert Scawen for the year ending 28 February 1659/60. 'Joyner to Robert Cleare for a blacke pedestall [5-0-0 *above*], 12 more at 30^s a peece [18-0-0 *above*], and 6 more [6-0-0 *above*] at 20^s a peece xxix^{li} . . . Carver to Richard Cleare for 6 pedestalles inriched with fowleage shieldes and Corronettes, and the vpper mouldinges inriched with lace at 46^s a peece xiij^{li}. xvj^d.'

110 See Wood, 'Van Dyck and the Earl of Northumberland'.

111 See Bold, *John Webb*, p. 13.

112 RIBA, Burlington-Devonshire Drawings, iv/7 (1). See J. Harris, *Catalogue of the Drawings Collection of the Royal Institute of British Architects: Inigo Jones and John Webb* (Farnborough, 1972), no. 164.

113 Allardyce, 'Patronage', p. 13, claimed that there were no payments for this work.

by Richard Cleare. The wainscot contained 'huskes and flowres', 'half-moones with flowres', 'Eggs and Anchores', as well as '7 Compartamentes with festoones' and '6 peeces of follidge'. The cornice contained leaves and lace as well as '136 Cartooses [brackets] in the ffreeze' and '134 festoones'.[114] The chimneypiece and door were not added until the next year, and an account for 1658/9 shows that they were constructed and carved by the same craftsmen.[115] Another sheet by Webb establishes that he provided designs for a chimneypiece in the Withdrawing Room (Fig. 29) in 1660,[116] and drawings for capitals in both these rooms survive in his 'Book of Capitols' formerly at Chatsworth and now in the collection of the RIBA (Figs. 30-31). The room to which Webb refers may be identical with 'my Lord Percy's withdrawing-roome' for which Robert and Richard Cleare provided the carved woodwork, together with the adjacent bedchamber, in 1660/1.[117]

Despite Northumberland's considerable expenditure, Petworth remained a medieval manor house, and the London mansion kept its old-fashioned courtyard plan. Although the Earl carried out little demolition at Northumberland House, he spent a great deal in order to classicise the interiors and the south front. In the late 1650s he was even prepared to have Webb redesign many of the rooms that Carter had completed less than a decade earlier. This suggests that the Earl, although architecturally conservative in some respects, was alert to the style of his buildings.

Syon House

The Earl of Northumberland inherited Syon House, outside London, from his father who had acquired the lease in 1594 on his marriage to Dorothy

114 Petworth House Archives, 5896. The Account of Robert Scawen for the year ending 20 January 1657/8. 'Carver to Richard Cleare for worke don in the wainscott of the dining roome viz! for 37 foote of huskes and flowres [2-9-4 *above*] at 16ᵈ the foote, for the halfe moones with flowres [11s *above*] 11 foote, 19 foote of halfe moones with a round in them [0-6-4 *above*] at 4ᵈ a foote, for 654 foote of beades [6-16-3 *above*] at 2ᵈ ½ a foote, 162 foote of Lace [1-7-0 *above*] at 2ᵈ a foote, 119 foote ½ of Eggs and Anchores [1-14-8 *above*] at 3ᵈ ½ a foote, for 94 foote of galloes [6-5-4 *above*] at 16ᵈ a foote, for 7 Compartamentes with festoones [22-15-0 *above*] at 3ˡⁱ-5ˢ a peece and 6 peeces of follidge [10-10-0 *above*], lijˡⁱ xiiijˢ vjᵈ to him more for worke don in the Cornice of the same room viz! for 135 foote of leaves [2-5-0 *above*] at 4ᵈ a foote, 135 foote of small lace [0-16-10 *above*] at 1ᵈ ½ the foote, 135 foote of beades [0-11-3 *above*] at 1ᵈ

a foote, 135 foote of water-leaves [2-16-4 *above*] at 5ᵈ a foote, 137 foote of great lace [1-6-2 *above*] at 2ᵈ a foote, 136 Cartooses in the ffreeze [6-16-0 *above*] at 12ᵈ a peece, and for 134 festoones [20-2-0 *above*] in the same ffreeze at 3ˢ a peece xxxiiijˡⁱ xiijˢ vjᵈ'

115 Ibid., 5906. The Account of Robert Scawen for the year ending 7 March 1658/9. 'Joyner Robert Cleere for 15 yardes of wainscott [5-5-0 *above*] over the Chimney peece and Dore in the Dining roome at 7ˢ a yard, for the pillers and frontispeece [3-0-0 *above*] . . . Carver to Richard Cleere for worke don about the Chimney peece in the dining roome ixˡⁱ xiiijˢ'

116 RIBA, Burlington-Devonshire Drawings, iv/7 (2). See Harris, *Drawings Collection of the R.I.B.A.*, no. 165.

117 Petworth House Archives, 5934. The Account of Robert Scawen for the year ending 16 January 1660/1.

Devereux, widow of Sir Thomas Perrot.[118] The 9th Earl was granted the fee simple by James I in 1604.[119] The character of the quadrangular house with four corner towers owed much to its origin as a Bridgettine monastery. A major rebuilding was begun around 1604 and the 9th Earl continued to direct the work from the Tower after his imprisonment in 1605.[120] The alterations to the house at this time included the removal of the gatehouse, construction of two lodges (which have survived), new fretting and wainscoting the main rooms, the construction of a series of rooms for the use of the Countess, and the building of a coachhouse, brewhouse and laundry.[121]

Following his succession to the title in 1632, the 10th Earl spent considerable sums on building work and on furnishings at Syon; work which he was prepared to have replaced twice within the next twenty years. In 1634/5 over £142 was spent on new doors and doorcases, new wainscoting, and repairs to fretwork ceilings in the north range.[122] Expenditure at this level continued for several years; the main focus of work being the construction of a new staircase and a 'greate windowe' overlooking the courtyard, completed in 1636/7.[123] Tapestries costing £45 were obtained from Antwerp, and some idea of the finished appearance of the staircase can be obtained from payments for '386 skinnes of gold & blew lether' and '153 borders of guilte lether' that decorated it.[124] These embellishments cost more than the construction of the staircase itself.[125] Splendid furnishings were also bought at this time, including a bed with black velvet curtains lined with 'incarnadine satten', and a 'crimosin clouded taffata' curtain.[126] Building work continued energetically in the period around 1638 to 1640 with masons making new windows and rebuilding chimneys, altering doors and removing part of the battlements in the east range, while carpenters and joiners made new doors and wainscots for the Long Gallery which was then painted and gilded.[127] The interior of the latter must have been magnificent, since 'gilding and painting the wainskott in the gallerie, drawing the ovall lightes, gilding the two chimney peeces, and colouring ye freize in Stone colore & oyle' cost no less than £170.[128] In 1641/2 a new

118 G.R. Batho, 'Henry, Ninth Earl of Northumberland and Syon House, Middlesex, 1594-1632', *Transactions of the Ancient Monuments Society*, iv (new series, 1956), p. 96.

119 Ibid., p. 102.

120 Ibid.

121 Ibid.

122 Alnwick MSS: Syon House, U.I.5. The Account of Thomas Cartwright for the year ending 12 January 1634/5.

123 Petworth House Archives, 478. The Account of Thomas Cartwright for the year ending 12 January 1636/7.

124 Alnwick MSS: Syon House, U.I.5. The Account of Peter Dodesworth from 16 January 1635/6 to 16 January 1636/7.

125 The total cost for building the staircase seems to have been £74 8s. 0d. (see Alnwick MSS: Syon House, U.I.5. The Account of Thomas Cartwright for the year ending 12 January 1635/6; and Petworth House Archives, 478), while the cost of the leather hangings and tapestries was £115 14s. 0d. (see the document cited at n. 124 above).

126 Alnwick MSS: Syon House, U.I.5. The Account of Peter Dodesworth from 16 January 1635/6 to 16 January 1636/7. The total cost of these furnishings for Syon was £208 6s. 0d.

127 Ibid. The Accounts of Thomas Cartwright for the year ending 12 January 1638/9, and the year ending 12 January 1639/40.

128 Ibid., U.I.6. The Account of Thomas Cartwright for the year ending 12 January 1641/2.

carved chimney-piece was made for the Earl's Closet, and carved wainscots were added to his Bedchamber, the Withdrawing Room, and the staircase.[129]

In 1639/40 a payment was made for '4 plottes made by the french gardyner',[130] perhaps to be identified with André Mollet, and in the next few years the gardens at Syon were entirely remade. Large sums were paid for work done by labourers,[131] and 'rampier' walls were constructed by bricklayers, who also made a fountain which was given a rim of black marble.[132] Appropriately, on 24 December 1644, John Christmas, the mason, was paid for 'the great fountayne garden and other work don there'.[133] The gardens themselves were planted with 180 cypress trees,[134] 400 laurel trees, 'plumb trees, cherrie trees, peach trees, & early Apricock trees'.[135] In 1643/4, a further sixty laurel trees were planted and £21 was spent on 'tulipps bought of Viana'.[136]

In 1643 royalist troops besieged Syon and took the opportunity to inflict vindictive damage on a house owned by one of the leading aristocratic supporters of Parliament. This must have given a piquancy to the visit that the King paid to Syon in 1647 while in the custody of Parliament.[137] Masons were paid for repairs to the north range 'where it was shott through with ordnance, and for mending the battlements'.[138] The soldiers also let off their guns in the interior of the house. It is difficult to assess the damage done to Syon at this time, but, though immediate large-scale repairs do not seem to have been carried out, it may help to explain why, in the mid 1650s, John Webb and Edward Marshall should have made structural surveys for the Earl, noting that the ashlar facing in the courtyard was separating from the brick walls, and that extensive repairs to the roofs, chimneys and cellars were necessary.[139]

The rebuilding of Syon was largely completed between 1657 and 1660, although the decoration of the interior continued for several years until 1663/4. John Webb was in charge during the main period of activity and received

129 Ibid. 'Joyners wainskotting one Bedchamber & with draweing roome. A staircase & doore and dore case in the Lord Conwaies chamber, for a chimney peece in yo.[r] Lo[ps]: closett, altering the closett dore, & doorecase goeing into the portague vnder the gallery, making a portall in the preserveing house and other small workes iiij [xx *above*] viij[li]. vj[s]. Carver, carveing in yo.[r] Lo[ps]: bedchamber at Syon the wth draweing roome, staircase & chimney peice in yo.[r] Lo[ps]: closet xxiiij[li].'

130 Ibid., U.I.5. The Account of Thomas Cartwright for the year ending 12 January 1639/40. The cost was £7 9s. 0d.

131 Ibid., U.I.5, U.I.6. The Accounts of Thomas Cartwright for the years ending 12 January 1639/40, 1640/1, 1641/2, and 20 January 1643/4, 1644/5. The maximum paid in any one year was £212 6s. 0d.(1641/2), and the minimum £107 0s. 6d.(1644/5).

132 Ibid., U.I.6. The Account of Thomas Cart-

wright for the year ending 12 January 1641/2. 'Mason viz.[t] for the r̄ȳmē [=rim] of the cesterne in the privy garden, being of black marble and the pedestall of touchstone, and for the modell of a flower pott to be sett on the Rampier xliiij[li] ij[s] vj[d].

133 Ibid. The Account of Thomas Carwright for the year ending 20 January 1644/5.

134 Ibid. The Account of Thomas Cartwright for the year ending 12 January 1639/40. The cost was £14 14s. 0d.

135 Ibid. The Account of Thomas Cartwright for the year ending 12 January 1640/1.

136 Ibid. The Account of Thomas Cartwright for the year ending 20 January 1643/4.

137 Ibid. The Account of Peter Dodesworth from 17 January 1646/7 to 17 January 1647/8.

138 Ibid. The Account of Thomas Cartwright for the year ending 20 January 1643/4.

139 Ibid., U.III.5. See Bold, *John Webb*, p. 170.

annual payments 'for surveying his Lordships buildinges and workes by his Lordships Comand'.[140]. He was assisted by Edward Marshall as mason, Gerald Strong as carpenter, Gideon Gibson and Maurice Emmett as bricklayers, John Embree as plumber, and William, Robert, and Richard Cleare as carvers. Emmett was a member of the Office of Works but was later to lose his post at the Restoration.[141] Embree (who was now Surveyor of the King's Works) and Robert and Richard Cleare had worked at Northumberland House in the late 1640s under Carter, but the remainder of the team were newly recruited by Webb, although Marshall and Emmett had worked previously on the new stairs in 1655-57, and must have moved directly from the Earl's house in London to his house in Middlesex.

The accounts show that a pear-tree model of Webb's project for the new roof at Syon was made by Richard Ryder,[142] who had worked on the new stairs at Northumberland House,[143] as well as under Webb's direction at Wilton around 1647-50.[144] Architectural models were seldom made in England during the first half of the seventeenth century,[145] and this suggests that the roof at Syon was of an uncommon type, perhaps a trussed design of the kind associated with Jones.[146] The rebuilding at Syon was probably more extensive (though less thoroughly documented) than that undertaken at Northumberland House in the late 1640s, and it required the removal of most of the roof in two stages of work datable to 1657 and 1658. In the first phase, seventeen bays of the 'old plattforme which was decayed' were taken down in the south range and in the west range as far as the end of the Hall. Gerald Strong was in charge of this work, while John Embree took up the leads.[147] In the second and larger phase, forty-three bays of the platform were removed from both the east and north ranges.[148] The difference in cost between these two unequal operations suggests that part of the roof in the west range was retained.

140 Petworth House Archives, 5896, 5906, 5915, 5934. The Accounts of Robert Scawen for the years ending 20 January 1657/8, 7 March 1658/9, 28 February 1659/60, and 16 January 1660/61. See also note 102 above.

141 See Colvin (ed.), *King's Works*, iii (part I), p. 167.

142 Petworth House Archives, 5886. The Account of Robert Scawen for the year ending 10 January 1656/7: 'to Richard Ryder for peare tree to make the modell of Syon house roofe'. See also Petworth House Archives 5906: 'to Mr Ryder for making a Moddell [2-10-0 *above*] for the plattforme of the house'.

143 Alnwick MSS: Syon House, U.III.3. See also Bold, *John Webb*, p. 164.

144 J. Bold with J. Reeves, *Wilton House and English Palladianism: Some Wiltshire Houses* (London, 1988), p. 42.

145 See M. Airs, *The Making of the English Country House, 1500-1640* (London, 1975), p. 75.

146 See D. Yeomans, 'Inigo Jones's Roof Structures', *Architectural History*, xxix (1986), pp. 85-101.

147 Petworth House Archives, 5896. The Account of Robert Scawen for the year ending 1657/8. 'To the said Gera Strong for sawing working framing and raising the platforme on the south side of the house and on the west side thereof soe farr as to the end of the hall containing 49 square 6 foote 9 inches at 25^s the square liij^{li} xvj^s viij^d.' Embree was paid £130 15s. 7d. for his work on the leads.

148 Ibid., 5906. The Account of Robert Scawen for the year ending 7 March 1658/9. 'For taking downe 43 bayes of the old plattforme which was decayed at 20^s the bay xliij^{li}.' 'For making framing and raising the plattformes on the east and north sides of the house containing 74 square ½ and 6 foote at 37^s a square Cxxxvij^{li} xviij^s ix^d.'

Edward Marshall was in charge of the refacing of the courtyard where, according to his own survey, damp had lifted the ashlar away from the brick walls.[149] This work was also undertaken in two phases, linked to the replacement of the roof. Marshall first took down all the old stone on the south wall of the courtyard and replaced it, renewing the ashlar parapet and the Portland stone coping.[150] The cornice, also of Portland stone, was made according to a drawing submitted by Webb as part of his proposals for the rebuilding (Fig. 32),[151] and contained thirty-nine 'Cartooses' (brackets). This is confirmed by the discovery of an early watercolour view of the courtyard (Fig. 33).[152] Marshall also added new mouldings to the five main windows in this wall. In the next phase, identical work was carried out on the east and north walls.[153] There is no record of payment for work on the west wall.

The most detailed payments for any of the exterior walls concern the north front, although there is little doubt that many unlocated items in the accounts relate to the east front (which was rebuilt with 14,000 new bricks),[154] and which is believed to have kept something of its seventeenth-century appearance despite Adam's remodelling of the 1760s.[155] Maurice Emmett took down a building attached to the north side of the house and rebuilt the wall.[156] Marshall then refaced this front, which is described as being 'towardes the fountaine garden', with ashlar and provided new surrounds for seven windows.[157]

Considerable work was undertaken on the two main staircases. Gerald Strong was paid for pulling down and rebuilding the 'old staires' by the Long Gallery, and the 'backstaires' in the south range leading to the garden.[158] In the Long Gallery itself the chimneys were altered and new doorways constructed,[159] including a balcony door which was 'wrought on both sides with an

149 See n. 139 above.
150 Petworth House Archives, 5896. The Account of Robert Scawen for the year ending 20 January 1657/8. 'Mason to Edward Marshall for takeing downe the old stone and setting vp againe the south wall of the principall Courte with supply of new Ashler 1062 foote at 2ˢ the foote Cvjˡⁱ iiijˢ.'
151 See Bold, *John Webb*, p. 170 and pl. 113.
152 Private Collection. I am grateful to John Bold for knowledge of this watercolour.
153 Petworth House Archives, 5906. The Account of Robert Scawen for the year ending 7 March 1658/9. 'Mason to Edward Marshall for taking downe the old stone and setting vp againe a greate part of the east and North walles of the principall Courte with supply of new Asteler cont 2072 foote 8 inches at 2ˢ a foote CCvijˡⁱ vˢ iiijᵈ.'
154 Petworth House Archives, 5896. 'Brickes viz!

14000 delivered at Syon this yeare for raising the walles of the south side of the house'.
155 Royal Commission on Historical Monuments, England, *An Inventory of the Historical Monuments in Middlesex* (London, 1937), pp. 86-88.
156 Petworth House Archives, 5906. The Account of Robert Scawen for the year ending 7 March 1658/9.
157 Ibid. 'For 1522 foote 2 inches of Asteler on the North side of the house towardes the fountaine garden at 2ˢ the foote Clijˡⁱ ijˢ iiijᵈ For 196 foote of Jambe and Soyle in seven windowes there at 14ᵈ a foote xjˡⁱ viijˢ viijᵈ.'
158 Petworth House Archives, 5896. The Account of Robert Scawen for the year ending 20 January 1657/8.
159 Petworth House Archives, 5906. The Account of Robert Scawen for the year ending 7 March 1658/9.

Architrave' by Edward Marshall.[160] Robert Cleare constructed, and Richard Cleare carved, a cedar panel for the decoration of the Gallery.[161] In the Hall, Gideon Gibson removed the old foundations,[162] Erasmus Armstrong took down the wainscot,[163] and Maurice Emmett raised 'the Chimney at the hall dore from the floore as high as the turning of the Arch'.[164] The Evidence House roof was removed by Gibson who raised the gable ends, and it received a new roof and tiling.[165]

Two of the most important and richly decorated suites of rooms were the Bedchambers and Closets of the Earl and Countess. These rooms received new floors and ceilings,[166] and, as late as 1662/3, both Closets were given 'Cases of Ceder' made by William Cleare which required '32 Revede [?reeded] Cullomes'. Richard Cleare carved 'two stringes of Tulippes and a peece of ffooledge', '18 foot of Lace', and '4 Ionicke Capitalles, 4 doricke Capitalles, and 4 Compostata Capitalles' in the Earl's Closet, and identical work was carried out in the Countess's Closet. The Earl's Bedchamber was decorated with '2 stringes of ffruite and a peece of ffooledge'.[167] William and Richard Cleare worked in at least seven of the main rooms at Syon at this time, of which the Bedchambers and Closets received particularly elaborate decoration. Although no drawings by Webb have so far been identified for the interiors at Syon, it is reasonable to assume that these would have looked something like the rooms at Northumberland House for which designs survive (Figs. 28-31). By 1662 the main

160 Petworth House Archives, 5915. The Account of Robert Scawen for the year ending 28 February 1659/60. 'Mason viz! to Edward Marshall for the Crest [8-4-3 *above*] about the balcony wrought on both sides with an Architrave molding 36 foote $\frac{1}{2}$ at 4$\frac{s}{}$-6$\frac{d}{}$ a foote'.

161 Ibid. 'To Robert Cleere . . . for the workemanshipp of one pannell of Ceder for the gallery cont 18 yardes $\frac{1}{2}$ [13-17-6 *above*] at 15$\frac{s}{}$ a yard . . . Carver viz! to Richard Cleere for Carving that pannell of Ceder xiiij^{li} xj^{s} vj^{d}.'

162 Ibid., 5896. The Account of Robert Scawen for the year ending 20 January 1657/8.

163 Ibid., 5915. The Account of Robert Scawen for the year ending 28 February 1659/60. 'To Erasmus Armstrong . . . takeing downe the wainscott at the North end of the hall and guilded gallery'.

164 Ibid.

165 Ibid., 5896. The Account of Robert Scawen for the year ending 20 January 1657/8. 'To Gera Strong . . . setting vp a roofe over the Evidence house'. 'To Gidion Gibson . . . for vncovering the Evidence house and new tyling it'.

166 Ibid. 'To Gera Strong . . . pulling downe the Ceelinges over my Ladyes Clossett and the pticones there'. Petworth House Archives 5915: 'To Gera Strong . . . takeing vp the

bordes in his Lo^{pps} Chamber and two roomes adioyning and new laying them, framing a double dorecase in his Lo^{pps} Chamber and setting it vp, takeing vp the boardes in the dining roome on the North side of the house and furring and new boarding it, the like don to my Ladies bedchamber and two roomes adioyning'.

167 Ibid., 5755. The Account of Robert Scawen for the year ending 28 February 1662/3. 'Carver viz! to Richard Cleare for 2 stringes of ffruite and a peece of ffooledge in his Lo^{pps} Chamber, two stringes of Tulippes and a peece of ffooledge in his Lo^{pps} Clossett, a shield with a Coronett and Garter two peeces of ffooledge two ffestoones and ringes for the Clossettes in the first [3-10-0 *above*] and second story [3-10-0 *above*], worke don in his Lo^{pps} Clossett viz! 18 foote of Lace [0-3-9 *above*], at 2^{d} $\frac{1}{2}$ a foote, 4 Ionicke Capitalles [0-12-0 *above*], 4 doricke Capitalles [1-14-0 *above*], and 4 Compostata Capitalles [2-0-0 *above*]; the like don in my Lady's Clossett [4-9-9 *above*], a picture frame in the roome next the Ceder viz! 27 foote of great leaves [1-7-0 *above*], 26 foote of Colosse with floweres [1-14-8 *above*] at 16^{d} a foote, and 26 foote of lace [0-5-5 *above*] at 2^{d} $\frac{1}{2}$ a foote, the like in the roome next the new staire head [2-7-1 *above*] xxx^{li} iij^{d}.'

apartments in the Earl's houses in London and at Syon would have had a measure of stylistic unity.

The fact that little visual evidence survives of Northumberland's architectural patronage makes it difficult to assess his taste and influence. The Earl's building projects are, however, well-documented, so that the household accounts establish not only the scope of the work undertaken, but also who carried it out. If something had survived of the mid seventeenth-century appearance of Syon or of Northumberland House, he would be more easily recognised as the equal, as a patron, of the 4th Earl of Pembroke, another of the aristocratic supporters of Parliament. Pembroke began the rebuilding of his country house, Wilton, in the 1630s, during the King's reign, but, though he commissioned designs for Durham House in London from John Webb in 1641 and 1649, neither of these projects were realised.[168] In contrast, Northumberland's rebuilding at Syon and Petworth in the 1630s does not seem to have been on such an ambitious scale as Pembroke's plans for Wilton. It may be that the 'unrealistic aspirations of the king encouraged architectural delusions in the subject',[169] but Northumberland was more effective both as a politician and a builder than Pembroke. The transformation of Northumberland House and Syon from Jacobean mansions into classical ones was achieved, as has been shown, in two main phases of activity, the first under Edward Carter, completed by 1649, and the second under the direction of John Webb from 1655 to 1662. The evidence suggests that Northumberland, unlike Pembroke, completed what he set out to achieve.

168 See Bold, *Wilton House*, p. 30.   169 Ibid., p. 35.

6

Hugh May, Clarendon and Cornbury

JOHN NEWMAN

In the years immediately after the Restoration the practice of architecture was dominated not by the ageing John Webb, whose bid to succeed his master Inigo Jones as Surveyor of the King's Works led only to the cul-de-sac commission for Greenwich Palace, nor by the young Christopher Wren, whose promise as a scientist was until the mid 1660s more apparent than his potential as an architect, but by two men in early middle age, Roger Pratt and Hugh May. It was their achievement, by drawing on their continental experiences during the years of the Civil War and Interregnum, to naturalise Jones's classicism among the English aristocracy and gentry.

Pratt's surviving notebooks enable us to appreciate in detail his grasp of architectural theory, his knowledge of continental buildings and in particular his deep involvement with the practicalities of house construction. Nothing comparable survives to throw light on the furniture of May's mind. His interest in the theory of classical architecture is demonstrated by his promotion of John Evelyn's English translation of Fréart de Chambray's *Parallel of the Orders* (1664). His capacities as an architectural impresario are evident in the fitting up of the state rooms at Windsor Castle (1678-83), where he brought Antonio Verrio and Grinling Gibbons together for the first time in a team which created what became the exemplar for apartments of state for a whole generation. About his activities as architect of country houses however we remain largely ignorant; in particular his practical capacities are extremely difficult to assess. The only firm evidence that he took an interest in constructional matters is John Aubrey's observation that he invented 'the Staff-moulding on solid right Angles'.

The purpose of this essay is to publish a small amount of documentation which clarifies a little further May's capacities, and limitations, as an architect.[1] The material concerns Cornbury Park, Oxfordshire, enlarged by him for the

---

1 The documents are noted in H.M. Colvin, *A Biographical Dictionary of British Architects, 1600-1840* (London, 1978), p. 544.

Earl of Clarendon from the spring of 1666, immediately after the completion of Clarendon's town mansion in Piccadilly under Pratt's supervision. At Cornbury, May had already designed the magnificent stables, completed by mid 1664. Attention thereupon turned to the house.

As was only to be expected, advice was sought from other quarters. Clarendon's son, Lord Cornbury, was on terms of friendship with John Evelyn, who, as noted above, also knew May. Evelyn's diary records a visit which all three made to Cornbury in October 1664.[2] As he noted, 'We design'd an handsome Chapell that was yet wanting, as Mr. *May* had the stables, which indeede are very faire'. His impressions and advice on that occasion are recorded in a notebook now at Christ Church, Oxford.[3] He made a plan of the existing house (a valuable record of Nicholas Stone's enlargement and regularisation of 1632-33), sketched his proposals for the siting and design of the chapel and took views of May's new stables from three directions and made a part plan (Fig. 34). The chapel was in due course erected in the position proposed by Evelyn, but the diarist's ideas for its form, with an apse and rectangular side windows, were not followed.[4]

It is clear that by the autumn of 1664 Lord Clarendon had not yet conceived the more extensive reconstruction of the house which he subsequently carried out. This is first heard of in a letter of Lord Cornbury to Evelyn dated 24 January 1665/6. After expressing his own and his father's satisfaction at Evelyn's favourable verdict on the new Clarendon House in Piccadilly, Lord Cornbury continued: 'Mr May (who you know governes at Cornbury) hath made a designe for a very convenient house there, & splendid enough, which will be begunn this Spring; & then we shall be very commode both in Towne & Countrey, though perhaps too much envyed'.[5]

If this refers to a design for a complete new house, it was soon cut down to a partial rebuilding. The chapel was built centrally at the back of the existing hall range, as Evelyn had suggested, but the south wing containing the main reception rooms, shown on Evelyn's plan to have been of single-pile form, was rebuilt largely as a double pile and given an eleven-bay front with a central pediment on pilasters (Fig. 35).

No architectural drawings by May are known. A document among the Clarendon State Papers suggests a reason for this: May did not make his own finished drawings. In an undated bill for work done since 26 November 1662

2 E.S. de Beer (ed.), *The Diary of John Evelyn*, 6 vols. (London, 1955), iii, pp. 381-82.
3 Christ Church, Oxford, MS Evelyn 44, p. 206.
4 See the illustration of the chapel in *Country Life*, cviii (22 September 1950), p. 92.
5 Evelyn MS 1, no. 44. I am grateful to Howard Colvin for bringing this volume to my attention.

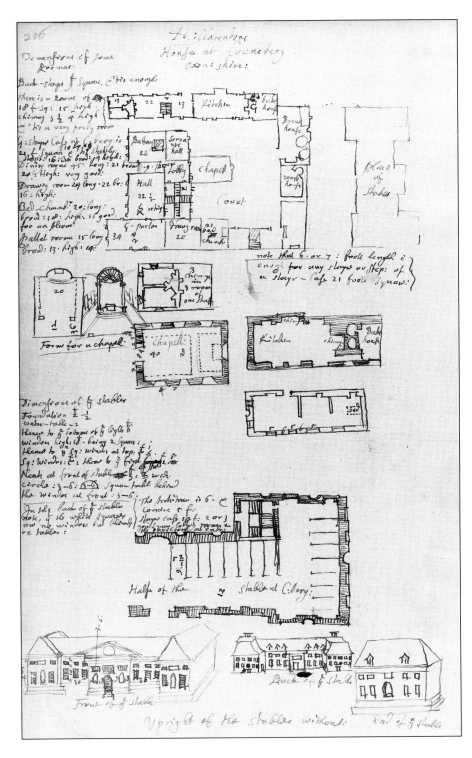

Fig. 34 John Evelyn, sketches of Cornbury, *c.* 1664: plan of house and proposed chapel (*top*); 'Forms for a chapell' and details of plan of house (*middle*); views and plan of new stables (*bottom*). (*Christ Church, Oxford, Evelyn MS 44, p. 206*)

Fig. 35 Hugh May, Cornbury Park, south range (1666-67).

an unnamed land surveyor, after charging for five estate maps costing between £16 and £5 each, added the items:

> for Drawing ye first Draft of Cornbury for Mr May   £2
> for Drawing ye 2d Draft of Cornbury for Mr May   £7[6]

Whatever sketch designs May was capable of producing, he committed the task of preparing fair presentation drawings to a professional draughtsman of a type familiar from the Elizabethan and Jacobean period but rendered obsolete by Inigo Jones's practice.[7]

During the construction works at Cornbury Clarendon was occupied with state affairs. Nevertheless he took a detailed, if long-range, interest in the progress of his country retreat, and through his London steward John Clotterbook transmitted instructions to the steward of his Oxfordshire estates, John Cary. It is through the survival in the Public Record Office of Cary's voluminous papers relating to his stewardships to the Earls of Clarendon at Cornbury and the Earls of Litchfield at Ditchley that we know something of the progress of building at Cornbury.[8]

6 Bodleian Library, Clarendon MS 78, fo. 167.

7 J. Harris and G. Higgott, *Inigo Jones: Complete Architectural Drawings* (New York and London, 1989).

8 PRO, C 104/109 contains the relevant material.

A summary account records monies paid out 'for my Lord Chancellors service in his building at Cornbury', totalling £698 4s. in 1664-65, presumably for the stables, and over £6,000 in 1665-67, covering the construction of at least the shell of the house. No details of this expenditure are given except for a closing memorandum under March 1667/8, which lists among other items:

To Thomas Strong for a casement for a patterne for Cornbury   £30 12s.
To Mr Joyner for the Moddell of the late new building   £5

The six letters from Clotterbook to Cary which relate to the construction of the house cover a period of a year, from August 1666 to August 1667, when the new chapel was being paved and the new south range had reached roof level. The extracts printed below give a good idea how the chain of command operated. Clarendon himself, in London, in a way typical of great men, took the keenest interest in the minutiae of the building works and was ready with advice even on technical matters; May, also in London, showed no sign of visiting Cornbury to inspect progress during the period covered by the correspondence and provided designs for chimney caps and dormer windows on the basis of measurements supplied by Cary; what made this long-distance control possible was Cary's own good sense and efficiency. These letters are clearly only part of a longer correspondence. All are directed to 'John Cary at Ditchley or Cornbury'; the first three were sent by Clotterbook from Worcester House, the last three after the move into Clarendon House had taken place.

2 August 1666
By yours of the 30th of the last moneth I understand that the work goes well on, which my Lord is well pleased withall and thanks you for your care thereof. When I shewed my Lord your letter Mr May was present, and he told my Lord that he would write now to Mr Deane,[9] that as soone as he hath done the Chappell[10] he shall Sett his Strength to helpe on the other worke with Strong about the Tarris &c.[11] But as to the ffountaine, my Lord is resolved that he shall not doe any thing in order to that worke untill the Spring, which he comaunds me to signifie to you, for his lordship will have nothing to be begunne in it.

---

9   This is presumably Anthony Deane of Uffington (Berkshire), who in 1673 undertook to act as general contractor for Holme Lacy (Herefordshire). Any dispute over its construction was to be submitted to 'the final Arbitrament and determination of Hugh May Esq.'. PRO, C 115/M24, no. 7789.

10   This would seem to dispose of the idea that the chapel was not built until the late 1670s, for which see *Country Life*, cviii (22 September 1950), p. 22 and J. Sherwood and N. Pevsner,

The Buildings of England: Oxfordshire (Harmondsworth, 1974), p. 555.

11   For Thomas Strong's participation in building the terraces at Cornbury, see R. Clutterbuck, *The History and Antiquities of the County of Hertford*, i (London, 1815), p. 167. When the local stone first used in the terrace walls failed, Strong repaired and new faced them with Taynton stone 'by directions of Hugh May esq.'

And it wilbe all one to Mr Deane, since he can imploy his Men in the dispatch of that other worke, by which meanes it wilbe the sooner out of hand, and that will please my Lord best.

Besides his Lordship would faine lessen his charge for the present. . . .
[postscript] I shall keepe the paper of the estimate of the Charge of the ffountaine by me untill you shall have orders to beginne it in the Spring. But Mr. May doth promise my Lord that it shall not cost above 100 li. which he must excuse me, if I say, I doe not believe.

30 August 1666
. . . your letter to Mr Maye my Lord hath likewise perused and hath returned it to me this morning againe with order to deliver it to him, which I shall doe as soone as he comes home this Evening, he being now at Hampton Court.

As for the 450 li. which you have now charged upon me to be paid here the next weeke, I will see it accordingly paid . . . But his Lordship hopes that this 450 li. will carry up the Roofe of the building.

20 September 1666
. . . My Lord is much troubled at the sad Accident you mett withall of the poore mans being killed at the Quarr and is very sorry that his Quarr is likely sodainly to faile him.[12]

You are still requested to presse them on the forward the worke. But his Lordship will at no hand heare that they shall cutt those long peeces which are of a fitt Length for Beames, for the service of the Windowes in the Roofe. But let them be all preserved and rather buy Timber for that use, which I pray be pleased to take notice of and let them be carefull to preserve all that Timber for Beames as it is most fitt for, and which you will peradventure want hereafter, and not be able to provide your Selfe withall when wanting.

As for the Patternes of the stone, it is agreed on all hands that your owne choise is the best couler and best grained Stone, which is neither the light nor the darke but the middle blewish Stone, and all of the same, and to be layed Diamond wise all of a Size with a border round the Chappell all of one Couler, and not to intermixe colours. To which end I have now by Willis returned you the same Patterne, and have kept the other two behind, because there may be no mistake. As to the price his Lordship referrs that solely to you, for the working pollishing and paveing, wherein he knows that your skill and good husbandry needs no direction.

. . . I have herein alsoe returned you the note of the valuation of the ffountaine, which my Lord gives me Comaund to tell you he will in no case have you meddle withall this yeare, for he is confident it will hinder some other worke, And that his lordship will not have done.

---

12 The very fine quality stone used for the south range was quarried from a bed 60 ft. down in a quarry in the park. See W.J. Arkell, 'The Building-Stones of Blenheim Palace, Corn-bury Park, Glympton Park and Heythrop House, Oxfordshire', *Oxoniensia*, xiii (1948), p. 51.

25 October 1666

. . . I have not time to write largely to you, being soe hurried up & Downe about the business of our new House . . . I have now by Willis returned the Patterne of the stone which my Lord hath chosen for the paveing of the Chappell, which is the darkest Colour of the two that you sent of the Langley Stone.[13] I have kept the other 2 Patternes that you may not mistake, and my Lord is satisfied in that you tell him that it will pollish (although this Patterne be not soe) as well as that of Bletchington. And soe his Lordship desires you to agree as cheape as you can for it.

1 August 1667

I have received both yours vizt of the 25th and 29th of the last Moneth, if that Wainscott you mention will doe the businesse of his Lordships Study soe well as you say it will, he is well contented to have it done, and to save the Charge of new, if it will not then it must serve somewhere else, but his Lordship wilbe very well pleased to have it serve there and that the same shelves that were in his former Closett may be put up in this. His Lordship knowes no reason why you should not keepe open both the Doores that are in his Closett, that he may as well goe out into the Tarris walke when he pleaseth, as into the Parlor.

   Your advise touching the Kitchen Garden Wall his Lordship hearkens to, and desires you to get it done as cheape as you can, and with what speed you shall think fitt. His Lordship referrs that worke as well as that of his Closett to your discretion and management which he is confident will prove for the best.

   I shall send you downe 100d. or 200d. of Deale Boards very shortly . . . I shall speake with Mr May sometime this day, and give you as speedy an Accompt as I can, as well of the Patterne for the Mouldings of the Chimneyes, as of the Patterne for the Casements in the Garretts.

8 August 1667

. . . I have now by Willys sent you three Patternes for the mouldings of the Chimneyes; But Mr May sayth that untill you shall Send him the exact Measure of the Heighth and breadth of the Windowes he cannot possibly send you the Patterne of a Casement, therefore I pray let those Measures by sent by the next, and I will give you a speedy returne from him.

---

13 The source of the misdating of the chapel mentioned in note 10 above is R. Plot, *The Natural History of Oxfordshire* (London, 1677), p. 134, where reference is made to a forest marble found at Langley in Wychwood, in which the 'cockles . . . are so closely knit, that the mass receives a very good polish, inso- much that his Lordship intends to pave the new Chappel now building at Cornbury with it'. Plot's book was not published until 1677 but clearly he here left unrevised a passage which he must have drafted over a decade earlier.

7

John Pollexfen's House in Walbrook

BRIDGET CHERRY

Although the story of the rebuilding of London after the Great Fire of 1666 is well known, surprisingly few details are available about the larger private houses that were constructed in the City at this time. This essay is an attempt to present the information available about one of these buildings, and to investigate to what extent it fits into what is known about comparable houses.

While subject to the general regulations regarding materials and external fire precautions, the form of the largest City houses was less strictly laid down than was the case of those houses fronting the public highways.[1] Their height was left to the discretion of the builders, providing they did not exceed four storeys, and as surviving surveys show, their planning was often eccentric, dependent on the intricate property boundaries which had developed in the medieval City, and which were in the main perpetuated in the post fire rebuilding.[2]

Houses for 'merchants and persons of repute' built in the years immediately after the Fire continued the tradition of the medieval courtyard house in the way they were set back from the street, approached by an alley or courtyard flanked by service buildings or lesser houses. Survey plans of the eighteenth century indicate that the placing of the main ground floor rooms (hall, main stairs, one or two parlours and kitchen, and often a 'counting' room or office), followed no set pattern.[3] The few elevational drawings that exist also suggest

* I am grateful to Frank Kelsall, to Dr Derek Keene and to Elizabeth McKellar for their helpful comments after reading a draft of this essay.

1 For the general character of City houses after the Great Fire see J. Summerson, *Georgian London* (revised ed. London, 1988), ch. 2. On the reconstruction see T.F. Reddaway, *The Rebuilding of London after the Great Fire* (London, 1940). The regulations for the different classes of house are usefully summarised in W. Maitland, *A History and Survey of London* (3rd ed. London, 1760), i, p. 441.

2 For London before the Fire see J. Schofield, *The Building of London from the Conquest to the Great Fire* (London, 1984). On the continuity of property boundaries: V. Harding, 'Reconstructing London before the Great Fire', *London Topographical Record*, xxv (1985), pp. 1-12.

3 See for example British Library, Crace Collection, portfolio ix, 141 (Garlick Hill); ix, 168 (King's Arms Yard). A design by Roger North for 'a citty hows lying backwards' shows a house set back from the street; the named rooms are hall, parlour, withdrawing room and closet on the ground floor; waiting room, bedchamber, great chamber and closet on the floor above. H.M. Colvin and J. Newman (ed.) *Of Building: Roger North's Writings on Architecture*, (Oxford, 1981), plate 11.

considerable variety, even if it was only variations on the 'robust and second rate', as Summerson has somewhat disparagingly described the architectural taste of the city. The heavy classical detail favoured by City craftsmen could be applied to asymmetrical frontages, as in the case of the houses built off Old Jewry by Sir John Frederick and by Sir Robert Clayton,[4] although other houses, such as Sir John Houblon's, were more elegantly regular.[5] These buildings reflected the fame of three of the richest merchants in the City, all of whom served as Lord Mayor in the later seventeenth century. At this time the Lord Mayor had no official residence, so the office holder's own house was of special significance, and this no doubt accounts for the artistic attention which they enjoyed. Other retired sites generally escaped the interest of topographical artists over the next two centuries. Late seventeenth-century houses did not have the allure of picturesque antiquity and their ponderous classical detail was no longer fashionable. Architectural taste had shifted in favour of compact houses which could make an outward show and the old tradition of the courtyard house declined. Already toward the end of the seventeenth century the wealthy were favouring sites less constricted than the old City centre, such as the newly laid out Hatton Garden to the west, popular with both merchants and professional families.[6]

The house which is the subject of this essay was built within the period when a City mansion was still the ambition of a rising merchant, although it did not satisfy this particular builder for very long. John Pollexfen (*c.* 1638-1715), the second son of a minor Devonshire landowner, was sufficiently prosperous early in his career to build himself a substantial house in Walbrook in 1668, shortly before his marriage in 1670 to the daughter of Sir John Lawrence, a wealthy haberdasher who was Lord Mayor in 1664-65. In the 1670s four of their children were baptised, and one buried, at St Stephen Walbrook. However, Pollexfen's future was not to lie in the City. In 1679 he entered Parliament as a Member for Plympton Earle in his native county, and in 1684 he leased his house in Walbrook to William Scawen. Soon after he established himself as a Devon country landowner by acquiring the estate of Wembury from the Duke

4 For Frederick's house see J. Imray, *The Mercers Hall*, (London, 1991), ch. 12. For Clayton's house, British Museum, Dept. of Prints and Drawings, Crace Coll., portfolio xxi, 21-23; F.T. Melton, 'Sir Robert Clayton's Building Projects in London, 1666-72', *Guildhall Studies in Local History*, 3 (1977-79), pp. 37-41.

5 Houblon's house (demolished 1733) is shown in a watercolour by T.H. Shepherd after an older drawing, British Musueum, Dept. Prints and Drawings, Crace Coll., portfol. xxii, 4.

6 The absence of the courtyard house in later seventeenth-century City property on the urban fringe is noted in F.C. Brown, 'Continuity and Change in the Urban House: Developments in Domestic Space Organisation in Seventeenth-Century London', *Comparative Studies in Society and History*, xxviii (1986), pp. 558-90. For Hatton Gardens see P. Hunting, 'The Survey of Hatton Gardens of 1694', *London Topographical Record*, xxv (1985), pp. 83-110.

of Albemarle.[7] He was re-elected as a Member for Plympton to the Parliaments of 1681, 1688-89 and 1689-90, the exception being the Tory Parliament of 1685, when Pollexfen and his colleague, the lawyer Sir George Treby, were replaced by the Mayor of Plympton, Sir Richard Strode and (less explicably) by Sir Christopher Wren. In Parliament Pollexfen made his name as an expert on trade and economics, supporting the cause of free trade against the interests of the East India Company, publishing pamphlets on this subject in 1697.[8] In his will made in 1713 there are bequests to the poor on his Devon estates, yet some feeling for his old City property must have remained, for at his request he was buried in his family vault in the south aisle of St Stephen Walbrook, immediately adjacent to his own house.[9]

The survival of the lease of 1684 together with Pollexfen's building accounts provide a remarkably full record of the house at the time of its creation and in the years which followed. These documents, together with later leases up to 1748, the year of death of John Pollexfen's second son, Woolcombe, who had inherited the house, are preserved as part of a Chancery deposit in the Public Record Office.[10] Unfortunately visual evidence is much more sparse. The site is shown on Ogilby's map published in 1677, the form of the windows in the rear wall are indicated on a sketch attached to a lease of 1746, and there is a small print of 1795 with a rather schematic elevation of the front in the Crace Collection in the British Museum.[11]

The chief eighteenth-century histories of London make no reference to the house, although Strype notes that Walbrook was 'well built and inhabited by merchants', a comment repeated by Maitland.[12] But Lambert's *History* of 1806 has quite a detailed although, as will be seen, a not wholly reliable description. He states, incorrectly, that the house was rebuilt the year after the Fire by Sir Henry Pollexfen, Chief Justice of the Common Pleas (who was John Pollexfen's elder brother) and continues:

> It stands on lofty brick arches, of exquisite workmanship and great antiquity, and may be reasonably supposed to stand on the site of some religious house formerly

7 For Pollexfen's career see *Dictionary of National Biography*, pp. 62-63, and B.D. Henning, *History of Parliament, the House of Commons, 1660-90*, 3 (London 1989), p. 259. On Wembury see B. Cherry, 'The Devon Country House in the Late Seventeenth and Early Eighteenth Centuries', *Devon Archaeological Society Proceedings*, xliv (1988), pp. 91-135.

8 See G.L. Cherry, 'The Development of the English Free Trade Movement in Parliament, 1689-1702', *Journal of Modern History*, xxv (1953), pp. 103-19.

9 Devon Wills, typescripts, West Country Studies Library, Exeter; W.H. Bannerman and W.B. Bannerman (ed.), 'St Stephen's Walbrook and St Benet Sherehog', *Harleian Society Publications, Register Section*, 49-50 (1919-20), p. 124.

10 PRO, C 106/149, C 106/150. I am grateful to Dr Derek Keene of the Centre for Metropolitan History for alerting me to these documents.

11 British Museum, Dept. Prints and Drawings, Crace Coll., portfol. xxi, 119 (missing from folder at time of writing, but recorded on microfilm). The small print (4 x 2 inches) is entitled Walbrook House, and is listed in the catalogue as 'a print by T. Prattent, 1795'.

12 J. Strype, *A Survey of the Cities of London and Westminster*, (London, 1720), i, pp. 198-99. W. Maitland, *The History and Survey of London* (3rd ed., London, 1760), ii, p. 1046.

dedicated to St Stephen. It is an elegant brick building, of the Corinthian order, with double windows. Nothing of the ancient grandeur of the house remains in the inside but the mouldings and a beautiful carved staircase.[13]

The account is repeated, with minor variations, in Thomas Allen's *History and Antiquities of London* (1828).[14] The house stood until *c.* 1875, ingloriously used in the earlier nineteenth century as a hat factory and by 1860 for a variety of offices including the printing works of Messrs McClure.[15] But its memory was still alive when J.G. White published his very thorough history of Walbrook in 1904. Drawing on his recollections stretching back fifty years (although no doubt assisted by the previous writers), he could recall the vestiges remaining of the 'ancient grandeur' of the old mansion of the Pollexfen family which included 'moulded ceilings and a remarkably fine old oak staircase'.[16]

The building accounts are neatly set out in the first five pages of a leather-bound book, most of the rest of which is concerned with rentals from the Wembury estates. They are entitled 'an account of ye cost and charges of ye ground and building of my house in Walbrook begun ye 13th March 1668', and are followed by a page headed 'memorandums'. The total cost of the building, as given in the accounts, was £3,351 6s. 8d. This is a substantial sum when compared for example with the £1,669 7s. 4d. spent by Sir Robert Clayton on a 'capital messuage in Cornhill', or with Clayton's smaller houses, which cost under £500 each.[17]

The accounts would appear to have been written up in roughly chronological order, as the first page is largely concerned with building materials and the last with painting. The major bulk expenses which appear at the start are £199 8s. for 200,000 bricks, with charges; £163 for timber for the warehouse; £151 for fifteen fothers of lead; £139 17s. for boards; £92 for slate; and £79 3s. for lime. It is not always possible to separate precisely the costs of building materials from labour, as sometimes individual items cover both, as well as carriage charges. In other cases special items are entered close to payments to individual craftsmen, suggesting the latter may have provided them. Thus the entry for 'rubbed bricks' costing £20 at 6s. per foot, is followed by payments totalling £49 13s. to Symon Foster for finishing the front of the house, the brick

13 B. Lambert, *The History and Survey of London and its Environs from the Earliest Period to the Present Time* (London, 1806), ii, p. 489.

14 T. Allen, *The History and Antiquities of London, Westminster, Southwark and parts adjacent*, iii (London, 1828), p. 773.

15 Post Office Directories, 1842, 1846, under No. 37 list Messrs Benjamin, William and James Wilson, hatmakers. Directories for 1860 onwards, under Walbrook House and 37 Walbrook, list around ten occupiers, including B. Wilson, 'French plush importer'

but also Messrs Maclures, lithographers and engravers, and several offices concerned with debt collecting and bankruptcy. The directory for 1878 omits No. 37, presumably because it was in course of rebuilding; in the directory for 1879, the entry for 'Walbrook House' lists twenty-five firms as occupants, on five floors.

16 J.G. White, *A History of the Ward of Walbrook in the City of London* (London, 1904), p. 73.

17 Melton, 'Sir Robert Clayton's Building Projects'.

arch, and 'several jobs of brickwork'. The more standard bricklaying was carried out by William Sifton, who was paid £94 3s. for fifty-two rods and a quarter, paid at the rate 36s. for fifteen foot. Although the most important craftsmen are named (see Appendix), others remain anonymous. It is not clear, for example, who was responsible for some of the other brickwork for which payments are recorded, such as the fourteen chimneys, and the 120 foot of straight arches. The bricks were brought by 'several persons'. 'Dutchmen' were paid for planing long boards, and the carpenter Robert Huett 'and Company' were paid for 'levelling and furring of floares'.

It is convenient first to consider the evidence for the site, then for the outbuildings in the yard, and finally for the house itself.

1. The Site

The first entry in the accounts records the purchase of the ground from Susanna Delabarr for £535. Susanna Delabarr had inherited the property from her father, John Delabarr, a merchant, who had acquired the site with the substantial mansion known as York Place only five years previously from the Duke of Richmond and Lennox (a characteristic example of the seventeenth-century shift of City property away from aristocracy).[18] It was described in Delabarr's will as a 'capital messuage or tenement with a warehouse and offices buildings cellars sollars and appurtenances' and was at that time let out to tenants. The Great Fire reduced the value of such investment properties; as so often, the tenants refused to pay the rent and the Fire Court had to adjudicate.[19] Susanna Delabarr, who in 1670 was living in Hackney, was no doubt glad to be rid of the troublesome city site and to put the money toward her marriage that year to Thomas Bird of Mattocks, Hertfordshire.[20] The Delabarr plot was supplemented by an additional piece of ground to the south, 19 × 9 ft, which was bought for £41 from William Tibbs, to provide additional depth for a warehouse.[21]

The boundaries of Pollexfen's plot were verified by Robert Hooke on 8 February 1668, as is recorded in both the building accounts and the memorandum, for the sum of 6s. 8d., the fee required for the registration of property after the Fire.[22] Hooke was the surveyor responsible after the Fire for the part

18 PRO, C 106/149. The sale of the Delabarr property to Pollexfen is dated 24 February 1667/8.
19 Philip E. Jones (ed.), *The Fire Court* (London, 1966), p. 73. Susanna Delabarr petitioned the Fire Court on 19 June 1667; Paul Priaulx, the tenant, was ordered to pay £100 and surrender the lease.
20 J.L. Chester and G.J. Armitage (ed.), 'Marriage Licences in the Registry of the Vicar-General of the Archbishop of Canterbury

1660-79', *Harleian Soc. Publications, Visitation Section* 23, p. 178.
21 PRO, C 106/149. The sale of William Tibbs's land is dated 16 January 1668/9. Disputes over William Tibbs's other properties in Walbrook were settled by the Fire Court; see Philip E. Jones (ed.), *The Fire Court*, document A 524.
22 This is confirmed by the list in Mills and Oliver's Survey, *London Topographical Society* (1967), i, 78.

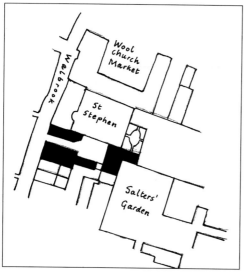

Fig. 37 Walbrook House, after a print of 1795.

Fig. 36 The site of Walbrook House in 1677 (after Ogilby and Morgan's map).

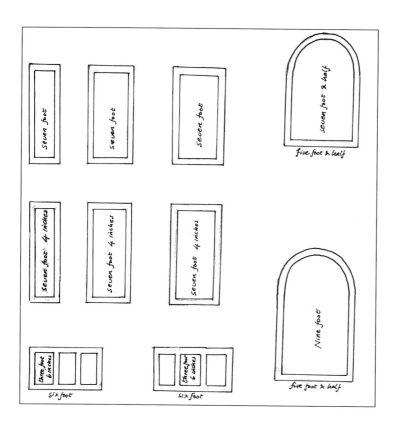

Fig. 38 Rear elevation of Walbrook House adjoining the Salters' Company gardens (from a lease of 1746).

of the city to the east of Walbrook. Unlike the records of Mills and Oliver, responsible for the western area, Hooke's ground plans do not survive and it appears to have been the absence of adequate documents that was in part responsible for later boundary disputes with the Salters' Company whose property lay immediately to the east.[23] Pollexfen's memorandum must have been intended to clarify the situation:

> That ye ground of ye said house . . . is an hundred feet long and fivety two foote and half broad beside ye garden of 35 foote broad and 45 foote long and a gateway of 8 foote 3 inches broad onely Sheffield's house between my gate and ye Church and his lowest house setts in about 8 foote which makes my ground but 92 foote on yt sides but in ye middle is 100f besides ye gateway'.

Ogilby's map of 1677 confirms the arrangement (Fig. 36). Along the east side of Walbrook, travelling from north to south, one passed first the Stocks or Woolchurch market; then the church of St Stephen, shown in 1677 still without its west tower, and immediately to its south a passageway between two street frontages. This led to a yard adjoining the south wall of the church, with large buildings on the south side. The house at the east end occupied the full width of the yard. At the back it overlooked the garden of the Salters' Company, but to the north it had its own small garden, abutting the east wall of the church.

Pollexfen's memorandum explained that:

> whereas the wall of my house toward ye Salters garden was formerly no higher yn a fence wall to ye said garden, wch fell down when I digged my sellar, I came to an agreement with ye said compn. (because it was disputable whether ye said garden wall did belong to ym or me) yt I should make it my house wall on condition I left ym a copeing, and because of a light which ye house had formerly from a closett which stood on said wall and other lights from ye house into said garden, they consented yt I should make what light I had occasion of, with the consent of their surveyor Wildgoose.

Pollexfen was clearly eager to exploit his limited site to the full by building up to the very edge of his boundaries, constructing the back wall of his house on the line of a wall which the Salters claimed was their property. Difficulties surfaced a few years later, when Pollexfen tried to avoid paying the rent of £4 previously agreed for the boundary wall. The memorandum records that in May 1678 the Master of the Company, the future Master and the Clerk met at Pollexfen's house and agreed that 'in consideration of a Bucke they would quit ye rent of

---

23 The Salters' Company, who had acquired their site in 1641, rebuilt their hall in 1667-68 on the north-east corner, with access from St Swithin's Lane, preserving the garden to the west. The property had previously belonged to the Earl of Oxford, and in the middle ages, to the priory of Tortington. See J. Steven Watson, *A History of the Salters' Company* (London, 1963).

£4 and I were to pay them and confirm all my lights for 99 years accordingly I sent ym in a fat Bucke at yr master's feast'. However, this was not to be the end of the story, as will be explained later.

Problems also arose with the north boundary, when the rebuilding of St Stephen's church began in 1672. The design of St Stephen, with its clerestory lighting and avoidance of lower windows to the aisles, is Wren's response to the problems of a site where there were already neighbouring buildings. Even so, Pollexfen (who had lent £50 for the rebuilding of the church) complained that Wren's intended design would obstruct his lights, and some mediation was necessary. A visit was arranged for 'aldermen and deputy' (*sic*) of the ward, together with Sir John Lawrence (Pollexfen's father in law) to see how the church could be continued 'in such a manner without altering the intended design' so that 'Mr Pollexfen would not be prejudiced'. Special arrangements had to be made for the guttering where the two buildings adjoined. At the same time Pollexfen's proprietary interest in the church was asserted by the establishment of a family burial vault beneath the south aisle.[24]

2. *The Buildings*

With the aid of the leases and the accounts a composite picture can be built up of the house and its outbuildings. The leases are particularly helpful because they list all the rooms in both house and outbuildings. The earlier leases (1684, 1704, 1728) also have an attached schedule listing certain fittings. The last lease in the Chancery deposits, dating from 1746, is arranged differently: the main part of the lease describes the repairs that are to be carried out at the owner's expense, after a survey carried out by Stiff Leadbetter (described as 'an experienced surveyor'). The descriptions, which are similar to those in the previous leases apart from a few minor changes, are relegated to a schedule. In the following description the quotations are from the lease of 1684 unless otherwise specified.

Buildings in the Yard

The layout of the yard was given some thought. The accounts record a payment to 'Sebett ye Surveyor for a draughte of the buildings in ye yard:

---

24 St Stephen Walbrook vestry minute books published in *Wren Soc.*, x, p. 112 and quoted by White, *A History of the Ward of Walbrook*, p. 372; L. Weaver, 'The Building Accounts of Wren's City churches', *Archaeologia*, lxvi (1915), pp. 48, 52. According to White (p. 72), the vault had a pre-Fire origin and lay beneath the house; he quotes a rhyme said to have been inscribed on a stone tablet before the Fire, beginning:

Who lies here, who don't ken
The family of Pollexfen
Who, be they living or be they dead
Like theirre own house over theirre head...

Without other supporting evidence this is difficult to interpret. It is possible that members of the family lived in the City before the Fire, but the site of the house was definitely acquired by Pollexfen only after 1666.

£3 6s.' It is notable that this small sum is the only indication in the accounts that any plans were drawn up. As was common at this time, the detail must have remained the responsibility of the individual craftsmen.

The gateway from Walbrook had a 'pair of gates toward the street made in wainscot with a wicket'. This must be the pair of wainscot gates that cost £12, and they must have stood within the brick arch for which the bricklayer Symon Foster was paid £20. At the inner entrance to the yard was a pair of 'perspective' gates with iron bars, flowers de luces and spikes at the top, which like the wainscot gates are included in the schedule of fittings attached to the lease. On the S side of the yard stood the 'great warehouse', occupying part of the extra land bought from William Tibbs. The accounts record that timber for the warehouse 'beside ye carpenter's account' cost £163 (£95 for fir, £50 for oak, £8 for elm, plus charges); 'Old ribs of ships for ye warehouse ground floor' cost £3, laying the warehouse floor and making stairs and doors £5. Eighteen window lights (confirmation that this was a large building) cost £1 4s.; six 'lutherne lights' (dormers) were more expensive, costing £3 12s. The lease mentions also on this side of the yard, a counting house, a washhouse paved with Purbeck stone, and a house of office paved with slate and white stone, and on the next floor 'over the said rooms' a large warehouse, the walls 'lined with deal six ft high half round the said room', and another counting house. The schedule lists 'in the upper warehouse' a packing press 'with hand spikes, blocks, boards necessary for working it', two large presses made of deal, with partitions, and a small windlass with a crane and brass shiner (?) and rope and iron hook. The 1684 lease further specifies that William Scawen was to add an extra floor to the great warehouse, at his own cost; the walls to be of brick, eight feet high, matching the dimensions of the existing building. In the counting house there were 'fixt tables for writing and shelves for bookes' and the washhouse was fitted with a copper for washing clothes, an oven, and a small dressing board. The washhouse was presumably the building, separated from the house by a small yard, shown on Ogilby's plan.

The buildings on the north side of the yard are not mentioned in the accounts and are not shown on Ogilby's map, so may be slightly later additions. By 1684 there was 'a stable with racks and manger and house of office. Also an open gallery with another house of office. In the next store over them an hayloft and a roome for servants to lodge in'. The gallery was perhaps a form of loggia which could have accommodated the '3 columns for ye yard' which appear among the joiner's work in the accounts (compare the view of Sir John Frederick's house which shows an arcade on one side of the yard).[25] The schedule completes the picture with a 'horse trough of lead 5ft 3 inches by 18 inches covered with deale painted leade colour' (which cost £12) and a 'pissing cistern of lead by the stable door'. Other leadwork was also included in the

25 J. Imray, *The Mercers' Hall* (London, 1991), p.262, fig. 48.

schedule: 'five pipes of lead which bring down the water from the house, a pipe which brings the New River water from the street and three pipes with cocks which carry it to the horse trough, wash house and kitchen'. The memorandum provides meticulous detail about drainage arrangements: the drain carrying the water from the house

> runs from ye washhouse door into ye common sewer, on ye inside of ye gate middle of ye gateway, inside ye Arch and middle of ye yard are left holes for a man to creep unto ye drayne to cleanse if necessary; and afterward made a hole of 5 foote which begins 12 foote from ye gate & crowne of ye drayne is about 3 foote underground.

The impression is of an active place of business, a gated and secure yard with two counting houses, well-equipped warehouses, stables, accommodation for servants, and no less than three 'houses of office' (privies), suggesting a workforce of some size.

The House

Lambert's account of 1806 suggests the house incorporated a substantial amount of pre-Fire work, but this seems very unlikely. This was one of the areas where the fire had raged most fiercely;[26] the story of the Salters' Company wall, the payments for clearing the ground and digging the kitchen cellar and for digging and carrying away 200 loads of rubbish, as well as the extensive quantity of new building materials, indicate that there was little on the site but rubble and broken walls, and that the house was a new building. It is possible that an older cellar was reused, as happened elsewhere in the City after the Fire, but it is equally likely that Lambert's romantic imagination was fired by the idea that the cellar vaults could be associated with a medieval monastic house, the origin of this rumour being inspired by the fact that the Salters' Company property, later Oxford House, had indeed been a medieval monastic possession.[27]

The lease mentions 'a vault of the length of the front of the house and Backwards a beer cellar and cellar for coale', and the schedule lists in the cellar 'two partitions, one to make a wett larder and the other a wine cellar'. From the lease of 1746, which specifies the repairs needed to the house, it is stated that twelve new brick steps were to be made down to the vault and that the oak frames and doors to the cellar were to be repaired. The number of steps implies a full cellar rather than a basement, and indeed in the print of 1795 the cellar was not visible.

The ground floor of the house was approached by 'a pair of stairs with rails and banisters . . . leading from the said yard to the hall'. The 1795 print (Fig.

26 J. Bedford, *London's Burning* (London, 1966), pp. 76-79.

27 See note 23 above.

37) shows a pedimented entrance, placed centrally in a five bay front, approached by a flight of stairs apparently flanked by freestanding columns, perhaps for lamps (possibly later additions). The print is too small and schematic to show much detail, but indicates an elevation which was symmetrical, but conservative in its detail, with three floors divided by plat bands, with paired windows all of the same height, a prominent cornice, end chimney stacks and a hipped roof with five dormers. The lease gives no further detail about the elevation but more can be gleaned from the building accounts. Some of the detail confirms the print: 'fourteen windows in ye front at 38s.', cost £26 12s. John Potter, a smith, was paid for casements 'from 4 to 5s. and double at 25s.'; which suggests that the old-fashioned double windows of the print are the original ones, although by 1795 the casements may well have given way to sashes. The windows must have been more elaborate than the print suggests, for a carver was paid £9 for windows in the front; as already mentioned there are also references to rubbed brick in the front and yard at 6s. per foot, totalling £20; and a payment to Symon Foster of £12 'for finishing ye front of ye house' and of £17 13s. 'for severall jobs of brickwork'. Possibly also for the exterior were the fifty five foot of 'mondillion ends' which at 8s. per foot came to £22; and 150 foot of cornice at 14d. which cost £8 15s. Both these items appear among the payments for carpentry work and so were presumably of timber. The entrance was an especially expensive item: the doorway must have been of stone, for there is a payment to a mason, James Flore, for £26 for the doorcase, while 'ye staires Railes and banisters comeing up' cost £50.

The ground floor rooms mentioned in the lease are the hall with a little closet, a kitchen with buttery, two parlours, an entry adjoining the parlour, a large buttery toward the garden, the great stairs, and a little stair 'leading from the bottom to the top of the house'. The next floor had a dining room with closet, a withdrawing room adjoining, and two chambers, each with a closet. On the third floor were four chambers with three closets, and a large closet 'in the front of the great stair'. Above this were four garrets. All this strongly suggests a straightforward double pile plan with four main rooms on each floor, some of them served by closets, with the kitchen at the south end of the house and the main parlour at the north end adjoining the garden. Such an arrangement would agree with the 1795 print.

The nature of the rear of the house is more problematic. The sketch attached to the 1746 lease (Fig. 38) which shows those windows which stood on the Salters' Company boundary wall, is confusing. It does not show the whole house, only the southern portion of it. One therefore cannot be certain if the back of the house was symmetrical, for the extension of the plot to the north east would have allowed for a projecting rear wing at this point, as Ogilby's map possibly indicates. The garden layout shown by Ogilby is centred on what would be the mid point of such a wing. The sketch of the Salters' wall shows on the right the two large arched windows at different levels from the other windows. It is likely that these are the 'two great windows' which cost 36s. each, and that they lit the stair hall. If so, the great stairs would have been in the centre of the rear of the house, directly behind the entrance hall. The low windows to the left are most likely to have belonged to the kitchen. (The conditions in the arrangements with the Salters, that no rubbish was to be thrown from the windows, would have been particularly necessary if the kitchen overlooked the Salters' garden.) The very narrow windows on the far left are comparable to the closet windows popular in London houses of the later seventeenth century. However, the tall proportions of the windows at the back of the house are noticeably different from the more old-fashioned square double openings shown on the 1795 print. The dimensions of at least some of the rear windows may be the result of early eighteenth-century alterations. A report of 1722 in the Chancery deposits explains that Pollexfen's tenant Scawen lowered the windows without permission and that in 1713 the Salters' Company 'blinded them up' (ignoring the former arrangements between Pollexfen and the Salters). Eventually, after two court cases, Woolcombe Pollexfen agreed in 1728 to pay the Salters £4 p.a. for the windows, and in another lease of 27 June 1728, between Woolcombe Pollexfen and Sir Thomas Scawen, reference is made to 'all those lights or windows as they are now fixt on the east side of the capital messuage'. The inclusion of a plan of the windows is mentioned in this lease, although it has disappeared. The surviving plan (possibly reused from the earlier lease) is attached to the lease of 1746. The intention was no doubt to make doubly sure that further unauthorised alterations would not take place.

A further slight piece of evidence about the nature of the rear of the house is provided by a painting of the Stocks Market, of *c.* 1730 by Josef van Aken.[28] Behind the east end of St Stephen's is a glimpse of a brick building with a cornice roughly level with the eaves of the church. To its left is a lower sloping roof, with a chimney rising behind. The main building must be Pollexfen's house; the sloping roof suggests a lower rear extension with a chimney on its south wall adjoining the Salters' garden. While one might expect a low rear extension to be a service wing, it seems unlikely here, given that the washhouse was at the opposite end of the site, and that the formal garden lay to the north, adjoining the churchyard. Perhaps the chimney served the fireplace of the parlour; if the parlour had its main windows and a door opening onto the garden to the north, the south wall of the room would have been a convenient place for the fireplace.

28 In the possession of the Bank of England; illustrated in M. Warner et al., *The Image of London: Views by Travellers and Emigrés 1550-* *1920* (Barbican Art Gallery, London, 1987), plate vii.

The Interior of the House

The accounts and 1684 lease are especially illuminating about the individual named rooms and their fittings, the levels of expense indicating the relative importance of the different rooms. The order in which they are mentioned here follows that of the lease. The hall was 'wainscoted all through with deal and painted with a little closett therein with shelves and a chimney sett with Flanders tiles the footpace of stone'. Wainscoting of hall and 'writing room' cost £50, the hall doors £5 10s. and 'two Spanish tables' for the hall £1 15s. Painting of the hall cost £12. The kitchen was paved with Purbeck stone and had a buttery in it with shelves. The schedule attached to the lease lists the kitchen fittings in detail: a lead cistern 5 ft 8 inches by 16 inches, 30 inches high, with 'plankes for a stande for it', an oak sink 5ft by 4 ft covered with lead, a dressing board 14 ft by 2 ft 'with cupboards under the most part of it' and 'several shelves fixt in the kitchen and the buttery'. Cupboards and shelves in the kitchen cost £34 5s. The first parlour is mentioned immediately after the kitchen, and so was perhaps the south-west room, looking out onto the front yard. It was 'wainscotted all through with deale and painted a chimney sett with white stone and marble and the floor pace of marble all one stone'. The second parlour was grander, for it was not only 'wainscotted all through' but had a carved cornice and chimneypiece, wainscot window shutters, and a chimney set with Flanders tiles and a floor pace of black and white marble. The wainscoting and carving of this room cost £42 10s. The parlour had also a 'great window' which cost £1 12s. (perhaps in the east wall of the rear wing) and one 'doorcase with a light over it' (perhaps in the north wall, opening onto the garden) which cost £1 12s. The entry adjoining the parlour was paved with black and white stone, the buttery 'by the garden' was fitted with shelves and cupboards. Payments for the entry and buttery appear at the end of the accounts among what appear to be late additions; other entries in this section refer to 'making ye counting house by ye hall' (£20) and 'altering ye counting house into withdrawing room' (£5), suggesting various minor changes, most probably to the closet off the hall, called the writing room earlier in the accounts.

The great stair was 'wainscotted on the sides of the walls two storeys high with deal painted' which cost £12; carving for the stairs cost £6. The little stairs had 'rails and banisters painted'. 'Two frontages to ye doors at the first flight of the stairs' cost £6. These were presumably the doors to the chief first floor rooms, the dining room and the great chamber. The dining room was 'wainscotted all through with a fretwork ceiling and cornish, a little closett in it. A chimney sett with Flanders tiles and a footpace of black and white marble'. Wainscoting the dining room and best chamber, with carving, cost £115, while Thomas Crooke was paid £17 for the special feature of the 'fretwork ceiling' (of plaster?). The withdrawing room was less important, for it was only wainscoted in front under the window, but the larger chamber had another Flanders tile chimney with marble footpace and a carved and gilded cornice and chimney-piece (the only reference to gilding in the accounts). As one would expect, there is less detail about the upper rooms. On the second floor 'four pairs of shutters to the windows' are mentioned, and the large closet at the head of the stairs had 'shelves all round'. The four garrets had shutters to three of the windows.

3. The Garden

Ogilby's map shows the small garden east of St Stephen's church formally laid out with an oval path. On the first page of the accounts there is an entry 'Pd a gardner for trees herbs and making garden, £3 5s.'; suggesting that the garden was prepared before the house was completed; a sensible move, as it would appear that once the house was built it would have cut off access to the garden from the yard. Late entries in the accounts, against the date 1680, are for payments for iron gates, brickwork and carpenters work; making the wall between garden and churchyard £20, and for grated gates £10. The barriers must have become necessary only after the churchyard had been laid out. In the lease the garden is described as 'five and thirty foot square with a dore and two windows perspective with iron barrs toward the churchyard'. The schedule adds 'in the garden a seat with back painted and covered at the top' and perhaps the birdcage which cost £23 was also a garden ornament (Sir John Frederick's garden had a large birdcage with a leaden fountain).[29]

Despite the lack of plans and detailed elevations, the available evidence provides a reasonably clear picture of Pollexfen's house. In many respects it was a traditional City merchant's mansion, built on a confined site at the back of a working yard. Although conforming to post-Fire building regulations in its use of materials, it was old-fashioned in some of its features. The 'double windows', pairs of casements within a square opening, were reminiscent of earlier seventeenth-century fashions, although eighteenth-century views of the City confirm that they continued in use after the Fire.[30] The symmetrical front with central entrance opening into a hall, and the double pile plan, also were not novelties, for they can be found already in those houses of the 1630s built for City men in the London countryside: Cromwell House, Highgate; Swakeleys, Ickenham; and Kew Palace. As at Cromwell House and Swakeleys, the main staircase at Pollexfen's house probably lay in line with the entrance. The siting of Pollexfen's kitchen on the ground floor, at the same level as hall and

29 Imray, *The Mercers' Hall*, p. 468 n. 72.
30 See for example the view of Cheapside illustrated in Reddaway, *The Rebuilding of London*, p. 192. A surviving example of a front elevation with a double window of this type, combined with narrow end windows, is 23 Highgate High Street, London N6.

parlours, is another feature found at Swakeleys, one that looks back to older traditions rather than forward to the arrangement of basement services that became standard in London houses in the new suburbs. The first floor 'dining room' is also prefigured in earlier grand houses and reflects usage that was becoming fashionable in the City as well. At Ham House the room above the hall is called the 'great dining room' in an inventory of 1654.[31] The large first floor rooms at Swakeleys and Cromwell House must have had a similar function.

Any ideal planning in the City was likely to be circumscribed by the exigencies of the site. The position of the garden to the north, overshadowed from both south and west, cannot have been ideal. The limited site may also explain the height of the house, three storeys apart from garrets and cellar, the same height as that prescribed for the second category of houses 'fronting streets and lanes of note'. Sir John Frederick's house, spread out over a larger area, appears to have had approximately the same number of rooms, but was one storey less in height.[32] Pollexfen's accommodation seems surprisingly ample for a builder who at the time of construction had yet to establish his own family, although possibly other relations also made use of the house.[33]

In its fittings the house was respectable but not among the very grandest. It could hardly compare with Frederick's house, where the parlour had a gilt ceiling and there were fretwork ceilings in five other rooms.[34] In Pollexfen's house the most elaborate joinery was reserved for the most important rooms: the ground floor hall and main parlour, the first floor dining room and great chamber. These rooms were also distinguished by fireplaces with Flanders tiles; fireplaces in the other rooms were simpler. Conspicuous expenditure was perhaps hardly to be expected by a man still only at the start of his career, who was only aged around thirty when building. His marriage to Mary Lawrence in 1670, who brought a dowry of £4,000, came after the house was completed.

As Pollexfen's wealth and his status as a Member of Parliament increased, a house in the crowded heart of the City may have proved inconvenient and

31 For City houses, see V. Harding and D. Keene, *Historical Gazetteer of London before the Great Fire* (Cambridge, 1987). For Ham House, see P.K. Thornton and M. Tomlin, *The Furniture and Decoration of Ham House*, Furniture History Society (London, 1980).

32 Imray, *The Mercers' Hall* figs. 47, 48.

33 There is no evidence to support the assertion by White, *A History of the Ward of Walbrook*, that John Pollexfen's elder brother, the lawyer Sir Henry Pollexfen, lived in Walbrook, but a Jane Pollexfen, perhaps a sister or cousin 'of St Stephen Walbrook, aged about twenty-four and at her own dispose, her parents being dead' was married at St Catherine Cree

in 1673. John Pollexfen's brother Nicholas, was described as 'a merchant, of Philpot Lane' and in his will as of Wad(d)on, Surrey, but two of his children were buried at St Stephen's (Grace in 1679, Reed in 1702, in the family vault). See W.H. Bannerman and W.B. Bannerman (ed.), 'St Stephen's Walbrook and St Benet Sherehog', *Harleian Society Publications, Register Section*, 49-50, (1919-20); J.L. Chester and G.J. Armitage (ed.), 'Marriage Licences in the Registry of the Vicar-General of the Archbishop of Canterbury, 1660-79', *Harleian Soc. Publications, Visitation Section*, 23, (1886), p. 223.

34 Imray, *The Mercers' Hall*, p. 468.

inappropriate, when compared, for example, with the suburban Hatton Gardens mansion of his parliamentary colleague Sir George Treby. It is also likely that by the 1680s Pollexfen's architectural taste had developed. The house in Walbrook may already have appeared old-fashioned. The sparse evidence suggests that the additions he made to his country seat at Wembury (demolished in the later eighteenth century) were both more architecturally sophisticated and more lavish. During the 1670s Pollexfen had come into close contact with Robert Hooke when he supervised the building of St Stephen's church. Hooke's diary records frequent visits to Pollexfen's house at this time, and it was Pollexfen who acted as intermediary when another Devonshire Whig Member of Parliament, Sir George Yonge, built his house at Escott to Hooke's design, a design which was reflected at Wembury.[35] Pollexfen's activities demonstrate how a combination of circumstances could lead to the spread of architectural ideas: opportunities and contacts arising from the rebuilding of the City after the Fire were developed further through association of like-minded merchants and politicians with both city and country interests.

A certain cautious frugality, or perhaps just self-interest, nevertheless accords with aspects of Pollexfen's later character revealed by other sources. His not particularly generous or helpful treatment of his orphaned nephew, the son of Sir Henry Pollexfen, is revealed in the (admittedly not impartial) Drake family records.[36] The sentiments expressed in his economic treatise published in 1697 display a somewhat self-righteous scorn of idleness and unnecessary luxury, with complaints that 'the people of this nation are of late years much changed for the worse in course of living'. He deplored, in particular, excessive wages, excessive apparel and other expenses, blaming the state of the economy in part on the import of luxury goods, especially from France.[37]

From 1684 the house in Walbrook yielded an annual rent of £100, a figure that remained constant in the later leases. By the middle of the eighteenth century the house not only must have appeared old-fashioned, but was also in need of repair. The elderly Woolcombe Pollexfen, by then living in retirement in Hampstead, had to agree to the work recommended by Stiff Leadbetter as

---

35 Escott and Wembury are discussed in B. Cherry, 'The Devon Country House' (see n. 7).

36 E.F.E. Drake, *The Family and Heirs of Sir Francis Drake* (London, 1911), 2, passim. Sir Francis Drake, 3rd baronet, married Elizabeth, the daughter of Sir Henry Pollexfen in 1689/90; John Pollexfen was one of the trustees, and was also the executor of Sir Henry Pollexfen, who died in 1691. Disagreements arose over outstanding debts and the terms of the will. John Pollexfen appears to have resented the influence of the Drakes over his young epileptic nephew Henry, who eventually married Gertrude Drake, the daughter of Sir Francis by his first wife.

37 (J. Pollexfen), *A Discourse on Trade, Coyn, and Paper Credit and of ways and means to Gain and Retain Riches* (London, 1697).

part of the conditions of a new lease to Samuel Swinfen in 1746.[38] It was these repairs that must have helped the house to survive for over another century, an increasingly anomalous reminder of the time when the City was a customary place of residence for affluent merchants.

Appendix

Craftsmen Mentioned in the Building Accounts

Baskervill, plumber
Mr Boase, painter
Thomas Crooke (fretwork ceiling)
Ellis, glazier
Evans, plasterer
James Flore, mason
Symon Foster (rubbed brickwork)

Hartrow, painter
Thomas Hodges, joiner
Robert Huett, carpenter
William Sifton, bricklayer
John Potter, smith
Thomas Pratt (roofing)
Watts, carver

38 Among the thorough and extensive recommendations in Stiff Leadbetter's survey were repair of the roof with one sixth part new tiles; three coats of paint for the garret windows, two coats for other exterior woodwork and ironwork; repairs to windows, ceilings, wainscot and floors. For the interior repainting it was specified that the wainscot should be painted a stone colour and the inside of the sashes wainscot colour. The house and yard appear to have changed little, but there are a few significant new names; a coach-house among the outbuildings, a servants' hall mentioned together with the kitchen, and three instead of two parlours on the ground floor, perhaps created by subdividing one of the older rooms.

8

Privacy and the Plan

JOHN BOLD

The first complete English translation of Andrea Palladio's *Quattro libri dell'architettura* was published by Giacomo Leoni between 1715 and 1720. This version was, on the author's own admission, not a faithful copy, but incorporated 'necessary corrections with respect to shading, dimensions, ornaments etc.' These alterations were remarked upon by Isaac Ware in the 'Advertisement' to his accurate edition of Palladio, brought out in 1738 with the sponsorship of Lord Burlington. Given the fidelity of Ware's edition, it might have been expected that when he came to write his own treatise he would have embarked upon a canonical justification of Palladian practice. But by 1756, when *A Complete Body of Architecture* was published, the high point of English Palladianism was past and Ware offered criticisms of the master in the light of national expectations and practice: 'We are not to take the Italians as our perfect model . . . because they adapted their edifices to their country, and so must we . . . let the builder remember that there is a great difference between Italy and England.' Even so, with regard to the laying out of houses, Ware tells us

Palladio lays down one excellent and universal rule; which is that in all buildings, the most beautiful and noble parts should be placed most in view; and those of a meaner kind as much concealed from sight as possible. This is one of those rules which is universal, for good sense is the language of all countries; yet we see this miserably transgressed.[1]

* Parts of this essay were given at Vancouver Art Gallery in 1989 in a symposium on Venetian and Anglo-Venetian themes in celebration of the opening of the exhibition 'Eighteenth-Century Venetian Paintings and Drawings in Canadian Collections', curated by Professor George Knox. I am grateful to Professor Knox for allowing a reworking of the material here, and to the British Council for assistance with travelling expenses. Some of the preparatory material for this essay was gathered in the course of work for the Royal Commission on the Historical Monuments of England with my colleague Nicholas Cooper. I wish to thank him for many illuminating discussions but stress that the views and interpretations offered here are my own.

1 I. Ware, *A Complete Body of Architecture* (1768 edition; facsimile Farnborough, 1971), p. 322. For a detailed discussion of Ware's treatise, see E. Harris, assisted by N. Savage, *British Architectural Books and Writers, 1556-1785* (Cambridge, 1990), pp. 468-76.

Ware's encyclopaedic compilation was the first detailed, illustrated architectural treatise to be written for an English audience: previous authors had produced practical guides to details, particularly the Orders, and some, such as James Gibbs, had produced volumes advertising their own work.[2] Ware's book, coming at the end of a century and a half of classical development, codified good English practice, by collecting 'all that is useful in the works of others . . . to make our work serve as a library on this subject . . . supplying the place of all other books . . . .'[3] As well as details – chimneypieces, windows, ceilings and so on – he published plans and elevations of houses, based on the two established plan forms, the double pile (two parallel ranges of building) and the tripartite arrangement based on the Palladian villa. He uses the double pile for a house near Bristol (with a central, transverse corridor); for a 'person of distinction' in Yorkshire; and, with a central corridor, at Wrotham Park in Hertfordshire. The villa arrangement is used for two houses in Scotland, and for 'a gentleman near London'.[4]

It is the purpose of this essay to look at the development of the seventeenth-century house plan, not as a stylistic phenomenon reflecting an increasing reliance upon Italian precedent, but as a response to national, planning requirements, particularly a strongly articulated demand for privacy and convenience. The seventeenth century was one of the most crucial periods of innovation and evolution in English domestic architecture and an understanding of the development of the concept of privacy, and the ways in which architecture sought to accommodate it, is fundamental to its assessment and to the charting of its development over the next two hundred years.[5]

'Privacy' is defined by the *Oxford English Dictionary (OED)* as, firstly, 'the state or condition of being withdrawn from the society of others'; secondly, in its plural form, as 'private or retired places; private apartments; places of retreat'. One of the sources for this second usage is Fielding's *Tom Jones*, published in 1749:

> Mrs Western was reading a lecture on prudence, and matrimonial politics to her niece, when her brother and Blifil broke in with less ceremony than the laws of visiting require . . . 'Brother', said she, 'I am astonished at your behaviour, will you never learn any regard to decorum? Will you still look upon every apartment as your own, or as belonging to one of your country tenants? Do you think yourself at liberty to invade the privacies of women of condition, without the least decency or notice?'

Later on, Squire Western resigns his family seat to his daughter and son-in-law and retires to a lesser house, better situated for hunting, but as a regular visitor

---

2 J. Gibbs, *A Book of Architecture* (London, 1728).

3 Ware, *A Complete Body*, preface.

4 Ibid., plates 39-42, 45, 47-49, 52-55.

5 The accommodation of privacy is fundamental for longer and over a wider geographical area than can be considered here; see M. Davis, *City of Quartz* (London, 1990), pp. 223-33, in which the author discusses the 'ingenious design deterrents' employed in Los Angeles.

to his former home he has the use of 'a parlour and anti-chamber to himself, where he gets drunk with whom he pleases'.[6]

1749 was a memorable year for English literature. John Cleland's *Fanny Hill*, alongside the main theme, gives us further useful insights into architectural expectations, here in an urban context:

> one day returning to my lodgings . . . the maid of the house . . . , as I passed by, told me Mr H. was above. I stept upstairs into my own bedchamber, with no other thought than of pulling off my hat, etc., and then to wait upon him in the dining-room, into which my bed-chamber had a door as is common enough.

Hearing sounds, she spies, through an opportune peep-hole, Mr H., her protector, with her maid Hannah, engaged on a couch in the corner of the room. Seeking to pay him back, the heroine later seduces his young servant on that same couch in the dining room. During a later, imprudent meeting in her closet, adjoining the bedroom and with no separate access, she and the servant are discovered by Mr H. who turns the key and locks the chamber door upon them, 'so that there was no escape but through the dining room'.[7]

The identification of the private space as the locus of morality was not, of course, Fanny Hill's discovery – she merely exemplifies the trend.[8] As early as the late sixteenth century, the historian Harrison was remarking in his *Description of England* on the improvements in lodgings and furnishings in houses and the increasing provision of separate service accommodation.[9] The need for comfort, convenience and private spaces was a common theme amongst those writers on both architecture and conduct who were describing current good practice. Francis Bacon argued for a separation of the banquet and household sides in grand houses and the separation of servants' quarters.[10] Sir Henry Wotton made a plea for the graceful and useful distribution of offices and reception rooms. He criticised Italian *en suite* lodging chambers on the grounds that only the last was private and that the user of the house should be able to 'avoyd Encounters'; for the same reason, the stairs should have 'no nigard Latitude'.[11] Thomas Fuller in 1648 made the same point rather more succinctly – 'let not the common rooms be several nor the several rooms common'; the hall, passages and stairs should be open; the chambers and closets private and

6 H. Fielding, *The History of Tom Jones* (Harmondsworth, 1966), pp. 763, 873.

7 J. Cleland, *Fanny Hill: Memoirs of a Woman of Pleasure* (London, 1964), pp. 95-110. It is worth noting, unsurprisingly in this context, that privacy was not always a prerequisite for sexual activity. In the houses of the less prosperous, particularly, the accessible space was as likely to be used as the private; see G.R. Quaife, *Wanton Wenches and Wayward Wives: Peasants and Illicit Sex in Early Seventeenth-Cen-*tury England (London, 1979), pp. 75-76.

8 See the important discussion in R. Evans, *The Fabrication of Virtue: English Prison Architecture, 1750-1840* (Cambridge, 1982), pp. 402-420.

9 W. Harrison, *Description of England* (1577-87), published with J. Norden, *Surveyor's Dialogue* (1608), ed. F.J. Furnivall (London, 1877-78).

10 F. Bacon, *Essays* (London, 1906), p. 134.

11 H. Wotton, *The Elements of Architecture* (1624; facsimile Farnborough, 1969), pp. 57, 72-74.

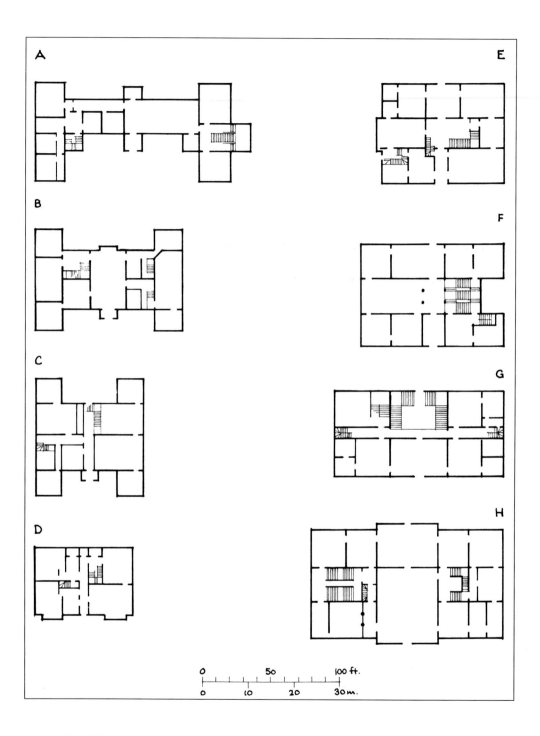

Fig. 39 Simplified ground plans of:

A. Doddington

B. Charlton House

C. Swakeleys

D. The Dutch House, Kew

E. Melton Constable

F. Tring (Wren)

G. Coleshill (Pratt)

H. Horseheath (Pratt)

(*Drawn by John Morrey*)

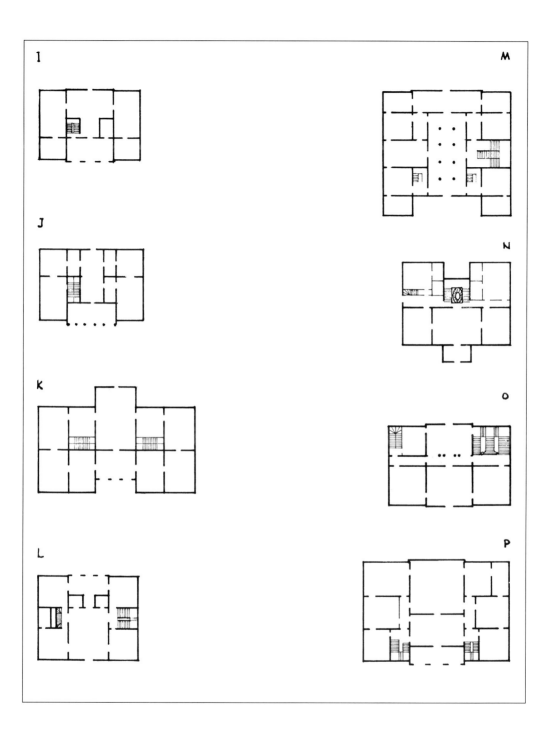

Fig. 40 Simplified ground plans of:

I. Villa Saraceno (Palladio)
J. Villa Badoer (Palladio)
K. Villa Godi (Palladio)
L. Maiden Bradley (Webb)

M. Gunnersbury House (Webb)
N. Amesbury Abbey (Webb)
O. Wrotham Park (Ware)
P. Amisfield House, Scotland (Ware)

(*Drawn by John Morrey*)

retired; the offices at a remove from the house.[12] These books did not offer detailed prescriptions for the designing of houses – theoretical writings on architecture in England in the seventeenth and eighteenth centuries were few: theory, in this case as in so many others, followed practice.[13]

How that practice evolved may be demonstrated by looking at the form of certain key houses, disregarding their relative size (Figs. 39 and 40) and by drawing on the writings on architecture of Sir Roger Pratt and Roger North. Their texts remained unpublished until 1928 and 1981 respectively, so they were not influential, but they are invaluable nevertheless in illustrating the intentions of seventeenth-century builders.[14] North's text is especially important because, writing at the end of the century, he was able to reflect upon a particularly dramatic period; one which saw the establishment and adaptation to English usage by Inigo Jones and John Webb of a fully developed continental classicism based on the buildings, drawings and published treatises of Palladio and Scamozzi; one which saw the supplanting, in fashionable circles, of the hitherto most common type of English country house plan, the hall and cross wings, by the double pile and villa plans which achieved their finest architectural expression in the work of Pratt and Webb.

Roger North was a lawyer who regarded himself as no more than a 'dabler' in the art of architecture, but he was well-versed in the literature and he did produce designs: the Great Gateway which gives access to the Temple from Fleet Street and various works at Wroxton Abbey, the seat of his brother Lord Guilford. It was the purchase of a house at Rougham in 1690 – an old-fashioned house in need of remodelling – which was to provide the greatest spur to his architectural ambitions. His 'Cursory Notes of Building' were occasioned by his 'Metamorfosis' of this 'old house in the Country'.

North's watchwords were 'convenience', 'decorum' and 'economy'. In his view, these were inadequately satisfied by the hall and cross wings as it developed in the years around 1600. Doddington in Lincolnshire, a house of *c.* 1595, with symmetrical façade and asymmetrical interior, represents the half-H plan in its canonical form, with entry at the centre of the house into the end of the hall, with a grand staircase beyond. North had this type of arrangement in mind when he wrote:

12 T. Fuller, *The Holy State* (2nd ed., London, 1648), p. 156.

13 D. Defoe, a century later, satirised the master/servant relationship which underpinned these arguments, inveighing against the 'insufferable Behaviour of Servants', a national grievance which 'calls aloud for a Remedy' in *The Great Law of Subordination Considered* (London, 1724); continuing the theme in the

following year: 'If I must have an Intrigue, let it be with a Woman that shall not shame me. I would never go into the Kitchen when the Parlour-Door was open', in *Everybody's Business is Nobody's Business* (London, 1725).

14 R.T. Gunther, *The Architecture of Sir Roger Pratt* (Oxford, 1928); H.M. Colvin and J. Newman (ed.), *Of Building: Roger North's Writings on Architecture* (Oxford, 1981).

This form is fit for a colledge or hospitall, to be devided into cells, and chambers independent of each other; but not for a dwelling house, that ought to have a connexion, and unity, without crossing to and fro from one part to the other, thro the air and abroad.[15]

Some of these problems were resolved in such full-H plan houses of the period as Charlton of 1607-12, in which the width of the central range was increased to allow for a transverse hall, with a great chamber above reached by a well staircase. However, the retention of the wings to provide space for a long gallery on the top floor did not solve the other fundamental difficulty identified by North, 'the great charge of walls, and roof', which made this an uneconomic form to build in comparison with the rectangular block which both he and Pratt recommended: the double pile.

The development of the double pile predated the introduction of the Jonesian classicism with which it has often been associated – examples can be found in the late sixteenth and early seventeenth centuries, a particularly good example being the Red House at Bourne, Lincolnshire, of 1615. During the period in which Jones was effecting his revolution in taste in the service of the Stuart court, substantial houses of double pile form were being built in the hybrid classical style exemplified by the Dutch House at Kew, built in 1631 by the merchant Samuel Fortrey; Swakeleys in Ickenham, completed in 1638 for Sir Edmund Wright; and Barnham Court in Sussex. These houses lacked the sophistication and discipline which was to characterise the work of Webb and Pratt when they attempted to solve comparable problems two decades later, but they survive as impressive representatives of a transitional phase in both stylistic and planning developments. All three have central entrances with off-centre halls, double-depth plans and classical, but not purely Italianate, decoration. These houses were all newly built, but a comparable form could be achieved by the simple expedient of doubling the central range of an existing H or half-H plan. Such a strategy was adopted at the Duke and Duchess of Lauderdale's Ham House, Richmond in the 1670s; an alteration which Roger North considered 'the best of the kind I have seen . . . For I doe not perceive any part of the old fabrick is taken downe, but the wings stand as they were first sett . . . joyned with a strait range intirely new'.[16]

The fundamental advantage of the double pile lay in its system of circulation which was flexible enough to allow for choices of route through the house, within an overall form which was architecturally coherent and compact. With the decline in importance of the great chamber and the long gallery, a compact rectangular plan combining communal and private spaces could be achieved without detriment to social requirements. There were, inevitably, problems inherent in the form, caused largely by that very proximity of rooms to one

15 Colvin and Newman (ed.), *Of Building*, p. 32.   16 Ibid., p. 144.

another which was the double pile's great advantage. Whilst more economic to build than the half-H, which was generally long in relation to its number of rooms, too great a contraction could result in the disadvantages identified by North: all of the noises of the house being heard everywhere; all offensive smells being a nuisance to all rooms; closets and interior rooms being hard to fashion without sacrificing a good room; some rooms being too low and others too high because floor levels needed to be constant; individual room temperatures being difficult to modify because of the proximity of other rooms.

These difficulties could be resolved in part by an increase in size. The type exemplified by Montagu House, a double pile with wings for offices, was recommended by North for those with 'full and luxurious purses', because 'it is the true way of composing the conveniences of a family in several orders without fraction and indecorum'.[17] The triple pile also, a potentially larger, variant form, was employed in the later seventeenth century by 'those of the best purses', being 'as much as can be practis't in a square figure', and therefore at first sight very desirable in offering many more rooms for relatively little more expense.[18] Here, with Melton Constable and Tring in mind, North pinpoints serious problems: how to light the central range, and how to organise circulation through it. At Tring, built by Sir Christopher Wren for Henry Guy, Groom of the Bedchamber to King Charles II, he found less to criticise than he did at Melton because much was 'excellently contrived', and the problems were those which were consequent upon attempting to accommodate 'several purposes in one and the same order of building'.[19] At Melton, however, the 'avaritious and mean-spirited' Sir Jacob Astley, employing a bricklayer as his architect, built a house which brought 'all inconveniences together': 'want of light in the middle'; 'the back stairs open to the great staires', which had no light apart from above the cornice; the whole appearing small 'tho it be large', and thus not humouring the 'proposition of a large country family'. 'So here was a mixture of the gentleman, usurer, and bricklayer, and the project proves accordingly'.[20]

We may infer from North's remarks on 'fraction and indecorum', and the desirability of shielding the main from the service stairs, a belief in the importance of private spaces and the need to separate the parts of the house occupied by owners and servants. That such an ordonnance could not be provided readily by the hall and cross wings, where many rooms were through rooms, is clear. North was not alone in his desire to use the house plan to guard against the possibility of accidental contact. 'The architect', he wrote, 'must

---

17 Ibid., p. 71.
18 Ibid., p. 73. The English version of the triple pile may be contrasted with the transverse, tripartite arrangement, commonly employed in Venice and comparable with the villa plan, in which the *pòrtego* ran back for the full depth of the house, with the accommodation leading directly from it; see R.J. Goy, *Venetian Vernacular Architecture* (Cambridge, 1989), pp. 123-49.
19 Colvin and Newman (ed.), *Of Building*, p. 74.
20 Ibid., pp. 9, 74-76.

truckle to his master of expenditor who will truckle to the mode of his time'.[21] The mode appeared to be changing, the architect being required to provide spaces which were geared to social fastidiousness: by the century's end, 'subservient accomodations and back staires' were essential. The main stair 'must not be annoyed with disagreeable objects, but be releived of them by a back-inferior staircase', for although 'it is no unseemly object to an English gentleman . . . to see his servants and buissness passing at ordinary times', 'if we consult convenience, we must have severall avenews, and bolting holes . . . to decline passing by company posted about by accident . . . For it is unpleasant to be forc't to cross people, when one has not a mind to it, either for avoiding ceremony or any other reason'.[22] Architecture is being recommended here as part of a defensive strategy against unwelcome and unpredictable territorial encroachments – a defence against potential violation. Service stairs, closets and corridors were all enabling devices in the pursuit of convenience, comfort and privacy.

Such defensive devices were not new in North's day. It is not their existence but the articulation of the need for them and the overall form of their accommodation which distinguishes the period. The earliest reference in *OED* to a 'Curridore, or private way' occurs in 1600, and to 'back stayres or private doores' in 1627, but these had long been present in domestic architecture. Maurice Howard has identified staircases in early Tudor country houses which 'were an essential part of the complicated arrangements for privacy and security, controlling access to different parts of the building', and corridors which 'gave shared access while at the same time preserving privacy'.[23] Recently, T.A. Heslop has demonstrated the sophistication of the planning arrangements at the twelfth-century Orford Castle, where we find 'a private chamber with its own entrance corridor . . . surmounted by a mezzanine chamber . . . with its own access staircase . . .'[24]

Each age must define and satisfy its own requirements in seeking an appropriate architecture. It would appear likely that the comparable needs and expectations of different periods prompt analogous solutions, but these may be only deceptive likenesses. Some of them will be exemplars for future generations, but others, because of divers, perhaps forgotten, contributory factors – formal, social and economic – will prove to be false trails. The architect may be conscious of what has gone before, yet fail to profit. He may lack the luxury of an historical perspective which would enable him to distinguish the directly relevant from the misleading simulacrum. In learning from past endeavours it is necessary to investigate the impulses which lay behind them as well as the

21 R. North, 'Of Building', British Library Add. MS 32540, fo. 46.
22 Colvin and Newman (ed.), *Of Building*, p. 137.
23 M. Howard, *The Early Tudor Country House* (London, 1987), pp. 85, 88.
24 T.A. Heslop, 'Orford Castle: Nostalgia and Sophisticated Living', *Architectural History*, xxxiv (1991), p. 42.

forms which they took, since one conditions the other.[25] The perception of the
need for privacy, and the architectural options for its satisfaction, appears to be
mutable yet recurrent, but we have insufficient evidence to gauge the extent to
which the requirements of earlier generations matched those which were
stated so strongly by the writers of the seventeenth century. It may be that the
satisfaction of the need for privacy in the plan of the house was subject to
continual reinvention over a long period of time, the architectural strategies
varying according to local expectations, means and inherited traditions. Certainly, the pursuit has not been confined by time, place or national boundaries.
Orest Ranum, writing on 'The Scene of Intimacy' in the collaborative *A History
of Private Life*, devoted mainly to France, observes: 'In the early modern era
architects provided new private spaces in the houses of the well-to-do, or,
rather, they increased the amount of private space by transforming into rooms
what had previously been mere objects of furniture.' While 'the inclusion of
distinctive rooms within the home is . . . not conclusive proof of privatisation,
. . . a man who once kept a locked writing desk could now closet himself in his
writing room and lock the door.'[26]

Such private spaces, disposed with impeccable logic, were provided by Sir
Roger Pratt in his design for the supreme, yet atypical, example of the double
pile form, Coleshill, built *c*. 1657 - *c*. 1662 for his cousin Sir George; a house
which manifested many of the principles expressed in his 'Certain Short Notes
Concerning Architecture'.[27] The bedchambers, 'must each of them have a
closet, and a servant's lodging with chimney both which will easily be made by
dividing the breadth of one end of the room into two such parts as shall be
convenient and to the servant's room a pair of backstairs ought to be adjoining
. . .'[28] The backstairs at Coleshill were situated at the ends of the central, spinal
corridor, adjacent to the services, an arrangement both symmetrical and
hierarchical, allowing for a build-up towards the centre in grandeur and
importance. Coleshill represents Pratt's most remorseless and uncompromis-
ing use of the corridor. The use of private rooms as through rooms (which
continued to be a problem in houses into the eighteenth century – Isaac Ware
deplored it) is here radically reduced; progress through the house is rapid and
effective; communication is at once facilitated and, paradoxically, impeded:
the chance encounter in the through room is no longer encouraged.

25 The problem of not having the complete
    story is discussed by Primo Levi who recalls
    adding chloride to a particular supply of
    paint as an anti-livering strategy. He predicts
    that as supplies of the raw materials improve
    in quality, so the additive will no longer be
    needed, but nobody will remember why it was
    introduced in the first place, so its use will
    continue, possibly harmfully, since formulas
    are as Holy Writ; *The Periodic Table* (London,

    1985), pp. 147-59.
26 R. Chartier (ed.), *A History of Private Life*, iii,
    Passions of the Renaissance (Cambridge, MA,
    1989), pp. 210-11.
27 For Pratt, see N. Silcox-Crowe, 'Sir Roger
    Pratt', in R. Brown (ed.), *The Architectural Out-
    siders* (London, 1985), pp. 1-20.
28 Gunther, *The Architecture of Sir Roger Pratt*, p.
    27.

Coleshill, symmetrical within and without, represented a perfect marriage of form and function. The less perfect Horseheath was designed by Pratt for Lord Alington in 1663. A combination of transverse, tripartite division, in the manner of the Palladian villa, and the triple pile, to accommodate the very large staircase compartments, the plan lacks the rigour of Coleshill, but nevertheless a separation of spaces is achieved between the double height entrance hall and the apartments set at the corners of the house. There are no corridors – the rooms are *en enfilade* – and circulation is hampered further by the provision of a chapel in the north-west corner.

In the early eighteenth century, Horseheath was attributed to John Webb; a highly implausible attribution since Webb's houses in both style and plan were indebted more closely to Palladian precedent than those of Pratt; a precedent which was not followed slavishly, but one upon which Webb drew in order to arrive at his own formulation.[29] In his design for a house for Colonel Ludlow at Maiden Bradley, he built on his earlier 'Lodge in a Parke' for Hale in Hampshire to produce a scheme clearly based on Palladio's Villa Saraceno. The choice of direction offered by the nexus of interconnecting rooms, a feature typical of Palladio's villas, provided here a freedom of circulation unusual, and probably unsought, in the English house at this time. Webb did not achieve in this plan an appropriate separation of public and private spaces. At Gunnersbury, the suburban villa built for Serjeant John Maynard, in the later 1650s, he drew on the work of Palladio and Inigo Jones to achieve just such a separation, producing a central sequence of public spaces, linked by the grand, processional staircase, with informal suites at the angles of the building. In taking elements from an inherited vocabulary and balancing them against functional requirements, Webb here produced a design of great typological significance, new to England. He refined this mode of planning at Amesbury. Again he looked back to Palladio and Jones, but produced a far more cohesive solution than before by retaining the interconnecting groups of rooms but providing linking corridors through the centre of the house. This was made possible by the alignment of the ground floor hall and first floor saloon across the front rather than being placed transversely as they were at Gunnersbury: the virtues of the villa type and the double pile were thus combined. Public and private areas were separated but interconnection was allowed. Spaces could be acted within and around; participation was optional. As C.R. Cockerell observed: 'for economy of convenience with proportion and effect, it may challenge any House in England ancient or modern'.[30]

The fluidity of planning at Amesbury illustrates the extent to which choices could be embodied in designs made to satisfy the demands of a comfortable,

29 For Webb, see J. Bold, *John Webb* (Oxford, 1989).

30 J. Harris, 'C.R. Cockerell's "Ichnographica Domestica",' *Architectural History*, xiv (1971), p. 7.

convenient and decorous existence. It requires a leap of the imagination to proceed from generalisation to visualisation, but to recreate that feeling of optional participation in domestic discourse, we cannot do better than position ourselves, unacknowledged, outside the door or window within certain Dutch paintings of the period and note the intimate transactions and activities taking place in the private realm. De Hoogh's *Interior Scene*, Metsu's *Man and Woman beside a Virginal*, Ochtervelt's *The Music Party* and Vermeer's *Officer and Laughing Girl* all provide tantalising glimpses of informal, fugitive moments in domestic settings.[31] To borrow from Svetlana Alpers, these are pictures of a world described, rather than a world ordered: 'It is here in the comfortable, enclosed, private setting of one's own home that experience is received and literally taken in'.[32] We are given to believe that we might choose to remain in the public realm and pass by, or to enter the private settings and participate in them ourselves. A comparable separation of spaces also occurs in two important Dutch houses of the 1630s, Van Campen's Huygens House and Mauritshuis, both in The Hague.[33]

The delicate and elegant balance achieved in seventeenth-century England between public and private was, as so often, the result of compromise. Neither the double pile nor the villa plan was perfect; both were constrained, in fashionable houses, by the desire for regularity behind a symmetrical elevation. For as long as architects and patrons continued to esteem these constraining factors – through most of the eighteenth century, until the emergence of Nash and Soane – no fundamental developments along the paths suggested by Roger North were possible. It was not by chance that his irregularly planned Rougham offered better answers to the problem of satisfying convenience and decorum than would have been provided by a newly-built house.

By the mid nineteenth century, the separation of domestic functions had become a firmly entrenched principle in house planning, but crucially, it was no longer considered necessary to compromise this aim by the imposition of symmetry.[34] Without this particular constraint, architects were not confined merely to prescribing and proscribing communicating routes through the house;[35] they were able to reflect social expectations and divisions much more

31 The De Hoogh, Metsu and Ochtervelt are in the National Gallery, London, nos. 834, 839 and 3864; the Vermeer is in the Frick Collection, New York.

32 S. Alpers, *The Art of Describing* (Chicago, 1983), p. 11.

33 W. Kuyper, *Dutch Classicist Architecture* (Delft, 1980), figs. 141-44, 148-52.

34 Cf. J. Franklin, *The Gentleman's Country House and its Plan, 1835-1914* (London, 1981), p. 39: 'the essence of Victorian planning was segregation and specialisation . . . Each group was allotted a separate territory . . . each territory except the nurseries subdivided into a male and female side; each room was designed to fit a single, precise function.'

35 Cf. Jane Austen's Catherine Morland, who is discovered by Henry Tilney in a passage which 'is at least as extraordinary a road from the breakfast-parlour to your apartment, as that staircase can be from the stables to mine'. This encounter in a remodelled courtyard house was described in 1798, but not published until 1818: *Northanger Abbey* (London, 1906), p. 157.

freely than before. These divisions had themselves become firmer. When the German cultural attaché, Hermann Muthesius, turned his forensic eye on English life and *mores* at the end of the century, he found it 'still a major concern in the English house that the paths of the servants and of the family and visitors shall never cross . . .'; still more remarkable, from his continental perspective, was the English room: 'a sort of cage, in which the inmate is entirely cut off from the next room'.[36] Philip Webb's eminently Victorian Red House, which Muthesius particularly admired, demonstrates very clearly this use of architecture to eliminate chance, enforce separation and foster solitude. The rooms do not communicate but are entered directly from corridors. The seventeenth century's desire to reduce through rooms, creating instead a separation between connecting groups of rooms and the routes between them, here reaches a rather barren climax. With the consolatory benefit of hindsight we may see such a conclusion, however regretable, as inexorably logical.

36 H. Muthesius, *The English House*, ed. D. Sharp (London, 1979), pp. 94, 79. In this account of the links in theme between Roger North and Hermann Muthesius I have borrowed from my review of both books in the *Oxford Art Journal*, v, 2 (1983), pp. 60-62.

9

Sanmicheli through British Eyes

PAUL DAVIES and DAVID HEMSOLL

Italian Renaissance architecture was a constant source of inspiration to British architects from the sixteenth century onwards, but the precise role that the works of individual Renaissance architects played in this is often more difficult to assess. Such is the case with the buildings of the talented and versatile Michele Sanmicheli (*c.* 1484-1559), who worked mostly in Verona and Venice. Indirectly Sanmicheli's buildings were to exert a considerable influence upon subsequent architecture since they undoubtedly constituted one of the foremost influences on Palladio. Many of the key ideas derived by later generations from the works of Palladio have precedents themselves in the works of Sanmicheli. This applies to entire compositional formats such as the two-storey palace façade with orders applied to both floors rather than just to the *piano nobile*, as well as to a whole repertory of motifs such as pilasters with tapering and curving sides, portals with cornices supported on elongated consoles, and arched openings recessed within larger arches. Directly, however, Sanmicheli's buildings had comparatively little impact on subsequent architecture outside the Veneto. The reasons are plain enough. Sanmicheli, unlike Palladio, wrote no treatise to circulate his designs; nor did he leave posterity with a corpus of his drawings; none of his works was illustrated in contemporary books or prints.[1] Yet later connoisseurs and architects, especially British ones, were occasionally impressed and inspired by what they saw of Sanmicheli's buildings. Indeed, the British seem to have played a considerable part in restoring his reputation. As tastes changed, especially in the eighteenth and nineteenth centuries, Sanmicheli's works began to be reassessed and appreciated in different ways and their robust and inventive style came to be seen as a quite distinct alternative to the more orthodox classicism of Palladio.

A very early example of Sanmicheli's impact in Britain is evident in the embellishments made by John Caius after 1565 to Gonville and Caius College

---

* We would like to thank Tim Knox, Margaret Richardson, Clare Robertson, Alexandra Wedgwood and Alan Windsor for their generous help and suggestions.

1 The main works are listed, however, in Vasari's *Vita* (1568), and this forms the basic catalogue used by writers from the time of B. dal Pozzo onwards; see B. dal Pozzo, *Le vite de'pittori, degli scultori, et architetti veronesi* (Verona, 1718).

in Cambridge.[2] John Caius had spent five years in Italy (1539-44), where he attended the University of Padua, so he doubtless would have been personally familiar with both the antiquities and the modern buildings of the Veneto.[3] His additions to his Cambridge college, especially the three impressive gateways, are indebted to a range of different sources, but in one of them, the Gateway of Virtue, the influence of Sanmicheli is clear. The learnedly classical stone ornamentation of the archway, with fluted Ionic pilasters, victories in the spandrels and an inscription in the frieze, seems to be derived from the entrance portal to the Palazzo del Podestà in Verona designed by Sanmicheli in 1533. Particularly close to Sanmicheli is the way in which the pilasters curve and taper in profile; Sanmicheli must be the source as it was he who promoted this kind of pilaster as an alternative to the more conventional pilaster with straight sides.[4]

From the end of the sixteenth century, after Sanmicheli had been eclipsed by Palladio, few connoisseurs or architects bothered to visit Verona and seek out his buildings. If travellers went there at all, it was first and foremost to admire the well-preserved amphitheatre and the other Roman antiquities.[5] Only exceptionally was an interest in the modern city expressed. The inexhaustible Thomas Coryate, who was there in 1608, viewed Sanmicheli's city defences with approval ('wonderfull strong fortifications, rampiers, and bulwarkes . . . incompassed with deepe and broad Trenches') and he seems to have been impressed by the Veronese palaces ('Gentlemens houses built with passing faire stone, and richly adorned with many goodly marble pillars'), yet he does not once mention Sanmicheli by name or draw particular attention to any of his buildings.[6] Visitors to Venice at this time would normally have looked principally at the works of Palladio and Scamozzi who were already familiar to them through their treatises. Sanmicheli's buildings, by contrast, were rarely deemed worthy of any attention. The exception was Palazzo Grimani which was vociferously criticised by Sir Henry Wotton for what he considered to be the excessive size of its upper cornice ('this magnificent errour'),[7] and liked by Sir

2 For the history of these works, see R. Willis and J.W. Clark, *The Architectural History of the University of Cambridge* (Cambridge, 1886), i, pp. 165-85.

3 For Caius, see e.g. L. Stephen and S. Lee (ed.), *The Dictionary of National Biography* (London 1908-9), viii, pp. 221-25.

4 On these pilasters, see P. Davies and D. Hemsoll, 'Entasis and Diminution in the Design of Renaissance Pilasters', in J. Guillaume (ed.), *L'emploi des ordres* (Paris, 1992), pp. 339-53. Similar pilasters also appear in other English buildings of the period, for example, the

porch of Charlecote Park (Warks) (1558), which likewise seems to be indebted to Italian architecture of the Veneto.

5 See N. Barker et al. (ed.), *In Fair Verona: English Travellers in Italy* (Cambridge, 1972).

6 T. Coryate, *Coryats Crudities Hastily Gobbled Up . . .* (London, 1611), pp. 311, 323. Palladio's Palazzo della Torre and the late sixteenth-century Palazzo Diamanti, on the other hand, are described in some detail (pp. 322-24).

7 Sir Henry Wotton, *The Elements of Architecture* (London, 1624), p. 42.

Roger Pratt, who singled it out as the finest palace in the city.[8] Despite the feelings of dislike or admiration that this building aroused, neither author mentions Sanmicheli by name.

A more sustained interest in Sanmicheli was awakened in the eighteenth century following the publication of two pioneering books by local Veronese writers: Scipione Maffei's *Verona illustrata* (Verona, 1732), which for the first time illustrates many of Sanmicheli's buildings (and which also discusses Wotton's earlier criticism);[9] and Alessandro Pompei's *Li cinque ordini . . . di Michel Sanmicheli* (Verona, 1735), which compares the proportions of the orders purportedly used by Sanmicheli with those set down in sixteenth-century treatises.[10] Drawings of Sanmicheli's buildings began to be made and circulated in Britain at around the same time or just a little later. Some drawings of the Veronese buildings were produced, *c.* 1730-40, in the studio of Antonio Visentini at the initiative of Joseph Smith (1682-1770), the future British consul in Venice, and these, like the many Visentini drawings of Renaissance buildings in Venice itself, are scaled in English feet and were apparently made for sale to a prospective British client.[11] Surprisingly, the architect of the buildings is named not as Sanmicheli but as the more fashionable Scamozzi, and the designs themselves, which for the most part are wildly inaccurate, have been brought more into line with the prevailing Palladian tastes of eighteenth-century Britain. In the case of the Porta Palio, for example, the gateway's exceptionally wide proportions have been reduced, the layering of the wall-surface is not indicated, the half-columns are shown as smooth rather than fluted and the openings have all been changed. Just a short time afterwards, however, enterprising British architects began to visit Verona and to see Sanmicheli's buildings for themselves. James 'Athenian' Stuart, who was acquainted with Smith, was there in 1750, and while there he drew Sanmicheli's

8 R.T. Gunther, *The Architecture of Sir Roger Pratt* (Oxford, 1928), p. 300: 'The best at Venice was that of Grimani, not much unlike to our banquetting house, but of lesser dimensions.' It seems that the late seventeenth-century porch to Castle Bromwich Hall, near Birmingham, may have been designed by an architect with a liking for Sanmicheli's Porta Palio in Verona.

9 The illustrations, drawn by Saverio Avesani and engraved by Francesco Zucchi, are of Palazzo Canossa, Palazzo Bevilacqua, Palazzo Pellegrini a S. Benedetto (Maffei's erroneous attribution to Sanmicheli), Palazzo Pompei, Palazzo Guastaverza, Porta Nuova and Porta Palio.

10 For a summary of the critical fortune of Sanmicheli in Italy, see L. Puppi, *Michele Sanmicheli architetto* (Rome, 1986), pp. 189-91. The first account of Sanmicheli's life from this period is by Dal Pozzo (as n. 1).

11 London, RIBA; see J. McAndrew, *Catalogue of the Drawings of the Royal Institute of British Architects: Antonio Visentini* (Farnborough, 1974). The buildings in Verona are cat. Visentini (196) S. Giorgio in Braida (1-4); (201) Palazzo Canossa; (203) Palazzo Pompei; (205) Porta Palio and Porta di S. Zeno (1-3); there is also a drawing (169) of the Palazzo Grimani in Venice. Other drawings of the Palazzo Grimani and also the Palazzo Cornaro a S. Polo are in the album entitled *Admiranda urbis Venetae* in the British Museum; see E. Bassi, *Palazzi di Venezia* (Venice, 1976), pp. 146-53; 324; yet further drawings of the Palazzo Grimani are in the British Library (Add. Ms. 26,107, fos. 24-25). For dating Visentini's drawings to the 1730s, see Bassi, p. 37, and for the relationship between Visentini and Consul Smith see F. Vivian, *The Consul Smith Collection* (Munich, 1989), pp. 108-9.

a San Bernardino a Verona
da Michel di San Michele

Fig. 41 James Stuart, Pellegrini Chapel, Verona. (*BAL, RIBA*)

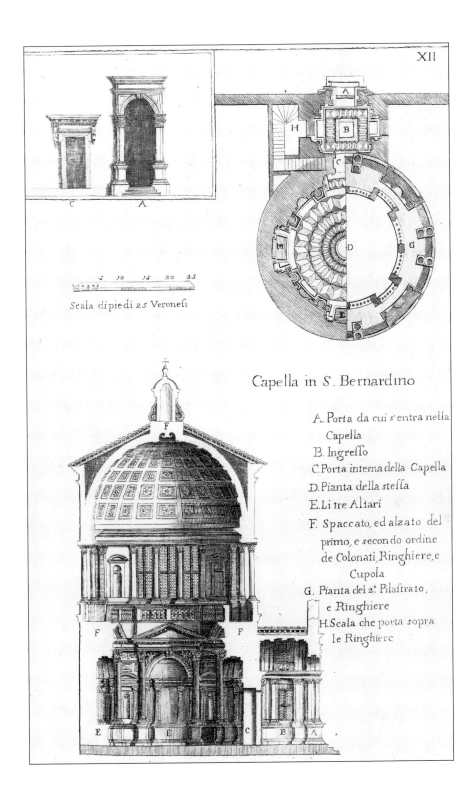

XII

Capella in S. Bernardino

A. Porta da cui s'entra nella
Capella
B. Ingreſſo
C. Porta interna della Capella
D. Pianta della steſſa
E. Li tre Altari
F. Spaccato, ed alzato del
primo, e secondo ordine
de Colonati, Ringhiere, e
Cupola
G. Pianta del 2°. Pilaſtrato,
e Ringhiere
H. Scala che porta sopra
le Ringhiere

Scala di piedi 25 Veroneſi

5   10   15   20   25

Fig. 42 An eighteenth-century engraving of the Pellegrini Chapel, Verona. (*British Museum*)

Fig. 43 Robert Adam, 20 Portman Square, London, stair-well. (*BAL, RIBA*)

Fig. 44 Circle of John Soane, Pellegrini Chapel, Verona. (*Sir John Soane's Museum*)

-THE - PELLEGRINI - CHAPEL -
- IN - VERONA -
-THE - ARCHITECTVRE - OF -
- MICHELE - SAN - MICHELI -

Fig. 45 Circle of John Soane, Pellegrini Chapel, Verona. (*Sir John Soane's Museum*)

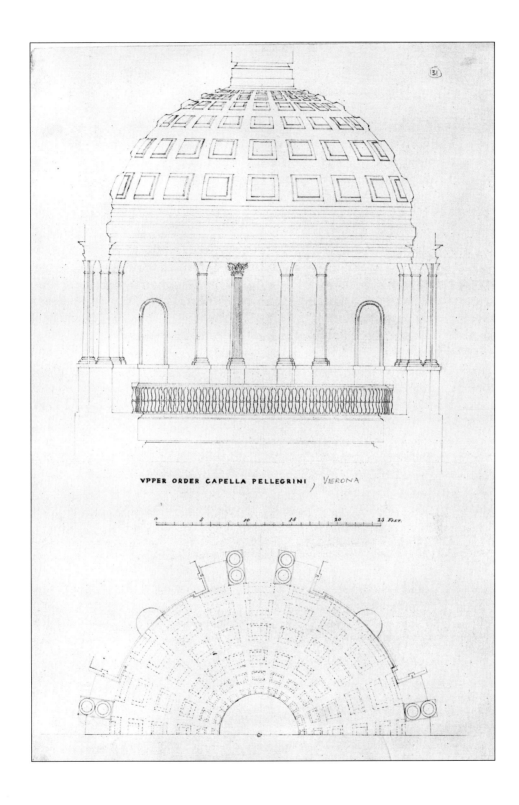

UPPER ORDER CAPELLA PELLEGRINI , VERONA

0   5   10   15   20   25 FEET.

Fig. 46 Charles Barry, Pellegrini Chapel, Verona. (*BAL, RIBA*)

Pellegrini Chapel (a building not illustrated in Maffei).[12] The drawing (Fig. 41) shows the interior elevation of the circular chapel as if unwound, but is far from accurate in detail. Stuart omits all the small-scale pediments, alters the shape of the coffers in the vault and the balusters and ignores the complex syncopation of vertical and spiral fluting of the chapel's lower order.[13] A little later, in 1757, Robert Adam visited Verona and said that he preferred Sanmicheli's buildings to those of Palladio.[14] Robert's liking for Sanmicheli, however, was subsequently only shared in part by his brother James who, while in Verona in 1760, 'saw a round church [i.e. the Madonna di Campagna], a chapel [the Pellegrini Chapel], and several other buildings of Michele San Michele, and really without much admiration'. Sanmicheli, he added, 'seems to have had rather more genius than Palladio in the ornamental part of architecture, and is sometimes bold and male in his decorations but is often very impure and trifling.[15] Although he was strongly urged by Count Girolamo dal Pozzo and Giuseppe Torelli, members of the local intellectual elite, to publish Sanmicheli's buildings, he felt too hard pressed to accept their invitation.

Yet despite these reservations, the buildings of Sanmicheli are clearly more in keeping with mid eighteenth-century British Neoclassicism than those of Palladio, especially in their sculptural and planar qualities as well as in their apparently greater licence.[16] They may well, in fact, have exerted some small influence on the works of Robert Adam and his contemporaries. The impact of Sanmicheli's Pellegrini Chapel (Fig. 42), a building to be explicitly singled out for its merit just a little later in L. Dutens's early and influential guidebook to Europe, will serve as an example.[17] Rotunda designs by Robert Adam come very close in their formal arrangement to that of Sanmicheli's circular chapel.[18] This applies to monumental projects such as his unexecuted hall design for

12 D. Watkin, *Athenian Stuart* (London, 1982), pp. 17-18.
13 London, RIBA, cat. Stuart (2), fo. 26. The drawing is labelled, 'a San Bernardino a Verona da Michele di San Michele'.
14 J. Fleming, *Robert Adam and his Circle* (London, 1962), pp. 241, 273-74.
15 See James Adam's journal (not Robert's as specified), in *The Library of the Fine Arts*, ii, (1831), p. 169. James later says, however, that he 'studied with great attention the work of Palladio and the celebrated modern masters at Verona, Venice and Florence'; see Fleming, ibid., p. 287.
16 Cf. G.A. Selva, *Elogio di Michele Sanmicheli architetto civile e militare* (Rome, 1814), where Sanmicheli's buildings are said to be 'più vario, meno ligio alle regole' in comparison with Palladio's.
17 L. Dutens, *Journal of Travels made through the Principal Cities in Europe* (London, 1782), p. 81: 'At S. Bernardino is the chapel of the family of Pellegrini, by Michiel San Michieli.

This architect was equal to Palladio, yet is nevertheless scarcely known. There are also other works of architecture at Verona by Michiel San Michieli: amongst others, the Porta Stupa [i.e. the Porta Palio], and the Palaces Canossa, Verzi, Bevilacqua, Pompei, and Pellegrini [cf. Maffei, n. 9]'. The first French edition of Dutens's work appeared in Paris in 1777 and records a journey of 1768-71. The Pellegrini Chapel was engraved in the eighteenth century (see London, British Museum, album entitled *Fabbriche diverse ed antichità di Verona*, King's Coll., 79/41 - a, fo. 12). A detailed set of engravings was eventually published by B. Giuliari, *Cappella della famiglia Pellegrini ... di Michele Sanmicheli* (Verona, 1816), who in the preface cites the example of Adam and his contemporaries.
18 J. Summerson, *Architecture in Britain: 1530-1830* (Harmondsworth, 1986), p. 370 compares Robert Taylor's Bank of England rotunda (1765-) with the Pellegrini Chapel although the similarities are not great.

Syon House (1762) and also to small-scale works such as the stair-well at No. 20 Portman Square, London (1775-77). With its two main storeys, the stair-well (Fig. 43) seems almost to be a straight reworking of the Sanmicheli prototype in its elevational composition and also in its surface layering, although Sanmicheli's Renaissance ornamentation, no doubt viewed as 'impure and trifling', has been replaced by a more modern architectural vocabulary.

A much more intense interest in Sanmicheli was fuelled by the Veronese architect Luigi Trezza, who in 1769 began to prepare a comprehensive set of detailed drawings of his works.[19] In the process, Trezza availed himself of the services of at least one Briton, an unidentified English architect who supplied Trezza with drawings of Sanmicheli's church of S. Margherita at Montefiascone to the north of Rome.[20] Trezza, in the preface to one of his drawing albums, also declares that the whole enterprise had been intended for the benefit of a 'raguardevole Personagio Inglese'.[21] The identity of this Englishman is subsequently established by Ferdinando Albertolli, whose published engravings of Sanmicheli's buildings were partly based on Trezza's drawings, and who states that Trezza's project had been commissioned by Count Girolamo dal Pozzo 'to satisfy the longings of the celebrated Signore Smith'.[22] Not long after completing his drawings, Trezza made them available to another Englishman with a great enthusiasm for Sanmicheli, the young architect John Soane. While in Verona in 1779-80, Soane made meticulous copies from several of Trezza's drawings, especially those of the three city gates, combining material in some of them from more than one of Trezza's originals.[23] At the same time, Soane seems to have also procured a series of drawings of Sanmicheli's palaces by the draughtsman Gaetano Avesani.[24] These include one of

19 See P. Carpeggiani, 'Disegni "mantovani" inediti di Luigi Trezza', *Civiltà mantovana*, viii (1974), pp. 136-54.

20 P. de la Ruffinière du Prey, *John Soane: The Making of an Architect* (Chicago and London, 1982), p. 161. The most prominent English architect working in Rome at this time was Thomas Harrison.

21 Ibid. Trezza adds (Verona, Biblioteca Comunale, MS 1010) that the commission was also financed.

22 F. Albertolli, *Porte di città e fortezze, depositi sepolcrali ed altre principali fabbriche pubbliche e private di Michele Sammicheli veronese* (Milan, 1815), preface.

23 P. de la Ruffinière du Prey, *Soane* (1982), pp. 160-64, and *John Soane's Architectural Education* (New York and London, 1977), pp. 305-8. The drawings (London, Sir John Soane Museum, drawer 45, set 2) bear Italian inscriptions in Soane's handwriting and depict as follows: (no. 1) Palazzo Grimani (Venice); (2) Villa Zani (Villimpenta; by a

follower of Giulio Romano); (3) Palazzo di Giustizia (Mantua; by A.M. Viani); (4 and 5) Palazzo Canossa; (6-8) Porta di S. Zeno; (9-11) Porta Nuova; (12-4) Porta Palio; (15) Porta Palio and Palazzo Guastaverza; (24) Cappella Pellegrini; (25) Madonna di Campagna. Soane also acquired one drawing by Trezza himself (drawer 44, set 6, no. 18) of D. Curtoni's Loggia di Gran Guardia in Verona; see also note 27.

24 London, Sir John Soane's Museum, drawer 44, set 10, depicting as follows: (no. 2) Palazzo Canossa; (3) Palazzo Pompei; (4) Palazzo Guastaverza; (5) Palazzo Bevilacqua. There is also a drawing of the Palazzo Pellegrini (no. 1), which, following Maffei's *Verona illustrata*, is attributed to Sanmicheli. Gaetano Avesani was presumably related to Saverio Avesani who drew the Sanmicheli illustrations in Maffei's work, and Gaetano's drawings would appear to be dependent on Saverio's originals. A watermark on one of the sheets has been dated tentatively to 1779.

the Palazzo Bevilacqua which shows the existing seven-bay façade reconstructed to a length of fifteen bays in accordance with an opinion (which seems
correct) that was put forward by Trezza but not actually illustrated by him.[25]
Soane subsequently had a number of drawings of Sanmicheli's buildings made
to illustrate his Royal Academy Lectures (1809-), and in one of these lectures he
publicly expressed his profound admiration for the architect by declaring that
Sanmicheli had a 'boldness of execution and originality of invention as has
seldom been surpassed'.[26]

The lecture drawings reveal some of Soane's own personal interests in
Sanmicheli's architecture.[27] Soane's fondness for domed interiors is reflected
in the spectacular renditions of both the enormous Madonna di Campagna and
the Pellegrini Chapel (drawn twice) which is given a second vestibule and is thus
turned into a circular hall with a cross-axis (Figs. 44 and 45). Although
seemingly less interested in the palaces (none of which were drawn), Soane
appears to have been greatly impressed by the gateways, and drawings were
made of all three. The low and wide Porta Palio, a building which Soane may
well have admired for its 'boldness of execution' (and which is the subject of two
drawings), has a particular affinity, moreover, with some of Soane's own
designs. The banded ashlar stonework, its combination with the delicate
detailing of the portals, and the use of square-sectioned pilasters (*antae*) to
conclude an elevational order, all have close parallels, for example in the low
exterior screen wall (1795-) of Soane's remodelled Bank of England.

Only a little later, a new and more critical perspective on Sanmicheli is
discernible in the observations and opinions recorded by Charles Barry.[28]
Barry, who visited Verona in 1820, gave Sanmicheli's buildings there considerable attention, producing measured drawings and filling his travel journal with
sketches and detailed notes.[29] His reactions were mixed. Of the Palazzo
Bevilacqua he wrote with vitriol: 'This has never been finished and would have
been much better for the reputation of Sanmicheli its architect had it never

25 See P. Davies and D. Hemsoll, 'Palazzo Bevi-
    lacqua e la tipologia del palazzo veronese',
    Annali di architettura, iii (1991), pp. 57-71.
26 Sir J. Soane, *Lectures on Architecture*, ed. A.T.
    Bolton (London, 1929), p. 86; cf. *Memoirs of
    the Professional Life of an Architect between the
    Years 1768 and 1835* (London, 1835), pp. 15-
    6: '. . . and I went on to Verona, Vicenza and
    Mantua, whence, after making drawings of
    the principal works of Michele San Micheli,
    Palladio, and Julio Romano, I returned to
    Rome to finish my studies.'
27 London, Sir John Soane's Museum, drawer
    22, set 7, as follows: (no. 1) Palazzo Grimani
    (Venice); (2-3) Loggia di Gran Guardia (by D.
    Curtoni but here attributed to Sanmicheli);
    (4) Porta di S. Zeno; (5) Porta Nuova; (6-7)

Porta Palio; (8-9) Cappella Pellegrini; (10)
Madonna di Campagna.
28 See M. Binney, 'The Making of an Architect:
    The Travels of Sir Charles Barry', *Country
    Life*, cxlvi (1969), pp. 494-98, 550-52, 622-24
    (for Verona p. 623).
29 Barry's drawings (London, RIBA) are in the
    album entitled *Sir Charles Barry and John Lewis
    Wolfe, i, Renaissance Architecture*, and depict:
    (fo. 131) the Pellegrini Chapel; (fo. 132) the
    campanile of S Giorgio in Braida; (fo. 136-7)
    the portal of the Palazzo del Podestà; (fo. 138)
    Porta Nuova (detail); and also (fo. 92) Palazzo
    Grimani. The relevant diaries of Barry (Lon-
    don, RIBA) are cat. 17 for the works in Ver-
    ona, and also cat. 16 for the works in Venice.

been begun. There are scarcely any beauties in it to set against its hideous deformities.' Generally, however, his opinions were much more favourable and he limited his criticisms to the handling of details, the Doric order of the Porta Palio, for example, not being 'of sufficient magnitude or simple enough to be imposing or to be in character with the walls of a fortified town'. In fact, he viewed some buildings, or at least parts of them, with considerable enthusiasm.[30] On visiting the Pellegrini Chapel for a second time and gaining access to the gallery, his praise of the upper story was indeed fulsome: 'from this situation the upper order with its incumbent dome is the most graceful and elegant thing of the kind I ever witnessed and is highly creditable to the taste of Sanmicheli who has not been ever equalled in a similar work by any of his successors Palladio not excepted.' In a drawing of the building (Fig. 46) Barry deliberately omitted the lower storey, which he considered 'very unpleasing in being broken up into so many angles and parts' and which he thought made the proportions of the building too tall; he also ignored the tabernacles framing the niches and most of the decorative detail. As a result of the chapel being truncated and simplified in this way, the design, with its wide proportions and its expanses of plain and unadorned wall surface, appears in a manner that is much more compatible with the academic classicism of the early nineteenth century.

Enthusiasm for Sanmicheli continued in some circles well into the nineteenth century. Following the publications of Albertolli (1815), and especially of Ronzani and Luciolli (1823), architects had ready access to Sanmicheli's designs and some may have been influenced by them.[31] The upper-floor balcony of Decimus Burton's Athenaeum (1827-30), for example, which is supported on brackets interpreted as substitutes for the triglyphs of a Doric frieze, would appear to be derived from the Palazzo Bevilacqua. Other architects produced drawings of Sanmicheli's buildings when they were in Italy. David Mocatta, a pupil of Soane, presumably based the series of exquisitely executed but often highly fanciful renditions (1839-40) of Sanmicheli's palaces and gates on sketches he must have made during his visit to Verona in 1830.[32] Frederick P. Cockerell also produced drawings of the palaces and gates during his travels in Italy in 1855.[33] After the middle of the nineteenth century interest in Sanmicheli declined but it did not dim entirely. Even though the champion of medievalism, John Ruskin, makes no mention whatever of Sanmicheli in his

30 The only building to win unqualified praise is the Palazzo Pompei: 'The best proportioned and most sensible front in Verona.'

31 F. Albertolli, as note 22; F. Ronzani and G. Luciolli, *Le fabbriche civili, ecclesiastiche e militari di Michele Sanmicheli* (Verona, 1823).

32 Mocatta's drawings (London, RIBA) are as follows: cat. Mocatta [102] Palazzo Canossa (1 and 2); [103] Palazzo Guastaverza; [104] Palazzo Pompei; [105] Porta Palio; [106] Porta Nuova; also [98] Palazzo Grimani in Venice (1 and 2).

33 Cockerell's drawings (London, RIBA, F.P. Cockerell, folders 3 and 4) are of Palazzo Bevilacqua, Palazzo Canossa, Palazzo Guastaverza, Porta Nuova, Porta Palio, Porta di S. Zeno, and also S. Giorgio in Braida (which he attributes to Sansovino).

eulogising *Verona, and its Rivers* (1870), elsewhere he had expressed a surprisingly wholehearted liking for the Palazzo Grimani ('simple, delicate and sublime').[34] The Palazzo Grimani also seems to have been one of the Renaissance models exploited by Gilbert Scott after he had been required to redesign the Foreign Office (1868-) in a classical style, especially the arched loggia framed by two blind pilaster-faced bays.[35]

After this, Sanmicheli was to return to fashion for one final spell during the interlude known as the 'Edwardian Baroque'. As architects turned to historical models for the rugged and heavily ornamented classical style that is characteristic of this period, they were again drawn to Sanmicheli, and some, among them the young Reginald Blomfield, inspected and studied his buildings at first hand.[36] Sanmicheli, in fact, seems to have been a particular favourite of the period's most successful architect, Edwin Lutyens, whose indebtedness is most evident at Heathcote, his house in Yorkshire (1906).[37] The lower storey is heavily dependent on the Porta Palio, not just in the adaptation of Sanmicheli's Doric order, as Lutyens himself later describes in a letter to fellow architect Herbert Baker, but also in the layering of the wall surface, the banded ashlar and the voussoir-faceted lintels over the main openings. It was with some justification, therefore, that Lutyens acknowledged this debt to his Veronese predecessor by affectionately referring to the Heathcote design as his 'Sanmichele'.

34 J. Ruskin, *The Stones of Venice* (1851), in *The Works of John Ruskin*, ed. E.T. Cook and E. Wedderburn (London, 1903-12), xi, pp. 43-45.

35 The architect in his memoirs mentions that he had previously 'bought some costly books on Italian architecture; see Sir G.G. Scott, *Personal and Professional Recollections* (London, 1879), p. 199.

36 London, RIBA: R. Blomfield's notebook (cat.

no. 20) with sketches and remarks of the Pellegrini Chapel and other buildings in Verona; also his sketchbook (ex cat.; numbered 20a) for a drawing of Palazzo Canossa; drawings also of the Pellegrini Chapel by P.E. Webb, the son of Aston Webb (cat. P.E. Webb, [12], 1-3), and by E.B. Musman (ex cat.).

37 C. Hussey, *The Life of Sir Edwin Lutyens* (London, 1950), pp. 128-33.

10

'Behold the Proud Stupendous Pile': Eighteenth Century Reflections of St Paul's Cathedral[1]

TERRY FRIEDMAN

St Paul's fame was established irrefutably by 1699, even though its most memorable features – the west front, twin towers and crossing dome – were still on the drawing-board when Walter Harris, the Royal Physician-in-Ordinary, proclaimed it in print as 'one of the most Spacious and *Magnificent Cathedrals* that ever yet was built in the World; and . . . which, in the judgment of Travellers, is like to emulate in its Structure, even *Saint Peter's* at *Rome*, and *Sancta Sophia* at *Constantinople*'.[2] The persistence of such laudatory literature, coupled with the building's universal inclusion in London guidebooks, the publication of innumerable engraved views (Fig. 47)[3] and rumours of an unimaginable cost (a reported £736,752 2s. 3d. at the time of completion in 1710),[4] all helped to fuel not only a constant stream of sightseers but also a climate in which architects were actively encouraged to offer their own Pauline homages.[5]

This essay concentrates on two such schemes dating from the 1760s, coinciding with the pioneering phase of British neoclassical architecture, when it might have been expected that the Baroque ideas epitomised in Wren's masterpiece would have long since been dismissed as legitimate models for imitation. However, Georgian church design was generally unadventurous compared to its counterpart on the Continent, and Wren's churches in particular survived as standard patterns well into the eighteenth century.[6] The cathedral, too, remained a potent image and in the face of stylistic innovation in

1 Anonymous, *St Paul's Cathedral* (London, 1750), p. 13.
2 *A Description of The King's Palace and Garden at Loo* (London, 1699), p. 2.
3 *Wren Society*, xiv (Oxford, 1937).
4 R. and J. Dodsley, *London and its Environs Described* (London, 1761), v, p. 160.
5 'How will the much-admiring artist then/ Applaud the builder? Yielding all the fame/ Of former masters to the greater Wren,/ That raised, and finish'd this majestic frame', J. Wright, *Phoenix Paulina* (London, 1709),

quoted in J. Lang, *Rebuilding St Paul's after the Great Fire of London* (London, 1956), p. 243.
6 In 1712 Wren recommended his modest, brick 'Auditory' box of St James's, Piccadilly (1676-84) as the most 'beautiful . . . convenient and cheapest of any Form I could invent', *The Letter of Sir Chr. Wren upon the Building of National Churches*, *Wren Society*, ix (Oxford, 1932), pp. 15-18. See T. Friedman, '"High and Bold Structures": A Georgian Steeple Sampler', *The Georgian Group Journal* (1991), pp. 10-15.

other building types continued to be regarded as 'one of the most magnificent modern buildings in Europe'.[7] The 1750s particularly saw an acceleration of interest, prompted by Christopher Wren Jr's detailed discussion of its design and construction history, published by his son, Stephen Wren in *Parentalia* in 1750.[8] This was soon followed by an anonymous sixty-four page poem entitled *St Paul's Cathedral* (price 1s. 6d.); then in 1753 by *An Historical Account of St Paul's Cathedral*,[9] Francis Price's technical analysis of the dome in *The British Carpenter*[10] and William Hogarth's accolade that it 'will scarcely admit of a dispute that the outside [of the cathedral] is much more perfect' than its Roman rival;[11] in 1755 by a brief but poignant reference in Andre Rouquet's *The Present State of the Arts in England*,[12] and in 1758 by a longer commentary in the anonymous *English Architecture: or, The Publick Buildings of London and Westminster*.[13] Meanwhile, in 1755 John Gwynn and Samuel Wale proposed a swagger redecoration of the interior, which they claimed was 'agreeably to the original INTENTION of Sr. Christopher Wren', and between 1754 and 1766 Thomas Gilbert, whose grandfather had supplied building stone for the cathedral, realised a modified centrally-planned, domed church with a St Paul's-like west tower at St George Reforne, Portland (Dorset).[14] In 1761 R. and J. Dodsley published a forty-six page history and description of the cathedral in the fifth volume of *London and Its Environs Described*.[15] The time was ripe for architectural re-assessment.

In February 1761 a Greenwich architect named Thomas Wiggens Jr won a 20 guineas premium from the Society of Artists in London for an engaging scheme to improve the west (entrance) front of St Stephen Walbrook (Fig.

7 J. Ralph, *A Critical Review of the Publick Buildings, Statues and Ornaments in, and about London and Westminster* (London, 1734), p. 17. J. Paterson called it 'the most ample and celebrated Piece of Architecture in the whole World', *Pietas Londinensis: Or, The Present Ecclesiastical State of London* (London, 1714), p. 217; the anonymous *A New Guide to London: or, Directions to Strangers; Shewing the Chief Things of Curiosity and Note in the City and Suburbs* (London, 1726), p. 33: 'the first in all the Universe . . . for Amplitude, Splendour, Solidity, Figure, and curious Architecture'.

8 *Parentalia: Or, Memoirs of the Family of the Wrens* (London, 1750), pp. 280-95 (the 'Heirloom' copy, reprinted 1965).

9 Reissued in the anonymous *An Historical Account of the Curiosities of London and Westminster* (London, 1759), pt. iii, pp. 1-38.

10 F. Price, *The British Carpenter* (London, 1753),

p. 30, pl. OP.

11 *The Analysis of Beauty; written with a view of fixing the fluctuating ideas of Taste* (London, 1753).

12 St Paul's is 'one of the largest structures in Europe [and] a compliment of the finest parts of ancient architecture', A. Rouquet, *The Present State of the Arts in England* (London, 1755, reprinted 1970), p. 95.

13 Included in the 'Heirloom' copy of *Parentalia* (see note 8).

14 *Wren Society* (Oxford, 1937), xiv, pl. xlv; E. Harris, *British Architectural Books and Writers, 1556-1785* (Cambridge, 1990), pp. 214-15, and H.M. Colvin, *A Biographical Dictionary of British Architects, 1600-1840* (London, 1978), pp. 69, 340, 346; M. Chatfield, *Churches the Victorians Forgot* (Ashbourne, 1979), pp. 29-31, respectively.

15 R. and J. Dodsley, *London and its Environs Described* (London, 1761), v, pp. 114-60.

Extends 248.

a Scale of 100 Feet

The West Prospect of S.T PAUL'S CHURCH *begun Anno 1675 and finish'd 1710 by*

S.T Christopher Wren K.T

Is most humbly Inscribed to the R.t Rev.d: Father in God IOHN *Lord* BISHOP *of* LONDON. *Dean of all Her* MAJESTYS *Chapels and one of Her* MAJESTYS *most Honorable privy Council.*

Elevation Occidental Del EGLISE *de* S.T PAUL *a* LONDRE. *Commencee 1672 et acherée 1710 par* Christophre Wren *Chevallier.*

Fig. 47 Sir Christopher Wren, St Paul's Cathedral, west front, 1675-1710, from Colen Campbell, *Vitruvius Britannicus* (1715), i, pl. 4.

Fig. 48 Thomas Wiggens Jr, St Stephen's Walbrook, design for west front, 1761, pen, ink and wash. (*Sir John Soane's Museum*)

Fig. 49 Colen Campbell, '*A new Design for a Church* in Lincoln's-Inn Fields', 1712, *Vitruvius Britannicus* (1715), i, pl. 9.

Fig. 50 Inigo Jones, St Paul's Cathedral, west front, 1633-42, from W. Kent, *The Designs of Inigo Jones* (1727), ii, pl. 55.

Fig. 51 Sir Christopher Wren, Great Model of St Paul's Cathedral, 1673-74, engraved by Jakob Schynvoet, probably in 1726.

Fig. 52 Timothy Lightoler, St Paul's, Liverpool. 1767-69, photograph prior to demolition in 1932-33. (*Liverpool City Libraries Archives, 804D*)

48).[16] Wren's church (1672-79) internally is a design of extraordinary originality (paralleling his early attempts to find a centrally-planned, domed solution
for the cathedral) and was applauded as his parish church masterpiece (the
Dodsleys in 1761 believed that 'Italy itself can produce no modern structure
equal to this in taste, proportion, elegance and beauty').[17] Its exterior, however,
is disappointingly bland and an obvious candidate for improvement. With
bare, rough walls and little decorative embellishment below the levels of
lantern and steeple, the main approach up to the glorious interior is by way of
a single flight of steps housed in an unprepossessing block stuck-on to one side
of the west tower projecting into the narrow Walbrook Lane. The church was
originally confined by buildings to the south and east and could only have been
seen to any advantage from the north, through a jumble of stalls forming the
Stocks Market. During 1679-82 Wren had proposed attaching an imposing,
pedimented portico with flanking colonnades to this side of the church (where
an existing door gave access directly in to the central lateral arm of the nave),
but this scheme was not adopted. Any similar solution to provide a grand
entrance would have become impractical once the decision had been made (in
1738) to build the new Mansion House (the Lord Mayor's palatial residence) on
the market ground, leaving the church separated from it only by a narrow
passage.[18]

These severe physical restrictions meant that Wiggen's proposal, which
entailed the wholesale demolition of the Walbrook Lane elevation (entrance
block, tower and vestry room) and its replacement by a monumental projecting
hexastyle temple portico approached by a broad flight of steps and flanked on
each side by grand towers, was never intended to be realised. It was, rather, a
competitive exercise and thus freed Wiggens to draw on a range of unlikely
sources, most especially St Paul's monumental west front. In doing so he

16 Sir John Soane's Museum, London, drawer
    47, set 9, nos. 1-2, front elevation and section
    through interior with key identifying princi-
    pal features, inscribed 'This Design of an
    Outside of St Stephens Walbrook London was
    presented to ye Society of Polite Arts Feby.
    1761 By Thos: Wiggens, Junior and was
    Adjudged ye best For Which a Premium of
    Twenty Guineas was given'. At least two other
    architects apparently submitted schemes for
    the premium: in 1761 'A design for the im-
    provement of St Stephen's Walbrook' by
    Jacob Le Roux; in 1762 'A design for the west
    front of St. Stephen's, Walbrook' by E. Belk,
    both untraced, A. Graves, *The Society of Artists
    of Great Britain 1760-1791 The Free Society of
    Artists 1761-1783* (London, 1907), p. 147, no.
    230 and p. 29, no. 164, respectively; H.M.
    Colvin, *A Biographical Dictionary of British
    Architects, 1600-1840* (London, 1978), pp.

    104, 514-15, 888.
17 *London and its Environs Described* (London,
    1761), vi, p. 66 (with an engraved plan, sec-
    tion and elevation), reiterating J. Ralph, *A
    Critical Review of the Publick Buildings, Statues
    and Ornaments in, and about London and West-
    minster* (London, 1734), pp. 12-13. The
    American architect, James Bridges, claiming
    that the church was 'esteem'd by all Architects
    that have seen it, as a matchless pile of Art',
    proposed adapting the interior for St Nicho-
    las, Bristol, *Four Designs for Rebuilding Bristol
    Bridge* (Bristol, 1760), p. 46, though the
    church as built (1758-61) was a wholly differ-
    ent, Gothic design.
18 V. Furst, *The Architecture of Sir Christopher
    Wren* (London, 1956), pls. 29-30; S. Perks, *The
    History of the Mansion House* (Cambridge,
    1922), pp. 109-24, pls. vi, xiv, plan 15.

appears to have responded to both the critical attacks and the proposed improvement schemes relating to the cathedral which were being aired among the London architectural fraternity. The most vocal of these appeared as part of a wider, acrimonious dialogue between the American critic, James Ralph, author of *A Critical Review of the Publick Buildings, Statues and Ornaments In, and about London and Westminster* (1734), and the architectural writer from Twickenham, Batty Langley, whose counterblasts appeared immediately after in a series of articles in the popular London newspaper *The Grub-street Journal*. Though Ralph, like the majority of commentators, applauded St Paul's west front (it afforded 'a very august and surprizing prospect'), he condemned as a defect 'abounding in absurdities' the division of the whole building (and the portico, by inference) into two stories of classical Orders without there being a corresponding internal arrangement.[19] It was claimed by Christopher Wren Jr that his father had been forced to abandon his preferred concept of a giant Order temple portico (as exemplified in the Great Model, 1673-4, and the Warrant Design, 1675) because of the unavailability of large enough blocks of Portland stone; but in conveying this technical insight the son was quick to award a Georgian classical respectability to the more complex Baroque solution of the executed front by citing Antique and Renaissance precedents for the use of double columns.[20] Langley (writing under the pseudonym of Hiram, the architect of Solomon's Temple at Jerusalem), argued that the 'most effectual way [to make the cathedral] truly magnificent' would be radically to refashion the anomalous exterior into a unified classical peripteral temple, 500 feet long from east to west, wrapped by ranges of giant columns, 71 along each of the north and south elevations and supporting straight entablatures, with pedimented and statued decastyle porticoes on the east and west. Wren's heroic crossing dome was to be kept but not his flamboyant west towers. Langley believed that the effect of such a colossal Antique temple atop Ludgate Hill would fill the eye with a 'solemn awe and surprizing grandeur . . . not to be paralleled by any building now subsisting in the world'.[21] These recommendations are of particular interest because Langley also found the exterior of the

---

19 J. Ralph, *A Critical Review of the Publick Buildings*, 1734, p. 18. The interior is articulated by a single Order of columns and pilasters reaching to the clerestory.

20 S. Wren, *Parentalia* (London, 1750), pp. 288-89: 'why were the Columns of the West Portico doubled? This . . . was followed in their [the Ancients'] greater Works; for Instance, in the Portico of the *Temple of Peace* . . . the Columns were very properly and necessarily doubled to make wider Openings . . . *Bramante* used double Columns without Scruple, as did *Michel Angelo* within and without the

Cupola of St *Peter's* . . . the like is done in the Portico of the Church of *Santa Maria Major* in *Rome* . . . The *French* Architects have practised the same to a good Effect, especially in the beautiful Facade of the *Louvre*'. For the earlier, rejected schemes for St Paul's see K. Downes, *The Architecture of Wren* (London, 1982), pls. 46, 56.

21 *The Grub-street Journal*, no. 243 (22 August 1734) p. 1. See Langley's closely related proposal for encasing Thomas Archer's Baroque church of St Philip's, Birmingham, in *Ancient Architecture* (London, 1736), pl. xii.

Walbrook church 'wanting [in] a very material [beauty]' and, following Wren, suggested the addition of 'a grand portico' on the north elevation.[22]

The extent to which Wiggens digested this material at St Stephen's is, of course, a matter of speculation. He clearly favoured at least a partial classicising of Wren's architectural vocabulary and an emphasis on the west front along Langleyan lines. Wiggens chose a prostyle temple portico of a type Wren had introduced in the Great Model for St Paul's (Fig. 51),[23] reducing and simplifying it to an unfluted Corinthian hexastyle, a form more befitting a small parish church and more straightforwardly Antique to Georgian sensibilities. It is pertinent that the unfluted Corinthian hexastyle portico of James Gibbs's St Martin-in-the-Fields (1721-26), to which Wiggens's structure may also owe a debt, was singled out among London churches in 1755 as having been 'borrowed from a Greek temple without any alteration' and that 'By this choice, the architect has shewn the elegance of his taste, and the solidity of his judgment'.[24] The rich treatment of pilasters, panels, niches and openings of the wall behind the Wren and Gibbs porticoes, however, was replaced in Wiggens's design by a sedate, windowless, continuously rusticated surface which is an almost exact copy of the west wall of the medieval cathedral refaced by Inigo Jones between 1633 and 1642. Though damaged beyond repair in the Great Fire of 1666 and subsequently demolished to make way for Wren's new fabric, this celebrated lost work was not forgotten. Dugdale's engravings of the pre-Fire building were, for Vertue, evidence of how much Jones had 'beautified that Noble Pile';[25] an accurate representation of the west front (drawn by Henry Flitcroft after the original manuscript design then in Lord Burlington's possession) was provided in William Kent's *The Designs of Inigo Jones* (1727) (Fig. 50),[26] and well into the century this spectacular recreation of Imperial Roman architecture remained fresh in the public's imagination as an example which 'stirred up a laudable zeal in others'.[27]

22 The porticoed church combined with the recently built Bank of England (1732-35) and a proposed statue of 'the ever glorious' William III for a site in the Stocks Market would make this 'the real *center of beauty to the city*', *The Grub-street Journal*, no. 241 (8 August 1734), p. 1. This solution was still possible in 1734, when the Mansion House's final appearance had not yet been resolved, though it would shortly become untenable, as we have seen.

23 Following the cathedral's completion in 1710 the Model was displayed in a room over the North Chapel, where it became a popular tourist attraction; it is now housed in the crypt, K. Downes, *The Architecture of Wren* (London, 1982), pls. 45-51. In or around 1726 its appearance was recorded in a set of four fine engravings, *Wren Society* xiv (Oxford, 1937), p. 164, pls. i-iv; see pl. 51 in the present essay.

24 A. Rouquet, *The Present State of the Arts in England* (London, 1755), pp. 95-96. For St Martin's, see T. Friedman, *James Gibbs* (New Haven and London, 1984), pp. 54-72.

25 *Vertue Note Books*, i, *Walpole Society* (Oxford, 1930), vol. 28, p. 150. Wren adapted the wall treatment for the external transept ends of his own rebuilding.

26 W. Kent, *The Designs of Inigo Jones*, ii, pls. 54-55, including a plan; J. Harris and G. Higgott, *Inigo Jones: Complete Architectural Drawings* (London, 1989), pp. 238-47; J. Summerson, 'Inigo Jones: Covent Garden and the Restoration of St. Paul's Cathedral' in *The Unromantic Castle and Other Essays* (London, 1990), pp. 41-62.

27 Anonymous, *English Architecture: Or, the Publick Buildings of London and Westminster* (London, 1758), p. 4.

Wiggens, however, was no revolutionary. He was content to reconcile the hybrid character of his elevation – neo-Jonesian yet preserving a Wrenian flamboyance in the broken silhouette of dome, lantern and towers above the main entablature – by subscribing to a well-publicised solution advocated by Colen Campbell in the influential first volume of *Vitruvius Britannicus* (1715). Condemning the Roman Baroque church façade, as represented by Carlo Maderno at St Peter's (1607-12), Campbell singled out as especially disreputable the 'trifling . . . Breaks [and] Parts without Proportion', the 'excessive Height' of the attic, and a central pediment 'supported by a Tetrastyle' portico which is 'mean for so great a Front, which at least would demand an Hexastyle'. In his own Palladian alternative, a *'new Design for a Church in* Lincolns-Inn Fields', dated 1712 (Fig. 49), he produced a building which was 'most conformable to the Simplicity of the Ancients' by reducing the plan to a square and circle ('the most perfect Figures'), introducing 'one single *Corinthian* Order', dressing the whole 'very plain' and removing the twin west towers 'at such a distance, that the great *Cupola* is without any Ambarass'.[28] Wiggen's towers are similarly isolated, pushed further out from the central axis of the dome than either Maderno or Wren had allowed; moreover, the tabernacle windows in the tower bases are set against flat, undecorated walls in a Campbellian manner. Campbell also observed that Maderno's excessively long extension of the nave from Michelangelo's original centrally-planned basilica 'extreamly injured the August Appearance of the *Cupola*, which is very much lost by being removed so far from the . . . Front'. At St Paul's, Wren solved what was substantially the same problem by lifting the crossing dome and its colonnaded drum on a solid masonary substructure, a solution which was by no means universally admired.[29] At St Stephen's, the drumless dome rising over the centre of the church was difficult to see from street level and at least one visitor complained that as a result it made 'no pleasing appearance'.[30] Here Wiggens suggested little more than cosmetic improvements, replacing Wren's lantern with a slightly taller, fuller, more complex structure crowned by a cathedral-like diminutive dome-on-drum.

Much the same Pauline repertory was used but with greater sophistication a few years later by a more experienced architect, Timothy Lightoler.[31] St Paul's, Liverpool, erected during 1767-69 (demolished 1932-33), was the most ambitious and novel of three new churches necessitated by a dramatic increase in

28　C. Campbell, *Vitruvius Britannicus* (1715), p. 3. Pls. 3-4 are devoted to St Paul's, a 'Noble Fabrick . . . beyond Exception . . . the second Church in the World' (p. 3).

29　The substructure, drum, dome and lantern together was 'abundantly too big for the rest of the pile', J. Ralph, *Critical Review of the Publick Buildings, Statues and Ornaments in, and about London and Westminster* (London, 1734), p. 19.

30　S. Markham, *John Loveday of Caversham, 1711-1789: The Life and Tours of an Eighteenth-Century Onlooker* (Wilton, 1984), p. 304. Loveday visited the church during 1737-38.

31　Lightoler worked *c.* 1758-79, mainly in the Midlands and the north of England, H.M. Colvin, *A Biographical Dictionary of British Architects, 1600-1840* (London, 1978), pp. 520-21.

population (from 5,741 in 1700 to 25,787 in 1760) following the town's rapid emergence as a major west coast trading centre (Fig. 52). The need, therefore, was for a large and imposing place of worship accommodating a prosperous, middle-class congregation. Constructed on a grand scale (80 feet square), entirely of yellow sandstone, at a cost of £12,000, the new church was described with some justification as 'one of the finest in England'.[32] Contemporary observers immediately recognised a kinship with its London namesake.[33] Lightoler had, in fact, returned not to the executed cathedral but to the dramatic ceremonial ensemble of west portico and domed vestibule of the Great Model (Fig. 51), which he detached from the main body to form an independent, centrally-planned building, in the process simplifying the Baroque prototype in compliance with current neoclassical ideas.[34]

The projecting west portico was reduced to tetrastyle, that is, half the number of columns, with an unfluted Ionic Order instead of Wren's richly fluted Corinthian.[35] The result resembles Gibbs's alternative Ionic 'round' design for St Martin's published in *A Book of Architecture* of 1728,[36] but with the more up-to-date, taller, slimmer columns and wider middle intercolumniation recommended by William Chambers in *A Treatise On Civil Architecture* of 1759.[37] Moreover, Wren's delicate and varied treatment of the external walls was replaced by sombre, severely delineated doors and windows set against a contrasting strata of smooth ashlar in the upper area and vigorously horizontal

32 P. Russell and O. Price, *England Displayed* (London, 1769), ii, p. 90. See also J.A. Picton, *Memorials of Liverpool Historical and Topographical* (London, 1873), ii, pp. 39-40, and *City of Liverpool Municipal Archives and Records, from A.D. 1700 to the Passing of the Municipal Reform Act* (Liverpool, 1886), ii, pp. 170-71, 276-78. The church is recorded in W. Enfield, *An Essay towards the History of Leverpool* (Warrington, 1774), pp. 45-46, including an engraved view of the exterior (reproduced in M. Whiffen, *Stuart and Georgian Churches* (London, 1947-48), pl. 56; C.H. Reilly, *The Liverpool Architectural Sketchbook* (September 1910), p. 28, and in pre-demolition photographs in Liverpool City Libraries Archives and *Transactions of the Historic Society of Lancashire and Cheshire*, lxxv (1923 for 1924), pp. 216-17.

33 A. Young, *A Six Months Tour Through the North of England* (London, 1771), iii, p. 167, referred to 'its namesake at London'. The 'architect appears to have had in view the construction of St Paul's in London', J. Wallace, *A General and Descriptive History of the Ancient and Present State of the Town of Liverpool* (Liverpool, c. 1794), p. 143; 'Howsoever the church . . . may pass for a miniature of the

original, the dome and cupola serve but to remind us of their inferiority', W. Moss, *The Liverpool Guide* (Liverpool, 1794), p. 77.

34 Nicholas Hawksmoor, who had assisted in the completion of the cathedral from 1691 to 1712, adapted the Great Model's vestibule lantern, with its colonnaded base and stepped spire, for the top stage of the steeple of St George, Bloomsbury (1716-31), substituting the crowning apostolic statue for one of King George I; K. Downes, *Hawksmoor* (London, 1959), pls. 68b, 69c.

35 'ST PAUL'S CHURCH . . . is a magnificent structure. It has a bold Ionic portico on the west side, the pediment of which, with its large projection, produces an agreeable recess of shadow upon the body of the building, and finely relieves the four columns which support the front . . . The stone work is finished at the top with plain vases', W. Enfield, *An Essay Towards the History of Leverpool* (Warrington, 1774), pp. 45-46. The engaged porticoes on the north and south fronts followed suit.

36 J. Gibbs, *A Book of Architecture* (London, 1728), pls. 13-14.

37 R. Chitham, *The Classical Orders of Architecture* (London, 1985), p. 35.

channelling in the lower.[38] In a Palladian building channelling of this sort normally was reserved for the supporting basement.[39] Lightoler employed it in a manner which suggests contact with progressive Parisian architecture of the time.[40]

St Paul's, Liverpool, with its brooding body and lofty, lanterned dome, was built on rising ground as the centrepiece of a newly laid-out domestic square of the same name, which together provided 'a noble addition to the view of the town, from whatever points it is taken'.[41] Arthur Young observed in 1771 how 'you may view it to much better advantage than its namesake in *London*'.[42] But in other ways it highlights the design and liturgical difficulties of adapting such idiosyncratic and complex Baroque central-planning to provincial parish church usage. Many contemporary commentators found Lightoler's building unsatisfactory. Young felt that, though 'handsome in several respects', it would not stand the test of critical examination:

> The cupola is by no means striking; it does not rise in a bold stile; its being ribbed into an octagon is disadvantageous; nor is there simplicity enough in the lantern. There is a great heaviness in the breadth of the space between the capitals of the pillars and the cornice. Within there . . . is much lightness, and a simple elegance . . . that is pleasing: but all is hurt by the absurdity of the square cornices above the pillars, which project so much as to be quite disgusting.[43]

While acknowledging an 'attempt at majesty and splendour', J. Wallace, a local historian writing around 1794, concluded that 'the scale of elevation seems greatly disproportioned to the plan, a confused heap of stone of gigantic dimensions . . . crouded together in one small spot'. He also regarded the interior as

> a positive satire on all order and design, it is neither calculated to hear nor to see, the immense masses of stone which rise in the shape of columns, are so thick and

---

38 The view published in Enfield and photographs of the church as built (see note 32) show that the proposed window pediments with their broken undersides were abandoned for a simpler detailing in execution.

39 As at John James's Wricklemarsh (Kent) (*c.* 1725), illustrated in J. Woolfe and J. Gandon, *Vitruvius Britannicus* (London, 1767), pls. 61-63.

40 For example, Ledoux's Hôtel d'Hallwyl, begun 1766, and Antoine's Hôtel des Monnaies (Mint), 1768-75 (A. Braham, *The Architecture of the French Enlightenment* (London, 1980), pls. 205-7 and 150-52, respectively). Specimens of this treatment appear in J.F. de Neufforge, *Recueil Elémentaire D'Architecture* (Paris, 1763) v, 56e Cayee, and *Supplément*,

XLIIe Cahier and XLIIIe Cahier (churches).

41 W. Enfield, *An Essay Towards the History of Leverpool* (Warrington, 1774), p. 46. In a 'Diagram or Series of Great Triangles by which the most eminent places in the Map of the Environs of Leverpool were projected' (following p. 116), the church is shown as the focal-point of seven radiating vistas.

42 A. Young, *A Six Months Tour Through the North of England* (London, 1771) iii, p. 167.

43 A. Young, *A Six Months Tour Through the North of England* (London, 1771) iii, pp. 167-68. Lightoler also designed the more conservative and internally successful domed Octagon Chapel at Bath in 1766-67, W. Ison, *The Georgian Buildings of Bath from 1700 to 1830* (London, 1980), pp. 54-56.

abundant, that one half the congregation is concealed from the other, while the clergyman is seen by few [hence the presence of a movable pulpit], the dome is gloomy, heavy, and unmeaning, the voice of the reader . . . so lost and unintelligible by reason of the lowness of the aperture of the (inner) cupola, which like a vortex swallowed all sound . . . eight little circular windows, which reflect a borrowed light from eight corresponding ones in the principal dome, aggravate an appearance already too dreary and monastic, and give the spectator a perfect idea of a compleat mausoleum . . . Eight enormous piles of stone, hewn into Ionic order support the dome, in addition to which two more are placed to the eastward, to conceal as much as possible the chancel from the congregation, these not only add to the gloomy horrors of the spot, but have a chilled and damp effect on the whole auditory.[44]

William Enfield had noted serious internal defects soon after the church's completion: 'The open dome renders the voice extremely indistinct, and in some parts almost unintelligible. Several attempts have been made to remedy this inconvenience; particularly by spreading oiled paper over the bottom of the concave, like parchment upon the head of a drum, but the ears of the audience are not so much benefited, as their sight is offended by this contrivance'.[45] This defect was still so conspicuous in 1794 that the church was 'but very thinly attended'.[46]

44 The 'south and north fronts [have] a heavy unmeaning effect' as well; *A General and Descriptive History of the Ancient and Present State of the Town of Liverpool* (Liverpool, *c.* 1794), pp. 142-44.
45 *An Essay Towards the History of Leverpool* (Warrington, 1774), p. 46. Wallace (see note 44) noted that this solution proved 'so extremely offensive, as to entirely disgust the eye of the observer' (p. 143).
46 W. Moss, *The Liverpool Guide* (Liverpool, 1794), p. 90. In 1873, J. A. Picton (see note 32) reported that though the church is large and imposing and 'in the midst of a dense population, it has, except for short intervals, few and far between been attended by the merest handful of a congregation' (p. 44).

11

Wren, Hawksmoor and the Architectural Model

JOHN WILTON-ELY

We . . . have commanded a Model . . . to be made in so large and
exact a manner, that it may remain as a perpetual and unchange-
able rule and direction for the conduct of the whole Work.[1]

With these sonorous words Charles II's commission for St Paul's Cathedral of
1673 defined the principal functions of what remains the most impressive
architectural model in British history. Wren's Great Model was intended to
embody both a definitive presentation of his ideal design to the commissioners
for rebuilding the cathedral as well as an effective demonstration of its
complete form to those responsible for its construction (Fig. 53).[2] Models,
however, also provided a variety of other functions in the work of Wren and his
colleagues – Nicholas Hawksmoor in particular – as developed in architectural
practice over many centuries.[3]

The recorded history of models providing a range of design functions can be
traced back at least to ancient Greece. They were undoubtedly of particular
value in periods of major structural innovation such as Imperial Rome and the
Gothic era. During the middle ages models were employed to work out and test
systems of masonry vaulting as well as for setting patterns of decorative carving

* This essay is based on a paper given at the
conference, *The Design and Setting of St Paul's*,
organised jointly by the Royal Academy of
Arts and the Centre for Metropolitan History
(Institute of Historical Research, London) in
April 1991. The author would particularly
like to thank the staff of the Conway Library,
Courtauld Institute of Art, and of the Photographic Archive of the Warburg Institute for
their help in obtaining photographs.

1 Quoted in M. Whinney, *Wren* (London,
1971), p. 86.
2 The Great Model is discussed at length in K.
Downes, *The Architecture of Wren* (London,
1982), pp. 68-72, and more recently in the
same author's exhibition catalogue, *Sir Christopher Wren and the Making of St Paul's* (Royal
Academy of Arts, London, 1991), pp. 10-13,
52-53.
3 Coverage of the history of architectural
models in general is scattered in various specialist works. For general historical surveys,
still with value, see M.S. Briggs, 'Architectural
Models', *Burlington Magazine*, liv (1929), pp.
174-83, 245-52; L.H. Heydenreich, 'Archi-
tekturmodell,' *Reallexikon zur Deutschen Kunst-
geschichte*, i (Stuttgart, 1947), col. 918-40. An
updated summary is due to appear in the
present author's entry on 'The Architectural
Model' in the forthcoming *Macmillan Dictionary of Art*.

Fig. 53 St Paul's Cathedral, Wren's Great Model from the north west. (*St Paul's Cathedral*)

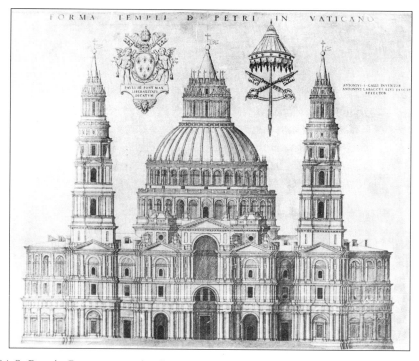

Fig. 54 St Peter's, Rome, engraving by Salamanca (1549) of Antonio da Sangallo the Younger's wooden model, east elevation, from A. Lafreri, *Speculum Romanae magnificentiae* (*c.* 1548-86).

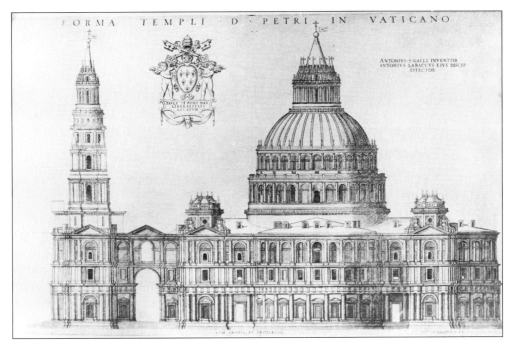

Fig. 55 St Peter's Rome, engraving of Sangallo's model, north elevation, from A. Lafreri.

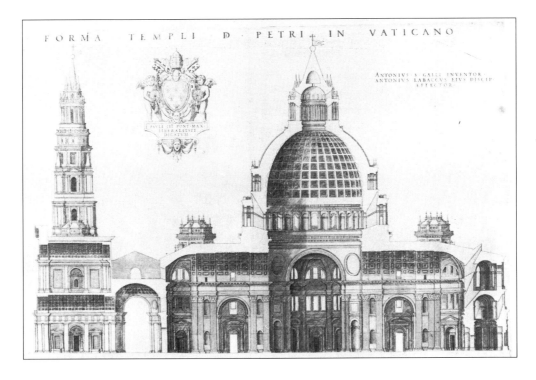

Fig. 56 St Peter's Rome, engraving of Sangallo's model, sectional elevation from the north, from A. Lafreri.

through templates and full-scale prototypes. The Italian Renaissance, however, gave a new stature to the model with the emergence of the architect as the co-ordinator of building operations as well as often the sole author of an evolving design. In the latter situation the model's uniquely three-dimensional nature enabled spatial and structural factors to be integrated in a way denied to drawings.

The first extensive record of models in operation is to be found in Brunelleschi's creation of the dome of Florence Cathedral.[4] There he developed a variety of model functions, from the presentation design to many improvised devices produced to instruct workmen in unfamiliar technical and ornamental details during the dome's construction.[5] At his death in 1446, Brunelleschi left a model behind to guide the completion of the lantern.[6]

Alberti was among the first theorists since Antiquity to define the importance of the model in *De re aedificatoria*, published in 1485.[7] By the following century the model's unique functions had been fully assimilated by western architectural practice, inevitably playing an important role in the protracted building history of St Peter's, Rome. While Bramante's model for the entire design has not survived, Antonio da Sangallo's ambitious model for the basilica can still be examined in the Vatican Museum.[8] Made to the unprecedented scale of one twenty-fourth of the intended building, this large wooden structure was begun in 1539 and took seven years to complete. Moreover, it was to establish a new level of importance in design techniques as the first 'walk-in' model with its ornamental character expressed as fully within as without, as portrayed in a set of engravings in Lafreri's *Speculum Romanae magnificentiae*, produced between 1548 and 1586 (Figs. 54-56).[9]

It was to be Sangallo's successor at St Peter's, Michelangelo, who was among the first designers to employ models extensively in the early stages of formal composition. Apart from his surviving wooden façade model for S. Lorenzo, Florence of 1520 (Casa Buonarotti) which originally involved wax sculpture which could be manipulated within this architectural framework, Michelangelo used clay models to shape his highly idiosyncratic staircase for the Laurentian Library.[10] He later went on to use the same techniques for the

---

4 *The Life of Brunelleschi by Antonio di Tuccio Manetti*, ed. H. Saalman, trans. C. Enggass (Philadelphia, 1970), pp. 80-81.

5 Ibid., p. 92.

6 Ibid., p. 116.

7 P. Portoghesi, *Leon Battista Alberti, l'architettura (De re aedificatoria)*, introduction and notes with Latin text and translation by G. Orlandi, (Milan, 1966), ii, 1, pp. 96, 98. See also the new English edition, *L.B. Alberti: On the Art of Building in Ten Books*, trans. and ed. by J. Rykwert, N. Leech and R. Tavernor (Cambridge, MA, and London, 1988), pp. 33-35.

8 The model made by Antonio Labacco of Antonio da Sangallo the Younger's design for St Peter's is discussed and illustrated in L.H Heydenreich and W. Lotz, *Architecture in Italy, 1400-1600* (Harmondsworth, 1974), pp. 198-200, pls. 205, 206 and fig. 52c. Another sizeable wooden model, approaching the same scale, was produced for Pavia Cathedral in the late fifteenth century and can still be seen there (reproduced ibid., pl.105).

9 Antonio Lafreri (1512-77), *Speculum Romanae magnificentiae* (Rome, c. 1548-86), iii, Q.301-303.

10 J.S. Ackerman, *The Architecture of Michelangelo* (London, 1961), pp. 304-5.

sculptural character of the façade for St Peter's.[11] When he came to evolve the monumental cornice for the façade of Palazzo Farnese in 1546, he had a full-scale wooden section placed *in situ* to determine its appearance.[12]

Taking these sculptural and plastic considerations even further, it was Michelangelo also who appears to have introduced the role of the sectional model where external and internal spaces could be evaluated and developed simultaneously. Several wooden sectional models were produced for his projected church, S. Giovanni de' Fiorentini, Rome.[13] One of them is recorded in an engraving by Jacques Lemercier of 1607, showing this substantial device set high for inspection on a trestle-table, complete with the full ground plan displayed (Fig. 57). Between 1558 and 1561 Michelangelo had a large sectional model made of his dome design for St. Peter's, also today in the Vatican.[14] This was to guide Giacomo della Porta and his contemporaries in completing the work, albeit with modifications to the model itself.

By this time model usage had inevitably accompanied the spread of Renaissance design to northern Europe. Models by Domenico da Cortona were produced for several châteaux of François I, including Chambord in 1509.[15] Philibert de l'Orme discussed their advantages at length in his *Premier tome de l'architecture* (1567), while Du Cerceau stressed the advantages of developing site models, including garden design, in his *Plus excellents bastiments* (1576). Meanwhile the earliest reference to models in England yet found occurs in 1567, when the French joiner Adrien Gaunt is recorded as making one for Longleat.[16] The word 'model' in documents, however, can prove misleading since the term, as derived from the Italian *modello*, frequently refers to a drawing. As Shakespeare succinctly put it in 1598: 'When we mean to build, we first survey the Plot, then draw the Modell', and Inigo Jones's recorded 'modell' for his Banqueting House, Whitehall, is likely to have been of this nature.[17]

The early architectural writers in England, paraphrasing Alberti, emphasised the practical value of the model to gentleman architects. Sir Henry Wotton in his *Elements of Architecture* (1624) saw its advantages in anticipating costly alterations in construction, while Sir Roger Pratt in his manuscript notebooks of 1660 gives practical instruction on the making of models. According to him the designer should prepare boards:

11 Ibid., p. 319. Michelangelo's clay models, supplementing a wooden model, are recorded for St Peter's in July 1557.
12 Ibid., p. 315.
13 Ibid., pp. 327-28. Other sectional models for the same commission were recorded by G.A. Dosio and V. Régnard (figs. 114 and 117).
14 Ibid., p. 319, fig. 96.
15 A. Blunt, *Art and Architecture in France, 1500-*

1700 (Harmondsworth, 1953), p. 12. Domenico da Cortona's wooden model is recorded in drawings made by Félibien in the seventeenth century.
16 M. Girouard, *Robert Smythson and the Elizabethan Country House* (London, 1983), p. 46.
17 P. Palme, *Triumph of Peace: A Study of the Whitehall Banqueting House* (London, 1957), pp. 2-3. W. Shakespeare, *Henry IV, Pt. II*, I, iii.

Disegno d'un Modello non messe in Opera fatto per San Giouâni [...] de i Fiorentini in Roma la reduttione del quale e di doi palmi per oncie la longhezza et larghezza è di [...] Pal'⁊ ⁊ et laltezza di Pal'⁊

Michel'Angelo Bonarota Inuentore

Iacobus Mercier Gallus fecit Romæ Aō 1607

Fig. 57 S. Giovanni de' Fiorentini, Rome, engraving by Jacques Lemercier of Michelangelo's wooden sectional model (1607).

Fig. 58 St Paul's Cathedral, Wren's Great Model, interior view looking south east.

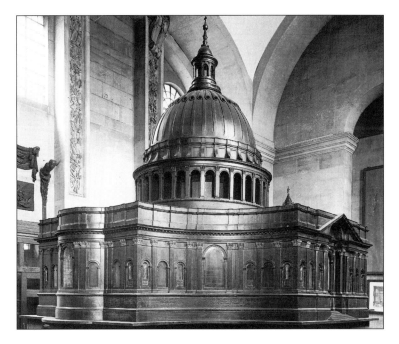

Fig. 59 St Paul's Cathedral, Wren's Great Model from the north east.

Fig. 60 Radcliffe Library, Oxford, Hawksmoor's model, sectional view without dome. (*Bodleian Library*)

Fig. 61 Royal Naval Hospital, Greenwich, sectional model for a cupola. (*National Maritime Museum*)

Fig. 62 Royal Naval Hospital, Greenwich, site model from the north west. (*National Maritime Museum*)

of some fine grained wood, as deal, pear tree, etc., exceedingly well smoothed, and so seasoned likewise, and upon them you are to draw just after the same manner as you did upon paper, and afterwards give them to some joiner to be neatly cut out, and to be put altogether, . . . and afterwards are all the ornaments to be made, and fastened upon it in their proper places; and lastly all things to be coloured after the same manner as they will appear at length in the building, . . .

Later, he went on to add that such a model should contain

all things both external and internal with all their divisions, connections, vanes, ornaments, etc, . . . there to be seen as exactly, and in their due proportions, as they can afterwards be in the work of which this is composed to be the Essay, . . . [18]

It was natural for Wren, with his technological concerns and empirical cast of mind, to exploit models throughout his career. His earliest surviving model for Pembroke College Chapel of 1663 (College collection) shows particular attention to the roof construction, and a similar emphasis appears to have been the case for the lost model of the Sheldonian Theatre, Oxford.[19] Wren is recorded as using this to demonstrate his ingenious vertical truss structure of the roof to fellow members of the Royal Society in April 1663.[20]

The design of St Paul's inevitably required the widest range of model usage in English architecture to date. Already in his report on the pre-Fire design of the cathedral in May 1666, Wren recognised the advantages of a visual aid to introduce the unfamiliar concept of a dome for the crossing to patrons and builders alike. He therefore recommended that:

for ye Incouragement & Satisfaction of Benefactors yt comprehend not Designes & Draughts on paper as well as for ye inferior Artificers clearer intelligence of their Business, it will not be amiss yt a good & careful large model be made, wch will also have ye use yt if ye work should happen to be interrupted or retarded Posterity will go on where it was left, pursuing still ye same designes.[21]

The need was all the greater when it came to advocating and explaining an entirely new building. The First Model of 1670, made by William and Richard Cleer, survives in the cathedral crypt today in a damaged and incomplete state, lacking its roof and domed vestibule. [22] The latter was clearly attached to the nave by a hinge at the base to enable the model to be opened for internal

18 H. Wotton, *Elements of Architecture* (London, 1624) (1903 edn.), pp. 51-52; R.T. Gunther, *The Architecture of Sir Roger Pratt* (Oxford, 1928), p. 23.

19 K. Downes, *The Architecture of Wren*, pp. 30-32.

20 T. Birch, *History of the Royal Society* (London,

1756), i, p. 230; Downes, *The Architecture of Wren*, p. 32.

21 *Wren Society*, xiii (Oxford, 1936), p. 17; Downes, *The Architecture of Wren*, p. 48.

22 Whinney, *Wren*, pp. 83-84; Downes, *The Architecture of Wren*, pp. 52-54.

inspection. When Pratt recorded his disparaging comments on seeing it in 1673, he clearly mistook it for the far more impressive production then nearing completion.[23]

Wren's initial designs for the cathedral having failed to meet the King's expressed wish for grandeur, his ambitious new design clearly required a model of comparable stature. Given Wren's considerable accumulation of books and engravings, it is likely that he was aware of the engravings of Sangallo's model in Lafreri, not only in terms of its grandiose scale and comprehensive detail but for its capacity to convey the nature of the internal space (Figs. 54-56).

In September 1672 Wren and his assistant Edward Woodroffe began scaling up the drawings for the Great Model and traced them on to oak boards to a dimension of one inch to two feet. The outlines were then cut out and assembled by a team of twelve joiners under the Cleers, the structure being sufficiently complete by February 1673 for Hooke to record that he had been 'at Paul's with Sir Chr. Wren, seen module and walked through it' (Fig. 58).[24] By late September the work was ready for the carvers, plasterers and the painter to render the model as realistic as possible. Richard Cleer himself undertook the decorative carving, and much of the 900 separate items mentioned in the accounts, such as the capitals and urns, were carved in softer woods such as pear (Fig. 59). The Dutchman, Simon Cheel, was paid for eighteen statuettes (long since lost to souvenir-hunters), the plasterwork inside was undertaken by John Grove, while the balconies and ball of the lantern in brass were produced by George Drew. Finally, Robert Streeter coloured the entire structure realistically according to stone or lead, touching in various passages of gilt ornament within, including the coffering of the dome (Frontispiece).

Looking at the surviving model in its depleted state without its colouring, it is hard to savour the full shock encountered by the conservative and staunchly Protestant clergy when first sighting this radical and alien statement (Fig. 59). As Kerry Downes has observed, the model's rejection can also be partly ascribed to the design's inability to be built by stages as funds permitted. [25] Wren clearly recognised the two-edged value of such an explicit statement of intent, as his son tells us in *Parentalia:* 'From that Time, the Surveyor resolved to make no more Models, or publickly expose his Drawings, which (as he had found by Experience) did but lose Time, and subjected his Business many Times to incompetent Judges.'[26]

Models, however, still continued to fulfill more prosaic and practical functions during the construction of Wren's final design. Regular payments to

23 Gunther, *Sir Roger Pratt*, pp. 213-14 [12 July 1673].

24 R. Hooke, *Diary* (London, 1935 edn.), p. 87 [21 Feb. 1674].

25 Downes, *Wren and the Making of St Paul's*, p. 11.

26 *Parentalia, or Memoirs of the Family of the Wrens* by Christopher Wren Jr, (London, 1750; facsimile reprint, Farnborough, 1965), p. 283.

joiners appear in the accounts for 'making Models and Molds, Templetts, etc.' Similarly models were also produced by the masons for parts of the building such as a substantial one in early 1691 for a quarter of the crossing. The cathedral still possesses a number of these detail models such as that reproducing Francis Bird's relief in the tympanum of the west front, a fragmentary model for an altarpiece with Salomonic columns, and another for a section of the choir stalls.[27]

By the final decade of the century Wren's office had become deeply involved in another major undertaking which involved debate, instruction and co-ordination through models – the Royal Naval Hospital at Greenwich. Nicholas Hawksmoor's emerging importance within the office, particularly as Clerk of Works at Greenwich, was to be closely associated with the production of models for the Fabric Committee. Looking over his later career, models appear to have possessed far greater significance in his exploration of those dynamic and sculptural qualities inherent in the Baroque. The physical character of his surviving models, such as those for Easton Neston, the west range of King's College, Cambridge, and the Radcliffe Library, Oxford (Fig. 60), all suggest a more personal function over and above their conventional explanatory role.[28] While much surface detail, especially in the latter, has been lost in those models, it is their basic finish as well as their registering of internal space, using sectional and detachable elements, that sets them apart from earlier works, including those of Wren.

In 1699 Hawksmoor was paid for having three models produced for the use of the hospital's Fabric Committee. The first 'according to the Designs and Directions of Sr. Chr. Wren' appears to be the site model now displayed at the National Maritime Museum (Fig. 62). Another surviving model made on Hawksmoor's initiative may be the large sectional model for one of the twin cupolas, also in the Museum (Fig. 61). The other two models referred to in the 1699 payment included one 'for the Infirmary to join to the First', and a third, also to join to the first, with the Infirmary, the 'Church' and the Queen's House.[29] Since the base of the first model is cut away at its southern end, it seems that the two attachments represented alternative schemes at this end of the site.[30]

In his pioneering research on Hawksmoor's visionary projects of 1711 for providing a Baroque climax at the southern end of the hospital's main axis,

27 Downes, *Wren and the Making of St Paul's*, p. 16.

28 J. Wilton-Ely, 'The Architectural Model: English Baroque', *Apollo*, lxxxviii (October 1968), pp. 250-59.

29 K. Downes, *Hawksmoor* (London, 1979 edn),

p. 87.

30 Ibid., one of the first opportunities to examine this model closely was during its display in the present author's exhibition of historic architectural models, *The Architect's Vision* (University Galleries, Nottingham, 1965).

Kerry Downes drew attention to three alternative designs for a majestic chapel or 'Church'.[31] Given Hawksmoor's response to the three-dimensional value of the model in design, it is not impossible to imagine the visual impact of his alternative designs being tested in this way.

31 Downes, *Hawksmoor*, pp. 88-98.

12

The Grand Bridge in Blenheim Park

HOWARD COLVIN and ALISTAIR ROWAN

It is only in the present century that Blenheim Palace has come to be generally admired as a work of architecture. In the eighteenth century its baroque rhetoric appealed neither to Palladian nor to neo-classical taste, and in the nineteenth appreciation of its picturesque qualities was nearly always coupled with deprecating remarks about the 'heaviness' of its structure and the 'over-loading' of its ornament. Even today, it requires more that a conventional liking for the baroque to understand the complex interplay of forms in the north front.

For the Grand Bridge, on the other hand, there has always been genuine, albeit sometimes rather grudging, admiration, especially after Capability Brown flooded the valley which it spans and converted a mere canal into a lake. Springing directly from the water, the great arch satisfied the taste for an *architecture ensevelie* (or in this case *engloutie*) that was fashionable at the end of the eighteenth century, and the spectacular landscape that greets the visitor as he passes through the Triumphal Arch could not fail to impress even those who were deaf to the language of classical architecture as spoken in the reign of Queen Anne. Whether it is seen light against darker water in the morning, or silhouetted against the glittering surface of the lake in the afternoon, the bridge in its setting forms one of the grandest architectural sights in Europe. Nevertheless it is, as Kerry Downes has put it, 'the most mysterious and the least understood part of all Blenheim'.[1] Only one original drawing for it appears to survive, and no written explanation of its puzzling interior spaces has been preserved, let alone any plan. Most of these spaces are now accessible only by boat, and exploring them is an adventure that requires some agility as well as

* We are grateful to His Grace the Duke of Marlborough, D.L., for permission to study the fabric of the Grand Bridge; to his Agent, Mr P.B. Everett, F.R.I.C.S., and to the latter's assistant, Mr Jonathan Sheppard, for their kindness in facilitating our exploration of its interior, and to Mr Christopher Rayson, F.R.I.B.A., for accompanying us on several of our visits, and for providing a set of draft survey plans. For access to a computer for architectural drawing we are indebted to Mr James Dunbar-Nasmith and to his assistant Mr Gordon Piper. Mr Alan Crossley kindly provided several documentary references.

1 K. Downes, *Vanbrugh* (London, 1977), p. 72.

indifference to bats, pigeons and other wild inhabitants of their dark recesses. What follows is an attempt to resolve some the problems that a study of the Grand Bridge poses for the architectural historian.

Today, the bridge is largely ornamental. But as originally conceived, it had the important function of conveying the principal drive up to the great forecourt. At the present day access to the palace is mainly from the east, either from the Hensington Gate or down the main street of Woodstock, through the Triumphal Arch, and round the eastern side of the lake (or Queen Pool, as this part of it is called.) The palace, however, faces north, not east, and it is clear that the original intention must have been for the grand approach to be down the great avenue from the Ditchley Gate, or perhaps, as Professor Downes has suggested, by a circuitous route from Woodstock that went past the site of the old royal manor house on the north side of the Glyme before turning south towards the new palace.[2] In either case a bridge would be needed to cross the valley, whose steep sides and marshy bottom would make difficult going for coaches and other large horse-drawn vehicles. For this bridge and its attendant earthworks not only Vanbrugh and his adjutant Hawksmoor were invited to submit designs, but also Sir Christopher Wren and the landscape-gardener Henry Wise. Of Hawksmoor's and Wise's plans nothing is known, but it appears that what Wren proposed was a low bridge only 15 feet high and a pair of curving ramps gradually rising to the level of the forecourt.[3] Vanbrugh, on the other hand, envisaged a bridge – or rather a viaduct – whose carriageway would be almost level with the forecourt of the palace rather than one which involved first descending into the valley and then climbing up again to enter the forecourt. Nothing was to interrupt this triumphal approach save the architectural pomp and circumstance of the bridge itself. In April 1706 there were several meetings at which these alternatives were considered by Lord Treasurer Godolphin and other of the Duke's friends and advisers. Wren's 'Modell', Vanbrugh later recalled, 'was quite rejected, and that I propos'd was resolv'd on'.[4]

Exactly what Vanbrugh's design implied in architectural terms we do not know: it may or may not have incorporated all the features of the grand scheme represented by an engraving made under Hawksmoor's direction in 1709, and by a previously unknown drawing almost certainly by Hawksmoor that must

2 Ibid., pp. 72-73. In a paper criticising the whole scheme, written probably in 1716, Sarah, Duchess of Marlborough, noted that the approach over the bridge was intended to be 'only the way for ourselves to go into the park, and not the way as people come to us from London or Woodstock' (Blenheim Muniment Room, Shelf G, box 10). For the topography of the park in the seventeenth and eighteenth centuries, see the maps in *Victoria County History of Oxfordshire*, xii, pp. 442, 462.

3 L. Whistler, *The Imagination of Vanbrugh and his Fellow Artists* (London, 1954), pp. 112-113 and Appendix III (this document is now BL, Add. MS 61354, fo. 1).

4 *The Complete Works of Sir John Vanbrugh*, iv, *The Letters*, ed. G. Webb (1928), p. 76.

have been made about the same time.[5] These agree in showing a huge central arch, two smaller ones to north and south, and four flanking towers linked at the level of the roadway by an arcade on either side (Figs. 63, 64).

What suggests that the design approved in April 1706 may in fact have been of a somewhat more modest character than the one represented in Figs. 63 and 64 is the fact that the northern arch was built in two sections which differ considerably from one another both in dimensions and in other respects. The eastern portion of the arch was intended not only to support the carriageway, but also to shelter a pumping apparatus designed to supply the palace with water drawn from the adjoining spring known as 'Rosamund's Well'.[6] As built by the Oxford mason Bartholomew Peisley in 1706, this arch was only about 36 feet in width from east to west, and was turned in rubble, not ashlar, like the great arch. When work began on the remainder of the bridge in 1708 this northern arch was extended westwards by a second arch built alongside it to make up the full width of the bridge, though to a larger radius and in ashlar masonry. That this was not merely phase two of a structure planned to be built in stages is demonstrated both by the differences in radius and masonry and by the awkward splayed junction between the two builds (Fig. 68). Moreover, a glance at the plan (Fig. 71) shows that the masonry of 1706 was continued southwards to form an internal space that does not conform to the otherwise symmetrical plan of the northern abutment of the great arch. All this suggests that the grand design as executed from 1708 onwards represented a revised and enlarged version of the one that had been approved in 1706, and that when Sarah, Duchess of Marlborough, complained in later years that designs connected with that 'ridiculous bridge' were being carried out that had never been 'shewn nor understood', her annoyance may have had some justification.[7]

5 Hawksmoor's account of £45 'For Copper Plates to engrave the plann of Blenheim house . . . and Front of the Great Bridge, and mony Disburst to the Engraver . . . ' is entered in the Blenheim building accounts under June 1709 (BL, Add. MS 19596, fo. 61). A variant form of the engraving is illustrated by D. Green, *Blenheim Palace* (London, 1951), where it is erroneously stated to have been published in *Vitruvius Britannicus*, i (London, 1717).

6 For the 'Water Engine under the Small North Arch of Blenheim Bridge' see S. Switzer, *Introduction to a System of Hydrostaticks and Hydraulicks*, ii (London, 1729), pp. 321-22 and *Universal System of Water Works* (London, 1734). It was capable of raising four tons of water an hour to a height of 120 feet, and was functioning by the end of June 1706 (BL, Add. MSS 19595, fo. 20; 19606, fo. 5). Screen walls were built on either side of the arch to enclose it, as seen in Fig. 65.

7 *The Letters* (as in n. 4), p.75. She may not always have known exactly what had been agreed between Vanbrugh and her husband. Thus it appears that it was not until September 1711 that she realised that the bridge was intended to have 'four Towers each of which is a little House' (Bodleian Library, MS Top. Oxon. c. 218, fo. 56). Yet Vanbrugh had had 'a large drawing' of the Bridge made for the Duke's inspection in August 1710 (*Letters*, pp. 42-43) and the whole scheme had presumably been made public by the print engraved under Hawksmoor's direction in 1709. As late as *c.* 1716 the Duchess wrote that she had been told by 'a Man that has looked after the Building of it' (the bridge) that 'he did not know how many stories there was to be more (in the towers), but he seemed to think two, because that would be necessary to make it look lofty and Great' (Blenheim Muniment Room, as in n. 2).

Fig. 63 The Grand Bridge, Blenheim, perspective drawing, probably by Nicholas Hawksmoor. (*Private Collection*)

Fig. 64 The Grand Bridge, Blenheim, engraving by P. van Gunst, published in 1709. (*Bodleian Library, Gough Maps, 26, fos. 53-54*)

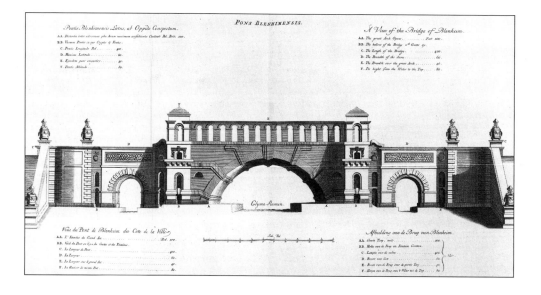

A North West View of Blenheim House and Park, in the County of Oxford, with Woodstock in the Distance. | Veüe Septentrionalle du Coté de l'Oust de la Maison et du Parc de Blenheim, dans le Comté d'Oxford, ayant le Village de Woodstock à quelque Distance.

Published according to Act of Parliament by I. Boydell Engraver at the Unicorn the corner of Queen Street Cheapside London 1752. Plate 1.

Fig. 65 The Grand Bridge, Blenheim, engraved view from the west by J. Boydell (1752). (*Bodleian Library, Gough Maps, 26, fo. 55 v*)

Fig. 66 The Grand Bridge, Blenheim, from the west (1991).

The progress of the works at Blenheim is chronicled fairly fully by regular reports written by Henry Joynes, the clerk of works, to Samuel Travers, M.P., who was in charge of the works at Blenheim with the title of surveyor-general, as well as by a series of annual accounts extending from 1705 to 1714.[8] At the end of July 1708 Joynes reported that 'the foundations of the Bridge are now Digging, and the first stone was laid the 28th of this instant'. By the end of September the foundations of the south side had all been brought up to the level of the meadow, and 'the foundations of the bridge North side the Great Arch adjoining to the Engine house' were 'bringing up'. The next year saw the 'Arch that answers to the Engine House' (i.e. the western extension of the northern arch) turned and the walls on the south side of the great arch 'considerably advanc'd above the springing of the Rustic Arches.' In 1710 work went on 'very vigorously', the great arch itself being successfully completed by Peisley in December.[9] However, in the absence of the Duke, all works at Blenheim were temporarily stopped by the Duchess in October of that year, and even when they were resumed, she held up work on the towers in the hope of getting the house finished first, so it was not until the autumn of 1711 that the two western towers and the spandrels of the great arch on the west side were in place.[10] The east side was still incomplete, and was to remain so for ten more years. For in December 1711 the Duke of Marlborough was dismissed by the new Tory government and the supply of money from the Treasury stopped, not to be resumed until the accession of George I and the return of the Whigs to power in 1714. Even then it was only the accumulated debt to the workmen that was (in principle) acknowledged by the Treasury. For any new works the Duke and Duchess would have to pay themselves out of their own considerable resources. In 1714 an estimate of £6,994 4s. 2d. was made for the completion of the bridge – £2,643 1s. 8d. for 'The stone and masonry', £851 2s. 6d. for 'The two Grand Acroterias', that is, the two arcades, and £3,500 for making up the ground to north and south with earth.[11]

In fact it was not until September 1721, when the palace was almost finished, that William Townesend and Bartholomew Peisley contracted to complete the east side of the bridge, cope the walls, pave the carriageway and finish the 'slope walls' at either end.[12] By that time the Duke had been incapacitated by a stroke and the direction of the works had passed to the Duchess, for whom the bridge

8 Joynes's reports are in BL, Add. MSS 19608-9, the accounts in BL, Add. MSS 19592-19601.

9 BL, Add. MSS 19608, fos. 37, 99, 103, 105, 111, 116; 19609, fo. 9, 10, 15, 19, 20, 34, 35, 40, 41, 45, 46, 67, 80.

10 BL, Add. MSS 19609, fos. 85, 88, 89, 93, 96, 99; 61353 (Travers' reports to Marlborough), fos. 49, 78-9, 107; *The Letters*, p. xxv; D. Green, *Blenheim Palace* (London, 1951), pp. 118-19, 331.

11 BL, Add. MS 61354, fo. 29.

12 BL, Add. MS 61354, fo. 83. A specification for some further works to be performed by Townesend and Peisley in 1724-25, mostly concerned with watercourses, but including iron railings for the two circular stairs inside the bridge, is in the Berkshire County Record Office (D/ESv (B), F 29/3). The iron railings were never made and the steps of the southern stair have at some date been deliberately destroyed.

was the maddest of the 'mad things' that Vanbrugh had set in motion either without her knowledge or against her wishes.[13] In November 1716 their epic quarrel had culminated in the architect's dismissal. So in the bridge, as in the palace, all unnecessary frills were now to be dispensed with. The panels of 'frostwork' that are a feature of the west side of the bridge were not to be repeated on the east side. As for the 'Acroterias', they were of course abandoned, and with them the upper parts of the four towers. By 1724 the Grand Bridge had assumed its present appearance as a great flat-topped arch flanked by two smaller ones. Precisely how much it had cost would be difficult if not impossible to calculate from the surviving documents, but contemporary guidebooks mention a figure of 'between 20 and 30,000 £' for bridge and causeway, and there is no reason to doubt that this is a fair estimate.

In Britain the Grand Bridge was unprecedented both in size and in design. Just over 100 feet in span, its central arch was by far the largest in the country at the time. In the 1730s the building of a bridge over the Thames at Westminster with substantially smaller arches was to tax British building technology to the utmost, but there the difficulty lay in constructing piers in the bed of a running river.[14] At Blenheim the masons were operating for the most part on dry land, where normal foundations could be dug without any difficulty, and the structure has never shown any signs of subsidence. Apart from its sheer size, the most striking feature of the design was the architectural superstructure, which again had no precedent in Britain apart from the dwellings that had been allowed to encroach on London Bridge. In Venice, however, an arcaded wall framed shops on either side of the sixteenth-century Rialto Bridge, while Palladio's published design for a grander bridge on the same site provided an example of what later in the eighteenth century would be called a 'bridge of magnificence'.[15] Vanbrugh's open arcade owed little or nothing to the Venetian example, but the similarity, such as it was, was enough to earn Blenheim's bridge the name of 'Rialto' in some guidebooks. The beauty of Palladio's bridge would have been the contrast between the enclosed courts at either end and the two open porticos facing up and down the Grand Canal in the middle. Vanbrugh's bridge had no such cross-axis to distract attention as one approached the palace, but the four towers were a characteristic stroke of genius that gave the bridge that 'movement' which Robert and James Adam rightly identified as a characteristic of his architectural compositions.

13 Bodleian Library, MS Top. Oxon. c. 218, fo. 55.
14 R.J.B. Walker, *Old Westminster Bridge* (Newton Abbot, 1979).
15 For Palladio's bridge design see his *Quattro Libri* (1570), Book III, ch. xiii and Howard Burns, *Andrea Palladio, 1508-1580* (Arts Council, London, 1975), pp. 123-28. Well-known designs for 'Triumphal Bridges' or 'Bridges of Magnificence' were made by G.B. Piranesi (1743), Sir John Soane (1779) and Thomas Sandby (*c.* 1780). A triumphal arch spanning the roadway like the Roman one still standing at Pola is a feature of the design for a bridge by Vanbrugh which he probably submitted in the Westminster Bridge competition in 1722, Colvin and Craig (ed.), *Architectural Drawings at Elton Hall* (Roxburghe Club, 1964), pl. xxiii b.

Fig. 67 The Grand Bridge, Blenheim, the underside of the great arch, showing the blocked-up windows.

Fig. 68 The Grand Bridge, Blenheim, the northern arch, showing the splayed junction between the two builds.

Fig. 69 The Grand Bridge, Blenheim, view from one of the lower openings in the north-west tower, looking south.

Fig. 70 View from one of the upper openings in the north-east tower, looking south.

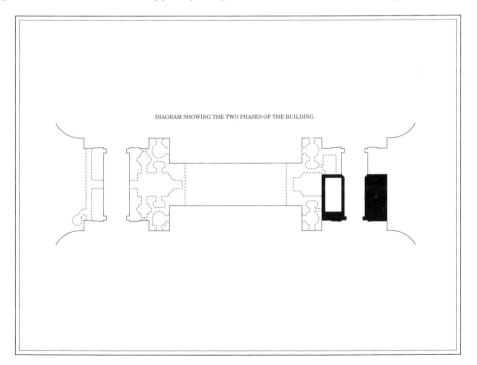

DIAGRAM SHOWING THE TWO PHASES OF THE BUILDING

Fig. 71 The Grand Bridge, Blenheim, diagram showing the two phases of the building. North is to the right.

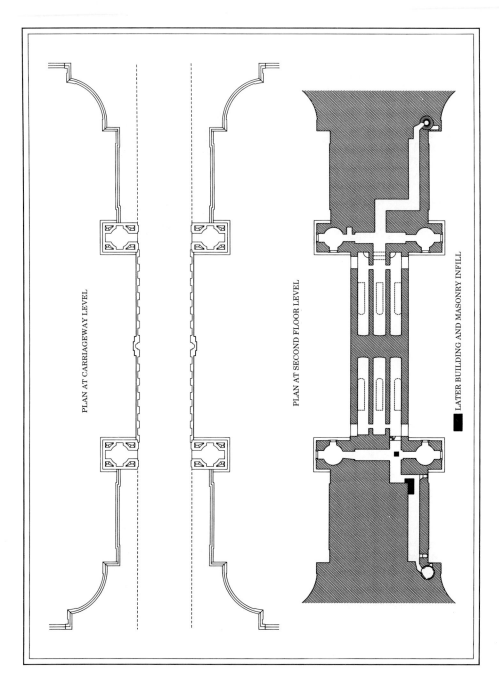

PLAN AT CARRIAGEWAY LEVEL

PLAN AT SECOND FLOOR LEVEL

LATER BUILDING AND MASONRY INFILL

Fig. 72 The Grand Bridge, Blenheim, plans at carriageway and second floor levels. North is to the right.

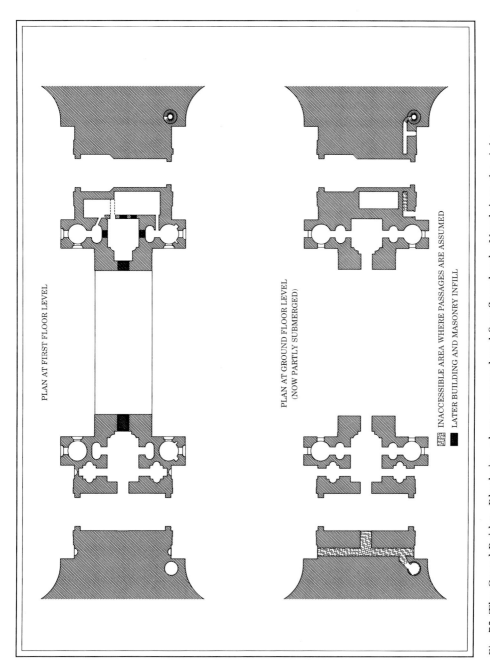

PLAN AT FIRST FLOOR LEVEL

PLAN AT GROUND FLOOR LEVEL
(NOW PARTLY SUBMERGED)

INACCESSIBLE AREA WHERE PASSAGES ARE ASSUMED

LATER BUILDING AND MASONRY INFILL

Fig. 73 The Grand Bridge, Blenheim, plans at ground and first floor levels. North is to the right. (*Scale* 1 inch: 66 feet; approx.)

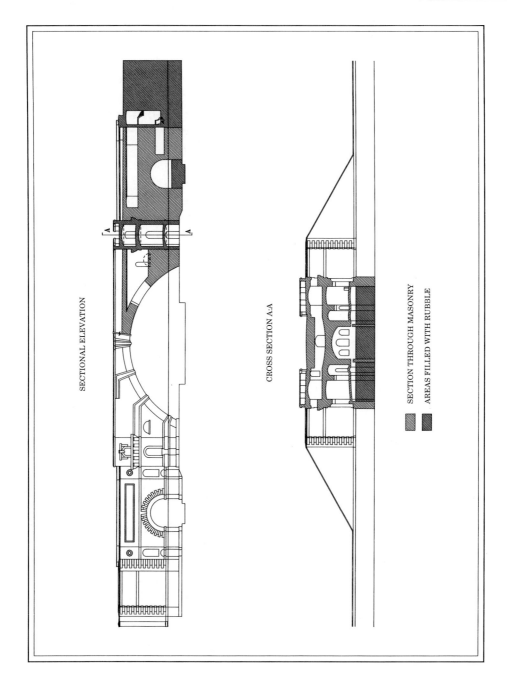

SECTIONAL ELEVATION

CROSS SECTION A-A

A

A

SECTION THROUGH MASONRY

AREAS FILLED WITH RUBBLE

Fig. 74. The Grand Bridge, Blenheim, sectional elevation from the east and cross section.

The most singular feature of the Grand Bridge was, however, the interior spaces. Duchess Sarah claimed to have counted thirty-three rooms inside the bridge,[16] and it is indeed possible to identify some twenty-eight spaces that might just qualify as 'rooms', though some of them have no light and others (in the towers) are open on two sides. There can be no doubt that the basic function of these voids was to save the cost of filling up the spaces between the arches and to reduce the pressure of superincumbent masonry on the latter. Voids were formed in the spandrels of other eighteenth-century bridges for the same purpose, for instance in William Edwards' celebrated one-arch bridge of 140 feet span over the River Taff in Glamorgan (1756) and they figure in at least one of the designs submitted for Westminster Bridge in 1736.[17] In such bridges as these, however, the voids were usually circular and often inaccessible. The complicated sequence of spaces within the mass of the Grand Bridge seems to have been quite without precedent in bridge architecture either British or European. They did, however, have analogies in the perforated-pier type of construction that had haunted the imagination of architects since Bramante's first plan for St. Peter's. In the Grand Bridge the mass of each pier is filled at its centre by a large rectangular room, barrel-vaulted and built of dressed ashlar, with a stepped segmental apse on the side towards the springing of the great arch. These two rooms were to have been entered by arches in their north and south walls opening onto the grassed or gravelled walkways bordering the watercourses (Fig. 63). They were flanked by a series of minor chambers whose axes crossed the central space. The round and square-headed openings at ground-level seen in Hawksmoor's drawing, blocked since the raising of the level of lake, mark the extension of these cross-axes onto the face of the building. In the southern pier the cross axes contain small, almost cruciform, chambers, with apsidal recesses, on either side of the main rooms and then a series of narrow oval lobbies leading to circular vestibules in the bases of the two towers. The resulting pattern recalls the fantastical sequences of rooms shown by the Italian architectural antiquary G.B. Montano in some of his reconstructions of Roman temples. His book was in Hawksmoor's library.[18]

In the northern pier the plan, though essentially similar, had to be modified to accommodate the plain rectangular room already built on the south side of the arch sheltering the water-engine. As a result the central room is considerably shorter from north to south and the second series of linked spaces is omitted altogether. Furthermore in the southern pier the subsidiary rooms rose to a considerable height as lofty two-storey chambers, whereas in the northern one it was only the central room that occupied two storeys, the subsidiary spaces (one of which is provided with a fireplace) being half its

16 Letter to Mrs Clayton, probably written in 1716, and printed in W. Coxe, *Memoirs of the Duke of Marlborough*, ed. Wade, iii (1848), pp. 414-15.

17 T. Ruddock, *Arch Bridges and their Builders*, 1735-1835 (Cambridge, 1979), figs. 4, 49, 52.

18 *Sale Catalogues of Libraries of Eminent Persons*, iv, *Architects*, ed. D.J. Watkin (London, 1972), p. 103.

height. There was also a difference in the way the two suites of rooms were finished. At the lowest level the cross axis in the northern pier – now only glimpsed as a series of vaulted ceilings a few feet above water level – has been finished throughout in hard wall plaster, still intact below as well as above water-level, while the great room with which it connected – also plastered, but probably at a later date[19] – was provided with wooden or metal gratings or overdoors within its connecting arches. There is no trace of plaster in the southern pier, whose rooms can now be explored only by boat. Before flooding their effect as cavernous spaces lit only by light seeping in from the outer chambers may well have been striking. Subtle effects of diffused lighting from the lunette windows in the spandrels of the bridge are also experienced at the upper levels, while the upper openings in the tower rooms afford dramatic views of the great arch (Fig. 70).

It is a curiosity of the plan that Vanbrugh did not attempt to link the uppermost floor of the bridge to the rooms below. A small stair might easily have been accommodated within one of the oval rooms or in one of the circular spaces within the towers. Instead he chose to provide access to the top floor by two circular cantilevered stairs constructed within the abutments on their eastern side. These stairs (the southern of which is now ruinous) are connected by long vaulted passages both to the uppermost rooms in the towers and to the six wedge-shaped spaces over the great arch, three on each side, formed by three longitudinal vaults that support the carriageway. In these spaces, light was provided at one end by the lunette windows in the spandrels, and at the other by great sloping openings, eleven feet long, pierced through six feet of ashlar masonry to the soffit of the arch itself. These were the windows out of which, as the Duchess wrote to her friend Mrs Clayton, you may 'set . . . and look out into the high arch, while the coaches are driving over your head'.[20] Now blocked, they are still clearly visible from a boat and even more so from the interior of the spaces they once lit (Fig. 67).

What, apart from the saving of weight and money, was the function of these strange speluncar spaces? According to the engraving by P. van Gunst (Fig. 64), which shows the complete design, the 'hollow of the Bridge' at ground level was destined to be occupied by 'Grotts etc.' (rendered in the French caption as *Grottes et Fontaines* and in the Latin one as *Cryptae et Fontes*). Grottoes have a long history going back to Antiquity.[21] In the seventeenth and eighteenth centuries they were often constructed in the sides of hills or beneath terraces, and the

19 The plaster, though prior to the rubble filling of the 1760s, is arranged in simple panels whose vertical divisions are unrelated to the lateral openings, which must have been at least partially blocked to accommodate the plaster.

20 Coxe, *Memoirs of the Duke of Marlborough*, pp. 414-15.

21 For grottoes in Antiquity, see H. Lavagne, *Operosa antra* (École Française de Rome, 1988), and for more recent ones, Naomi Miller, *Heavenly Caves* (New York, 1982).

empty spaces inside the Grand Bridge may well have been planned by Vanbrugh and Hawksmoor as grottoes or nymphaea through which fashionable ladies and gentlemen would wander on warm summer days in the course of a promenade along the banks of the canalised Glyme. Indeed, there is confirmatory evidence of this in the form of a letter that Hawksmoor wrote to the Duchess in 1722, in the course of which he ventured to remind her 'how fine a Grotto may be placed under the bridge finished with Rocks and Shells and a plentiful command of water', and to suggest that Bernini's fountain might be placed in it, 'being too tender to stand without doors in the Frost and violent weather of this Climate'.[22] A more sympathetic patron than the Duchess of Marlborough might have fallen in with this idea and commissioned not only some rock-work but also an appropriate statue of Thetis, Egeria, Calypso, or even 'Fair Rosamund', presiding over some ingenious water-effects powered by the near-by pumps.

As it is, there is no trace of that rough tufa, or of those patterned shells or glistening spar or quartz with which empty caves or cellars were transformed into magical grottoes. On the contrary, the walls of the large rectangular room on the north side were at some time covered with smooth plaster,[23] and there are clear traces of a collapsed cornice and of some sort of moulding round the arch of the entrance-tunnel on its south side. Was this, perhaps, the 'very large' room which the Duchess sardonically observed might be used 'for a Ball if there were occasion'?[24] As for its southern counterpart, that served as a cold bath, a facility whose value had been emphasised by recent medical opinion.[25] A French traveller called Fougereau who visited Blenheim in 1728 reported that the bridge contained 'deux massifs . . . ou l'on a pratiqué d'un coté un appartement frais pour les bains at de l'autre coté un moulin à l'eau'.[26] The latter was of course the water-pump, which was actually beneath the northern arch rather than in the adjoining *massif*,[27] but Fougereau's reference to freshwater baths in the southern *massif* is confirmed by an account left by Charles Richardson, a native of nearby Coombe, in which he states that the bridge contained 'a fine bath, the entrance to which is under the small south arch and in its north side'. 'I have reason to believe', he adds, 'that this bath was never used as such owing to the shore [i.e. the sewer] from Blenheim being opposite

22 Printed by D. Green, *Blenheim Palace* (London, 1951), p. 309. For the model for Bernini's fountain in the Piazza Navona in Rome, now in the lower water-terrace garden, see D. Green, 'The Bernini Fountain at Blenheim', *Country Life* (27 July 1951).
23 See note 19 above.
24 In her commentary on the state of the works, written probably in 1716 (n. 2 above).
25 A. Lennard, 'Watering Places', in *Englishmen at Rest and Play, 1558-1714* (Oxford, 1931), pp. 74-6.
26 Victoria and Albert Museum Library, MS 86 NN 2, fos. 111-12.
27 A sketch-plan in Fougereau's manuscript in fact shows the pumps in their correct position under the northern arch.

its entrance'.[28] 'Good accommodations for bathing' are also mentioned as a feature of the bridge in a guidebook of 1748,[29] and some small vents high up in the walls of the southern complex could possibly have been connected with some system of heating now under water.

Whatever facilities the lower spaces provided, they were drowned in 1764 by the rising waters of Capability Brown's lake, which gave the bridge a visual justification that it had previously lacked. No longer would topographers like Defoe or wits like Horace Walpole be able to make quips about a bridge without enough water to justify its existence. What had been the steep sides of a marshy valley were now transformed into 'the bold shores of an noble river'.[30] The loss of the dubious amenities afforded by the interior of the bridge was more than compensated for by the creation of a landscape in which the bridge became the focal point of one of the finest picturesque prospects in Britain.

The flooding of the valley raised the water level by at least fifteen feet. This necessitated some consequential alterations to the bridge. As the pumping engine could no longer function, it was removed, first to 'Queen Elizabeth's Island', and ultimately to Woodstock Mill,[31] and the walls that had screened it (Fig. 65) were taken down, opening up the northern arch. In order to protect the foundations and the lower courses of masonry from erosion, the remaining ruins of the manor – already extensively pillaged for rubble with which to build the bridge – were finally levelled to the ground and the stone was 'sunk all round below the foundations at great expense'.[32]

The visual consequences of submerging the lower portions of Vanbrugh's great bridge must have been very much in Brown's mind, and the new water level was calculated with some precision to coincide with the platband between the ground and the first-floor rooms. To allow for seasonal fluctuations in the level of the lake the band was deepened so that it now reads as a plinth extending below water level. At the same time the bold keystones beneath the lower tower windows were removed. On the underside of the great arch the six windows were blocked up with masonry, as were the entrances immediately below them which had led to the rooms in either pier. The floor of the central room on the north side was raised above water level by half filling it with rubble, but the southern one (the former cold bath) found a new use as a boat-house until a new and more convenient one was built on the shore of the lake in

28 Bodleian Library, MS Top. Oxon. d. 173, fos. 176-78. Richardson died in 1827, aged 67: *Gentleman's Magazine* xcvii (1827), pt. 1, p. 571.

29 T. Salmon, *The Foreigner's Companion through the Universities of Cambridge and Oxford and the Adjacent Counties* (London, 1748), p. 6.

30 T. Whately, *Observations on Modern Gardening* (London, 1770), p. 78.

31 V.C.H., *Oxfordshire*, xii, p. 466.

32 Charles Richardson in Bodleian Library, MS Top. Oxon. d. 173, fos. 176-78. The carting of rubble from the ruins of the old manor house is mentioned in the building accounts from 1708 onwards, and numerous fragments of medieval carved and moulded masonry, dating from the twelfth century to the fifteenth, can be seen in the interior of the bridge.

1888.[33] Within, the elegant sequences of interconnected spaces were lost, interrupted either by water or by blocked-up arches, thus creating that 'warren of dark tunnels, oddly-shaped rooms and winding stone staircases' that has puzzled those few who have been privileged to explore it ever since.[34]

33 The conversion of the bath into a boathouse is recorded by Richardson as in n. 32.

34 D. Green, *Blenheim Palace* (London, 1951), p. 255. In a letter written to her friend Lady Cairns on 29 Sept. 1721 (BL, Add. MS 61466, fos. 99-102), Sarah, Duchess of Marlborough, tells her of the completion of the bridge, which was 'not to be finished as Sir John intended but only to be made useful to pass over'. 'All those rooms', she added, 'which he made in the towers . . . are to be stopt up.' No such stopping up is mentioned in the masons' contract of 28 Sept. 1721 (Add. MS 61354, fo. 83). Nevertheless it is possible that some of the blockings date from 1721 rather than from 1764.

13

St Lawrence, West Woodhay: A Church by Vanbrugh?

PETER SMITH

In their article 'The Rebuilding and Repair of Berkshire Churches during the Seventeenth, Eighteenth and Early Nineteenth Centuries', Basil F.L. Clarke and H.M. Colvin include an entry on the demolished eighteenth-century church at West Woodhay.[1] They state that 'the old church . . . had an embattled brick tower whose character, so far from suggesting the work of Inigo Jones, rather resembled that of Vanbrugh'. They were refuting a statement taken from an anonymous history of Newbury published in 1839, which stated, 'The church, although small, is a very superior building, from the design of Inigo Jones'.[2] The author continued: 'it is justly considered the finest specimen of brick building in this part of the country. West Woodhay house, the residence of Mr Sloper, was also erected by the same celebrated architect.' Since the church was built for William Sloper, after he was granted a faculty on 17 April 1716 to 'pull down the old church and substantially rebuild it againe', it cannot possibly have been designed by Jones.[3] Clarke and Colvin go on to state that the church tower 'bore a certain resemblance to the tower of the water pavilion at Carshalton House in Surrey (c. 1720), whose architect is thought to have been Henry Joynes, the Controller of Works at Blenheim Palace under Vanbrugh from 1705 to 1715'.

In a recent article by Gervase Jackson-Stops devoted to the architectural history of West Woodhay House, he explores the possibility that the house was designed by Inigo Jones.[4] He concludes that though the building, which survives today, was built in 1635 as the surviving datestones suggest, it was more likely to have been designed and built by Edward Carter, Inigo Jones's deputy in the repair of Old St Paul's Cathedral, from 1633 to 1641, and his successor as Surveyor of the King's Works, from 1643 to 1653. The advanced nature of the design of this house explains the nineteenth-century attribution

1 Basil F.L. Clarke and H.M. Colvin, 'The Rebuilding and Repair of Berkshire Churches during the Seventeenth, Eighteenth and Early Nineteenth Centuries', *Berkshire Archaeological Journal*, liv (1954-55), pp. 58-118.

2 Anon, *The History and Antiquities of Newbury and its Environs* (London, 1839), pp. 289-96.

3 A copy of this faculty survives in the present church and at Salisbury Diocesan Registry.

4 Gervase Jackson-Stops, 'West Woodhay House, Berkshire', *Country Life*, clxxxi (1987), pp. 44-48.

to Inigo Jones, but the design of the church shows no such Jonesian characteristics. Jackson-Stops illustrates the church, demolished in *c.* 1880, with a photograph taken *c.* 1860, and states that 'the remarkable Baroque tower . . . suggests that it may have been designed by a disciple of Vanbrugh, such as Henry Joynes'. In this essay I intend to reconstruct the appearance of this church, so far as that is possible, and to explore the possibility that the building may not have been designed by a disciple of Vanbrugh, but by Vanbrugh himself.

The estate of West Woodhay was acquired by Sir Benjamin Rudyard in 1634 and it was he who set about the immediate rebuilding of the house. Rudyard was a wealthy courtier, a poet and a friend of Ben Jonson, as well as an intimate of the Earls of Pembroke.[5] He was a member of the most cultured court circles and it is not surprising that the house he commissioned was in the most advanced style. In fact it is one of the earliest examples of the Renaissance house in England. Rudyard died in 1658 and his grandson sold the estate at the beginning of the eighteenth century to William Sloper. The exact date is not recorded but in the correspondence of Lord Bruce, Marquis of Aylesbury, a letter dated 6 September 1714 states 'Mr Sloper . . . has recently bought Captain Ruddier's estate at Woodhay'.[6] Two years later Sloper applied for the faculty to demolish the medieval church and build anew. This new church, like its medieval predecessor stood to the south-east of the house, and as the faculty stated, was to be built 'again in the place and as near as may be to the same dimensions it is now of, as may be done with solidity and ornament, and so finish the inside thereof according to the best methods that are now used in buildings of that nature both for decency and worship'. The estate remained in the hands of the Sloper family throughout the remainder of the eighteenth and much of the nineteenth centuries. In 1880 it was purchased by William Henry Cole, who demolished the brick church and employed Sir Arthur Blomfield to build a new church, erected in 1882-83, on a new site well away from the house.[7] This church, a careful essay in the Gothic Revival style, built of local flint with stone dressings, survives to-day virtually unaltered, with a fine set of stained glass windows by Morris and Co.

The church also contains, more importantly for our purposes, three photographs of the demolished church.[8] Both the exterior photographs are general views of the house and the church but they are of high enough quality to produce usable enlargements of the sections which show the church. The first

5 J.A. Manning (ed.), *Memoirs of Sir Benjamin Rudyard, Knt.* (London, 1841).
6 Historical Manuscripts Commission, fifteenth report, appendix, pt. vii (London, 1898), p. 217.
7 Victoria County History, *Berkshire*, iv, pp. 242-45.

8 On my original visit to the church all three photographs were in the vestry but when I returned recently one was missing. Fortunately, Mr J. Henderson of West Woodhay House rediscovered the third photograph and has kindly allowed all three to be reproduced here.

(Fig. 75) shows a clear view of the church from the south. It has a massive square brick tower with applied buttresses articulated as plain brick pilasters on the lower stage.[9] Most of this lower stage is obscured by trees, but on the south side a large circular blind opening in darker brick with a raised keystone is clearly visible. The upper portion of the tower has large round-arched bell-openings with raised keystones and raised aprons below, plus a continuous impost band which wraps around the buttresses. The protruding square top has a further band and battlements. The main body of the church is obscured by vegetation, and by a small addition made of knapped flint with a plain tile hipped roof, but the cornice, brick parapet and pantiled hipped roof are clearly visible above. It is important to note that this view of the church is slightly misleading; the building was sited in a dip and it was much taller than this photograph suggests. The true height of the building is more clearly visible in the second photograph.

This second photograph (Fig. 76) shows the east end of the church, which has a short projecting chancel defined by single brick pilasters, with a large round-headed east window with raised keystone between. Also visible are the similar brick pilasters which define the wider nave behind and the cornice and parapet which tops both the nave and chancel. Beyond the pantiled roof is the tower, showing a further round headed opening to the east side.[10] The third photograph (Fig. 77) shows the interior of the church. Clearly visible is the short projecting chancel, with its large east window partly obscured by probably later commandment boards. It has a concave segmental chancel arch and plaster ceiling, with a deeply moulded cornice at impost level. There are small windows visible high up in the walls of the easternmost bays of the nave; that to the right appears to be blocked. The impost level of these windows corresponds with the east window and they may well have been circular, like the blocked openings on the tower. Further west, just visible, are the edges of tall, deeply set windows presumably also round-headed. Most of the original church fittings are clearly identifiable in this photograph. The altar rail remains, with its barley-sugar turned balusters and to the right the octagonal double-decker pulpit with its bolection mould raised and fielded panels and turned baluster staircase. All the box pews survive, including on the left the Sloper family pew with its higher sides topped by a small balustrade. Even the original brass candlestick holders are still in place on some of the pews.

Clarke and Colvin reproduce a seating plan of the former church: 'Preserved in a petition to the Archdeacon of Berks dated February 1717/18'.[11]

9 This is a detail of the same photograph published by Gervase Jackson-Stops.

10 I am most grateful to Dr Tim Mowl for allowing me to use his negative for this photograph. It clearly shows no addition to the south side of the nave and was presumably taken some time before the first photograph (fig. 76).

11 Clarke and Colvin, *Rebuilding and Repair*. This plan is also reproduced in Basil F.L. Clarke, *The Building of the Eighteenth Century Church* (London, 1963), appendix I, pp. 214-15.

Fig. 75 St. Lawrence, West Woodhay (Berkshire), from the south. Enlargement of photograph taken pre-1882.

Fig. 76 St Lawrence, West Woodhay, from the east, enlargement of photograph taken *c.* 1860.

Fig. 77 St Lawrence, West Woodhay, interior looking east, photograph taken pre-1882.

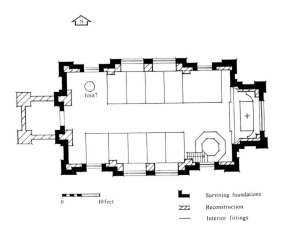

Fig. 78 St Lawrence, West Woodhay, reconstructed ground plan, based on the remaining foundation outline. (*Drawn by Mary Kerr*)

This illustrates clearly social structure and relative status within an estate village in the early eighteenth century, though it does not match exactly the pew arrangement recorded in the photograph. The pew of the Sloper family is not recorded in the seating plan but presumably, since Sloper paid for the church, there was no question as to which pew was his. The plan records three pews on the north and four on the south; the photograph shows four on the north and a probable five on the south, presumably reflecting the final resolution of the petition. The photograph shows that there was a space at the north-west corner, which is presumably where the font stood. The hierarchy of the village is reflected in the seating plan, with on the north side, first the Sloper family, then 'William Sloper's servants', then 'Henry Durnford for the farm' (presumably the estate farm suggesting that Durnford was Sloper's agent), and finally various 'Lease or copy holds' (the tenant farmers). On the south side, the Rector comes first with the other tenant farmers behind. 'The servants of the said parish' are accommodated on benches with the children of those who 'pay no Scot or Lot in the said parish' to either side of the tower at the back of the church.

In a short guide to the history of the church, written by a former incumbent, it is stated that 'the foundations (of the former church) . . . have been preserved. To-day they form the setting of an intimate small garden sur-rounded by flowering shrubs and paved with ancient tombstones'. The founda-tions of the nave and chancel of the eighteenth century do indeed survive, preserved as a garden feature within a gravel walk and planted with roses.[12] A maximum of seven courses of brick are visible, mostly nineteenth century, but enough of the original brick-work is visible lower down, to confirm that this is the exterior outline of the former church. Having measured these founda-tions, as well as the roses allowed, it has been possible to produce a ground plan, within which I have attempted to reconstruct the internal layout of the church, using the evidence provided by the interior photograph.[13] This plan (Fig. 78) shows a slightly more complex arrangement than is discernible from the photographs themselves. The nave has single bays set back to the east and west of the main nave, which contain the high, probably circular windows, just visible at the east end of the nave in the interior photograph (Fig. 78). The projecting central section of the nave presumably had two round-headed windows with raised keystones like the east window. The tower photograph (Fig. 75) clearly shows the central nave cornice and parapet breaking forward on the south side but the addition and the ivy obscure the remainder of this façade.

12 I am most grateful to Mr J. Henderson, the present owner of West Woodhay House, for allowing me permission to inspect and mea-sure these foundations.

13 I am most grateful to Mrs Mary Kerr for drawing this ground plan.

Fig. 79 St Lawrence, West Woodhay, detail of an engraving illustrated in *Memoirs of Sir Benjamin Rudyard Knt*, edited by J.A. Manning (1841).

Fig. 80 Design for a church, possibly by John Vanbrugh, related to his designs for the Fifty New Churches Commission. (*Victoria and Albert Museum*)

Fig. 81 Water Pavilion Tower, Carshalton (Surrey), probably designed by Henry Joynes, *c.* 1720.

One further, possibly misleading, illustration of the demolished church has also come to light. Illustrated in the memoirs of Sir Benjamin Rudyard, which were published in 1841, it is a view of the house and church from the south west.[14] This drawing (Fig. 79) is not accurate, the general proportions of the tower and its buttresses being incorrect and some of the details wrong. For instance, no circular opening is shown on the south side of the tower and the bell-openings are drawn with pointed heads. But this view does show the lower stages of the tower, not visible in the photographs, with large open arches at the base. These arches are pointed in this drawing but it is possible that like the bell-openings, they have been incorrectly drawn, and that the base of the tower had a large round-headed opening to each face.

William Sloper was born *c.* 1658, the son of William Sloper of Great Bedwyn in Wiltshire, not far from West Woodhay. He graduated from New College, Oxford in 1679, and then disappears from view until he is recorded as a Clerk to the Paymaster-General in 1702. He married Rebecca Abbot some time before the birth of his eldest son and heir, also William, at Great Bedwyn in 1708. In 1714 he was promoted to Deputy Paymaster, a post he held until 1720, when he and Henry Clinton, 7th Earl of Lincoln, one of the Joint Paymaster Generals, were both dismissed. It seems that Lord Lincoln was his patron, for in 1726 he was appointed Deputy Cofferer, after the Earl's appointment as Cofferer of the Household in 1725.[15] William Sloper retained this post until his death in 1743. It seems that William Sloper's fortunes were slowly rising in the early years of the eighteenth century, largely thanks to his responsible and lucrative post in the Paymasters' Office. At about the same time as his promotion in 1714 he was wealthy enough to purchase the estate of West Woodhay. In the following year he was elected, unopposed, as the Member of Parliament for his family seat of Great Bedwyn. He was elected M.P. a further four times, in 1722 for Camelford, in 1729 for Great Bedwyn again, and in 1742 and 1743 for Whitchurch.[16]

In 1716 he was appointed by the Privy Seal, along with William Lowndes, the Secretary of the Treasury, and James Craggs, Secretary of State, to examine the Blenheim accounts, and it was from their recommendations that Vanbrugh was finally to receive the overdue payments for his work at Blenheim.[17] At the same time that Sloper was working on these accounts he was embarking on the expensive task of rebuilding the church on his newly acquired estate. Between the faculty dated April 1716 and the petition containing the seating plan dated February 1718 the design for the new church must have been decided; by this

14 Manning (ed.) *Memoirs*, frontispiece.
15 John M. Beattie, *The English Court in the Reign of George I* (Cambridge, 1967), pp. 154-55.
16 Romney Sedgwick, *The History of Parliament: The House of Commons 1715-1745*, ii (London,

1970), pp. 425-26.
17 *The Complete Works of Sir John Vanbrugh*, iv, *The Letters*, Geoffrey Webb (ed.) (London, 1928), appendix I, pp. 204-05.

latter date in fact, the building work may have been nearing completion. Since he was studying the Blenheim accounts, full of references to both Henry Joynes and John Vanbrugh, whilst considering the design for his new church, he may well have been prompted to approach them for advice. Sloper may also have consulted his patron Lord Lincoln, who would have been more likely to recommend Vanbrugh, since he was being employed by his new brother-in-law the Duke of Newcastle at Claremont in Surrey. The Duke married Lord Lincoln's sister Lucy in May 1717. These two noblemen were fellow members with Vanbrugh of the Kit-Cat Club, and chose to be painted together in the only known Kit-Cat double portrait.[18] Interestingly, in the background of this portrait is a view of the park at Claremont with the Belvedere, built to Vanbrugh's designs in 1715, displayed prominently on the skyline, suggesting a shared interest in architecture. The Duke had purchased Vanbrugh's country estate at Chargate in 1714, renamed it Claremont and employed him to enlarge the house over the following years. The original house was designed and built as a country retreat in the brick castellated style which Vanbrugh was experimenting with at the time, and the enlargements were carried out in a similar style.[19] There are two particularly significant features of the Claremont design which also appear at West Woodhay, firstly the circular windows, and secondly the corner towers with round-headed openings and an impost band wrapped around the buttresses.

John Vanbrugh's name is almost exclusively associated with the design of country houses but for a short time, between 1711 and 1715, he was directly concerned with the design of churches. On 21 September 1711 he was appointed as one of the commissioners for the fifty new churches, and on 10 October he was appointed to their building committee with Sir Christopher Wren and Thomas Archer. He was obviously interested in the problems of church design and in the architectural opportunities that this appointment offered, for he regularly attended meetings, doing his share of site inspections, report presentations and discussion of proposed designs. We know for certain that he produced two unsuccessful designs, for the sites of St Mary-le-Strand and St George's Bloomsbury. The committee minutes record that on 2 November 1714, 'Vanbrugh and Gibbs submitted two designs for the church to be erected near the Maypole. Both designs are proper to be put into execution. Referred to Commissioners to make choice'.[20] This they did two days later,

18 National Portrait Gallery. This portrait is one of the forty-one canvases of members of the Kit-Cat Club, purchased from the heirs of Jacob Tonson in 1945.

19 Kerry Downes, *Vanbrugh* (London, 1977), pp. 50-52, fig. 6, pp. 100-101, plate 118. Downes illustrates the drawing of Claremont by J.F.

Rigaud now in the Royal Collection. A similar view, is illustrated in John Harris, *The Artist and the Country House* (London, 1979), p. 186, plate 192a.

20 M.H. Port (ed.), *The Commission for Building Fifty New Churches*, London Record Society Publications, xxiii (1986), p. 174.

when the minutes record 'resolved that it be built to Mr Gibb's design'.[21] More hopefully the committee minutes for 17 May 1715 record that the 'Church on Lady Russel's ground in Bloomsbury to be built to Vanbrugh's design: and built north and south, as it cannot conveniently be built any other way'.[22] But even this apparent success was eventually superseded by Hawksmoor's ingenious solution to the orientation problem, for the commissioner's minutes on 9 May 1716 record that an estimate was required for 'Hawksmoor's design for Bloomsbury new church',[23] so Vanbrugh's hopes for designing at least one of these new churches were finally dashed. He was not appointed to the new commission in December 1715 and his name does not appear in the subsequent minutes.

Vanbrugh may well have submitted designs previously and he was certainly involved in the commission's early preoccupation with finding a 'general model' for all these churches. As part of this debate he produced, probably with Hawksmoor's assistance, a detailed set of 'Proposals about Building ye New Churches', which deals mostly with large-scale urban churches and the importance of their town settings, but also gives some general clues to his ideas about church design. He states that the design of these churches 'shou'd generally be express'd in plain but Just and Noble Stile', that 'every Church may have a Tower . . . of Stone or Brick; High and Bold Structures', and 'That for the Lights, there may be no more that what are necessary for meer use; many Windows . . . take off very much, both from the Appearance and reality of strength in the Fabrick; . . . which shou'd ever have the most Solemn and Awfull Appearance both without and within, that is possible'.[24] All these ideas are clearly visible in the much smaller rural church at West Woodhay.

The only visual evidence we have for Vanbrugh's church designs survives in two drawings now in the Victoria and Albert Museum. These are inscribed in a later hand 'possibly by N. Hawksmoor', but they do not correspond with his or any of the other architects' known projects; they are in a hand close to Vanbrugh's known drawing style.[25] The design (Fig. 80) is for a large-scale church built in stone, resplendent in detailed architectural articulation, and dominated by a massive western tower. The shape of this tower is very close in outline to the tower of the brick church at West Woodhay; strip away the architectural detail and you are left with the form of the tower of Mr Sloper's church.

The suggestion that Henry Joynes may have been responsible for the design of West Woodhay church, rests exclusively on its similarity to the tower of the

21 Ibid., p. 38.
22 Ibid., p. 42.
23 Ibid., p. 50.
24 Downes, *Vanbrugh*, appendix E, pp. 257.
25 Victoria and Albert Museum, D 104 and 110/

1891. The tower in this drawing does share similarities with other Hawksmoor church designs, but overall it shows none of his other complex aesthetic preoccupations.

water pavilion at Carshalton (Fig. 81)[26] Whilst it is obvious that there is a similarity, there are also very distinct differences. The basic proportions are different, the Carshalton tower is rectangular, the buttresses are much smaller and far less significant, and the overall design does not have the tightness and power of the West Woodhay design. The details also differ: Carshalton has refined, rather thin and almost fussy stone detailing with curved battlements and obelisk finials, whilst the details at West Woodhay are bold and plain, stripped down to an absolute minimum in order to emphasise the powerful simplicity of the basic design. Though these two towers may be similar in outline, their distinct differences in detail suggest that they were designed by different architects.

The boldness, simplicity and maturity of the overall design of the church at West Woodhay suggests an architect of real quality and confidence, someone of the stature of John Vanbrugh. After several years of discussion concerning church design with his contemporaries, Vanbrugh no doubt would have eagerly accepted the opportunity to design even a small rural church. Certainly William Sloper had the connections which would have given him access to Vanbrugh's services, either through his work on the Blenheim accounts or through his patron the Earl of Lincoln. At the same time, Vanbrugh was completing Claremont for the Earl's brother-in-law in his new brick castellated style, the same style as the church in West Woodhay; a style which Vanbrugh was still creating for himself and one which virtually no other architects were exploring. The design of this church also fits well within the general ideas that Vanbrugh outlined in his proposals, being in a 'Just and Noble Stile', with a 'High and Bold tower', and of a 'Solemn and Awfull Appearance'. Altogether the evidence examined here, though circumstantial, points clearly in Vanbrugh's direction, making him the most likely candidate for the authorship of this remarkable lost church.

26 H.M. Colvin, *A Biographical Dictionary of British Architects, 1600-1840* (London, 1978), p. 447. Henry Joynes received payment for unspecified works at Carshalton House in about 1720, possibly for the design of the water pavilion. For a more detailed discussion of this attribution see Derek R. Sherborn, 'Carshalton House, Surrey', *Country Life*, cvi, (1949), pp. 480-83, and 'The Landscape Garden and Water Pavilion at Carshalton', *Country Life*, cvi (1949), pp. 1254-55.

14

Sir William Strickland's Hunting Lodge at Malton

ALISON SINCLAIR

It has long been accepted in Malton that the Talbot Hotel in Yorkersgate was converted in 1740 from a late seventeenth-century hunting lodge belonging to Sir William Strickland (1665-1724), third Baronet of Boynton. The Talbot is said to have been created by Lord Malton, later the first Marquess of Rockingham, as a place of resort for county gentry visiting Malton for the races at Langton Wold, established some thirty years earlier. There are however few signs in the present Talbot of any structure earlier than mid nineteenth-century date, other than the fine tunnel vaulted cellars beneath the rear half of the building, and the lavish bolection moulded panelling with which the public rooms on the ground floor are fitted. To accept without question the claim of the Talbot's origins appears to overlook a house only yards away from the hotel, the surviving architectural evidence of which makes it a much likelier candidate for Sir William Strickland's hunting lodge. The house is known as York House (Figs 82 and 83). Most of the above would be of little interest to anyone other than a local historian were it not for the people associated with the hunting lodge, and one extraordinary feature which must arouse the curiosity of the architectural historian.

York House is a small H-plan house of late seventeenth-century appearance on the outskirts of Malton, standing on the south side of the main road to York, some eight miles from Castle Howard. It is separated from the road by a courtyard bounded by fine wrought-iron railings on a low stone wall with a pedestrian gate between rusticated gate piers with ball and pedestal finials. The gate is spanned by an overthrow incorporating the entwined initials WS, the import of which seems never to have been acknowledged, nor even perhaps recognised. Above the monogram, the motto *Vince malum bono* forms the arched head of the overthrow.

In 1684, the year in which he succeeded to the title, Sir William Strickland married Miss Elizabeth Palmes of Malton. The match must have been considered eminently suitable, as Elizabeth was daughter and heiress of Mary Palmes, herself co-heiress, on the death of her cousin William, Lord Eure, in

1652, to half the Eure estate at Malton.[1] Elizabeth was also a distant cousin of the third Earl of Carlisle through the marriage of her great-aunt to his great-grandfather. Both the Strickland and Eure families must in any case have been well acquainted since both owned deer parks at Hildenley and Easthorpe to the west of Malton, between the town and Lord Carlisle's Castle Howard estate. It was to Sir William's trees at Hildenley that Nicholas Hawksmoor referred when he wrote to Lord Carlisle in May 1701 that he heartily wished 'the woods in the front of the house belonging to Sr Wm Strickland' could be secured in his Lordship's possession in order that the view from Castle Howard might be improved.[2] In the event, the Howards had to wait until the end of the nineteenth century for Hawksmoor's wish to be fulfilled. It is not clear whether Sir William already owned a hunting lodge at Malton as well as the house at Hildenley, or whether a lodge came to him, perhaps as part of Elizabeth's marriage settlement. The repetition in the York House overthrow of the motto found also in the relic of the Eure mansion tends to suggest that York House was part of the Eure inheritance.[3]

The entrance to York House (Fig. 82) is in the middle of the north side of the recessed central range, between tall sash windows which light the entrance hall. The door is of eight fielded panels in an eared architrave with a keyblock. All the window architraves are fasciated but, as they were renewed in the early years of this century, it is not certain that they reproduce the originals. This side of the house is built mostly of coursed rubble stone on a chamfered plinth, with flush quoins dressed with a scutching hammer starting about one metre above the plinth. The first floor of the centre range is of scutched stone and has a coved ashlar cornice at eaves level, continuing across the returns of both wings. Ground floor window sills in both wings break into the plinth, suggesting the windows have been altered and lowered. The likelihood of substantial alteration, and perhaps rebuilding, is strengthened by the different stonework and the position of the scutched quoins, beginning some distance above the ground.

1 In 1674 a dispute over their inheritance between Mary and her sister Margaret had led to a memorable legal decision by the High Sheriff of Yorkshire that the great Eure mansion at Malton should be demolished, the materials to be divided between the two sisters, stone by stone. This house, built in 1604 by Ralph, third Lord Eure, was likened in his diary for 1640 by Sir Henry Slingsby to Theobalds and Audley End, see D. Parsons, *The Diary of Sir Henry Slingsby of Scriven, Bart.* (London, 1836), p. 52. The extraordinary gatehouse, surviving today as Malton Lodge, together with its arched forecourt wall, remains as a tantalising relic of the prodigies of architecture torn down upon this decision.

There must however have been some degree of compromise in the settlement since it seems Mrs Palmes and her husband continued to live in the converted gatehouse. Celia Fiennes records in 1697 that she was entertained by Mrs Palmes in her 'pretty house', and that Mrs Palmes operated a linen manufactory for poor persons of the town in the outbuildings, see C. Morris (ed.), *The Journeys of Celia Fiennes* (London, 1947), p. 93. The motto *Vince malum bono* appears in a splendid plaster overmantel in the Lodge.

2 K. Downes, *Hawksmoor* (London, 1979), pp. 234-35; C. Saumarez Smith, *The Building of Castle Howard* (London, 1990), p. 120.

3 See note 1.

Fig. 82 York House, Malton, entrance front.

Fig. 83 York House, Malton, garden front.

Surviving internal fittings provide further evidence of alteration and remodelling, probably of more than one phase. Towards the rear of the stone-
flagged entrance hall is an arcaded screen of keyed round arches on either side
of a wide flat arch, with panelled square piers. Behind this, built against the
rear wall around an open well, is a fine close string staircase with shallow stairs,
turned balusters, square newels and heavy moulded handrail. Beneath the
stairs is a pair of glazed and panelled double doors, the panels enclosed in
fluted surrounds with angle rosettes.

In the east wing there are fittings of various periods. Both ground floor
rooms have coffered ceilings formed by heavy beams with coarse mouldings,
guilloche in the front room, Greek key in the back, and both have had
semicircular-headed niches cut into the thickness of the wall. In the back room
the cornice is enriched with egg-and-shell mouldings and the stone chimney-
piece has a pulvinated frieze carved as a bayleaf garland with a festooned
centre panel. Upstairs a round arch, at the end of what was perhaps originally a
gallery across the stair-well, leads to two chambers, of which the back one
retains substantial portions of square-panelled wainscoting, the front one
vestiges of bolection moulded panelling. Over the front part of the entrance
hall there is another room, now subdivided, again with a coffered ceiling. Here
the walls are entirely covered in four heights of panelling, incorporating a
fireplace with overmantel flanked by sunk-panelled Ionic pilasters.

In the west wing were the service rooms, separated by the secondary staircase
which gives access to the first floor and the attics. The lower flights of this
staircase are boxed in but the top flight to the attic has turned column-on-vase
balusters, square newels and a moulded handrail. At the south end of the wing
a room has been subdivided to form a parlour or breakfast room overlooking
the garden. Here the walls are still covered with raised and fielded panelling in
two heights, and there is a neat little corner fireplace in a bolection moulded
wooden surround. Two original doorcases are incorporated in the panelling,
one providing access from the entrance hall through a doorway with panelled
double doors, inserted to the side of the original entrance to the service wing,
now blocked. The second doorway, now converted into a cupboard, gave on to
a small lobby with a door leading to the garden. On the first floor there is a
small fireplace with a pulvinated frieze in the front room and, in the back room,
a bolection moulded fireplace and substantial remains of panelling. In this
wing all the doors on the first floor are of three panels, in the attic of two panels.

Each of the rooms overlooking the garden in both wings has a small closet,
three of which now serve as lavatories or small cloakrooms. The fourth,
adjoining the parlour in the west wing, provides the lobby through which the
garden was reached, either from the parlour, or from the entrance hall by
means of the doors beneath the staircase.

The existing fittings of the house, with the exception of the main staircase
and the coffered ceilings of some rooms in the east wing, are substantially of

the early eighteenth century. It would appear therefore that whatever the form of the house at the time of Sir William's marriage to Elizabeth, an extensive campaign of refurbishment was carried out some twenty or thirty years later. The probable reason for this is to be found on the garden side of the house (Fig. 83). Here the original front was a repetition of the entrance front, except that the centre, like the crosswings, was gabled. At the time we are considering the façade underwent a dramatic transformation by the construction of a two storey block-like extension between the two wings. In the centre of the block is a giant arch, rising the full height of the two storeys, formed of rusticated voussoirs and with a massive keystone. Beneath the arch a round-headed window, designed to light the staircase, is shaded almost permanently from natural light. On either side are tall, narrow sash windows, one on each floor, lighting the closets attached to the garden side rooms; in the left return an eight-panel door gives access to the lobby adjacent to the little parlour. On this side of the house both door and window architraves differ from those on the entrance front, being simply moulded with keyblocks. The arch block is quoined at the angles and breaks forward slightly from the plane of the flanking cross wings. At the top a sharply moulded cornice projects, forming a low parapet masking a flat roof behind which the original attic gable rises intact. The cross wings of this front are constructed almost entirely of scutched ashlar, although there are small areas of squared masonry towards the east end, where the quoins at the south-east angle are irregular. At the south-west angle quoins are raised and chamfered like those of the arch extension.

Other alterations were carried out within the house later, most notably sometime in the middle of the eighteenth century when the ground floor rooms in the east wing appear to have been refitted. It could have been at this time that the alcoves were constructed in both, and the back room overlooking the garden received its new fireplace and ceiling cornice. In the nineteenth century the service wing chimney was rebuilt, perhaps signifying other modifications to the wing, but the rooms, still in domestic occupation, have lost most of their fittings in the course of this century. In recent years conversion of part of the house to offices has resulted in the subdivision of other rooms with light partitions. But with the construction of the giant arch at the beginning of the eighteenth century, the house had reached the form in which we find it today. Confirmation of this is provided by a perspective of Malton drawn by Samuel Buck around 1720, in which, though the sketch is badly faded, the heavily-shadowed front of York House is clearly identifiable.[4]

The evidence suggests one, and perhaps two, periods of extensive rebuilding and probably three phases of redecoration before the status of the house began to decline. It seems likely that, when he married Elizabeth Palmes, Sir William decided to rebuild a house he may already have owned, or which he acquired as

4 Wakefield Historical Publications, *Samuel Buck's Yorkshire Sketchbook* (Wakefield, 1979), p. 38.

part of Elizabeth's marriage settlement. The surviving rough masonry and irregular quoins at the east end of the garden front, together with the raised position of the scutched quoins on the entrance front, suggest the existence of fragments of a house earlier than the late seventeenth century. Coffered ceilings in rooms in the east wing and fragments of square-panelled wainscotting tend to support this proposition. Assuming that the renewed window architraves of the entrance front, which differ from those on the garden side, reproduce their predecessors, it is likely that a late seventeenth-century campaign of modernisation involved the wholesale rebuilding of this side. Further, it is reasonable to assume that the garden side was largely rebuilt at this time as well, though clearly it was remodelled again in the early eighteenth century.

During the first five years or so of the new century Sir William was engaged in alterations to Boynton Hall. In 1708 he ceased to be M.P. for Malton, a function he had performed, with his father-in-law, from the year after his marriage. For the next two years he represented Yorkshire, after which there was a break of six years before he re-entered Parliament, sitting as Member for Old Sarum between 1716 and 1722. For the last two years of his life, from 1722 to 1724, he was again returned for Malton, in company with Thomas Watson-Wentworth. In 1713, while out of Parliament, he and his wife, whose inheritance they were, had sold the titles of the Malton manors to Thomas Watson-Wentworth, in settlement of his father-in-law's debts, whilst retaining for themselves estate property. In the same year Sir William was one of the founders of a Plate to be run for annually on the Langton Wold racecourse. He was clearly expected to be on the spot at the time of the races, since one of the articles for the Plate stipulates that 'if any difference shall arise upon account of this plate, it shall be referred to Sir William Strickland, Bart'.[5] It seems reasonable to suggest therefore that, in about 1710, having completed the work at Boynton and no longer having to attend Parliament, Sir William began actively to prepare for greater involvement in the social life of Malton and turned his attention to further improvements at York House.

To this second phase of building would belong the rebuilding of the garden front and the addition of the arched extension. This massive structure appears to have been designed solely to improve the accommodation by providing closets for the rooms overlooking the garden. It seems likely, however, that the opportunity was taken at the same time to make the little parlour in the service wing, with access to the garden through the lobby and door provided within the arch. Such modifications would account for the replacement of the doorway from the service wing to the entrance hall by new panelled doors leading from the entrance hall to the parlour. Another improvement was the construction of the arcaded screen at the foot of the staircase, the piers of which are encased

---

5 N.A. Hudleston, *History of Malton and Norton* (Scarborough, 1962), p. 161.

in the same fielded panelling as that fitted to the closet door reveals. This had the effect of making arrival in the entrance hall more impressive and progress up the staircase more ceremonial. Finally, many of the rooms must have been fitted with the surviving bolection moulded panelling, including both first floor rooms in the service wing, which were thus upgraded. Access to these rooms was contrived by the insertion of a panelled door at the head of the main staircase, which opened on to the first floor landing of the service staircase, whence new doors opened into the chambers on each side. The upgrading of first floor chambers in the west wing may account for the fitting up at the same time of the attic in that wing as usable rooms.

The third baronet died in 1724, when the title was inherited by his son, also Sir William, responsible for the extensive alterations carried out at Boynton Hall in consultation with Lord Burlington.[6] The fourth baronet died in 1735. In 1739 the 'late Strickland mansion and estate at Malton' was sold to Thomas Watson-Wentworth's heir, Lord Malton, created first Marquess of Rockingham in 1746, and father of the more famous second Marquess, twice Prime Minister.[7] It is to the first Marquess that the establishment of Malton's first hotel is attributed, through the conversion of the Strickland hunting lodge. If, however, the existing Talbot Hotel and York House are carefully explored and analysed, it is difficult not to conclude that York House is in fact the Strickland hunting lodge. The present Talbot Hotel is perhaps built on the site of the lodge stableyard, engulfing what were its stables and coach-houses. In support of this argument, the existence of an arched Vanbrughian gate a little further up the road opposite the hotel may be cited. Traditionally, this led to the Talbot's stables of which little remains except a range of altered nineteenth-century buildings, including a lofted barn. No Rockingham residence has been recognised or identified in Malton and it is tempting to wonder whether the first Marquess was responsible for the mid eighteenth-century work at York House, if perhaps he retained it for his own use after 1740.

Whatever happened to York House following its sale as part of the Malton Estate to Lord Malton, it eventually descended through the female line to the third Earl Fitzwilliam in 1782. It remains part of the Fitzwilliam Estate. Only access to the archives could establish with any certainty the identities of those responsible for successive phases of alteration, including the building of the giant arch, and their precise dates. Unfortunately, gaining access to the archives is not a straightforward matter. A preliminary enquiry established there is no relevant reference in the index to the Fitzwilliam archive. Some Strickland papers are deposited with the Bryn Mawr Jones Library at the University of Hull, but these relate to that part of the family which inter-

---

6 A. Oswald, 'Boynton Hall, Yorkshire', *Country Life*, cxvi (1954), pp. 280-83, 356-59.

7 Hudleston, *History of Malton*, p. 142.

married with the Cholmley family, eventually taking their name. Documents relating to the Stricklands of Boynton Hall were removed to Canada some years ago and are now held there privately by a descendant of the family.

There remains the puzzle of the great arch to be addressed. Whatever possessed its builder, whoever he may have been, to solve the problem of providing his house with new fangled closets in such a prodigious fashion? What was the source of the solution? Who or what inspired it? It is not possible to resist the temptation to speculate that the builder cast his eyes toward activities at Castle Howard and sought the advice of his neighbour's architects. Whoever the builder was he must have known Lord Carlisle: if it was indeed Sir William Strickland, the possibility of advice from that direction is even more likely. In February and March 1724, and September 1725 Vanbrugh wrote three letters to Lord Carlisle in which he speaks of joining with 'Mr Strickland, Mr Frankland and others in persuading my Lord Morpeth to go on' with a 'Bill for Reforming the Streets'.[8] Details of this Paving Bill are obscure, but it appears that Vanbrugh was actively engaged in promoting a parliamentary bill for improving the condition of London streets by having them paved. Whether or not the Bill ever reached the Statute Book is uncertain, and it is possible that Vanbrugh died before the outcome was known. The second of the letters referred to above, dated 26 March 1724, was written six weeks before the death of Sir William Strickland. The 'Mr Strickland' mentioned in it was probably his son. Clearly Vanbrugh was acquainted with the family. Could Vanbrugh have been the originator of the great arch?

If not Vanbrugh, then Hawksmoor must be the alternative, and perhaps more likely, originator. The arch has something of the maverick quality associated with Hawksmoor's work and bears some resemblance to the tall arches framing the outer windows in the Kensington Palace Orangery. The third Baronet's son had followed in his father's footsteps as M.P. for Malton from 1708 to 1715: in 1715, he was brought in by Lord Carlisle as Member for Carlisle, which he represented until 1722, when he was returned for Scarborough, under the patronage of Horace Walpole, Secretary of the Treasury, and brother of Sir Robert. From 1725 to 1727 the fourth Baronet served as a Lord of the Treasury under Lord Carlisle, and from 1727 to 1730 he acted as Treasurer to Queen Charlotte. He was one of those to whom Hawksmoor addressed appeals for help in his efforts to regain his appointment with the Office of Works. On at least one occasion he sought the good offices of Lord Carlisle. In September 1725, he wrote to Carlisle, 'I hope your Lordship will also write to Sir William Strickland, who being one of the Lords of the Treasury, I doubt not will at your Lordship's instance zealously assist me'. The following year he recorded that 'Sir William Strickland is exceeding kind to me,

---

8   *The Complete Works of Sir John Vanbrugh*, iv, *The Letters*, G. Webb (ed.) (London, 1928), pp. 156, 159, 168.

and I have hopes that I may obtain some favour': and finally in May 1726, 'I am extremely obliged for your Lordship's own, and the interest you have made me and in particular for Sir William Strickland, who has treated me with all imaginable goodness and patronage'.[9] Clearly, a climate of mutual goodwill existed between Sir William and Hawksmoor, in which it would not be surprising to discover that architectural works had played their part.

No definitive evidence may ever come to light to show that either Vanbrugh or Hawksmoor carried out work for the Stricklands at York House. It is, however, entirely within the bounds of possibility that one or other of Lord Carlisle's architects could have had a hand in the construction of the giant arch. The puzzle awaits a solution.

9 Downes, *Hawksmoor*, p. 249.

15

The Building Practice of the English Board of Ordnance, 1680-1720

NIGEL BARKER

The Board of Ordnance was the supervising body of the government depart-ment charged with supply of the army, at home and abroad, and with supplies of ammunition to the Navy. It had its origins, like many other departments, including the Office of Works, in the Wardrobe of the medieval monarchs of England and Wales, and its ancestry can be traced back to the reign of Edward I when it was acting as the 'Household Armoury' during his campaigns in Wales. The development of the Ordnance from the Privy Wardrobe based in the Tower of London occurred during the fourteenth century with the appoint-ment of the first Master Keeper of the Ordnance, so that by the Tudor period an embryo Office of Ordnance had evolved. In the later sixteenth century efforts were made to provide proper rules for the running of the department. The Ordnance in 1589 received the Board which it was to keep until the reforms of 1683 which established the pattern of Ordnance activity until the early eighteenth century, when revisions were made during the reorganisation undertaken by the Duke of Marlborough in his capacity as Master General of Ordnance in 1714. This last reorganisation stemmed from the failure of Ordnance credit and the extraordinary demands which were placed on the office at that time. The result was the development of a military establishment within the Ordnance which provided a stable framework for the creation of unprecedented complexes at Woolwich, Chatham, Plymouth, Portsmouth and Berwick.[1]

The Ordnance's responsibility for the manufacture, storage and protection of materials meant that they were one of the three government departments, with the Office of Works and the Admiralty, which had considerable building requirements. The range of commissions was extensive, from vast earthworks

1 I would like to acknowledge the assistance of Richard Hewlings and Geoffrey Parnell who kindly read through this essay and made some useful points. Much of the article was based on the surviving Ordnance records kept in the Public Record Office at Kew. For a more detailed assessment see: N.P. Barker, 'The Architecture of the English Board of Ordnance 1660-1750' (unpublished Ph.D. thesis, University of Reading, 1985).

around such strategically important towns and cities as Portsmouth and Berwick, to routine maintenance at such minor garrisons as Clifford's Tower in York. Allowing for fluctuations and repeated attempts by the Treasury to restrain Ordnance finances, the annual allowance for building was very similar to that of the Office of Works. Rising from approximately £10,000 p.a. in 1660, it reached £30,000 p.a. under James II, and £50,000 under Queen Anne. Whilst the average annual allowance for building remained reasonably constant, the pattern of expenditure varied considerably, partly because the cost of labour and materials fluctuated, despite the efforts of the Ordnance Board to control it, and partly for political reasons. The Board had to plan and allocate its expenditure carefully to obtain the best value for money. It could not afford to have large-scale works in progress at all of its garrisons at the same time.

Money was a perennial problem for the Ordnance, the root of many problems experienced with labourers and craftsmen employed on building projects. The Board became adept at financial juggling and usually built on credit, using its expected income as security in the same way that Parliament funded land purchase by raising tallies with government revenue as security. Thus tallies raised in 1678 on the Hearth Tax paid for the purchase of land required at Portsmouth for fortifications, and were used again in 1680 for the works at Gosport. An alternative, subscription to the South Sea Company, was used in the 1720s to pay for the buildings at Woolwich while the sale of 'dotard' trees and timber from the Crown forests paid for the construction of the army hospital at Portsmouth sponsored by Charles II.

In the period 1680-1714 a standard procedure was established for Ordnance building projects and this was contained in *The Rules, Orders and Instructions for the Government of His Majesty's Office of Ordnance* (1683).[2] These regulations contained a section of common duties for all members of the Board, thus involving all of the principal officers in some responsibility for the building works of the office. Significant by his absence was the Master General who was the link between the 'professional' officers of the Board and the court. Appointed by the monarch as nominal head of the service, his actual involvement in the day-to-day running of the department depended very much on personal inclination. In theory, the post of Master General of the Ordnance was a recognition of military prowess, and indeed many distinguished soldiers were appointed in the eighteenth century, but in practice most remained relatively aloof from administration. The significant exception was John Churchill, Duke of Marlborough, who was Master General in 1702-1712 and again in 1714-1722.

2 PRO, WO 55/1789. These were 'Instructions for the Government of our Office of Ordnance under our Master General thereof, committed to the five Principal Officers vizt. our Lieutenant General, Clerk of Ordnance, Keeper of Stores and Clerk of Deliveries . . .'

The common duties of the Board, outlined in the regulations, can be divided into two sections; the first which established general office procedure for all activities, including buildings and fortifications, and the second, which established office procedure for building and fortification alone. The first, general responsibilities included living in lodgings provided in the Tower of London, and meeting twice a week on Tuesdays and Thursdays at 8.00 a.m., or more often if required. These meetings could take place in the lodgings of a principal officer, in the old Elizabethan office behind the chapel of St Peter ad Vincula or the new office in Coldharbour built in 1672-3. After the completion of the complex at Tower Place in Woolwich the new Board Room could be used. At various times the Board also had access to rooms adjoining the Banqueting House in Whitehall, which were used when Parliament was in session, and they also had use of a house in Downing Street. The Board's major function was to execute all warrants from the Master General, which were in turn the result of information they had compiled and sent to him which indicated what was required to carry out their duties with an estimate of the cost. These lists were produced by the Clerk of Deliveries and the Clerk of Ordnance and were signed by the whole Board. In the case of buildings and fortifications the requirements would often be based on a survey carried out by an engineer who also appended his estimate of the costs, which were then ratified by the Board.

All transactions, including payments for building work, had to be recorded in the Ordnance Treasurer's 'Particular Instruction Book'. The Clerk of the Ordnance and the Surveyor General were also required to keep account, or 'cheque' books. Payment of creditors was also regulated; a bill had to be presented to the office within ten days of completion of the task, there to be signed and 'made up' by the Storekeeper. For those bills relating to buildings and fortifications the deadline of ten days was counted from completion of construction as certified by an engineer or purveyor, the bill then being passed on to the Storekeeper. Once received, the bills were entered into the 'Bill Book', hence their usefulness in dating buildings, and a further ten days was allowed for a 'debenture' or official order for payment to be made out. The whole process was designed to be completed within one month of work being finished and payment was to be 'in due course of the office', i.e. on a rota with the oldest outstanding bills paid first out of whatever money came into the office, unless that money was specifically ordered to be spent elsewhere. In theory this was a fair and efficient system, but because of the irregular supply of funds it often failed in practice and there are numerous petitions in the Ordnance records for payment of long standing debts.

In addition to these general duties there were regulations related specifically to buildings and fortifications, mainly concerning the employment of craftsmen and labourers and the care of materials. The Board was given the responsibility for deciding on the best method of payment for building, by day work or by the yard, and it also appointed the relevant clerk of works to provide detailed daily and weekly accounts to be ratified. Great emphasis was placed on the need to prevent embezzlement, and a separate 'Embezzlement Book' was kept by the Board. Although all of the principal officers were involved in various aspects of Ordnance building projects, three of the six working members of the Board had specific responsibilities outlined in their individual instructions. The Surveyor General was directed to supervise the Chief Engineer, and the engineers below him, and was also responsible for the craftsmen and labourers. He supervised the Clerk of Works and prepared estimates. He had to visit the site during construction and had to certify satisfactory completion of work before the major bills were paid.

The Clerk of Ordnance kept the 'Journal Book' containing all the warrants for supplies as well as all orders, warrants and minutes issued by the Board. He drew up all letters and instructions, commissions and contracts and any other necessary agreements. If any enquiries were made into procedure or precedent he was the officer responsible for finding the answer. The third officer directly involved was the Treasurer who was responsible for financing the works, ensuring all payments were made in the approved manner and recording all such transactions carefully. It is the combination of various ledgers and journals kept by these three officers that provide much of the surviving information on Ordnance buildings, although the records are far from comprehensive.

The link between the Board and the workmen on site was provided by the engineer, reporting to the Chief Engineer. At times the latter, although subordinate to the Surveyor General, was treated as a principal officer; he was after all required to be:

> skilled in all parts of Mathematics, more particularly in Stereomestrie, Altemestrie, and Geodisie to take distance, height, depth, surveys of land measures and solid bodies, and to cut any part of the ground to a proportion. He should be skilled in all manner of foundations, in the scantling of all timber and stone, and of their several natures, and to be perfect in Architecture, civil and military, and to have always by him the descriptions and models of all manner of engines useful in the foundations fortifications or seige.[3]

However, he was not formally admitted onto the Board as a full member until 1714, thereby correcting the previous ambivalent attitude displayed by the Ordnance, which had been a reaction to the dominance of an earlier Chief Engineer, Sir Bernard de Gomme.

The regulations laid out in 1683 were to allow the Office to control building activity from design and planning, through acquisition of land and contracting of men and materials to construction and completion. In the event, they were

3 PRO, WO 55/1789.

used to control the design and construction of large-scale fortifications that were the principal Ordnance building activity during the later seventeenth century. The modest number of buildings erected were largely utilitarian. So strong was the control of the Board that by 1710 a standard design for each building type had evolved and in each case, although external decoration varied, basic features of planning and construction remained constant.[4] Despite this, problems were experienced at every stage of the construction process.

The decision to undertake a project could only be made once the Board had been made aware of a need for it, usually by direct petition from one of the garrison governors or by outside events. General surveys of all sites undertaken in 1660-61 formed the basis for the programme of work over the next two decades, but general surveys were usually too large an undertaking to be carried out with any frequency. However, individual garrisons were inspected by engineers sent by the Board. For instance in 1682 the engineer Martin Beckman was sent to report on the state of the buildings and fortifications at Berwick. He recommended various repairs and, more importantly, suggested the building of a new powder magazine.

Requests from outside the office were not unusual: at Carlisle in 1718/19 the mayor and aldermen of the city petitioned for new barracks; the request was referred to Michael Richards, Surveyor General, with instruction to consider it, prepare plans and estimate the cost. Not all petitions were successful, as the Board could not afford it, and some were attempts by city aldermen or other authorities to get the Ordnance to pay for work that in fact was their responsibility or were claims for expenditure on work not authorised by the Board. The schemes which the Board usually resisted strongly were those put forward by other government departments, notably the Victualling Office and the Admiralty, as funds were not usually provided, leaving the Ordnance to foot the bill. The Admiralty in particular was notorious for non-payment and even resisted paying statutory dues for the Sea Service, i.e. for guns, ammunition and stores provided for its fleets by the Ordnance. The records are peppered with claims and disputes between these two departments at various garrisons. Occasionally there were times when their interests coincided; notably in Admiralty demands for new storehouses and wharves close to their dockyards, which brought improvements for both departments.

---

4 The development of standard designs for the main Ordnance building types – magazines, storehouses and lodgings/barracks – was complete by the end of the seventeenth century. Magazines were usually rectangular, stone, or occasionally brick, with brick barrel-vaulting under a pitched roof. The walls were double-skinned and the floor raised to ensure good ventilation; it was usually buttressed and was ideally surrounded by a fence wall. Storehouses were usually rectangular, with a minimum of internal partitions, with the main stairs centrally placed, often under a cupola. Barracks or lodgings were based on the designs of De Gomme used in the 1660s at Portsmouth. A simple rectangular building with two beds to each room and a partitioned privy at the end. The main development in barrack design was the use of communal stairs rather than the individual spiral stairs used by De Gomme.

Whilst the Ordnance preferred to decide for itself whether any project was necessary, there are some examples of events beyond its control. The Dutch raid on the English fleet in the Medway, for example, resulted in Parliament deciding to refortify the river, ordering a large-scale building programme with new forts at Upnor, Gillingham, Howness and the refortification of Sheerness and Gravesend. Fortunately Parliament also allocated the funds. Similarly, in 1708 the House of Commons petitioned Queen Anne for new defences at Chatham and Portsmouth Dockyards, because of fear of invasion, and money was found for fortifications to be built by the Ordnance.

Once a project was approved in principle, estimates were prepared. This was usually done by an engineer, sometimes working with local officials. The Board routinely commissioned several estimates for any one project and all were checked by both the Surveyor General and Chief Engineer before approval was given and contracts drawn up. The design for new work was usually prepared by Ordnance personnel; before 1683 the majority were carried out by the Chief Engineer, Bernard de Gomme. Alternatively, designs could come from the site engineer or be provided centrally by the Board if an engineer was not considered experienced enough, or if the project was especially important. It was not unknown for people outside the Office to be asked to supply a design. Christopher Wren was offered, and declined, the task of designing the 'mole' at Tangiers; he did, however, accept the commission for the Royal Observatory at Greenwich, which came under Ordnance jurisdiction.

Once estimate and design had been approved, if the land required was not already in crown ownership the site had to be purchased, which could prove very difficult with negotiations lasting several years. In some cases, rather than pay the price asked by private owners for their land, the Board relocated their planned buildings; at Portsmouth they even moved the barracks after the foundations had been begun. Whilst negotiations over land were in progress, contracts were drawn up with the main contractors for the works, although the scale of some projects was such that finding adequate contractors was difficult. At Hull in 1681, Martin Beckman reported to the Board:

> I have made up my estimate for the repair of the South Blockhouse and other necessarys for this year, the particulars of which I have offered to Mr Cattelyn who is the man Mr Watkinson, Mr Baker, Mr Fareside and the Master Gunner have presented to be the ablest man for the undertaking of it, to make his demand, but he did declare he would not meddle with it . . .

and two days later reported:

> I went to Cattelyn again Saturday and he again declined, so sent to one Robert Trollope who hath hitherto been the undertaker of the King's works in these northern parts and has commission from the Ordnance, he built Clifford's Fort, and

is indeed a choice workman and able architect to employ him or Mr Fitch as both are sufficient for the work, but the season shortens so I wish a beginning was made . . .[5]

Unfortunately, the Board rarely had a choice: from 1680 until the early eighteenth century their principal contractors were the Fitch family. The Fitches obtained the lucrative Ordnance contract largely because of a patent granted them by Charles II which appointed John Fitch as 'Workmaster' for building and repair of all forts for his lifetime. The Board complained that such a sweeping patent gave Fitch licence to charge high prices, so most of the contracts with the Fitches, who had proved unreliable, included penalty bonds payable if work fell behind schedule.

The major contractor was expected to supply both skilled and unskilled labour, although the Ordnance also provided men and quite often the bulk of materials. The Ordnance men were usually hired employees and craftsmen already based at the garrison involved. At the larger garrisons outside London, such as Plymouth, Portsmouth, Hull, Berwick and some on the Medway, the Ordnance built up corps of resident craftsmen who maintained the buildings at their home garrison and surrounding bases. This gradually superseded the previous practice of sending the master craftsmen down from the central base in the Tower. On the Scillies and Isle of Wight, special problems were posed because of the scattered nature of the bases, which were small and needed frequent repair but out of range of the nearest large garrison. As the repairs were not usually large enough to warrant the establishment of a permanent workforce on the islands, the Board occasionally employed local craftsmen but more usually sent both men and materials from central stores. This added greatly to the cost, as the Board had to request transport from the Admiralty.

On such large projects as the fortifications at Hull and Portsmouth, the main requirement was for bricklayers and 'scavelmen', or labourers to dig foundations and raise the earthworks. The labourers were placed under the supervision of one or more overseers at the ratio of 60 men to one supervisor. The overseers were under the command of an engineer and were occasionally trainee engineers themselves, or local craftsmen who had been recommended to the controlling site engineer. The choice of site engineer was subject to approval by the Board. The choice of overseer for large projects was particularly important in large projects and one with experience, such as John Duxbury, could be called upon to supervise all the work on a temporary basis in the absence of the site engineer. At smaller garrisons the resident storekeeper

5 Clifford's Fort was built in 1672 to strengthen defences on the River Tyne under the direction of Martin Beckman. The craftsmen were supervised by Robert Trollope, a local 'architect' who was also involved in supervising Ordnance building at Hull. The design, a square redoubt with lower gun platforms facing the river, is old-fashioned; a separate rectangular building of no great distinction served as storerooms or lodgings. Plans of the fort survive in the British Library, King's Top. Collection.

usually filled the post, as he was already conversant with Office procedure and was moreover involved as a supplier of tools for the work.

Ordnance overseers were required to provide weekly progress reports. These would have provided valuable detailed information on procedures and problems but unfortunately only two survive, for work at Hull in 1680-85. Exceptionally, they deal with a project carried out by Commissioners for Fortification, appointed by the Board. This was an added complication, as it meant that an unusually close relationship was required with civic officials at Hull and that conditions were different from a lot of other garrisons. However, the journals provide such an attractive and interesting spectacle of quarrelling officials, rebellious workforces and shifty contractors that they are well worth discussing.[6]

A major programme of fortifications was undertaken at Hull in the 1680s. Designed to protect the city and its river approaches, it was drawn up by Beckman with Duxbury as his chief overseer. The contractors, inevitably, were Thomas and John Fitch, but Beckman also had to work with the Commissioners for Fortification and the aldermen of Hull, who were endeavouring to get the Ordnance to complete most of the town's defences so that they would have to pay as little as possible. Beckman appears to have been at the centre of most disputes. The Board in London was bombarded with claim and counterclaim about the problems and failures besetting the work. Despite his undeniably argumentative nature, Beckman appears to have been both able and intelligent, as well as a master of character defamation. His opinion of the Commissioners is typically expressed: 'These gentlemen as many does, [*sic*] love to make a great noise where one word is not needed and for all their zeal one shall as soon meet a devil on the ramparts as a Commissioner.' He held a similarly contemptuous opinion of the paymaster for the works, Alderman Lambert. When Lambert attempted to get his nephew appointed an overseer Beckman informed the Board that: 'he is a drunken sort and one who has his livelihood only by running about with letters [I refuse to make him] an overseer, and therefore I expect his good word as he has mine . . .'

Beckman also clashed with Fitch, declaring stoutly that he expected nothing but a battle and was ready to strike the first blow. He also had a poor opinion of the workers employed, describing them as: 'rabble members who live merrily and lug and tug one another's ears . . . and if paid on Friday were addicted to become debauched and be absent from the works . . .' At least in this he was in agreement with Fitch who, excusing himself for delays, described the labourers as: 'a dull lazy sort of people which makes me very out of love with them but I will still manage all things with as much expedition as possible . . .'

6 PRO, WO 46/1 and 46/2, journal books for Hull containing letters and instructions concerning the fortifications built in the 1680s.

Beckman and Duxbury were themselves not popular with the workforce. Beckman, a Roman Catholic, was dubbed the 'Pope's unnatural bastard' and he and Duxbury, it was claimed, could scarce go out for fear of being threatened and abused. This was a result of Fitch's having dismissed labourers without payment and Beckman's alleged collusion in cheating the sub-contractors. The problems of labour shortages and disputes merely added to this already contentious situation. In 1681 Fitch wrote:

work goes very well considering the time of year and the Harvest not being in, we have not the number of men in I had expected but in a little time I hope to have hands enough out of all parts since I have made proclamation in several market towns whereby it is not to be doubted but in a very short time I may have 300 men at the graft . . .

The problem of labour shortages at harvest-time affected all of the building undertaken by the Office. Labourers were in great demand by local land-owners and the Ordnance could not, or would not, compete for available men. Engineers were instructed not to pay above specified rates and severe labour shortages were the result. Payment was officially set at 10d. per day for earth wheelers, 1s. for 'rammers' and 6d. per day for boys. At Hull, Alderman Lambert as Paymaster, could make payment only on receipt of a written order signed by the engineer, Beckman, and had to submit weekly accounts. Money was sent in the form of 'imprests', certificates empowering him to spend a specified sum, which would be honoured by the office. For the payment of labourers, an overseer presented the weekly wage bill to the paymaster and together they sat at the pay table on Saturday and paid the men in hard cash, obtained by cashing imprests with customs or other government departments. The payment of labourers took some time, especially as Lambert insisted on having lunch before paying the men. This caused great discontent as the process took six or seven hours, swallowing up large amounts of the workmen's free time.

The working day was from seven in the morning until five at night with no 'half-hours'. Men were hired on a daily basis and only paid for hours worked. This system also added to the problems, since when work was disrupted by bad weather or lack of materials they were not paid. In 1682 Duxbury reported:

the country men are so hard put to it having but 10d. per day and sometimes not getting two days work per week that they are begging in the street for victuals and money to carry them home, and many of them are quite gone, which brings great scandal on these works . . .

To overcome the labour shortages the works were advertised throughout the surrounding countryside, Jeremy Bulkely being paid to go 'into the country to proclaim the works'; some labourers were drawn from up to seven miles away. But, following the problems experienced in 1682, labour was even more difficult to recruit the following year and the Board had to order the major contractors to bring their labourers with them rather than rely on a local supply.

Inevitably attempts were made by labourers to exploit the shortages, by trying to force wages up to 18d. per day in 1681 but the Board refused to pay. It adopted a similarly inflexible attitude when the workforce mutinied in July 1683, directing that: 'whoever offends in that [mutiny] or any other nature is to be discharged without any further punishment and those who refuse to work this harvest shall not be employed at any other time.' The contractors then tried to overcome the problem by employing women. When this was discovered by the Board and an explanation was required they wrote:

> it is harvest time and the employment of women is not forbidden in the instructions and in time of danger we felt it wise to hasten the works and expected thanks not reproof, we will suspend the lessening of wages that you request until we receive further instructions as we advise you that we feel we will lose all of them [labourers] if we do so.

Although the Board did employ women in other capacities, Jane Hill, for example being 'paintress' to the Ordnance, and wives of former contractors who inherited their husband's businesses being given contracts, the use of women as labourers was not allowed at Hull, the Board dismissing the attempted justifications. The only other solution approved was the use of garrison soldiers.

As the Board would not compensate the contractors for time lost during strikes or shortages the pressure on them could be considerable. The building season could not be extended into the winter because of dangers of flooding or frost damage to exposed masonry, so the works were usually covered with a protective layer of earth by October. A token workforce then remained, to protect the works and deter vandals, until the opening of the building season in the spring of the following year. This residual workforce was usually under the supervision of an experienced overseer whilst the site engineer presented the accounts to the Board in London.

Compared with the labour problems, difficulties with materials were less frequent. As most garrisons were on the coast and could be supplied by water, the delivery of heavy building materials was made easier. Most inland garrisons could often be supplied by river, although with greater difficulty. In 1684 the Roach Abbey stone contracted for the work at Hull could not be delivered as drought had made the river too shallow. Seaborne supply was not without its problems. Portland stone contracted for Ordnance work was frequently delayed because of attacks by French ships and the Board had to rely on naval escorts for its transports. There are numerous requests for protection in the records, and when two hoys were actually captured, and a third driven to take refuge in Portland Harbour in 1709, it became absolutely vital that naval protection was provided, as the hoymen refused to travel without it. With supply occasionally difficult, the Board had to be flexible about allowing substitute material. Thus in 1682 when the specified Purbeck stone could not be 'gott for money' the Board allowed 'best Isle of Wight stone' to be substituted with a suitable reduction in the estimate. Another alternative often practised was the reuse of materials from demolished garrison buildings and other obsolete structures. Thus at Berwick in 1717 the castle was plundered for building stone with which to construct the new barracks.

Use of materials was carefully controlled with an eye to value for money. Frequently the site engineer would prepare a report on the estimated price of several types of material from different sources before the Board would negotiate a contract. At Berwick in 1717 there is a particularly well-documented example of this process. A letter was first sent to Captain Phillips, the engineer in 1716/17:

> and to Capt. Phillips with the draughts and estimates of the barracks ordered by His Majesty to be built for the reception of thirty six officers and 600 men amounting to upward of £4,900 (with observations thereupon) for him to inform the board of the prices of several materials requisite, the quantity of them, and the number of workmen that can be produced, so as to report what can be done this year . . .

A further letter to Phillips ordered him to prepare his report on the barracks and to 'consult proper artificers for what price bricks etc. can be had upon the spot, or at Hull, since materials are not be sent from hence [London] . . .' Following a month of negotiation Phillips was sent instructions: 'it is now proposed to contract here for all the timber to be sent directly from Norway to Berwick, and he is to inform the Board what quantity of bricks and tiles he can provide and at what prices'. It took a further month for the Board to decide that slates were not to be used for the roofs but that tiles or pan tiles would be considered.

Assuming that all problems were overcome and that the work was eventually completed, the Board then had to maintain the new buildings and fortifications. All repairs over a fixed sum of £5 had to be estimated for in the same way as the large projects. Repairs were a constant drain on finances, the Board having to cope with cattle grazing on earthworks, ramparts being turned into gardens or kennels and dunghills being created against walls. Soldiers bringing their families into barracks, where they then kept poultry, or cadets damaging fittings and furnishings all occur in Ordnance records; there are even examples of buildings being pulled down and materials being sold off. The Admiralty caused damage to Ordnance wharves by dumping heavy loads of timber on them. All of these problems were in addition to the constant problem of maintaining buildings that were frequently on exposed sites, subject to storms, as well as the occupational hazard of being blown up by careless workmen in powder magazines.

In the period 1680-1714 the Ordnance Board exercised control over construction with increasing confidence having minimised the role of the Chief Engineer. The major problems left to be solved were the contractual system and the virtual monopoly of the Fitches. These were tackled in reforms introduced by Brigadier Michael Richards, Surveyor General, in 1714, under the auspices of the Duke of Marlborough. The reforms separated the military and civil functions of the Ordnance and reflected a new situation, where the buildings of the Office became as important as the fortifications. Indeed, the emphasis switched in the period 1714-20 from fortifications to buildings, with the creation of a number of new complexes at the larger Ordnance outposts. The previous, informal practice of engineers dealing with a main outpost and its surrounding smaller garrisons was formally incorporated into the system with the establishment of the ordnance divisions, based on major garrisons, each having its own divisional engineer and hierarchy of craftsmen, with master craftsmen supervising ordinary, or trainee craftsmen below them. The divisional building estimates were all to be prepared at the same time to be sent annually to the Board to be incorporated into the General Estimate that was presented to Parliament. The divisions were at Plymouth (including Pendennis and St Mawes), Portsmouth (including Gosport, Portsea Bridge, Southsea Castle and the Isle of Wight), the Tower (including Woolwich, the Medway and Thames garrisons, Harwich, Guernsey, Jersey and the Scillies), Hull (including Clifford's Fort, Tynemouth, Chester and Carlisle) and the North Britain Division (including Edinburgh, Stirling, Fort William, and occasionally Berwick when it was not included in the Hull Division). The divisional engineer would prepare designs, or implement those sent by the Board and supervise the body of craftsmen built up within the division. Contractors were to be local with no monopoly possible. A trainee engineer from each division would be sent to study at the drawing office established in the Tower as part of Richards's proposals for streamlining building procedures. Other reforms included simplification of the payment of bills and, significantly, the appointment of an Architect to the Ordnance.

The appointment of Andrews Jelfe as Architect to the Ordnance in 1719 is interesting, particularly since the post was allowed to lapse in the mid 1720s shortly after Marlborough ceased to be Master General. Following apprenticeship to Edward Strong the mason, Jelfe went into partnership with Christopher (Kit) Cass, a mason employed on St Pauls and other major commissions during the later seventeenth and early eighteenth centuries, including Hawksmoor's house, which he built in 1727. In 1715 Jelfe had obtained the post of Clerk of Works at Newmarket and Clerk Itinerant to the Surveyor of the Office of

Works, which he held until 1728. His appointment as Architect and Clerk of Works to the Ordnance is not explained in the minutes, but it is possible that he was recommended by Richards. Previously the Board had not felt it necessary to have an 'Architect' or other officer responsible solely for buildings and this appointment indicates a significant change in attitude. It is a recognition of the importance and unprecedented scale of construction being undertaken by the Ordnance in the period 1714-20.

At Plymouth the decision to extend the old gunwharf at Mount Wise was taken in 1715, the year following the reforms. This was then abandoned in favour of a more ambitious scheme to create a new gunwharf, with Colonel Lilley, Divisional Engineer, instructed to find a site and design the buildings. His scheme for a wharf projecting out into the river with central powder magazine, flanked by two cranes and a cooper's shop to one side and carriage sheds and storehouse behind was standard, as was his design for the storehouse with a central pavilion. However, the final wharf as built on the Hamouze at Morice Yard (Fig. 84) is very different. It was sent by the Board to Lilley, although whence it originated is not clear. The wharf is now sheltered by two half docks curving round at each side and the buildings are placed much more deliberately with the idea of the central powder magazine retained but flanked by both cranes and storehouses on the wharf. The officers' terrace and lodgings are placed up on the hill looking down on the more utilitarian buildings. The arrangement and design of the buildings is of a quality not previously evident in Ordnance work. The unusually elaborate gateway, the great arched panels on the ends of the storehouses and, most intriguingly, the officers' terrace, are entirely foreign to the standard Ordnance building types evolved in the seventeenth century.

An even clearer instance of this new, outside influence may be found at Chatham. Surviving drawings of April 1717 (Fig. 85) of a grand storehouse to replace an older building, show a standard Ordnance design. Surviving bills indicate that this was largely complete by the following year. With its central pavilion and applied decoration, including an anachronistic giant order, the Grand Storehouse was typical of Ordnance storehouse building of the seventeenth century. This may be compared with the New Storehouse at Chatham (Fig. 86) completed in 1720 and, sadly, demolished in 1950. This much more sophisticated and rhythmic elevation, with massive pier buttresses imposing strength and regularity to the long façade, was alien to previous Ordnance design.[7]

Unlike the majority of the large projects carried out in the seventeenth century, these eighteenth-century complexes were mainly buildings rather

7　It should be noted that in the early eighteenth century the Ordnance named the first storehouse 'The Grand Storehouse' and that the building we now call the Grand Storehouse acquired that name later due to its superior size, quality and longevity in comparison to the original.

Fig. 84 The Gunwharf, Morice Yard, Plymouth. (*PRO, W.O., 78/1564*)

than fortifications and, as such, may have required special skills. However, since Jelfe was not employed until 1719 he could not have played a major role in the design of many of the new buildings. His disappearance from Ordnance records in the mid 1720s coincides with the completion of these new projects and, significantly, until the later eighteenth century no schemes of comparable size or importance were carried out by the Ordnance in England.

Although the problems encountered by the Ordnance in its building practice have been explored at some length, it is only by such examination that the effectiveness of the regulations of 1683 and the reforms of 1714 can be ascertained. It must be concluded that despite the many problems encountered, the system as set enabled the Board to complete most building with a reasonable degree of success. The completion of the defensive fortifications around Portsmouth, Chatham and other ports, whilst modest on a European scale, is nevertheless impressive. But the extraordinary buildings erected at several garrisons in the early eighteenth century cannot be said to be representative of Ordnance building. They were not designed by the Ordnance and do not represent the typical Ordnance building types. That the Ordnance for the first time employed an architect whilst they were being constructed is surely of interest, but his relationship to them is unclear. The problems of poor workmanship which dogged Ordnance projects in the late seventeenth century are

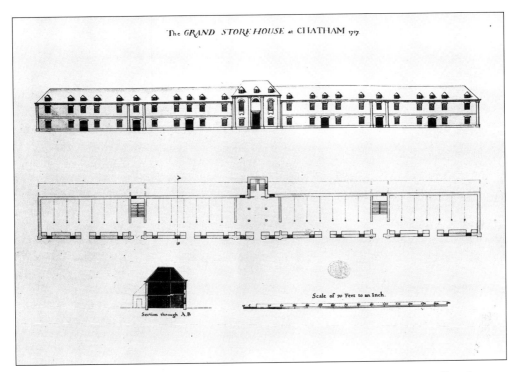

Fig. 85 The Grand Storehouse at Chatham (1717). (*British Library, King's Top. Coll., xvi, 16.42.f*)

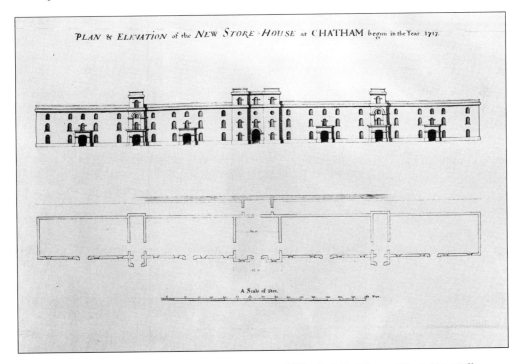

Fig. 86 The New Storehouse at Chatham (begun 1717). (*British Library, King's Top. Coll., xvi, 16.42.g*)

largely attributable to the dominance of the Fitches and the lack of competition for principal contracts because of the sheer size of most projects. In this respect, the first Ordnance regulations and all subsequent pragmatic measures failed to solve the problem which was exacerbated by irregular financing. It was only with the reforms of the early eighteenth century and the formal establishment of the divisional system that the dependence on outside contractors could be reduced and Ordnance building practice could become established in the form it was to retain until the nineteenth century.

16

Hawksmoor's 'Brave Designs for the Police'

RICHARD HEWLINGS

The idea that Vanbrugh designed a group of non-military buildings of the Board of Ordnance which were erected between 1715 and 1724 was first systematically expressed by Laurence Whistler in 1952.[1] He worried at it, but found no written record to support his hypothesis. The appearance of the buildings, however, prevented his idea from going away, and he eventually set out all the evidence, both for and against, in *The Imagination of Sir John Vanbrugh and his Fellow Artists* in 1954.[2] This evidence was only circumstantial, and it favoured Hawksmoor equally. Encouraged by his discovery of Hawksmoor's designs for Ockham, Whistler then published the stylistic evidence in favour of Hawksmoor, separately, in 1955.[3] More detailed evidence of the workings of the Board have subsequently been published by Howard Tomlinson in 1973 and 1979,[4] of the Board's principal seat, at Woolwich, by O.F.G. Hogg in 1963,[5] and of the construction of the Board's buildings in royal dockyards by Jonathan Coad between 1981 and 1989,[6] but none of these authors found evidence to modify Whistler's contentions.

* I am grateful to the Earl of Pembroke for permission to photograph and discuss the drawing in his collection, and to Miss Penelope Rundle, Archivist, Wiltshire Record Office, for making the collection available to me. I have benefited greatly from discussions with my colleague Geoffrey Parnell, who is writing a book on H.M. Tower of London and a dissertation on the Board of Ordnance. Mr Parnell drew my attention to the Guard House, Carriage Store and Office at the Tower, and to the Magazine in Hyde Park, all of which were previously unknown to me, and by showing me his transcriptions of the Board's archive made it possible for me to provide the dating evidence referred to in notes 7-12, 15, 16, 19, 76 and 77.

1 Laurence Whistler, 'Ordnance Vanbrugh', *Architectural Review*, cxii (December 1952), pp. 377-83.

2 Laurence Whistler, *The Imagination of Sir John Vanbrugh and his Fellow Artists* (London, 1954), pp. 212-26.

3 Laurence Whistler, 'Hawksmoor and the Ordnance', *Architectural Review*, cxviii (October 1955), pp. 237-39.

4 Howard Tomlinson, 'The Ordnance Office and the King's Forts, 1660-1714', *Architectural History*, xvi (1973), pp. 5-25. H.C. Tomlinson, *Guns and Gunmen* (London, 1979).

5 O.F.G. Hogg, *The Royal Arsenal: Its Background, Origin and Subsequent History*, 1 (London, 1963).

6 Jonathan G. Coad, 'Historic Architecture of H.M. Naval Base, Portsmouth, 1700-1850', *Mariner's Mirror*, lxvii, 1 (1981); idem, 'Historic Architecture of Chatham Dockyard, 1700-1850', *Mariner's Mirror*, lxviii, 2 (1982); idem, 'Historic Architecture of H.M. Naval Base, Devonport, 1689-1850', *Mariner's Mirror*, lxix, 4 (1983); idem, *Historic Architecture of the Royal Navy* (London, 1983); idem, *The Royal Dockyards, 1690-1850* (Aldershot, 1989).

Laurence Whistler found no record of designs furnished by any one individual – neither a payment, nor a Board minute recording the presentation of draughts, nor an out letter instructing someone to prepare them. In the course of searching for such a record he identified the Ordnance engineers who managed individual works and some of the contractors who carried them out; but none was recorded as a designer of these works, any more than Vanbrugh was. Few of them were designers at all, and none of them is known to have designed in the same style as Vanbrugh. Furthermore, although each engineer or contractor was responsible for one or two of the Board's buildings in no more than one locality, all the Board's buildings from Berwick to Plymouth have the same idiosyncratic style in common. The only designer identified by Whistler whose activities may have been common to all the Board's works was the well-known masonry contractor (and occasional architect) Andrews Jelfe, appointed Architect to the Board in 1719. Whistler discounted Jelfe's contribution to the design of these buildings as Jelfe's appointment was only made in January 1719, by which time all but those at Plymouth were under construction. This has to be modified in view of Geoffrey Parnell's discovery that Jelfe was casually employed in the Drawing Office of the Board from as early as July 1716, before his permanent establishment.[7] Nonetheless there is no record that Jelfe furnished these particular designs, and Jelfe lacks the stylistic candidature which distinguishes Vanbrugh or Hawksmoor.

Whistler noticed three connections between Vanbrugh and the Board apart from style. First, its Master-General (the senior officer) was the Duke of Marlborough, who might have been expected to exercise judgement in favour of an architect whom he had privately employed, in choosing an architect for the Board's first prestige buildings. Secondly, the Surveyor-General (the officer responsible for the Board's buildings, who 'presented the draughts' to it)[8] was Brigadier-General Michael Richards, who lived near Vanbrugh in Blackheath, and who acted as an intermediary between him and the Duchess of Marlborough in 1716. Thirdly, outstanding among the surviving drawings of the Ordnance cadets done in the 1780s is a drawing of the Temple of Bacchus at Stowe, designed by Vanbrugh; Whistler interpreted this as an exercise in draughtsmanship on the part of the cadets, copying an original drawing in the office collection. The Stowe drawing had inadvertently joined this collection, he suggested, because it had once been among other drawings of Vanbrugh.

Whistler also made an equally circumstantial case for Hawksmoor. Hawksmoor had the same connections with Marlborough as Vanbrugh; but, unlike Vanbrugh, who was dismissed from Blenheim in 1716, Hawksmoor maintained his. Hawksmoor also had relations with Brigadier-General Richards, which are more precisely known than those of mere neighbourly proximity:

7 PRO, WO 51/101, fo. 3.   1718, PRO, WO 47/31.
8 For example, those for Woolwich on 7 March

it was in Richards' house that Hawksmoor and the Duchess of Marlborough met and were reconciled in 1716. Thirdly, Vanbrugh wrote thus in praise of Hawksmoor in 1721:

> What wu'd Monsr Colbert in France have given for Such a Man? I don't Speak as to his Architecture alone, but the Aids he cou'd have given him in almost all his brave designs for the Police.

The buildings which Whistler was discussing were certainly Architecture, and thus presumably not those to which Vanbrugh referred; instead it appears that he was writing of military engineering. Whatever he meant, it is certain from this statement that Hawksmoor provided designs of some kind for the military (the 'Police'). On balance, Whistler's 1954 speculation on the identity of the designer of these buildings slightly favoured Hawksmoor, although appearing in a book on Vanbrugh.

The buildings which had aroused Laurence Whistler's interest were in the Royal Arsenal at Woolwich, in the naval dockyards at Chatham, Portsmouth and Plymouth, and at Berwick-upon-Tweed. There are other Ordnance buildings of these years displaying similar features, which were perhaps unknown to him. They are the Magazine at Tilbury Fort (begun in 1716),[9] the Guard House, Carriage Store and Office at the Tower of London (all three begun in 1717),[10] the Barracks and Storehouse at Upnor Castle (begun in 1718),[11] the Magazine in Hyde Park (begun *c*. 1718),[12] the Governor's House at Berwick (begun in 1719)[13] and the Master Gunner's House at Carlisle Castle (complete by 1725).[14] At the Tower of London the Board also altered the windows of the White Tower in 1715-16,[15] giving them round arches with broad unmoulded Portland stone architraves. It has sometimes been suggested that this work (occasionally attributed to Wren, perhaps on the incorrect presumption that it was the responsibility of the Office of Works) was intended to look Romanesque, to complement the style of the great fortress. Yet in 1718 identical

9 A.D. Saunders, *Tilbury Fort, Essex*, (London, 1980), pp. 11 and 26. BL, K.Top., xiii, fo. 57e; PRO, WO 51/102, fo. 84.

10 BL, K.Top, xxiv, fo. 23. PRO, WO 47/29, fo. 104; 30, fos. 108, 128; 31, fo. 13.

11 For the Barracks see A.D. Saunders, *Upnor Castle, Kent* (London, 1967), p. 16; British Library, K.Top, xviii, fo. 58c; and PRO, WO 51/102, fo. 68. For the Storehouse see British Library, K.Top., xviii, fo. 58d.

12 PRO, WO 44/299.

13 John Cornforth, 'Opportunities for History: Berwick upon Tweed, Northumberland – II' *Country Life*, clxvii (17 April 1980), p. 1200, and fig. 6. PRO, WO 47/31, fo. 92; 32, fos. 173, 250, 289.

14 M.R. McCarthy, H.R.T. Summerson and R.G. Annis, *Carlisle Castle* (London, 1990), pp. 115-16, 239-40. British Library, K.Top., x, fos. 14-15.

15 PRO, WO 47/20A, fo. 78.

windows were provided for the Middle Tower,[16] built by Edward I in 1278-79,[17] and, if a complementary appearance had been intended, these would have been Gothic, just as Wren's St Mary Aldermary was, or Hawksmoor's All Souls College. Concordance with the style of the host buildings does not therefore explain these windows.

The White and Middle Towers were not the only medieval military buildings to be given windows of this design. At Westminster, the Jewel Tower was given similar windows two years later, beginning in September 1717. The officials of the Board of Ordnance were then housed within sight of the Jewel Tower and could not have avoided watching the works.[18] Yet it was not their responsibility, for the Palace of Westminster was maintained by the Office of Works, and the official responsible for the works at the Jewel Tower in 1717 was the Clerk of Works for Westminster, Nicholas Hawksmoor. The windows can therefore be no better explained as the house style of one discrete branch of government.

The elusive common element could be the architect. Hawksmoor, the Works officer responsible at Westminster, had no responsibility to the Ordnance, and that Board's papers do not mention him. It was Brigadier-General Richards, the Surveyor General, whom the Board of Ordnance instructed, on 8 March 1715 to 'give directions for making what Lights may be Necessary to the Rooms in the White Tower'.[19] Richards, formerly Chief Engineer, was promoted to Surveyor General on 19 November 1714,[20] by Marlborough, who had himself been appointed Master General on 4 October.[21] Richards died on 5 February 1721,[22] and Marlborough on 16 June 1722.[23] All the buildings under discussion were begun within this period, and indeed all were completed save those at Plymouth, which, although designed by 1718, were begun in 1722 and occupied in 1724.[24] The chronological coincidence strongly indicates Richards's responsibility and Marlborough's support. However, Richards need not have presented his own design. The Tower, in particular, was a building for which he might have been encouraged to have presented designs by either of his friends Vanbrugh or Hawksmoor, since its Constable, whose wishes the Board

16 PRO, WO 51/105, fo. 63.
17 H.M. Colvin (ed.), *History of the King's Works*, ii, (London, 1963), p. 721.
18 Ibid., v (London, 1976), pp. 409-11; O.C. Williams, *The Topography of the Old House of Commons*, (London, 1953), p. 12.
19 PRO, WO 47/20A, fo. 78.

20 *Dictionary of National Biography*, xvi, p. 1103. Tomlinson, *Guns and Gunmen*, gives 2 December as the date of his appointment.
21 Ibid., p. 223.
22 *Dictionary of National Biography*, xvi, p. 1103.
23 Ibid., iv, p. 338.
24 Coad, *The Royal Dockyards*, pp. 250-51.

would doubtless have had to respect, was a long-standing patron of them both, the Earl of Carlisle.[25]

For another of these buildings there is a drawing which is demonstrably by Hawksmoor. This drawing, from the collection of the Earl of Pembroke at Wilton, is entitled *'Apud Bervicences'*, and endorsed 'Barraks at Berwick May 20 1717' (Fig. 87).[26] It is not signed, but Hawksmoor's authorship can be demonstrated by the architecture, the draughtsmanship, the handwriting and the annotations. First, its architectural style appears to be his. In general terms it is apparently deliberately unharmonious. The main range is sub-divided into a short block and a long block, whose relationship is made as abrupt as possible: the link between them has a flat roof at a lower level, which, rather than graduating the transition, abruptly emphasises it.[27] The entrances to the officers' quarters, presumably the most important in the building, are located in these links, not in a location made conspicuous by its projection, but in a corner, shrinking back from the visitor, a part of the building which appears to owe its existence only to expedience. Such a location ignores the Aristotelian idea of *decorum*. So do the most prominent windows of the buildings, which light the least important rooms, in the third storey and garret.[28] The two elevations which the drawing illustrates were intended to sport no fewer than ten different window types, without any harmonic consistency or graduated progression to one superior type.[29] The plat bands which are continued around the projecting porches at the upper level are broken by them at the lower level. Deliberate inconsistency appears to be an aesthetic objective.

The drawing illustrates several features which Hawksmoor used elsewhere. They include egg-shaped urns (apparently smoking),[30] a raised panel with lugs below it,[31] rusticated quoins of an unusual length,[32] and open segmental

---

25 G[eorge] E[dward] C[ockayne], *The Complete Peerage*, iii (London, 1913), p. 35.

26 Wiltshire Record Office, Wilton Estate Records (2057), F6/27.

27 Hawksmoor separated the towers from the naves of St Alfege, Greenwich, and St Anne, Limehouse in a similar manner.

28 Hawksmoor placed the most important windows on the top floor of the east front of the Queen Anne Block at Greenwich, and in Proposition IV for The Queen's College, Oxford.

29 Few elevations with so many window types can be found after *c.* 1680 except in Hawks-

moor's work; the north front of Easton Neston, for instance, has eight.

30 Hawksmoor designed egg-shaped urns for Kensington Palace, Castle Howard, The Queen's College chapel, and All Souls College (in two different proposals).

31 Hawksmoor designed similar panels for King's College Provost's Lodge, and for the 'first' and 'third' projects for Greenwich.

32 Rusticated quoins are obviously not unusual, but the length of these can only be equalled by those Hawksmoor designed at St Anne, Limehouse, or those framing the niches on the side walls of St Mary Woolnoth.

pediments, only one bay wide, supported on consoles, and framing a round-arched window.[33]

Hawksmoor's contemporaries may have used some of these features also. But readers of Kerry Downes's books will inevitably notice that the drawing illustrates features used both by Hawksmoor and Vanbrugh, but by few others. These include the pyramidal roof of the entrance gate,[34] the machicolated cornice which runs around gate and guardhouse,[35] and the latter's cylindrical stacks.[36]

But the stacks in the barrack ranges, cruciform in the lower stages, square or rectangular above, cannot be found among Vanbrugh's designs.[37] The arched windows set in sunk oblong panels are particularly characteristic of Hawksmoor alone,[38] and so is the carriage arch set in a similar panel.[39] The semicircular lunettes, which were later (and with the addition of mullions) to be much used by Lord Burlington, were unique to Hawksmoor in 1717.[40] The imposts of the arched windows, a feature much used by Hawksmoor,[41] are

33 Hawksmoor designed open pediments for Christ's Hospital Writing School, All Souls College, The Queen's College Proposition IV, St George's, Bloomsbury, and in the 'first' and 'third' projects for Greenwich. He designed segmental pediments on the west front of the King William Block at Greenwich and in the proposal for the west front of Windsor Castle. It is the particular combination of these features over one bay, with the consoles and the round-arched window which is unusual; Hawksmoor used it on the Kitchen Court towers at Blenheim, and over the doors in the flanking walls in one of the garden front designs for Worcester College.

34 Vanbrugh designed pyramids over gates at Castle Howard (the Pyramid Gate), Eastbury (in both square and octagonal-planned forms) and the Nunnery at Greenwich. Hawksmoor designed two pyramidal roofs in the first design for St Anne, Limehouse, built a form of pyramid as the spire of St George, Bloomsbury, and built a real pyramid in the Pretty Wood at Castle Howard.

35 Vanbrugh designed machicolated cornices for Claremont, Vanbrugh Castle and the Nunnery at Greenwich. Hawksmoor designed one for the internal elevation of the street range of All Souls College, although in the event he used a more decorative cusped version, on the tower. On a larger scale, the round-arch-on-corbel element of which the machicolations are composed was used by Hawksmoor internally at St Alfege, Greenwich, and in the tower of the Long Library at Blenheim. In the form proposed by this drawing it occurred also on the water tower at Kensington, attributed to Joynes, but probably Hawksmoor's idea.

36 Vanbrugh designed cylindrical stacks at Grimsthorpe and at Seaton Delaval (at least in the *Vitruvius Britannicus* illustration). Hawksmoor designed cylindrical Roman altars as finials for The Queen's College Proposal IV and the tower of St George in the East, at the top of the east perron of St Alfege, Greenwich, at the top of the garden pedestal at Castle Howard, and as a statue pedestal surmounting the spire of St George, Bloomsbury.

37 Hawksmoor designed a cruciform lower stage to the cylindrical garden pedestal at Castle Howard.

38 Hawksmoor designed arched windows in sunk oblong panels for the Clarendon Building, The Queen's College chapel, All Souls College, Christ Church, Spitalfields and one of the models for King's College, Cambridge.

39 Hawksmoor designed carriage arches set in sunk oblong panels for the North Gate at Blenheim, and the west gate of All Souls College.

40 Hawksmoor designed semi-circular lunettes for the Clarendon Building, The Queen's College chapel, King's College, Cambridge (both in the model and the drawn design), Greenwich Hospital (both in the 'first' and 'third' projects), St George in the East, St Anne Limehouse, St Mary Woolnoth, Christ Church, Spitalfields (at both east and west ends) and Worcester College.

41 Hawksmoor designed imposts both moulded and plain. The former include those at Blenheim, in the design for the north lodging at All Souls College, in the design for St Paul's Cathedral Baptistery, in both the circular and square-planned designs for the Radcliffe Library, in the design for the steeple of St

illustrated by this drawing in an unusual variant form: on the arched doors a second pair of imposts repeats at a lower level those in the conventional position. This feature is certainly peculiar to Hawksmoor among his British contemporaries; indeed he only used it in two other designs.[42]

The drawing also illustrates features for which exact comparisons with Hawksmoor's work cannot be found. Conspicuous among these is the gable end, crow-stepped with scrolled flourishes at the bottom. Hawksmoor inevitably designed scrolls,[43] as did most of his contemporaries. But he did not design crow-stepped gables elsewhere, although he was undoubtedly interested in stepped features.[44] Nor is it possible to find among Hawksmoor's designs similar gablets over the semi-circular lunettes. Few pen strokes, however, are required to transform these gablets into the open pediments which he frequently designed,[45] sometimes in conjunction with semi-circular lunettes,[46] or into the Gothick gablets which he designed at least once.[47] Although Hawksmoor designed large and distinctive brackets in many cornices, he did not design eaves with prominent rafter ends like those illustrated on the end blocks of the barrack ranges. But the drawing has an explanatory note, reading 'All Gutters are Avoyded, because of ye Snow, and Only an Eves projecting 18

Giles in the Fields, in the Queen Anne Court at Greenwich, at Christ Church, Spitalfields, St George, Bloomsbury and St Mary Woolnoth. The latter include those in the Stable Court at St James's Palace, at St Anne Limehouse, in the square-planned designs for the Radcliffe Library, and in the proposal for Worcester College.

42 At St George in the East, and on a proposal for lodges to flank the North Gate at Blenheim.

43 Hawksmoor designed scrolls for the Hensington Gates to Blenheim, for instance, or the west entrance proposal for All Souls, but scrolls like those, with the inward-spiralling volute at the bottom, were common ornament of the day. Scrolls with the bottom volute spiralling outward, as in this drawing, were common in the sixteenth century, but uncommon in 1717. Vanbrugh designed some scrolls like this on a drawing for the forecourt wings at Blenheim. So did Hawksmoor, on a drawing for the base of his proposed steeple for St Giles in the Fields. The scrolls in the drawing appear surprising because they flank a feature which is otherwise so rectilinear. Vanbrugh used scrolls in comparable positions at Kings Weston, and Hawksmoor did the same on the Kensington Orangery and The Queen's College entrance gate.

44 Hawksmoor designed stepped domes for the Radcliffe Library, the 'first' and 'third'

designs for Greenwich Chapel, the Castle Howard Belvedere design, and the Castle Howard Mausoleum. The kitchen court towers at Blenheim also terminate in stepped features. The rusticated masonry framing the south door in a proposal for St Mary Woolnoth is not surmounted by a single flat course, but by progressively diminishing courses, to give a stepped effect. The steeple of St George, Bloomsbury diminishes in steps, each step marked by a projecting course comparable to a tread end. The coping of the crow steps illustrated in the Berwick drawing is partly continued under the succeeding step in a manner also comparable to tread ends. One of Hawksmoor's sketches for St George in the East illustrates what may have been a proposed crow-stepped gable, combining features both of St George, Bloomsbury and of the Berwick drawing: the steps have vertical risers (as at Berwick, but unlike the raked risers at St George), and the tread ends are continued across the full width (as at St George, but unlike the discontinued tread ends at Berwick).

45 Hawksmoor's open pediments are noted in note 33, above.

46 Hawksmoor designed open pediments framing semi-circular lunettes in both the 'first' and 'third' Greenwich proposals.

47 Hawksmoor designed a pointed gablet with Gothick ornament at All Souls College.

inches on ye Ends of ye Rafters'. The note implies that the exceptional climate engendered an exceptional feature.

The style of the draughtsmanship is also Hawksmoor's. Characteristic of Hawksmoor are the smoking chimneys, whose smoke is indicated by two curved pen strokes on its under side and a splash of thin wash,[48] the indication of carving by a freehand line of bubbles,[49] the simultaneous representation of the building in elevation and in perspective (the guardhouse and arch),[50] the vigorous and confident hatching, although hatching itself is obviously not peculiar to him,[51] and the inconsistency by which some windows are shown shaded and others are not.[52]

The handwriting is also Hawksmoor's. The especially individual forms of some of the letters are also found on other Hawksmoor manuscripts. The *I* of *Infirmery* and *Inches*, and the *S* of *Steps* can be found on the sketch for an obelisk proposed at Blenheim, and on the drawing for the west end of the garden front at Castle Howard. The *E* of *Ends* can be found on the Blenheim obelisk sketch and on the St Paul's Baptistery proposal. The *B* of *Bervicences* can be found in Hawksmoor's drawing of the office pavilion at Castle Howard. The terminal *k* of *Berwick* can be found in his drawing of the office yard. The *A* of *Apud* can be found in a letter explaining the design of the obelisk at Ripon.[53] The less individual letters do not conflict with Hawksmoor's regular usage of these letters in other manuscripts.

Finally the Latin title (*Apud Bervicences*) is consistent with Hawksmoor's use of Latin titles on his drawing of the Monument (*Columna Londinensis*), the Radcliffe Camera proposal (*Pinacetheca Radcliffiana*), the Oxford town proposal (*Regio prima . . .* , with *Forum Civitatis, Elaborator[ium], Domus Architypograph-[hici]*, and *Pausilyp*), the Greenwich proposals (with a *Via Regia* and *Pausilippo*), the Cambridge town proposal (with a *Vallum, forum, basilica* and *Pety Cury ampliat*), and on the drawing for the north lodging at All Souls (in which the scale is marked in *Pedes Ang*). The use of Latin titles generally, and for as inappropriate a building as utilitarian modern accommodation on the Scottish border in particular, is consistent with Hawksmoor's enthusiasm for Roman civilisation.

48 Hawksmoor represented smoke in this way on a drawing of an unidentified country house (Christie's, Lot 42, 19 December 1989), and with hatching instead of wash on a drawing of the kitchen block at Ockham.

49 This notation can be seen on Hawksmoor's drawings of the west end of the garden front of Castle Howard, All Souls College, St Paul's Baptistery, the Radcliffe Library, and St George in the East.

50 This idiosyncrasy can be seen on Hawksmoor's drawings for the hall at Blenheim, St Anne Limehouse and the Belvedere at Castle Howard.

51 Hawksmoor only used hatching on sketches; for example, on sketches for St George in the East, and for an unidentified palace, illustrated in Kerry Downes, *Hawksmoor* (London, 1969), ill. 138.

52 Hawksmoor's unidentified palace design also has this inconsistency.

53 Leeds Archive Department, Vyner MS 5742 (245/3).

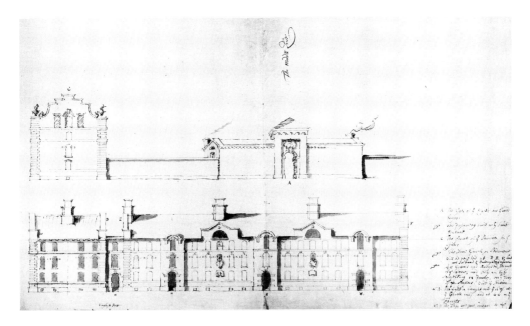

Fig. 87 Sketch proposal for Ravensdowne Barracks, Berwick-upon-Tweed (1717), drawing attributed to Nicholas Hawksmoor. (*Earl of Pembroke Collection, Wiltshire Record Office*)

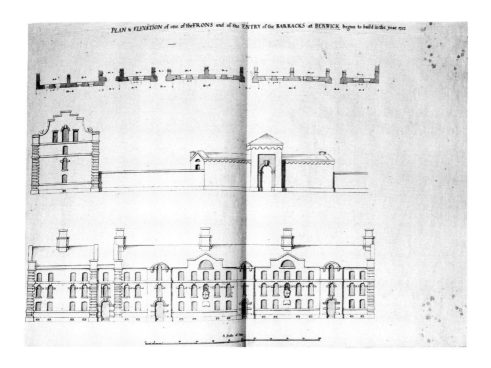

Fig. 88 Proposal for Ravensdowne Barracks, Berwick-upon-Tweed (*c.* 1717), drawing attributed to the staff of the drawing office, Board of Ordnance. (*British Library*)

Fig. 89 Thomas Phillips, Ravensdowne Barracks, Berwick-upon-Tweed (1717-20), after a proposal attributed to Nicholas Hawksmoor.

The drawing has enough inconsistencies to indicate that it is a sketch, albeit a dimensioned sketch. The use of both perspectival and elevational representation and the random shading of windows have already been mentioned. The hatching is also inconsistent. It is used to indicate recession on the roof, the pyramid, the left-hand side of the left-hand stack, and the right-hand part of the arch. Elsewhere it is used to indicate shade, for example, to the right of the stacks, below some eaves, in the windows of the gable end and in the lunette. Its precision is also inconsistent. It is scaled, partly ruled (on the right-hand side), and some of the arches (chiefly on the right) are drawn by compass. Elsewhere it is sketched; and the quoins on the left, the plinth of the wall, most chimneys, most arches, and the panel with the royal cypher are sketched most rapidly.

There is a version of the Wilton drawing among the King's Topographical Collection in the British Library (Fig. 88).[54] This drawing does not display any of Hawksmoor's characteristic draughtsmanship,[55] is apparently not a

54 BL, K.Top, xxxii, fo. 47h.
55 It does not have the smoke, the rendering of carved ornament, nor the loosely applied wash characteristic of Hawksmoor. It retains one inconsistency found in the sketch, namely its representation of the building both in perspective and in elevation, the different types of representation being applied to the same parts of the building in both drawings. Hawksmoor's finished drawings do not have the inconsistencies of his sketches, and thus substitution of ruled for hand-drawn lines, regularly shaded windows and the elimination of hatching, might not be incompatible

sketch,[56] and thus logically post-dates Hawksmoor's drawing.[57] It was presumably made by the Board of Ordnance drawing office as a finished version of the latter.

The barracks were not executed exactly as either drawing proposed. The gatehouse was built to an alternative design, for which another sketch, dated February 1719, survives in the King's Topographical Collection.[58] It is difficult to establish the authorship of this drawing. It does not share the buttoned up, unconfident, draughtsmanship of the Ordnance drawings. The handwriting is not Hawksmoor's but it could be Jelfe's,[59] who was involved at Berwick by March 1719, when he was instructed to alter the draught by adding the King's arms to 'the Gateway in the Fence wall of the Barrack'.[60] The architectural style, however, is compatible with Hawksmoor's.[61]

In execution some of the more distinctive features of the rest of Hawksmoor's drawing were omitted (Fig. 89). These include the break in the roof line between the blocks, the bracketed eaves, the cruciform stacks, the arched first floor windows set in recessed panels, some of the segment-headed windows on the ground floor, the doors with second (lower) impost blocks, the segmental pediments on brackets, the gablets, the lunettes, the carved cartouches on the side blocks, the scrolls and flaming urns on the end gables. But the general arrangement follows Hawksmoor's drawing, both in plan and elevation, and some of his distinctive detailing was retained – for example, the round-arched windows with unmoulded architraves, the elongated quoins and (most distinctive of all) the crow-stepped gables, reduced from Hawksmoor's three steps to two. Nor does the gatehouse exactly follow the drawing of 1719. Its buttresses

with Hawksmoor's authorship of this drawing also. But the inconsistency which does survive is not found among Hawksmoor's finished drawings, so this drawing is therefore unlikely to be his.

56 It is consistently ruled throughout, the windows are consistently shaded and there is no hatching, and thus no opportunity for hatching to represent more than one thing.

57 It is not dated. On May 21, the day after Hawksmoor signed his drawings, Brigadier Groves, Governor of Berwick 'attended and represented the Board that . . . the Barracks . . . might be more commodiously Built on the King's own Ground by the Town Wall', where it was eventually built [PRO, WO 47/30, fo. 138]. It is unlikely that the finished drawing would have been available before the site was chosen, so it may be later than Hawksmoor's sketch. It is possible that the Hawksmoor drawing is a copy of the Ordnance drawing, but unlikely. It is unlikely that Hawksmoor would reproduce its representational solecism, which stands out more clearly

in the finished drawing, partly by virtue of being the only solecism. It is still more unlikely that Hawksmoor would find himself copying architectural features characteristic of his own work, which in this case had been conceived by an anonymous Board of Ordnance draughtsman. It is particularly unlikely that his sketched copy would be to scale. Dimensioned sketches are usually first draughts. It is therefore more likely that the Ordnance drawing was copied from the Hawksmoor sketch.

58 BL, K.Top, xxxii, fo. 47i.

59 BL, Add. MS 27587, is Jelfe's letter-book.

60 PRO, WO 47/32, fo. 91, 6 March 1719.

61 Both the raised central part and the clustered buttresses each side are found on a Hawksmoor proposal for the north gate of Blenheim, and the grouping of buttresses is found on the Carrmire Gate at Castle Howard. The fluted frieze of the outer buttresses was used by Hawksmoor round the Kitchen Court towers at Blenheim, and on the pilasters of the tower of St Alfege, Greenwich.

are not channelled, the flanking buttresses do not have fluted friezes, the upper part has a simplified cornice, and the rear omits the sunk panel, triple keystone and imposts.

The Berwick buildings cannot therefore have inspired the use of the more distinctive features of Hawksmoor's design on other Ordnance buildings. Yet these features were used, and it is their use which gave the contemporary Ordnance buildings the character which Laurence Whistler was to identify. The most distinctive is the gablet with a semi-circular lunette. This feature was used on the central house of the Ordnance officers' houses at Morice Yard, Plymouth. With *serlianas* instead of semi-circular lunettes, gablets were used on the Ordnance Storekeeper's and Clerk's houses at Portsmouth. In the less distinctive form of the Guardhouse at Berwick, on an end elevation (where the gablet is an actual gable end), the semi-circular lunette was used on the Ordnance Carriage House at Portsmouth and on the Barracks at Upnor. A similar combination, not of semi-circular lunette and gablet, but of semi-circular arch and gablet, equally distinctive and doubtless similarly inspired, was used for the south entrance of the Grand Square at Woolwich. This form is close to the open pediment with an arch below, used in the frontispiece of the Royal Military Academy at Woolwich. The one-bay open pediment on block brackets was used on the Master Gunner's House at Carlisle. The distinctive cruciform stacks were used on the Ordnance Storekeeper's and Clerk's houses at Portsmouth, and, in a variant form, on the Royal Military Academy at Woolwich. The cylindrical stacks were used in the upper part of the latter, and, as ornaments alone, at the four corners of the Ordnance Carriage House at Portsmouth and on the buttresses of the River Gate at Woolwich. The Carriage House and the Landport Gate at Portsmouth have flaming grenades for finials, similar to the flaming urns of the Berwick drawing. Machicolation ornaments the piers flanking the south entrance to Grand Square at Woolwich and the central towers of the Ordnance Storehouse at Chatham. Impost-like blocks, used not in the position of an impost, but lower, were used on the River Gate at Woolwich and on the doors in the end elevations of the Ordnance Carriage House at Portsmouth. Porches with internal steps were built in the Ordnance Storekeeper's and Clerk's houses at Portsmouth. Porches breaking forward and carried upwards beyond the eaves line were used on the Ordnance Storehouse at Chatham. A break in the continuity of the roof occurs in the Ordnance officers' houses at Morice Yard, Plymouth. Lugged aprons were used on the storehouses in Morice Yard. An arch set in a panel (though itself a basket-arched panel) was used at the River Gate, Woolwich.

The use of these features, unrealised at Berwick, indicates one of three possibilities. The least likely is that some were copied from other Hawksmoor buildings. It is the least likely because others among them were not. For instance, the Ordnance officers' houses and the Ordnance storehouses at Morice Yard, Plymouth, are ornamented with crow-stepped gables. These may have been copied, either from the drawing for Berwick or from the barracks as realised, but there is no other building by Hawksmoor from which they could have been copied, and it seems unlikely that his sketch for St George in the East (in which he made his only other known use of the feature) was available to the Board's staff. The second possibility is that other Hawksmoor drawings which included these features were made for these other Ordnance buildings and no longer survive. This hypothesis is sustained by the occurrence of features commonly used by Hawksmoor, although not on the Berwick sketch, among other buildings of the Board of Ordnance. They include *serlianas* in the Royal Military Academy, Woolwich, in the Carriage House, and the Storekeeper's and Clerk's houses at Portsmouth.[62] They include blind attics above the frieze at the Woolwich Academy, in a stepped form on the Storehouse at Upnor, and attics with arches set in them in the Officers' terrace at Plymouth.[63] They include *oculi* with plain architraves at Woolwich Academy, the Carriage House at Portsmouth, the Hyde Park magazine and the Great Storehouse at Chatham.[64] They include pilaster strips without capitals on the Storekeeper's and Clerk's houses at Portsmouth, on the Storehouse at Upnor, on the Officers' terrace at Plymouth, on the Carriage House at Portsmouth, on the Governor's House at Berwick, on the Hyde Park magazine and on the magazine *enceinte* at Tilbury.[65] The third possibility is that the Berwick drawing served as a quarry for all the Board's designs during these years. If the latter is the case, its discovery provides evidence of the authorship not of one, but of twenty-nine previously unattributed designs.

The influence of the drawing, or of Hawksmoor, whichever may be the case, was quite circumscribed, however. After the completion of Morice Yard at Plymouth in 1724, to a design first considered in 1718 and certainly fully worked out by 1720, the Ordnance Board virtually ceased to erect buildings in the Hawksmoor style. The conspicuous exception is at Berwick. Hawksmoor's drawing illustrates the entrance range, on the north, and one of two flanking ranges. The fourth (south) side of the quadrangle was filled by a magazine, known only from plans of 1717[66] and 1725,[67] and from Macky's reference to it

62 *Serlianas*, at that date still a novelty for Burlington and Campbell, were used by Hawksmoor in proposals for All Souls, Brasenose and Worcester Colleges at Oxford, at Christ Church, Spitalfields, at Ockham and in the proposal for a belvedere at Castle Howard.

63 Hawksmoor used similar blind attics on Kensington Palace and Kensington Orangery, and an arrangement similar to the Plymouth one in the kitchen block of Ockham.

64 Hawksmoor used similar *oculi* in the design for Easton Neston published in *Vitruvius Britannicus*, at St George in the East, St Luke Old Street, but most of all at Christ Church,

Spitalfields.

65 Hawksmoor used such pilaster strips at Christ's Hospital Writing School, Kensington Palace, the east front of the King William Block at Greenwich, one model for the Fellows' Building at King's College, Cambridge, one proposal for the Radcliffe Library, Christ Church, Spitalfields and Ockham.

66 BL, K.Top., xxxii, fo. 47f ('Plan of the Barracks at Berwick begun to build in the year 1717').

67 Ibid., fo. 46 ('A Plan of Berwick upon Tweed 1725').

in 1724.[68] Two survey plans of 1749,[69] however, show the magazine rebuilt in its present position on the eastern ramparts of the town, and its place on the south side of the barrack quadrangle taken by the building which is in that location today.[70] This building therefore falls outside the date range of the other buildings discussed, 1715-24. It has, however, features in common with the Hawksmoor drawing, which are, moreover, executed more faithfully than Hawksmoor's other features are on the two flanking ranges. It has crow-stepped gables, three (as Hawksmoor proposed), rather than two (as were built on the flanking ranges). It has a semi-circular lunette (not realised on the flanking ranges) set below what may be regarded either as the gablet of Hawksmoor's drawing or as the open pediment which he made such frequent use of elsewhere. It has capital-less pilaster strips at the angles, broad unmoulded architraves and the combination of round-arched and segment-headed windows so characteristic of Hawksmoor. Indeed, were it not for the evidence of Hawksmoor's drawing, it is this rather than the flanking ranges which might most readily be attributed to Hawksmoor. Nothing but a guess can explain this. It was evidently built between 1725 and 1749, perhaps to Hawksmoor's design, perhaps to a design of Hawksmoor's supplied some years before, perhaps to Jelfe's interpretation of other designs by Hawksmoor. The more perfect realisation of Hawksmoor's style than that of the flanking ranges may well be due to the mediation of Andrews Jelfe, who was not in office when the flanking ranges were built, under the supervision of Thomas Phillips, Captain of Engineers and not otherwise recorded as an architect.[71]

The residual legacy of Hawksmoor's style may also be observed in magazine design. Magazines typically had barrel vaults abutted by massive and unadorned buttresses and few windows. Semi-circular lunettes set high in the end gables satisfied the requirements of their specialised function, and thus a favourite motif of Hawksmoor's can be found (together with open pediments) as late as the 1760s in magazines, like those at Purfleet in Essex.[72] Apart from these exceptions, however, the Board abandoned the style of Hawksmoor after 1721. The barracks at Landguard Fort, Suffolk, for instance, designed by John Peter Desmaretz in 1732, show no sign of it.[73]

Hawksmoor's style was institutionally as well as chronologically circumscribed. One other institution predictably influenced by it was the Navy, but only rarely. The Navy's adoption of it is most apparent on the Dockyard wall at

68 John Macky, *A Journey through Scotland* (London, 1723), pp. 24-25.
69 PRO, MPHH/703 (21 and 23).
70 Iain MacIvor, *The Fortifications of Berwick upon Tweed* (London, 1972), p. 29, dates this range specifically to 1739-41.
71 Whistler, *The Imagination of Sir John Vanbrugh*, pp. 224-26.
72 Coad, *Historic Architecture of the Royal Navy*, p.

129 and pl. 134. Mr Coad dates these magazines to the 1770s. The Act of Parliament for building them received royal assent on 15 April 1760 [33 Geo.II, c.11], however, and four drawings for them in the King's Topographical Collection are dated between 1764 and 1768 (British Library, K.Top., xiii. fos. 48b-48cc).
73 PRO, MPHH/703.

Chatham, built in 1718.[74] There the main gate has the machicolations of the guard house block in Hawksmoor's Berwick drawing; and they are repeated on the towers which punctuate the wall. Understandably Whistler regarded this wall as built by the Ordnance Board, and so it might have been had it been a defensive structure. But it was no more than a dockyard boundary, built to prevent thieving, and as such built by the dockyard authority, the Navy Board. Nor did the Navy entirely shake off the Hawksmoor influence for half a century: between 1763 and 1771 it built three ropehouses at Plymouth with the crow-stepped gables of Berwick-upon-Tweed.[75] This influence was, however, exceptional. Even in close proximity to Ordnance wharfs in the royal dockyards, naval buildings were largely uninfluenced by the Hawksmoor style.

One building erected by the Office of Works, a Carriage Store belonging to the Mint in the Tower of London, has a gablet with a semi-circular lunette.[76] Here, under the windows of its drawing office, the influence of the Ordnance must have been difficult to avoid, especially as the Office of Works used the Board of Ordnance's craftsmen for the Mint's buildings.[77]

It would be generally correct, therefore, to identify this style as that of the Ordnance Board alone, and of that institution between 1715 and 1724 only. Richards, Hawksmoor's friend (or at least acquaintance), died in 1721, and Marlborough, his patron, died in 1722. It is perhaps not a coincidence that no Ordnance building in Hawksmoor's style was begun after the latter date apart from the south block at Berwick. The adoption of Hawksmoor's style by the Board may therefore specifically be connected with them. They took up their posts almost simultaneously in 1714 and had no opportunity to initiate works until the Jacobite Rebellion of 1715. Proposals were put in hand during 1716 and designs drawn up between 1717 and 1720.[78] The Board's buildings at Plymouth were the last of the group and, although they were designed before Richards's death, work only began in 1722, just after it. The abundant surviving archive of the Board does not record Hawksmoor's efforts on its behalf, but he may have contributed them by private arrangement with Brigadier-General Richards. The existence of a sketch by Hawksmoor and a finished version of the same subject by a Board draughtsman indicates that Richards had the opportunity to lay either before the Board. That being so, he would obviously have presented the neater version and the Board need have had no direct contact with Hawksmoor or his drawings. It is perhaps for this reason that Hawksmoor's participation has remained undetected until now.

74 Coad, *The Royal Dockyards*, pp. 82-83.
75 Ibid., pp. 199-200, and pl. 149.
76 PRO, WORK 31/129.

77 This information was given to me by Mr Geoffrey Parnell.
78 PRO, WO 47/30-33, passim.

17

The Payment Book of William Baker of Audlem (1705-71)

RICHARD MORRICE

William Baker was born in 1705 in the parish of St Bride in London, the son of Richard Baker of London and later of Leominster in Herefordshire (d. 1749). He married twice, first Eliza Evelyn and then, following her death, in January 1736/37, Jane Dod, the daughter and sole heiress of George Dod of Highfields near Audlem in the county of Cheshire. The couple at first settled in Bridgnorth but in January 1743/44 Jane succeeded to Highfields, a sizeable timberframed house built by the Dod family in 1567 and altered in 1615. Baker was to lead the life of a gentleman farmer, while combining it with that of architect and surveyor. His payment book for the years 1748-59 survives as evidence of other interests apart from architecture; the majority of payments and receipts concern farming while others tell of other business, including a number of loans. Baker owned a brickfield at Highfields and a number of payments relate to it, including a number to a Mr Plant and a Mr Barber who may have been the brick-makers. Much later, in 1767, Baker purchased the manor and estate of Fenton Culvert in Staffordshire as well as a pottery works in Fenton for his younger son, William, no doubt because his elder son, Richard, also an architect, was to succeed to the Highfields estate.

On a slip inserted into this payment book is written (very faintly in pencil) '8 April dined Mr David Hiorn. Daventry Church is built with a Bad yellow couler Stone the Windows to Small – the body of the Church to Low the Steeple crowded with work yet Clumsy – no Connection between the Cornice & of pillars . . .'[1] That Baker could have written such criticism is not as surprising as its survival; such comment in the eighteenth century must have been more

* I would like to thank Michael Bullen with whom most of the buildings considered in this paper were visited and discussed and Andor Gomme who read the paper and has generously given me much information on Baker's early years with the Smiths of Warwick as well as his thoughts on Baker's practice. I would also like to thank Mr and Mrs Bellyse Baker for kindly allowing me to make a complete transcript of the Baker payment book. I am grateful to the Royal Commission on the Historical Monuments of England for permission to publish the photographs in figs. 92, 93 and 95.

1 Holy Cross, Daventry (1752-58). See A. Gomme, 'William and David Hiorn', in R. Brown (ed.), *The Architectural Outsiders* (London, 1985) pp. 53-54.

common than one would guess from its infrequent discovery today.[2] It underlines William Baker's perception of himself as an architect as well as a craftsman contractor. Baker appears first to have worked as a joiner and later as foreman at a number of houses on which the Smiths of Warwick contracted; he first appears on the record in 1727 as a joiner at Ditchley in Oxfordshire.[3]

Baker contracted infrequently. More common in his payment book are details of work sub-contracted to such craftsman contractors as Roger Eykyn, Gabriel Featherstone and Charles Trubshaw, with Baker operating as the supervising architect. It suggests, moreover, that Baker worked for clients in a variety of ways. His use of the term 'survey' appears old-fashioned, that is in denoting inspection of work, but it may also indicate 'measuring'. As it was usual for the client to employ a measurer separately it is unlikely that he was employed in this latter capacity at many sites.[4] On contracts, the payment book does not give much indication beyond plenty of hints. In most cases he appears only to have provided plans, in many cases he supervised work in some way and sometimes he provided craftsmen and materials. Although he records the supply of building materials and/or labour at a number of sites, he generally sub-contracted; it is not surprising, given his background as a joiner that many payments relate to the supply of timber. Baker also contracted on specialist matters. It appears that while the client would supply the more mundane materials and crafts, Baker would often arrange for fireplaces and church monuments, marble and alabaster, including their preparation by Hiorn, Trubshaw, Eykyn or others.

In the small number of cases where he himself contracted he negotiated singly with one contractor but provided some of the materials through separate

2 Baker also notes: '5 Orders of Fools: 1st, The Blockhead; 2nd, The Coxcomb; 3rd, The Vain Blockhead; 4th, Grave Coxcomb; 5th, The Half-Witted Fellow; the last is the Composite Order.'
   Baker regularly used the payment book for news of personal or national importance; thus 'Mem that on this 1st day of November the Water at Sherton (?) was observed by Mr Jackson to move from Side to Side at Swinnerton and other places although no Wind yett the Water was much agitated – ye City of Lisbon' (rest in pencil and very faint) and, in July 1756, 'Island of Minorca was taken by the French after being bravely defended by Gen:1 Blakeney Admiral Bing is disgract for running away with 13 men of War from 12 French – he is brought to England and Tryed and Shott to death for his Cowardice'.

3 Baker's long connection with Francis Smith, probably ending at his second marriage, culminated in his role as foreman on a number of buildings. It would also probably explain his continuing work at various Smith-related houses – Mawley, Etwall, Swynnerton, Wingerworth, Catton and Patshull.

4 Regular payments for surveys are noted, for instance, for both Stone and Wolverhampton parish churches. In both cases it appears that Baker was not the contractor; Trubshaw and Webb shared that role at Stone and Roger Eykyn at Wolverhampton. Stone church was designed by William Robinson but Baker regularly inspected work on site; 'Mr Hiorn' was also paid for one survey by Baker, who presumably had the lead. For work at Stone, on 30 August 1757, he received '£10 for my seventh paiment and £10 in part for the Survey of Joyner's work', no doubt evidence of 'measuring' of some kind. At Wolverhampton Baker was also inspecting work but there he was presumably also the designer of the building; there is circumstantial evidence to support his authorship.

contracts with suppliers. This of course allowed him the possibility of negotiating discounts with both craftsmen and suppliers and also assured him of certainty of quality and supply. Indeed he notes addresses of favoured craftsmen and suppliers within the book. His favoured contractors appear to have been Gabriel Featherstone, Roger Eykyn and, to a lesser extent, Charles Trubshaw. It was almost certainly to them that he passed over the foreman's role in the small number of cases where he appears to have contracted directly (Wood Eaton Hall, Woodhouse Farmhouse, The Coppice, Penkridge, Astbury Rectory and the College of Vicars Choral at Hereford). None were of such great size that they would require a separate clerk of works and it is unknown whether a measurer was employed by the client in each case. It appears that only once did he follow that other eighteenth-century model for the employment of labour, the direct contract, apparently at Norton-in-Hales church, where Baker notes the payment week by week of all workmen and suppliers – except for stone.

The payment book appears to suggest that Baker favoured building by the great and, probably, by measure, though the book is not specific enough to suggest which in each case.[5] Other than those cases noted above, William Baker was paid by the client directly for plans and perhaps for supervision. Unfortunately, in most cases the exact terms of contract are lost and estimates are rare; one survives, among the Powis papers, for the building of a new town hall in Bishop's Castle (it is quoted in full in Appendix 2).

The payment book is one of the few surviving documents which allow detailed consideration of the general practice of an eighteenth-century provincial architect. Study of it, and the different types of work it illustrates, allows a preliminary listing of sites by the kind of work which appears to have been carried out.[6] The present list goes one further than Arthur Oswald's 1954 survey because, as he admitted, he had not been able to inspect many of the sites mentioned in the payment book.[7] While recognising that a lot more may be discovered from clients' surviving papers, that some 'surveys' appear not to

---

5 During the eighteenth century there were three contractual arrangements in use: 'building by the great', 'by measure' and 'by day'. 'By the great' refers to a system where the whole work, or discrete parts of it, were contracted separately. 'By measure' required contracting usually for parts of the work at a fixed price and the work then measured by an independent surveyor or architect. 'By day' refers to contract for payment at day-rates, the direct contract. See F. Jenkins, *Architect and Patron* (London, 1961), pp. 128-29 and H.M. Colvin, *A Biographical Dictionary of Bri-*

tish Architects, 1600-1840 (London, 1978), pp. 20-21.

6 It also underlines the regularity with which he uses these words to mean the same thing; his use of language might be expected to have been a little wayward, but inspection of the sites show this not to have been so in the majority of cases.

7 A. Oswald, 'William Baker of Audlem, Architect', in *Collections for a History of Staffordshire* (Staffordshire Record Society), vol. for 1950-51 (1954), pp. 109-35.

have been inspections of work completed but the survey of pre-existing buildings and, of course, that many of the buildings with which he was concerned have been rebuilt or demolished or indeed both, the survey given in the appendix shows the variety of Baker's practice.[8] A further lacuna, as with so many eighteenth-century provincial architects and craftsmen, is a general lack of knowledge on Baker's fitting out of interiors. A different problem has been thrown up by inspection of the sites; in a number of cases where Baker contracted or supervised, the book does not mention the provision of plans. The rest of this essay is devoted to those buildings, some already mentioned, which can be attributed to Baker on stylistic grounds.

Although nothing is known of Baker's architectural training, his use of pattern books, foremost among them Gibbs's *Book of Architecture* (1728), has often been noted.[9] Indeed on one occasion he notes the purchase of 'half-pennys books/Chinese books – 17s. 6d.' – books supposedly published for just such as he, provincial practitioners seeking the latest in metropolitan styles.[10] Ludlow Butter Cross (1743-44) is often given as an example of his use of pattern books but within the limits of Georgian classicism he was fully capable of independent creation.[11] Such, for instance, is his design for Bishop's Castle Town Hall among the Powis papers, with its crestings and gables and a lower forward projecting and pedimented loggia. The main block is set back and is topped by a clockface set in a decorative surround, which turns into a Baroque gable with concave sides rising from an eaves band. Directly behind he put a louvred cupola.[12]

Like many of his ilk, his debt to Gibbs was great; this included the church of St John in Wolverhampton (1755-60) and the north range of Patshull, where

8 It is particularly interesting to note that, outside the years of the payment book, Baker can be identified with only nine commissions, whereas fifty-two sites can be identified for the eleven years covered by the book (and that excludes the thirty-nine uncertain cases). A number of pieces of work of the years 1748-59 can be identified independently from the payment book.

9 Baker took over from Gibbs as the architect of Patshull Hall, whose owner, Sir John Astley, seems to have been a personal friend.

10 Payment noted for 9 October 1752.

11 The Butter Cross in Ludlow, which makes such an effective terminal feature in the view from the bottom of Broad Street, is certainly based on a design by Gibbs. Plate 62 in his *Book of Architecture*, one of a series of designs for Whitton Place, Middlesex (itself based on a design for the Villa Pisani at Bagnolo in Palladio's *Quattro libri*), distinctively combines

a pedimented single-storey *tetrastyle* portico with a wide thermal window above. It is typical of Baker's conservatism that he should have reduced the width of the thermal window. The three-bay façade, framed by pilasters carrying a heavy entablature and balustrade, is topped by an octagonal cupola on a clock-face flanked by scroll-volutes carrying an open segmental pediment-like hood, a feature derived from various of Gibbs's designs for towers for the churches of St Martin-in-the-Fields and St Mary-le-Strand.

12 An estimate for the building of a new town hall at Bishop's Castle, with two sheets of drawings, including plans, elevations and a section, is lodged in the Powis papers at Shropshire County Record Office (552/14/ box 465). That these vary from the form of the town hall as built should not surprise; indeed the plans as drawn do not match the elevations shown.

he apparently followed Gibbs as architect.[13] Yet, to take one example, whereas the pavilions at Morville Hall (1748 or first half of 1749) showed Gibbs's influence, the main block, which was subject to a Baker remodelling, certainly did not (Fig. 90). Though the house was again remodelled after his intervention, and is now very plain, its earlier form is known from a painting of the entrance front, thought to date from the 1740s, which was sold at Christies in December 1971 (rather naive in execution but, as a representation of the house before late eighteenth-century alteration, probably accurate) (Fig. 91).[14] It shows a U-plan house as now but with very tall octagonal stair-towers in the angles of the U and pairs of three-quarter columns carrying open pediments, articulating the ends of the wings. The roof line is enlivened by the cupolas on the towers, arch-linked chimneys and a central motif of a thermal window capped by an open pediment. This all appears rather crude but his canting out of the Gibbsian end-pavilions to give the impression of greater depth to the forecourt by false perspective is both subtle and effective.

William Baker could also manage a workmanlike Gothick; apart from the classical St John's Church, Wolverhampton, he was responsible for work (most often including new towers) at Stone, Staffordshire (1754-58), where William Robinson, the surveyor to Greenwich Hospital was the designer and Baker only the surveyor; Seighford, Staffordshire (1754-57, new tower, west end and north wall of nave) (Fig. 92); Norton-in-Hales, Shropshire (1756-58, general repairs); Ellenhall, Staffordshire (1757, a small new church with west tower); Wybunbury, Cheshire (1758, inspection of the steeple which was, and still is, leaning); Norbury, Staffordshire (1759, general repairs and new tower); Acton, Cheshire (1757, inspected repairs to the upper stage of the tower – it is likely that he was responsible for the rebuilding); Kenmore, Perthshire (1760, a design for the Earl of Breadalbane apparently reduced in building); and Penn church in Staffordshire (1765, the casing of the tower in brick). In all of these cases Baker chose a simple 'Gothick' style for his new work. Stone Church, a boxy version of the St Martin-in-the-Fields/St Giles-in-the-Fields type of church in Gothick dress, must be due largely to William Robinson rather than Baker. We will probably never know for certain how much, if at all, Robinson's design was altered in execution by Baker. His probable rebuilding of the upper part of Acton church tower, therefore, was the only occasion where he used a

13 Baker's authorship of St John's is not entirely certain but it would appear very likely, attribution being supported by the patronage of the church. It is recorded that donations to the building fund were sluggish until the Earl of Stamford offered £1,000 in return for his family's right to the presentation of the living. He probably suggested Baker, who had not only worked for him at Enville in Staffordshire but was also working for other members of his circle.

14 Baker was paid by the owner, Arthur Weaver, on a number of occasions in 1748 and 1749 and also for a chimney-piece commissioned from 'Mr Hiorn'. See J. Harris, *The Artist and the Country House* (London, 1979), p. 205, fig. 212. Fig. 91 shows the detail of the main block of the house; the picture is in a private collection.

Fig. 90 Morville Hall (Shropshire), forecourt pavilion (1748/49).

Fig. 91 Morville Hall, detail of painting (late 1740s). (*Private Collection*)

Fig. 92 Seighford church (Staffs.) (1754-57).

more elaborate decorative Gothick vocabulary.[15] Here he took his cue from the highly decorative nature of this church; he decorated the uppermost stage of the tower with arched panelling above a band of lozenge derivation directly below a crenellated parapet which used (probably reused) crocketed corner pinnacles and rather oddly taller central merlons carrying globe finials.

At Seighford church Baker used one rather peculiar decorative device, not seen on any of his other churches, by giving the pilaster quoins of the tower, and the tall merlons of the parapet, tall, deep, rectangular panels. In this context two other Staffordshire towers should be mentioned, with one of which Baker was almost certainly concerned. The first is attached to a farm building next to Seighford Hall (Baker, according to the payment book, worked not only on the church in Seighford but also on the Hall and was paid on 20 August 1755 for a 'survey of a dovehouse'). It consists of a one-and-a-half storey crow-stepped gabled range with a two-storey tower attached symmetrically at one end. It is probable that the gabled block consisted of a ground-floor wagon-

15 Baker noted, on 26 March 1757: 'Paid Expense to Acton and Nantwich when I was agreed with to Inspect the repair of the Church of Acton (ruind by the wind on 15 Instant) for 42 Pound.'

shed with stowage over. The tower is more obscure in purpose though it certainly appears dovecote like; the interior has not been investigated. The feature to be noted in this context is a parapet with corner merlons and triple central merlons with raised centre, all with slab abaci tops. Although these merlons appear to have been rebuilt recently, it may be assumed that they mimic the original pattern.

Although altered, and either restored or rebuilt, the design of this peculiar building, which we can assume Baker inspected during building, is very likely to be his own work; the tower at Oakley near Tutbury, even though more convincingly Baker-like in aspect (its niched pilaster-quoins are very similar to those of Seighford church tower), has no such association and any ascription must be tentative. The most Bakerish features are those tall pointed recessed panels in the pilaster quoins and the parapet with tall corner and central block-like merlons (with more recessed panels) and pairs of lesser merlons between, all with plain slab-like abaci.

Baker used such parapets on only one other known farm building. This was the barn at Bevere, just north of Worcester, built between 1748 and 1749 for a Mr Brodribb.[16] A standard West Midlands brick and timber barn was here given crenellated and stepped gable-parapets with slit breathers and at one end a circular pitching hole (now blocked).

Baker enjoyed crenellation; four houses mentioned in the payment book are characterised by their use of similar parapets. These are Lady Dorothy's Cottage at Enville, Staffordshire (1748-50, possibly the recasting of an earlier building) (Fig. 93); Wood Eaton Hall, Staffordshire (1753-56) (Fig. 94); Wood-house Farm, Peplow, Shropshire (1754-58) (Fig. 95); and Burnhill Green Farm, Patshull, Staffordshire (1754-58) (Fig. 96). All four are variations on the mid eighteenth-century brick farmhouse, so common in the Midlands. All are of three bays and two storeys with the roof-space lit by small garret-lights; both Lady Dorothy's Cottage and Burnhill Green Farmhouse have ridge-roofs with gable-parapets.

The four buildings have in common a crenellated parapet rising above the eaves, on all except Lady Dorothy's Cottage rising from a shallow central projection. That these crenellated features are all of the same form, with five merlons, capped by abaci-like flats, of which the outer ones are at a lower level than the three in the centre, shows that Baker was thinking in terms of these

---

16 Baker's farm buildings included the now rather altered stable block at Hanmer Hall, Flintshire (1756), with its central thermal window; the stables at Mawley Hall, Shropshire (1748) (if by Baker), with its Venetian window-type entrance; the larger and part quadrangular stables at Enville Hall, Staffordshire (1748-50), and the estate farm, (both of which may be by Baker, at least in part); the pedimented stables at Aldenham House, Shropshire (1750-51), very probably by Baker; and the large and presumably altered stables at the Woodhouse at Wombourne, Staffordshire (1758-59).

gables as particular features; he used an identical gable at Powis Castle (on the north range in the outer bailey, altered between 1748 and 1754).[17] As we have seen, related, though not identical, crestings appear on the towers at Seighford Hall and Oakley, and on the barn at Bevere. They can also be seen on Sibdon Castle in Shropshire and, at one time, on the Swan Hotel at Woore, Shropshire (the last two do not appear in the payment book). Furthermore, Baker used other kinds of cornice-level projection to give emphasis (at Morville Hall, for instance, and in the alternative design for Bishop's Castle Town Hall) and, as we have seen, in a more generalised way, his church towers display various combinations of merlons and pinnacles. These all reveal a general interest in crestings.

Sibdon Castle is at Sibdon Carwood, a couple of miles to the north west of Craven Arms. This little-known house, formerly of U-plan like Morville Hall though not of medieval origin, was somewhat irregular externally and like Morville was remodelled, probably during the mid 1740s.[18] The alterations consisted of tidying up the fenestration, interpolating a single-storey entrance block within the U, reworking the south front and more or less completely refitting the interior. The elevations to north and west were tidied up and towards the south Baker converted a broadly disposed five-bay front into seven bays by the insertion of windows, sometimes awkwardly for internal planning, and giving the whole front considerable character by adding a panelled and crenellated parapet. This parapet, combining an idiosyncratic rhythm of crenellations with one thermal and two round windows, makes an attribution to Baker convincing.[19]

One rather more tentative attribution is worthy of mention: the Swan Hotel in Woore, just over the border into Shropshire from Audlem (Fig. 97). The building today appears to be a two-storey hotel with parapet and slight central projection. However, a photograph of *c.* 1910 shows that the parapet replaced a second storey with three pointed-arched windows, incongruous in view of the segment-headed windows below – but typically Baker – and three gables with variations of the Baker stepped gable above. The central one is lower and it

17 The interior of this range, which already contained a gallery, was converted by Thomas Farnolls Pritchard in 1775-77 for use as a ballroom and picture-gallery on the first floor.

18 The house had been bought by Edward Fleming, a barrister of the Inner Temple, from his father in 1744 and it was to Sibdon Castle that he retired from the law to lead the life, if not of a major landowner as he desired, at least of a squire with pretensions. He immediately set about improving the house. It is very likely

that he turned to Baker, the chosen architect of most of those whom Fleming was trying to impress. There are receipts throughout the payment book from a Mr Stubbs, one of which, 8 May 1753, was 'on acct Mr Fleming', a possible indication that Mr Stubbs acted as Fleming's agent; but Baker also received a payment for surveying at Ranton Abbey, Staffordshire, from a Mr Stubbs.

19 Noteworthy are the pairs of merlons which intervene between the end and centre features.

Fig. 93 Lady Dorothy's Cottage, Enville (Staffs.) (1748-50).

may be that it began life more or less as identical to the outer pair and was partially taken down later.[20]

Appendix 1

The Buildings and Sites Mentioned in the Payment Book

This list is derived from analysis of the use of the words 'plan', 'draught' and 'survey', backed up by inspection on site. Furthermore, contracting is noted where Baker received payment for services or materials, including sub-contracting. Survey is taken to mean inspection of work; no attribution of design to Baker is made here, though it may be assumed that where he is noted as preparing plans he was the designer. Known cases where he prepared plans and was *not* the designer are noted. The client's names, usually Baker's identification of a payment in the book, are noted.

20 Rather like the Swan at Woore, the Town Hall at Clun has a skinned look; the façade breaks forward in the centre with a central first floor thermal window, but the tall hipped roof looks as though it would be better relieved by some kind of projection above the cornice-line.

Fig. 94 Wood Eaton Hall (Staffs.) (1753-56).

Fig. 95 Woodhouse Farm, Peplow (Shropshire) (1754-58).

Fig. 96 Burnhill Green Farm, Patshull (Staffs.) (1754-58).

Fig. 97 Swan Hotel, Woore (Shropshire), photograph taken *c.* 1910.

Baker as Main Contractor
(with Plans and Supervision Except Where Noted)

Hereford, College of the Vicars Choral (1750-53), 'the Vicars of Hereford' – repairs and possible alterations; no plans.

Wood Eaton Hall, Staffordshire (1753-56), for the Revd William Astley – new house (see Fig. 94).

Woodhouse Farm, Peplow, Shropshire (1754-58), for Charles Pigot Esq. – new house (see Fig. 95).

Norton-in-Hales, St Chad's Church, Shropshire (1756-58) – repairs.

Astbury Rectory, Cheshire (1757-59), for the Revd Joseph Crewe – repairs and possible alterations.

The Coppice, Penkridge, Staffordshire (1757-59), for Sir Edward Littleton, Bt. – new house; no supervision but building work was continuing when the payment book finished and such work may have come later than 1759.

Contracting and Supervision

Powis Castle, Montgomeryshire (1748-54) for the Earl of Powis, formerly Henry Arthur Herbert, Lord Herbert of Chirbury, of Oakley Park, Shropshire – alterations to north range and other works, almost certainly repairs and minor alterations.

Bellaport Hall, Shropshire (1755-57), for William Cotton Esq. – alterations, including a new chimney-piece.

Brand Hall, Shropshire (1756-57), for Robert Davison – contracting for alterations to interior.

Dorfold Hall, Cheshire (1757-59), for James Tomkinson Esq. – alterations, possibly internal, and addition of wing.

Plans and Contracting

Morville Hall, Aldenham, Shropshire (1748-49), for Arthur Weaver – alterations and wings; plans probably produced before payment book begins (see Figs. 90, 91).

Montgomery, Town Hall (1748-51) – new building.

Acton Scott, St Margaret's Church, Shropshire; Acton monument (1751-52), for Sir Richard Acton, Bt.

Hankelow Hall, Cheshire (1755-57), for Mr Wettenhall – alterations, including refitting of drawing room; may also refer to exterior alterations.

Norton-in-Hales, St Chad's Church, Shropshire; Davison monument (1757).

Plans and Supervision, without Contracting

Penn Hall, Staffordshire (1748-54), for Thomas Bradney – drawing and surveying – probable refronting of house and new stables.

Bevere, Worcestershire (1748-49), for Mr Brodribb – barn.

Patshull House, Staffordshire, including Burnhill Green Farmhouse (1748-58, see Fig.

96), for Sir John Astley, Bt. – flanking courtyard pavilions and forecourt, library, stables, chapel and new house.

Swynnerton Hall, Staffordshire (1750-56), for Thomas Fitzherbert – outbuilding and other works unknown.

Acton Burnell Hall, Shropshire (1753-58), for Sir Edward Smythe, Bt. – house enlarged and lodge.

Wingerworth Hall, Derbyshire (1753-54), for Sir Henry Hunloke, Bt. – unspecified work; house (but not service blocks) demolished.

Seighford Hall, Staffordshire (1754-55), for Mr Elde – miscellaneous works including weathervane, dovehouse and bridge.

Seighford, St Chad's Church, Staffordshire (1754-57) – supervision of rebuilding (see Fig. 92).

Wolverhampton, St John's Church (1755-59) – new church.

Hanmer Hall, Flintshire (1756), for Humphrey Hanmer Esq. – barn.

Acton, St Mary's Church, Cheshire (1757) – rebuilt tower ('Mar 15 – An Excessive high wind which Blew down abundance of trees unthatch houses and threw down a number of barns and overturned the to of Acton Steeple upon the roof of the Church which fell in upon the pews in a ruinous *Condition*').

Norbury, St Peter's Church, Staffordshire (1759) – survey and, almost certainly, rebuilding of tower.

Surveying and Inspections (Largely of Repairs)

Ranton Abbey, Staffordshire (1748-55), for Sir Jonathan Cope, Bt. – it is possible that Baker provided plans for this building before the payment book begins.

Brewerne Abbey, Oxfordshire (1749), for Sir Jonathan Cope, Bt. – unspecified work.

Catton Hall, Derbyshire (1753-59), for Mr Horton – unknown works and 'survey of dovehouse vault'.

Stone, St Michael's Church, Staffordshire (1754-58) – acted as Clerk of Works.

Etwall Hall, Derbyshire (1756-58), for Mrs Cotton – work unknown; house entirely demolished. Baker did receive two guineas on June 30 1756 'of Mrs Cotton Etwell for Surveying the Altarpiece at Etwell'.

Whitmore Hall, Staffordshire (1756), for Edward Mainwaring Esq. – unspecified work.

Newport, Shropshire, school (1756) – unspecified work.

Wichnor, Staffordshire, bridge (1757) – noted as an inspection.

Wybunbury, St Chad's Church, Cheshire (1758) – inspection of tower; noted as an inspection.

Newcastle-under-Lyme, St Giles' Church, Staffordshire (1759) – survey of steeple.

Plans Only

Enville Hall, Staffordshire (1748-50), for the Earl of Stamford-farmhouse (Lady Dorothy's Cottage, see Fig. 93) and other unspecified work; possibly stables and estate farm.

Tixall Hall, Staffordshire (1751), for Lord Aston – unknown work though Oswald mentions notes given in the diary of Charles Trubshaw, the builder, which mention the contemporary rebuilding of the quadrangle, a new coach-house and stables.

Darlaston Hall, Staffordshire (1751), for John Jervis – survey.

Pattingham House, Staffordshire (1753), for Sir John Astley of Patshull – new house, whereabouts unknown.

Stanage Park, Radnorshire (1755), for Mr Johns – unspecified work, house altered.

Egginton Hall, Derbyshire (1756), for the Revd Sir John Every, Bt – Andor Gomme suggests that Baker's design may have 'formed at least the basis for the house that the Wyatts built and that he recommended them to Every on the strength of previous knowledge'. Benjamin Wyatt and Sons began work in 1755, the house was altered by Samuel Wyatt (1782-83) and demolished in 1955.

Terrick Hall, Whitchurch, Shropshire (1756), for Mr Watson – unspecified work.

Butterton Hall, Staffordshire (1757), for William Swinnerton – unspecified work.

Teddesley Hall, Staffordshire (1757-59), for Sir Edward Littleton, Bt – service blocks (?); demolished 1954.

Keele Hall, Staffordshire (1757-59), for Ralph Sneyd Esq. – alterations to south front and new kitchen garden walls.

The Wodehouse, Wombourne, Staffordshire (1758-59), for Samuel Hellier – stables (?) and cheeses.

Kenmore Church and pavilion, Perthshire (1759), for the Earl of Breadalbane – the church was built to a reduced scheme.

Contracting Only

Mawley Hall, Shropshire (1748), for Sir Edward Blount, Bt. – unspecified work; new stables?

Oakly Park, Shropshire (1748-58), for the Earl of Powis – rebuilding of early eighteenth century house, rebuilt by John Haycock (*c.* 1784-90) and C.R. Cockerell (1819-36). Baker produced various designs for the house, including a book of designs kept there; other papers are at the National Library of Wales (Powis Papers 21129-45).

Leighton, St Mary's Church, Davison monument (1756-59), for Robert Davison.

Sidway Hall, near Maer, Staffordshire (1758-59), for Mr Elde of Seighford – unspecified work.

Uncertain

Mr Littleton; library (1747).

Mr Woodhouse; plan (1747).

Mr Guest of Bridgnorth'; 'sash stuff' for library and surveying (1747).

Mr Wooley of Worcester; 'draughts' (1747).

Mr Ashwood of Liverpool; elevation (1747).

Mr Blondall of Worcester; plan (1748).

Mr Brown of Hampton; plan (1748).

Liverpool, houses for Ashwood, Pardoe, Fletcher and Cunliffe; new houses (?) (1748).

Mr Cunliffe of Liverpool; plans (1748).

Dr Cronk; survey (1749).

Mr Mackworth; plan (1750) and plan of farmhouse (1751).

Mr Davies of Ludlow; survey of gallery (1750).

Mrs Read; plan (1750).

Mr Bough of Ludlow; 'for trouble and jiorney to make affidavitt concerning the repairs of Stone House' (1751).

Sir Richard Acton of Aldenham; drawing (1751) – it has been suggested that Baker was responsible for the stable block at Aldenham Park.

Mr Talbot; 'plan of an office near Ats Bromley' (1751).

Dr Attwood of Worcester; surveying (1751).

Mr Dicken; plans (1752).

Mr Nichols; plan (1752) – possibly related to Patshull – and 'alteration of plan' (1753).

Mr Stubbs; surveying, 'Walkenstone and Walkenwood'(?) (1752).

Mr Gretton; 'for the Survey and attending assizes at Stafford for delapidation of Bloreroy(?) agt Mr Lee (1753).

Mr Woodhouse; survey of roof of house (1753).

Mr Andrews; plan (1753).

The Earl of Shrewsbury; 'deal etc, freight & Alabaster' (1754).

Mr Webb of Brewood; 'for the block of black Marble' (1754).

Capt. Baldwyn; plans and estimate (1755) – a Capt. Baldwyn appears to have acted as agent for Lord Powis so this receipt may relate to Powis Castle or Oakley Park.

Mr Wade of Market Drayton; 'for a plan of a Window etc' (1756).

Mr Knight of Whitchurch; plans (1757).

Mr Tollet of Betley; survey (1757).

Mr Broom of Trysull; plans (1758).

Mr Lea of Newport; survey (1758).

Mr Wallhall; 'for a horse & for drawing plans' (1758).

Mr Coyney; 'for plan & jiorney' (1759).

Mr Stubbs; 'for Brinton plans' (1759).

Mr Hollier; plans (1759).

Mr Prebendary Jackson; 'for Surveying the Delapidations of Prees', (1759).

Mr Willson; 'for a plan of Sandbach House, (1759).

'Bishop of Litchfield'; 'for a Small advice', (1759).

Buildings which can be connected with Baker
through evidence other than the Payment Book

The Butter Cross, Ludlow (1743-44).

No. 52, Broad Street, Ludlow; house for Richard Salwey, drawing in Shropshire Record Office – 2505-7 (1743)

Elton Hall, near Ludlow, Herefordshire; house remodelled for Richard Salwey 174? – information from Richard Hewlings.

Town Hall, Bishop's Castle; unexecuted designs, building varied in execution – Shropshire Record Office, Powis Papers SRO 552/14/box 465 (1745) – information from Richard Hewlings.

Shropshire Infirmary, Shrewsbury; unexecuted designs – minute books of the Infirmary (1745).

Hosyer's Almshouses, Ludlow; unexecuted designs – VCH, *Shropshire*, ii, 109 (1756).

English Bridge, Shrewsbury; unexecuted designs – minute book of the bridge trustees in SRO (1767).

Upper Penn, St Bartholomew's Church, near Wolverhampton, Staffordshire; recasing of tower (1765).

Aston Hall, Warwickshire; interior alterations – house accounts (176?) – although Baker does record a payment for expenses to Aston 18-20.xi.1759.

Appendix 2

The Town Hall, Bishop's Castle, Shropshire

2d Nov:1745
An Estimate of the Town Hall at Byshopscastle according to plans Given in – Mr Will: Baker.

To pull down the old building leaving only the walls about the water Reservoy – to Digg the foundation & to lay the same with the old Stone cased with brick & to turn a brick arch over the Goal – to build all the rest of the Walls of brick (except Such Stone ornaments as is here named viz: the Goal door and the [illegible] and Imposts of the Arches and Key Stones Attick windows [illegible] Balusters and Pediment at the end of the building & flagging of the Cross floor) To new frame the timber of the old floors for the Town Hall and to lay the same with sound Oak boards, bradded down – to frame & put on the Old roofs fitt for tileing & to tile the same with the old tiles and find which areas will be wanted – to Cover the Stone of the Pediment att the end of the building with Lead & a [illegible] for the both – to frame and paint an index for the Clock – to make & Glaze nine Sash windows for the Hall – to put up a plain stairs – to frame deal doors & Oak Cases for the Goal the Reservoy the foot of the Staircase town Hall & Councel room & to paint the Same finding Locks and Hinges – to put a skirting board round the Hall & boards in the bottom of the windows – to plaster the Ceiling of the Hall Councel room & Cross & the Walls of the Councel room – all which work to be done in a good substantial & workmanlike manner & find all manner of materials (except what timber may be wanted for the floor & roof) will be worth four hundred and ten pounds – Together with all materials of the old Building (except the barrs belonging to the Court – £410 0s. 0d. PS: Note that what Carrige will be given I will deduct(?) the Value of it.

18

Charles Bridgeman and the English Landscape Garden: New Documents and Attributions

PETER WILLIS

Recent years have witnessed a burgeoning of scholarship in garden and landscape history, including a reappraisal of such eighteeenth-century English figures as Charles Bridgeman and William Kent. Since the publication of my book, *Charles Bridgeman and the English Landscape Garden* (London, 1977), further discoveries have been made which add to our knowledge of Bridgeman's connection with various estates and enable us to ascribe additional layouts to him. The purpose of this essay is to present such material as a pointer to further research and as a contribution to a greater understanding of Bridgeman's role in the establishment of *le jardin anglais*.

Charles Bridgeman's achievement was publicly recognised on Friday 18 May 1984 when the Mayor of Westminster unveiled a blue plaque on Bridgeman's former house, 19 Broad Street, Westminster (now 54 Broadwick Street). Today this forms part of the Dufours Place development of offices and apartments by

* Among those who shared with me the results of their researches during the preparation of this essay I am particularly grateful to Howard Colvin, Andor Gomme and Gervase Jackson-Stops.

The Duke of Beaufort permitted me to use and cite material on Badminton, the Earl of Scarbrough showed me drawings of Lumley at Sandbeck Park, and access to other material was given by the National Trust at Kedleston and Wimpole. Permission to quote from manuscripts was granted by the British Library, the Lewis Walpole Library at Yale University, the National Library of Scotland and Warwickshire County Record Office.

For help with research on specific landscapes I am indebted to David Adshead (Wimpole), T.E. Alasdair Barclay and Leslie Harris (Kedleston), George Clarke (Stowe), Katie Fretwell (Lodge Park, Sherborne), Peter Goodchild (Lumley), Christine Hodgetts (Wroxall), David Lambert (Gobions), Margaret Richards (Badminton), and Chris-

topher Wall (Cliveden). At Hoares Bank in London I was helped by Victoria Hutchings and Maurice Lloyd, and for Goslings material at the Barclays Bank archive, Wythenshawe, by Victoria Wilkinson.

Others whose assistance I gladly acknowledge are Mavis Batey, Geoffrey Beard, Camilla Beresford, Briony Blackwell, Michael Bott, Iain Gordon Brown, Iain Campbell, Kerry Downes, Pierre du Prey, Terry Friedman, Keith Goodway, Maggie Grieve, Frances Harris, John Harris, Richard Hewlings, Charles Wheelton Hind, Alison Hodges, Sally Jeffery, Dorothy B. Johnston, John Lord, Arline Meyer, David Neave, John Phibbs, Malcolm Rogers, Kathryn M. Thompson, Deborah Turnbull, Jan van der Wateren, Tom Williamson and Magnus Willis.

Publication was supported by a generous grant from the Small Grants Research Subcommittee at the University of Newcastle upon Tyne.

Haslemere Estates, completed in 1984, for which the architect was Quinlan Terry. The plaque was erected by the Greater London Council and bears the inscription 'CHARLES BRIDGEMAN/Landscape Gardener/lived here/1723-38'.[1] Haslemere Estates divided the terrace of six houses in Broadwick Street into three self-contained units, the two end pairs bearing the names Phipps House and Dufours House respectively. The central pair have been linked to form Bridgeman House which offers, in the view of Haslemere Estates, 'a blend of period offices with modern open planned accommodation in the new building at the rear'. In Bridgeman's day his house in Broad Street was modest in scale and character: the new Bridgeman House 'incorporates three lifts, central heating, and basement car parking'.[2]

Less dramatic changes have taken place at the Bell Inn, Stilton, which Bridgeman owned and bequeathed to his son Charles: after a period of neglect, the architects Saunders Boston completed extensions and upgrading of the Bell in 1990, including the incorporation of the 'Marlborough Suite'.[3]

The most striking acknowledgement of Bridgeman's work has come through the extensive publications on Stowe, and the conservation of the buildings and landscape there, although little documentary evidence of a Bridgemanic kind has come to light. Similarly the few additional comments by eighteenth-century observers which have appeared tend to reinforce existing assessments: thus Horace Walpole (in a little-known manuscript) describes Kingsmill Eyre as 'One of the first Improvers of Gardens in the Style of Bridgman [*sic*] before Kent perfected the new & quite natural Taste', an opinion familiar from Walpole's *The History of the Modern Taste in Gardening* (1780). 'Mr Eyre planted for Sr Rob. Walpole the Garden at Houghton', Horace Walpole continues, 'which was in a much greater manner than the ancient formal Gardens in the Dutch Style.'[4] Elsewhere specific features of Bridgeman's landscapes are

1   At the Greater London Council, Mr Frank Kelsall in particular was instrumental in promoting the erection of the plaque.

2   The source for this description is primarily 'Broadwick Street London W1', a folder prepared by Haslemere Estates Plc in conjunction with Refuge Assurance Plc and presented to those who attended the reception to mark the completion of the 'restoration' of 48-58 Broadwick Street on Friday, 18 May 1984.

See also the coverage of Dufours Place in the chapter 'Offices and Gentlemen' in Clive Aslet, *Quinlan Terry: The Revival of Architecture* (London, 1986), pp. 146-58. Terry's 1983 linocut of Dufours Place (plate 142) was exhibited in the Royal Academy Summer Exhibition in 1984.

The site of Bridgeman's house in Marylebone at 11 Henrietta Place (formerly 8 Henrietta Street), demolished in 1956, is now occupied by Henrietta House, an office building designed by the Building Design Partnership for the joint developers Nationale-Nederlanden Intervest XII Bv and Lynton Plc, and completed in 1992.

3   I am grateful to the current proprietor of the Bell Inn, Mr Lian McGivern, for his assistance.

4   This is taken from four pages of manuscript notes in Horace Walpole's hand, pasted into Volume ii of Daniel Lysons, *The Environs of London*, . . . (1795), now in the Lewis Walpole Library, Farmington, Connecticut, and quoted with permission. Walpole's observation refers to Lysons's record on p. 161 that Kingsmill Eyre died in 1743 and that his undated tomb was in the burial ground of the Royal Hospital, Chelsea. Eyre was a Fellow of the Royal Society and secretary to the Commissioners of Chelsea College. My visit to Farmington was made possible by Judith Colton, and Catherine Jestis assisted my research there.

endorsed: on 2 October 1723 Lord Orkney writes that 'Bridgeman mackes difficultyes of nothing' in his construction of the amphitheatre at Cliveden,[5] and Joseph Spence, on his grand tour, finds that the fortifications at Geneva 'look extremely neat and the earthworks are like Bridgeman's slopes', and that at Mount Vesuvius the 'slides sloped off for about four mile [*sic*] each way, as prettily as Bridgeman's slopes do in a garden'.[6] More expansively, on 11 March 1733/4 the Duchess of Beaufort exclaims that Bridgeman's 'draught' for Badminton 'is one of the Grandest things' she has seen.[7]

The Duchess's letters also confirm Bridgeman's collaboration at Badminton with Wootton, William Kent, and Francis Smith of Warwick – indeed there are significant connections between Bridgeman and Smith at Chicheley, Kedleston, Shardeloes, Wimbledon, and perhaps Dallington or The Rolls House.[8] Other evidence strengthens the links between Bridgeman and his fellow-artists: apart from Wootton and Kent, these include Archer, Gibbs, Leoni, and John James,[9] not to mention Vanbrugh, with whom Bridgeman may have worked (conceivably with Stephen Switzer) at Lumley Castle in County Durham. Vanbrugh's treatment by Sarah, Duchess of Marlborough, is called to mind by a group of eight letters written by Bridgeman's widow, Sarah, to the Duchess, pathetically seeking redress for unpaid debts.[10] Little fresh light has been cast on the royal gardens,[11] but speculation continues that Charles

Nowhere in The History of the Modern Taste in Gardening *or in his correspondence does Walpole give 'Mr Eyre' a first name; he notes the death of 'Mr Eyres of Chelsea' when writing to Horace Mann, 25 March 1743, and the work of 'M. Eyre' at Houghton in a letter to the Duc de Nivernais, 6 January 1785. See Wilmarth S Lewis, et al., ed., The Yale Edition of Horace Walpole's Correspondence, 18 (1955), p. 201; 42 (1980), p. 131.*

For a reappraisal of Bridgeman's work at Houghton and other Norfolk landscapes see Anthea Taigel and Tom Williamson, 'Some Early Geometric Gardens in Norfolk', which is a special double issue of the *Journal of Garden History*, 11, nos. 1–2 (January-June 1991).

5 National Library of Scotland, Edinburgh, Fraser Collection, MS 1033, fo. 157. Letter from Orkney to one of his brothers, 2 October 1723. Quoted by permission of the National Library of Scotland.

6 Slava Klima (ed.), *Joseph Spence: Letters from the Grand Tour* (Montreal and London, 1975), pp. 70, 373-374. On p. 420 one 'Bridgeman' is listed by Spence as among those whom he met in Paris in 1733.

7 Letters at Badminton received by Lord Noel Somerset, later 3rd Duke of Beaufort. Quoted by courtesy of His Grace the Duke of Beaufort.

8 Professor Andor Gomme has generously shared with me the results of his research on Smith of Warwick. See also Howard Colvin, 'Francis Smith of Warwick, 1672-1738', *Warwickshire History*, ii, no. 2 (Winter, 1972-73), pp. 3-13.

9 For James see Sally Jeffery, 'English Baroque Architecture: The Work of John James', (unpublished Ph.D thesis, University of London, 1986). Possible Bridgeman-James connections at Standlynch are explored in Dr Jeffery's article, 'An Architect for Standlynch House', *Country Life*, clxxix (13 February 1986), pp. 404-6.

10 BL, Add.MS 61478, fos. 9-12, 17-18, 31-34, 43-44, 47-48, 51-52.

Other references which seem to refer to Bridgeman's widow support the possibility that the Royal Gardener worked for Lady Elizabeth (Betty) Hastings at Ledston, Yorkshire. See *Bridgeman*, pp. 61, 180-81, and plate 48b. Accounts at Hoares Bank, London (Ledger K, fo. 304), record two payments from Lady Betty to 'Mrs Bridgeman' of £5. 19s. 6d. on 27 March 1731, and £21 on 5 April 1731. See also Peter Willis, 'William Kent's Letters in the Huntington Library, California', *Architectural History*, xxix (1986), pp. 158-167.

11 Mr Andrew C. Skelton and Miss J. Coburn have kindly drawn my attention to the

Bridgeman's father (or Bridgeman 'Senior' as he was called on occasion) was a gardener active in the late seventeenth and into the early eighteenth centuries.[12]

No new signed drawings by Bridgeman have come to light, and those which may be ascribed to him generally support existing documented landscapes rather than indicate additional attributions: the group of plans of Wimpole, apparently varying from surveys to finished drawings, is the prime example of this.[13] Most striking visually are the two drawings of Lumley which point to the possible partnership there of Bridgeman and Vanbrugh, and which stylistically look to such dramatic Bridgeman set-pieces as Amesbury and Stowe.[14]

All in all the mixture of drawings and documents presented here adds usefully to our knowledge of Bridgeman's life and career. Doubtless in the future further material will emerge: his own bank account has not yet been found, nor has a copy of the catalogue for the sale of his possessions (including 'Pictures, Drawings, and Prints') held by Aaron Lambe in London on Tuesday, 9 December 1741 onwards. The search for such Bridgemanalia has not lost its fascination.[15]

[Further material emerged about Marble Hill, Middlesex, as this book was going to press. Bridgeman's client here was Henrietta, Countess of Suffolk; three estate plans forming additions to the Lothian (Blickling) papers were deposited in 1992 in Norfolk Record Office, Norwich. Two of these drawings (MC 184/10/1 and 2) are likely to be in Bridgeman's hand, although the third (MC 184/10/3) not so. See *Bridgeman*, pp. 36, 56, 58, 59, 67, 77, 78, 129, 131, and plate 71. For help with Marble Hill I acknowledge Miss Jean Kennedy, the County Archivist, Jan Hodges, Paul Rutledge, and Andrew Wimble.]

minutes of the Court of Directors of Chelsea Waterworks, April 1728-April 1731, in the Greater London Record Office and Library, Acc 2558/CH/1/2-4, which contain references to Bridgeman. Mention is made here of Hyde Park and St James's Park.

12 For instance, Briony Blackwell informs me that a gardener William Bridgeman appears in the accounts of the Dutton family of Sherborne of *c.* 1693-1710 in Gloucestershire Record Office, D678(55N) and D678(148); and Dr Keith Goodway refers me to another gardener by the name of William Bridgman, of Spittlefields, Middlesex, whose title deeds of 1738/39 are now in Derbyshire Record Office, Matlock, Deposit 157, Snelston Hall.

In addition Mr Howard Colvin tells me of a payment of £5 11s. 6d. in 1694 to 'Bridgman the gardener' in volume 41, 'An Account Book of the Archer Family, Commencing in the Year 1691', in the James Orchard Halliwell-Phillips Collection, Library of Congress, Washington, DC. This probably relates to Coopersale, Essex. I must thank Mr Charles J. Kelly, Manuscript Reference Librarian at the Library of Congress, for his help.

13 A drawing excluded from the following catalogue is in the Bodleian Library, MS Maps, Misc.a.l; it has been suggested that this may be a Bridgeman plan of Amesbury, Wiltshire, but this is doubtful.

14 The largest single collection of Bridgeman drawings remains that in MS Gough Drawings A3 and A4 in the Bodleian Library, Oxford. For a catalogue see my 'Charles Bridgeman: Royal Gardener' (unpublished Ph.D. thesis, University of Cambridge, 1961), appendix F(b), pp. 396-423. A copy of this appendix has been deposited in the Bodleian Library.

15 A landscape with Bridgemanic features, though apparently with no documentation linking it to the royal gardener, is Castle Hill, Devon. See *Bridgeman*, p. 62, and Plates 54a, 54b, and subsequently Kenneth Woodbridge, 'Landscaping at Castle Hill', *Country Life*, clxv (4 January 1979), pp. 18-21; Robin Fausset, 'The Creation of the Gardens at Castle Hill, South Molton, Devon', *Garden History*, xiii, no. 2 (Autumn 1985), pp. 102-125; and the correspondence in *Garden History*, xv, no. 2 (Autumn 1987), pp. 167-171, which includes a 'reply' by John Harris.

CATALOGUE

The following catalogue is confined to documentary and published sources of Bridgeman's work, with cross-references to Peter Willis, *Charles Bridgeman and the English Landscape Garden*, Studies in Architecture, xvii (London: Zwemmer, 1977).

Gardens or landscapes which were not ascribed to Bridgeman in this book – and which now may be suggested as new attributions – are marked in the catalogue with an asterisk. These are Dallington (Northamptonshire) or The Rolls House (London), Esher (Surrey), Lumley Castle (County Durham), Lodge Park at Sherborne (Gloucestershire), and Wroxall or Wroxhall Manor (Warwickshire).

BADMINTON (Gloucestershire)

Bridgeman is referred to in four letters written to the 4th Duke of Beaufort (1709-56) when he was Lord Noel Somerset, preserved at Badminton and arranged by him in bundles; each letter is endorsed with the name of the correspondent and date. They are published here by courtesy of His Grace the Duke of Beaufort, and were drawn to my attention by Mrs Margaret Richards and Professor Andor Gomme (who initially transcribed them).

From the 3rd Duke of Beaufort, 8 February 1733/34

> As to Wootton & Bridgeman I can't tell what to say for Smith was here yesterday & shakes his Head sadly abt a Pediment[,] the Walls of ye House being very narrow & draw'd in at [the] Top; & likewise queries how it will look in all ye other Fronts since there can be nothing to back it, for it will be much Higher than the Cupillo is now.

From the Duchess of Beaufort, 11 March 1733/34

> The draught Bridgeman sent down for Badminton is one of the Grandest things I have seen, and will I believe answer in the execution as well as it does upon paper. My Ld: seems much please'd with it, and I hope it meets with your favourable opinion, least I shou'd be oblige'd to call my own judgement in question.

From the 3rd Duke of Beaufort, 17 March 1733/34

> I am glad to find the Drawings got safe to Town, and must beg you to get either Wootton or Bridgeman to draw me out a Plan of ye Foundations of ye Temple & Gateway that I may know ye size of 'em in order to [start] ye setting out [of] ye Ground for levelling it to be ready for planting next Season . . . Pray put Bridgeman in mind yt ye Temple is broader than the Plan of ye House he put into ye Design which he left here.

From the 3rd Duke of Beaufort, 30 March 1734 [A postscript]

> pray send ye Plans of ye Ground Plots of ye Houses from Bridgeman as soon as you can for I want 'em sadly.

For the context of these letters see Andor Gomme, 'Badminton Revisited', *Architectural History*, xxvii (1984), pp. 163-82.

See *Bridgeman*, pp. 71, 84, 88, 118 n. 46, 135, and plates 86, 87.

BLENHEIM (Oxfordshire)

Frances Harris, 'Charles Bridgeman at Blenheim?', *Garden History*, xiii, 1 (Spring 1985), pp. 1-3, casts doubt on Bridgeman's work at Blenheim.

Her view is based on the correspondence between Sarah, Duchess of Marlborough, and Mrs Sarah Bridgeman, of ?1739-41, which she believes refers not to Blenheim but to Bridgeman's landscaping at Wimbledon. See below the catalogue entry under WIMBLEDON, Surrey. Two of the three letters from the Duchess to Mrs Bridgeman of 6 July, 26 July and 10 September 1741 (published in *Bridgeman*, pp. 157-60) are now in the BL, Add. MS 61478, fos. 39-40 (6 July), 45-46 (10 September). Eight unpublished letters from Mrs Bridgeman to the Duchess ?1739-1741 are in Add. MS 61478, fos. 9-12, 17-18, 31-34, 43-44, 47-48, 51-52.

See *Bridgeman*, passim, and Frances Harris, *A Passion for Government: The Life of Sarah, Duchess of Marlborough* (Oxford, 1991).

CLIVEDEN (Buckinghamshire)

Bridgeman's work at Cliveden is referred to in the correspondence of George Hamilton, 1st Earl of Orkney (1666-1737), and his family, in the National Library of Scotland, Edinburgh (Fraser Collection, MS 1033).

On 2 October 1723 Orkney writes to one of his brothers from Cliveden about the landscape there (MS 1033, fo. 157), commenting:

> I must doe the best I can but it is a greater work than I thought but I still think it will be much better than was Intended (but the Amphitheatre is quite struck out) wher[e] to get turfe and trees for la grand machine, beside ther[e] is great difficulty to get the slope all that side of the Hill where the precipice was, but Bridgeman mackes difficultys of nothing[.] I told him if I had thought [it] had been the one Half of what I see it will cost, I believe I never had done it, he says the *begining* is the worst . . .

The suggestion here is that Bridgeman may well have designed the amphitheatre at Cliveden, and that 'la grand machine' may have been a hydraulic machine, later abandoned.

For an interpretation of Bridgeman's work at Cliveden see the following three articles by Gervase Jackson-Stops: 'The Cliveden Album: Drawings by Archer, Leoni and Gibbs for the 1st Earl of Orkney', *Architectural History*, xix (1976), pp. 5-16; 'Formal Garden Designs for Cliveden: The Work of Claude Desgots and Others for the 1st Earl of Orkney', *National Trust Year Book, 1976-77* (London, [1977]), pp. 100-17; 'Cliveden, Buckinghamshire', *Country Life*, clxi (24 February, 3 March 1977), pp. 438-41, 498-501.

See *Bridgeman*, p. 127 n. 84.

*DALLINGTON (Northamptonshire) or *THE ROLLS HOUSE (London)

Dallington Hall was built or rebuilt about 1726-30 by Francis Smith of Warwick for Sir Joseph Jekyll (1663-1738), the Master of the Rolls, and accounts of Goslings Bank indicate that Jekyll paid Bridgeman £10 on 17 March 1721/22. Jekyll's agent, Professor Andor Gomme believes, was Charles Frewen, and Goslings's records show that he paid Bridgeman £20 on 31 May 1735.

Jekyll was also the client for The Rolls House, Chancery Lane, London (1717-24), designed by Colen Campbell, and the possibility that the earlier Bridgeman payment refers to this should not be discounted.

*ESHER (Surrey)

Payment is made to Bridgeman of £52. 10s. on 17 March 1734/35 by the Hon. Henry Pelham (1695-1754) in his account at Hoares Bank, London, presumably for Esher Place. Kent worked at Esher from about 1729. His landscaping is covered in John Dixon Hunt, *William Kent, Landscape Garden Designer: An Assessment and Catalogue of his Designs* (London, 1987).

See *Bridgeman*, pp. 48-49, 140.

GOBIONS or GUBBINS (Hertfordshire)

Gobions or Gubbins was the seat of Jeremy Sambrooke (*c.* 1677-1754), who became a baronet in 1740. There is an undated plan of the estate in the Gloucester Record Office, Gloucester (D/1245.FF75), which bears the inscription 'Surveyed by Tho: Holmes' in the lower left-hand corner (Fig. 98). The drawing itself (on which Sambrooke's name appears) is the work of several hands; part of it is in Bridgeman's style and could well have been added by him.

Although no plan of Gobions of Bridgeman's date exists in the County Record Office, Hertford, there is a layout of *c.* 1815 (34137) which shows the park and ornamental water 'as done by Bridgeman'. The County Archivist, Dr Kathryn M. Thompson, told me of this.

See *Bridgeman*, pp. 18, 84, 86-87, 132, and plates 83, 84.

Fig. 98 Gobions or Gubbins
(Herts.), detail attributed to
Bridgeman of undated plan by
Thomas Holmes and others, ink,
pencil and water-colour; 1555 ×
690 mm. (*Gloucestershire Record
Office, D/1245.FF75*)

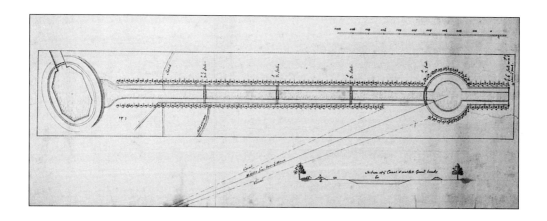

Fig. 99 Kedleston (Derbys.), plan of canal and cascades attributed to Bridgeman (*c.* 1725), ink,
pencil and water-colour; 685 × 273 mm. (*National Trust, Scarsdale Collection, Kedleston Hall*)

KEDLESTON (Derbyshire)

Payment is made to Bridgeman of £51 11s. on 10 November 1722 by Sir John Curzon, 3rd Bt (*c.* 1674-1727) in his account at Hoares Bank, London. See *Bridgeman*, p. 87 for payments to Bridgeman in 1722 and 1726, and other references on pp. 33 n. 41, 84, 118 n. 46, 128, 132.

Francis Smith of Warwick had built the Kedleston in existence at this time and was back doing alterations between 1724 and 1734. A plan showing a canal with cascades at Kedleston (Fig. 99), attributed to Bridgeman, *c.* 1725, is at the house and is reproduced as pl. 52 in Leslie Harris, *Robert Adam and Kedleston: The Making of a Neo-Classical Masterpiece* (London, 1987).

LONGFORD CASTLE (Wiltshire)

Bridgeman's work on the grounds at Longford in about 1737 for Sir Jacob Bouverie, 3rd Bt (?1694-1761), created 1st Viscount Folkestone and Baron Longford in 1747, was noted in *Bridgeman*, pp. 58, 88, 118n. 46.

This is confirmed by Helen Matilda, Countess of Radnor, and William Barclay Squire, *Catalogue of the Pictures in the Collection of the Earl of Radnor*, ii (London, 1909), pp. 33, 45. Mr Howard Colvin kindly told me of this.

*LUMLEY CASTLE (County Durham)

Two drawings of Lumley Castle, now at Sandbeck Park, Yorkshire, in the collection of the Earl of Scarbrough, may be dated *c.* 1721 and attributed to Bridgeman; the better of the two is entitled 'Lumley Castle' (Figs. 100, 101), otherwise the drawings are virtually identical.

These drawings may well have been completed in collaboration with Vanbrugh, who remodelled the south and west ranges for Richard Lumley, 2nd Earl of Scarbrough (*c.* 1688-1740) from 1722 onwards (as attested, for example, by Kerry Downes, *Vanbrugh* (1977), especially pp. 106-7). Making at least one if not two visits to Lumley, Vanbrugh wrote in August 1721 that he found the castle 'a Noble thing' and that he was able 'to form a general Design for the whole, which consists, in altering the house both for state, Beauty and Convenience; and making the Courts, Gardens, and offices suitable to it' (Webb, ed., *Letters*, pp. 138, 142). Could not Bridgeman have been involved in these proposals?

It is worth noting that Vanbrugh prepared designs for a house for John Hedworth at Chester-le-Street, near Lumley (Downes, *Vanbrugh* [1977], p. 278), which Howard Colvin suggested in *A Biographical Dictionary of British Architects, 1600-1840* (1978), p. 184, may have been a rival scheme to one of 1716 by Colen Campbell.

Stephen Switzer may have been involved at Gateshead Park and Gibside (County Durham), and he mentions Lumley Castle in *An Introduction to a*

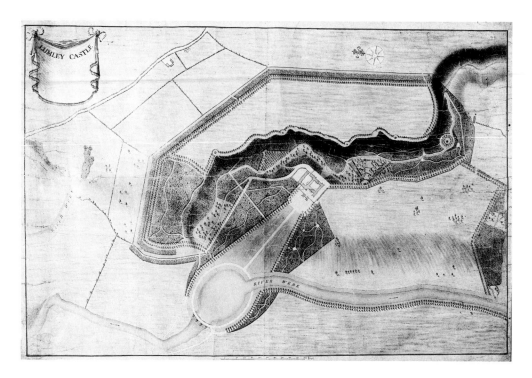

Fig. 100 Lumley Castle (Durham), plan attributed to Bridgeman (*c.* 1721), ink. pencil and water-colour; 1205 × 775 mm. (*Sandbeck Park, Yorks.*)

Fig. 101a and b (*opposite above and below*) Lumley Castle (Durham), details of plan attributed to Bridgeman (*c.* 1721).

a

b

RIVER WERE

General System of Hydrostaticks and Hydraulicks, Philosophical and Practical (1729), i, p. 274.

At Sandbeck there are also drawings of Lumley in Vanbrugh's manner, and designs for a gothick fisherman's lodge.

SACOMBE (Hertfordshire)

Payments are made to Bridgeman of £30 on 2 July 1715 and £60 on 16 June 1716 by Edward Rolt (1686-1722) in his account at Hoares Bank, London (Andor Gomme).

See *Bridgeman*, pp. 59, 60, 118 n. 46, 131, 176, 182, and plates 46a, 46b.

SHARDELOES (Buckinghamshire)

Payment is made to Bridgeman of £50 on 27 January 1725/26 by Montagu Garrard Drake (1692-1728) in his account at Hoares Bank, London (Andor Gomme). Drake's private account book for 1722-27 was donated to Hoares in 1979 and also contains this payment, which endorses Loudon and Felton's ascriptions of the landscape at Shardeloes to Bridgeman noted in *Bridgeman*, p. 63 n. 104. See also p. 79 and plate 72a.

*SHERBORNE, Lodge Park (Gloucestershire)

Work by Bridgeman at Lodge Park, Sherborne, for Sir John Dutton, 2nd Bt (1684-1743), is noted in Dutton's will, dated 30 March 1742, published in *Historical and Genealogical Memoirs of the Dutton Family, of Sherborne, in Gloucestershire . . .* (1899), compiled by Morgan Blacker, with an introduction by Lord Sherborne.

A transcription of the will is on pp. 236-246, and on p. 244 we read:

> I strictly enjoin and desire every person in whom my estate shall vest by this my will to finish and perfect the plantations I have begun at my new park [Lodge Park] and all the other work I intended there pursuant to a plan made by Mr. CHARLES BRIDGEMAN for that purpose which plan I desire may be strictly pursued excepting only in those particulars which I shall direct to be varied from in a paper in my own handwriting which I will leave enclosed in this my will and when the same are finished I desire they may be always kept in good order.

The will itself (with others of Sir John Dutton) is in the Dutton of Sherborne collection at Gloucestershire Record Office, Gloucester (D678.FAM.57).

Sir John Dutton's accounts are also at Gloucester (GRO.D678.FAM. SETT.148). Miss K.M. Fretwell summarises those between 1723 and 1742 in appendix 5 of her *Sherborne and Lodge Parks: Park and Garden Survey* (National Trust, 1990), pp. 43-53.

We find here that on 22 December 1729 Bridgeman is paid £70 'for his journeys to Shireborn and making a plan for [Sir John's] New Park', which may well be the drawing referred to in the baronet's will. Apart from minor Bridgemanic payments for transport and miscellaneous expenses in 1725, 1729 and 1731, on 24 April 1734 Sir John records payment of two guineas for his 'subscription for Mr Bridgeman's Prints of Ld. Cobham's Gardens' at Stowe. Kent and Wootton also appear in the accounts: Kent is paid three guineas on 3 March 1723/4 for a subscription for 'Inigo Jones' works', and thirty guineas on 29 October 1728 for 'his trouble making plans for me at My Lodge & House'; John Wootton thirty guineas also (on 6 July 1725) for 'a landskip for my Drawing Room Chimney'.

STOWE (Buckinghamshire)

Three MS account books kept by the steward at Stowe, William Jacob, and covering part of Bridgeman's period there, are in the University of Reading Library, Estates of the Dukes of Buckingham and Chandos, BUC 11/1/2-4. Jacob was steward to Viscount Cobham, formerly Sir Richard Temple, 4th Bt, of Stowe (1675-1749). The accounts cover outgoing payments for carpenters, carters, etc., from Michaelmas 1717 to Lady Day 1718.

Manuscripts at the British Library and the Henry E Huntington Library, San Marino, CA, are cited in George B. Clarke, 'Where did All the Trees Come From? An Analysis of Bridgeman's Planting at Stowe', *Journal of Garden History*, 5, no. 1 (January-March 1985), pp. 72-83.

See *Bridgeman*, passim.

WIMBLEDON (Surrey)

Frances Harris, 'Charles Bridgeman at Blenheim?', *Garden History*, xiii, 1 (Spring 1985), pp. 1-3, proposes that correspondence between Sarah, Duchess of Marlborough and Mrs Sarah Bridgeman of ?1739-41 refers to Wimbledon rather than Blenheim, as I had supposed. See *Bridgeman*, pp. 45, 58-59, 88, 157, 159, 184, and plates 43a-44b, and the catalogue entry above under BLENHEIM.

Dr Harris informs me that on 1 March (?1748) the Duchess of Marlborough's executors 'Paid Mrs Sarah Bridgeman in full of what was due from her Grace to Charles Bridgeman her late Father deceased at the time of his Death' (BL, Althorp Papers, temporary no. D32, fos. 146-147). The sum was £880 17s. 0d. which is close to the disputed figure of £897 25s. 8½d. mentioned in the Duchess's letter to Mrs Bridgeman of 26 July 1741. As Bridgeman's widow Sarah had died in 1743/44, could the executors have been making payment to the Royal Gardener's daughter Sarah (born 1720)? See Dr Harris's article, '"The Best Workmen of All Sorts". The Building of Wimbledon House, 1730-1742', *Georgian Group Journal* (1992), pp. 87-90.

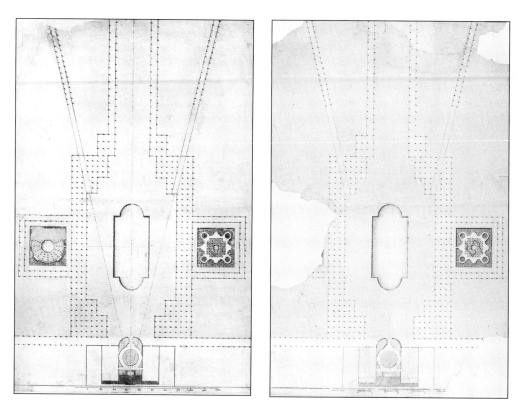

Fig. 102a and b Wimpole (Cambs.), plans attributed to Bridgeman (*c.* 1721-24), ink and wash; 750 × 520 mm. and 755 × 520 mm. (*National Trust, Bambridge Collection, Wimpole Hall*)

Fig. 103 Wimpole (Cambs.), plans attributed to Bridgeman: (a) (*c.* 1720), ink and pencil; 420 × 325 mm. (*top*); (b) (*c.* 1721-24), ink and pencil; 560 × 535 mm. (*bottom left*) (*both National Trust, Bambridge Collection, Wimpole Hall*); (c) (*c.* 1721-24), ink; 600 × 515 mm (*right*) (*British Library, Add MS 36278, M1*)

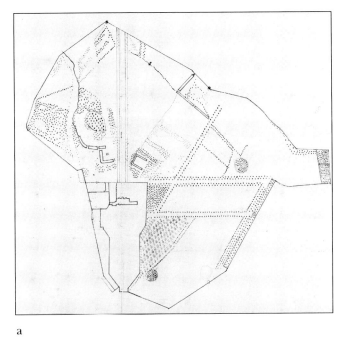

a

b

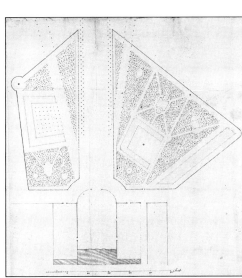

c

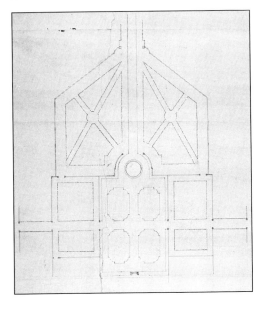

WIMPOLE (Cambridgeshire)

Five Bridgemanic drawings of Wimpole (Figs. 102, 103) may be added to the four in the Bodleian Library, Oxford (MS Gough Drawings, A4, fos. 30, 31, 35, 69), four being at the house and the fifth in the BL (Add. MS 36278, M1). Their context is considered in John Phibbs' survey for the National Trust, *Wimpole Park, Cambridgeshire* (1980). Another drawing at Wimpole which may possibly be by Bridgeman is reproduced in David Souden's National Trust guide, *Wimpole Hall, Cambridgeshire* (London, 1991), p. 14.

Other relevant published accounts are Gervase Jackson-Stops, 'Exquisite Contrivances: The Park and Gardens at Wimpole', *Country Life*, clxvi (6 September 1979), pp. 658-61; Dorothy Stroud, 'The Charms of Natural Landscape: The Park and Gardens of Wimpole', *Country Life*, clxvi (13 September 1979), pp. 758-62; and Eric Parry, 'Wimpole Hall', *Architects' Journal*, clxxxiii (26 March 1986), pp. 36-55.

On p. 70 of *Bridgeman* it is assumed that the ballad celebrating an excursion to Wimpole in 1721, entitled 'A Hue and Cry after Four of the King's Liege Subjects, who were Lately suppos'd to be seen at Roystone in Hartfordshire', was written by Thornhill, and that the participants were Bridgeman, Wootton, Gibbs, and Thornhill himself.

As Professor Pierre du Prey pointed out to me, this was questioned by William Pinkerton in *Notes and Queries*, 3rd series, vi (17 December 1864), pp. 490-91, where Wootton is replaced by the engraver Christian in the identifications, and Bridgeman is given as the author of the ballad. The last two lines of it read:

> Surrounded with Pickax, wth Maddox, and Spade,
> The Ballad is ended, in Wheelbarrow made.

'From the last two lines', writes Pinkerton on p. 491, 'we may conclude the piece was written by Bridgeman, who, it will be observed in the notes, which are in the original, does not give his own name, but merely "The Gardiner".' Pinkerton's 'original' is in the BL, Lansdowne MS 846, fos. 165-166, and is undated.

Two other manuscript versions of the poem formerly at Welbeck are now in the Portland literary collection in Nottingham University Library (Pw V, 416-417). The ascription of authorship to Thornhill is based on Francis Needham's attribution when he published 'A Hue and Cry' in *A Collection of Poems by Several Hands, Never before Published*, Welbeck Miscellany, no. 2 (1934), pp. 53-56; this text was adopted by the *Wren Society*, xvii (1940), pp. 11-13. However the Keeper of Manuscripts and Special Collections at Nottingham, Dr Dorothy B. Johnston, kindly informs me that 'there is no reference to Thornhill on either copy [of the poem]' and that indeed Francis Needham must have realised that the copies were not in Thornhill's hand. This can be seen from the opinion expressed in a letter of 1934 by Robin Flower of the British Museum, which is kept with them at Nottingham.

See *Bridgeman*, passim.

*WROXALL or WROXHALL MANOR (Warwickshire)

Dr Christine Hodgetts has drawn attention to the possibility that Charles Bridgeman was involved at Wroxall Manor. This is based on an illustration (Figs. 104, 105) in John William Ryland's *Records of Wroxall Abbey and Manor, Warwickshire* (London, 1903), which bears the following caption:

> This plan and survey of the Manor of Wroxhall was made by Mr. Bridgman in the year of our Lord one thousand seven hundred and fourteen: I have known this plan and survey for upwards of sixty-two years when in the possession of my grandfather Christopher Wren, Esqr. Wroxhall February the Eighteenth 1831. Chris Wren.

In 1714, the date of the map, the estate had just been bought by the architect Sir Christopher Wren, though he may never have lived there, and it became the home of his son, Christopher. According to the caption the original drawing by Bridgeman measured 6 ft by 2 ft 11 in, and Ryland notes on p. xli that it was 'in the possession of J. Broughton Dugdale, Esq.' Its present whereabouts are unknown.

Warwick had connections with both Bridgeman and Henry Wise, who retired to Warwick when his period as Royal Gardener came to an end in 1728. Bridgeman and James Fish, the Younger (1673-1740), had produced a drawing of Warwick town and priory in 1711, and about 1727 a further Bridgemanic plan of the priory was completed.

See *Bridgeman*, pp. 31 n. 30, 33, 35, 37, 175-176, 184, and plate 18.

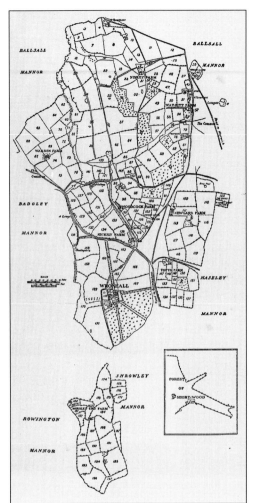

Fig. 104 Wroxall [Wroxhall] Manor (Warks.), plan and survey by 'Mr Bridgman' (1714), from John William Ryland, *Records of Wroxall Abbey and Manor, Warwickshire* (1903), facing p. lxviii.

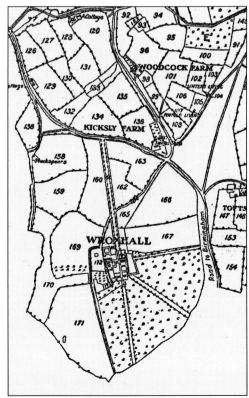

Fig. 105 Wroxall [Wroxhall] Manor (Warks.), detail of plan and survey by 'Mr Bridgman' (1714).

19

Sir James Thornhill's Portrait of Stephen Duck (1731)

GEORGE KNOX

Thornhill's portrait of Stephen Duck (1705-56), the 'thresher poet', has always been a matter of record, for it was engraved by George Bickham the younger, for the folio edition of Duck's *Poems of Several Occasions* (London, 1736) (Fig. 106)[1], unequivocally inscribed 'Thornhill, Eq. Pinx:'. As such it is noticed in the *British Museum Catalogue of Engraved British Portraits*. It was remarked upon, and reproduced, thirty years ago, in a most admirable and amusing account of Duck by J.L. Nevinson in the *Country Life Annual* of 1961, as '2. Stephen Duck: An Engraving after a Lost Portrait by Thornhill'.[2]

Thus it is pleasant to be able to report that this lost portrait (Fig. 107) came to light in a sale in Vancouver in 1984, in perfectly good condition.[3] It has been relined and on the relining is an inscription, no doubt copied from a similar inscription on the original canvas, reading 'Rev.d Stephen Duck/The Poet/ Painted by Sir James Thornhill/and Hogarth/for Queen Caroline/Wife of George. 2nd 1731'.

This is perhaps not the right place to go into the full details of the career of Stephen Duck, but the writer of the inscription seems to be in adequate possession of the facts. The most crucial of these are set out in the title-page of perhaps the first printing of a selection of his poems, which reads:

Poems on Several Subjects, Written by Stephen Duck, Lately a poor *Thresher* in a Barn [at Charlton, added in MS] in the County of *Wilts*, at the Wages of Four Shillings and Six Pence *per* Week: Which were publickly read by The Right Honourable the Earl of *Macclesfield*, in the Drawing-Room at *Windsor* Castle, on *Friday* the 11th of *September*, 1730, to Her MAJESTY. Who was thereupon most graciously pleased to take the Author into her Royal Protection, by allowing him a

---

* It is a happy occasion when a person mostly concerned with Venetian painting and drawing of the eighteenth century must search around for an English topic, preferably in the age of Vanbrugh and Hawksmoor. This must also be my excuse for doing the inexcusable, in drawing attention to a work of art in which I 'have an interest', as the politicians would say.

1 Many copies appear to lack the frontispiece.

2 J.L. Nevinson, 'Stephen Duck, the Thresher-Poet', *Country Life Annual* (London, 1961), pp. 144-47. I am grateful to Dr John Bold for drawing my attention to this article. See also *The Gentleman's Magazine*, vi (1736), pp. 316-19.

3 Maynard's sale, Vancouver, 9 October 1984, lot 48 (reproduced), oil on canvas, $21\frac{1}{4}'' \times 15\frac{1}{4}''$.

Fig. 106 *Stephen Duck*, engraving by George Bickham after Sir James Thornhill (*c.* 1735).

Fig. 107 *Stephen Duck*, portrait by Sir James Thornhill (1731). (*George Knox*)

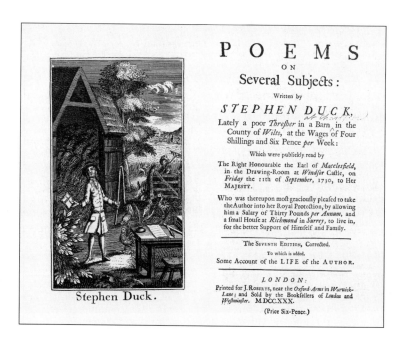

Fig. 108 Frontispiece and title-page of Stephen Duck, *Poems on Several Subjects* (London, 1730).

Fig. 109 John Sheppard, engraving by George White after Sir James Thornhill (1724).

Fig. 110 Speaker Onslow in the House of Commons by Sir James Thornhill (1730). (*National Trust, Clandon Park*)

Fig. 111 Sarah Malcolm, portrait by William Hogarth (1733). (*National Gallery of Scotland, Edinburgh*)

Fig. 112 Sarah Malcolm, engraving by William Hogarth (1733). (*British Museum*)

Salary of Thirty Pounds *per Annum*, and a small House at *Richmond* in *Surrey*, to live in, for the better Support of Himself and Family'.[4]

The frontispiece shows the young poet, aged twenty-five, standing in a farm-yard with a copy of Milton in his right hand, and a flail in his left, and a writing desk nearby (Fig. 108). After the death of the Queen he did indeed take holy orders.

It is not at all improbable that the Queen should command her Sergeant Painter to paint a likeness of her protégé in 1731,[5] and not even impossible that Sir James (1675-1734) might have delegated the task to his son-in-law, William Hogarth (1697-1764), then aged thirty-four. However, when the time came for Bickham to make his cut, it would be natural to use Thornhill's name rather than Hogarth's.[6]

Thornhill's reputation rests upon his vast decorations but he did paint some formal portraits, life-size, among them one of Sir Isaac Newton, dated 1710.[7] He is recorded as having done some smaller portraits of a more popular character, the most celebrated of them being that of the highwayman John Sheppard (1702-24), more often known as Jack, in his cell at Newgate. This was engraved in mezzotint, no doubt in the year 1724, with the inscription 'J Thornhill Eques delin/ G White fecit' (Fig. 109). George White (*c.* 1671-1732), 'one of the first of the real artists among the mezzotinters', according to Hind, was a far more impressive performer than Bickham, and had he lived, he might well have been entrusted with the engraving of Duck. Even so the two designs are clearly related, with a similar relationship of sitter to space, and a similar *contraposto* – though young Jack Sheppard, with his face turned towards the daylight of the past, and his finger pointing to the darkness of his future, is the more moving image.[8]

4 I quote from a copy of 'the Seventh Edition, Corrected' (London, 1730), in the library of the University of British Columbia. This edition is referred to by Nevinson as pirated. He reproduces the frontispiece and title-page of the 8th edition (1731).

5 Sir Oliver Millar tells me that there is no record of such a painting in the inventories of the time.

6 A second smaller engraved portrait of Duck, inscribed 'Bickham sculp' is used as the front-ispiece of an octavo edition of Duck, *Poems on Several Occasions* (London, 1737). Little is known of the Bickham family of engravers. George Bickham senior receives a brief note in Horace Walpole, *Lives of the Painters*. His son is very briefly noted by Arthur M. Hind, *A Short History of Engraving and Etching* (London, 1911), p. 379, as the author of the *Universal Penman*, died 1769. See also, George

Bickham, *The Universal Penman*, facsimile edition with a foreword by Philip Hofer (Jericho, New York, 1941); Ambrose Heal, *The English Writing Masters and their Copy Books, 1570-1800* (Cambridge, 1931); P.H. Muir, 'The Bickhams and their *Universal Penman*', *The Library*, xxv (1945), p. 192; George Bickham, *Deliciae Brittanicae* (London, 1742); George Bickham, *The Beauties of Stow* (London, 1750) – The Augustan Reprint Society, nos. 185-86 (1977), with an introduction by George Clarke.

7 C.H. Collins Baker, 'Antonio Verrio and Thornhill's Early Portraiture', *Connoisseur*, cxxxi (March 1953), pp. 10-13 (IV).

8 There is a pen and wash drawing , possibly by Thornhill, in the London Museum: John Kerslake, *Catalogue of the Eighteenth Century Portraits in the National Portrait Gallery* (London, 1977) [732].

Another painting by Thornhill, which must surely be taken into account here, is the *Portrait of Speaker Onslow in the House of Commons*, at Clandon Park (Fig. 110), according to the inscription written on the scroll, bottom right: 'Done by/ S.r James Thornhill/ then a member/ of the/ House of Commons/ 1730'.[9] There is also a related drawing at the Yale Centre for British Art, with a key, identifying '4. M.r Staples ye first Clerk', and '8. S.r Ja: Thornhill', on the right of the first row, and on the scroll: 'J. Thornhill An.D. 1731'.[10] In the portrait of Mr Staples, one of the three principal figures, in the right foreground, the close resemblance to that of Stephen Duck is very striking.

This may be sufficient grounds to discard once and for all the notion of Hogarth's involvement in the *Portrait of Stephen Duck*, but unfortunately there is also some question of Hogarth's involvement with the *Speaker Onslow*. This is generally thought to be confined to the portrait of Thornhill and his two associates in the first row of seats.[11] At Clandon Park it is not possible to examine the painting at all closely, and I might be wise to leave the issue in the hands of specialists in Hogarth. But I feel that the early tradition indicated on the back of my portrait should not be too hastily dismissed.

There is an additional aspect to the problem. We have noted that only one secure full portrait in oils by Thornhill appears to be on record, *Sir Isaac Newton*, dated 1710, though there are others of the same period which can be linked with it. In 1720 he was able to buy back his family estate at Thornhill in Dorset and to rebuild the house, and in 1722 he became the Member of the House of Commons for Melcombe Regis. At this point he appears to have effectively abandoned large-scale decorative painting,[12] and had begun to try his hand at architecture.[13] Thus the portraits of Speaker Onslow and Stephen Duck are the only documented portraits subsequent to 1710 and the only new paintings, apparently, later than 1722. Meanwhile Hogarth was in his early thirties and very close to Thornhill, in spite of a brief rift following his marriage to Jane Thornhill in 1729, at the age of thirty-two, and with some claim to be regarded as heir to Thornhill's position as a painter. Moreover one must take into

9   The National Trust, Clandon Park, 50" x 40". Coll. Earl of Hardwick, 1888; Colville sale (anon.), Christie's, 24 February 1939 [52], as by W. Hogarth and Sir J. Thornhill. Exhibited: National Portrait Exhibition, 1867, no. 285; 'Early Georgian Portraits', catalogue by John Kerslake, National Portrait Gallery, 1977, as: *The House of Commons 1730, with Portraits of the Speaker, Arthur Onslow Esq., Sir Robert Walpole, Sydney Godolphin Esq., Sir James Thornhill and others*. There are other versions of the picture at Wimpole, and in the Victoria and Albert Museum.

10   312 x 163 mm.; 'English Portrait Drawings and Miniatures', Yale Center for British Art,

1979-80 [27], with reference to other drawings: a. *Speaker Onslow in a Chair*, Colnaghi 1948, now at San Marino (Wark), and b. in the British Museum (Binyon).

11   R.B. Beckett, *Hogarth* (London, 1949) [21]; Ronald Paulson, *Hogarth: His Life, Art, and Times* (Newhaven, 1971) [66].

12   This has been linked with William Kent's success in securing the appointment to decorate Kensington Palace in March 1722, though the work on the Painted Hall at Greenwich was not completed until 1727.

13   H.M. Colvin, *Biographical Dictionary of British Architects* (London, 1978), pp. 824-26.

account Hogarth's other House of Commons paintings of these years, admittedly of a less formal character. In spite of the clear way in which Thornhill's name is linked with these two works, one cannot dismiss the possibility of Hogarth's intervention in both of them, to a greater degree than the written evidence implies.[14]

Finally one should consider briefly the matter of Hogarth's *Portrait of Sarah Malcolm* (Fig. 111) in the National Gallery of Scotland.[15] Sarah's crime of murder was reported on 5 February 1733 and she was hanged on 7 March.[16] Thornhill and Hogarth visited her in her cell on 5 March and the portrait no doubt followed closely after. It was also engraved by Hogarth (Fig. 112) in a manner which is in no way remote from those of Jack Sheppard and Stephen Duck.[17] It is most unfortunate that Stephen Duck should find himself in this rogues' gallery, but he shared with them both youth and celebrity, as well as lowly origins.[18]

14 Another item which obviously demands some reconsideration in this context is the drawing, *The Thornhill Family with Hogarth and Others* in the collection of the Marquis of Exeter – Paul Oppé, *Hogarth Drawings* (London, 1948) [fig. 1]. This is obviously a study for an ambitious portrait group, presumably to be carried out by Hogarth.

15 It is a full length (measuring $18\frac{1}{2}''$ x $14\frac{1}{2}''$), hence a little smaller than the *Stephen Duck*. cf. Frederick Antal, *Hogarth and his Place in European Art* (London, 1962), p. 56 [39a], as 1735;

Beckett [60].

16 For full details, see Paulson, *Hogarth: His Life, Art, and Times*, pp. 309-11.

17 British Museum, 1868-8-22-1212: Ronald Paulson, *Hogarth's Graphic Works* (London, 1989) [129]. The engraving cuts the image down to a three-quarter length. See also *Hogarth: His Life, Art, and Times* [112a, 112b].

18 Stephen Duck was twenty-six in 1731, Jack Sheppard and Sarah Malcolm were hanged at the age of twenty-two.

20

The Simeon Monument in Reading by Sir John Soane

ALAN WINDSOR

The anonymous author of a little book published in 1810, entitled *The Stranger in Reading*,[1] was an early example of the layman trying to come to terms with the Soane Style. He describes the Market Place as possessing, at its centre:

> a large stone lamp-post if such it may be called, of a triangular form to correspond, I suppose, with that of the market-place, but of what order of architecture, I was not able to discover; some of the ornaments however are British, some Roman and some Egyptian. The base or pedestal is, as you may conclude from its shape, divided into three compartments, in one of which, composed of the same kind of gingerbread work I mentioned before, are the town arms . . . In another compartment are the arms of the founder and in the third an inscription on a brass plate, recording the time of its erection.

(The inscription reads: 'Erected and lighted forever at the expence of Edward Simeon Esq. as a mark of affection to his native town AD 1804 Lancelot Austwick Esq. Mayor'.)

> The three facets, or corners of the base, are ornamented with what I first mistook for bundles of sticks or fagots with a woodman's axe thrust into the ends of each of them . . . On the pedestal is raised a triangular shaft, with facets ornamented in the Egyptian style, and surmounted at the top with something like an acorn. At each corner of the pedestal is a large lamp, for the maintenance whereof, for ever I am

* My thanks to Susan Palmer and Christine Scull at the Archive and the Library of Sir John Soane's Museum, to my colleagues, especially Paul Davies, for their advice and comments, and, for their help, to the staff of The Bank of England Archive; Blandy & Blandy, Solicitors, Reading; Berkshire Record Office; The British Museum; The Corporation of London Records Office; The Guildhall Library; Lambeth Palace Library; The National Register of Archives; Reading Public Library; Reading Museum and Art Gallery.

1 *The Stranger in Reading: In a Series of Letters from a Traveller to his friend in London*, printed by Snare and Man, Reading; the author is believed to have been John Man. It immediately provoked an indignant book by H. Gauntlett, calling himself 'Detector', *Letters to the Stranger in Reading*, published by Powell & Co., London, later in 1810. In this book, any suggestion that Edward Simeon's endowments might not be altruistically motivated is scornfully dismissed, but the monument is not discussed.

a   b

c   d

Fig. 113 Drawings for the Simeon Monument: (a) No. 58, fo. 4 (*top left*); (b-d) Nos. 10-12, set 3, drawer 65 (*top right, bottom left and right*), (*Sir John Soane's Museum*)

Fig. 114 The Simeon Monument, Reading.

told, the founder has funded a sufficient sum of money in annuities, under the management of the Corporation. It is surrounded by a handsome iron railing, and may, upon the whole, be called a pretty, rather than a correct, design for a lamp post.[2]

The monument he was describing had been commissioned a few years earlier by Edward Simeon, (c. 1755-1812) a successful City merchant and a director of the Bank of England. He was a director of the Bank from 1792 to 1811, and appears to have become very rich indeed. In London he lived in Salvador(e) House, a large early eighteenth-century house which stood at the end of White Hart Court off Bishopsgate Street.[3] He maintained contacts with Reading, where he had been married (1792) and where he was eventually buried.[4]

Mr Simeon wrote to the Mayor of Reading (Lancelot Austwick, who had been sworn in the previous month, and for whom Soane had designed a house in c. 1796) on 24 January 1804, to make known his desire to erect, at his own expense, 'an obelisk in the center of the Market place. The obelisk to have four lamps'. He had long felt, he wrote, a secret wish to improve the lighting there; he argued that the project would also rationalise the circulation of traffic by obliging the drivers of waggons to take 'a regular line' on market days. If the corporation would agree to this proposal, he promised, 'The architect will be directed to present the proposed plan and carry the same into immediate effect'. He did not name Soane.[5]

---

2 *The Stranger*, pp. 40-43. Simeon gave £1,000 on 7 July 1805 in Reduced 3 per cent Annuities to pay for the expenses of lighting and maintenance. This stock was transferred in 1883 into the name of the Official Trustee; the dividends were then used in paying for gas supplied to the three lamps. W. Blandy, *A History of the Reading Municipal Charities* (Reading, 1962), p. 41.

3 Soane (who had just begun his first major work at the Bank of England) surveyed a gateway for Mr Simeon on 23 May 1792, a month after he had been elected Director of the Bank (*Day Book*, 1792 and *Journal*, ii, 1792-93, Soane Museum). He also saw to other minor work in 1793. He noted that he gave directions 'about stair, windows and chimney in hall' in November 1804 (*Journal*, iv, 1797-1804). The house was described by the Rev. Thomas Hugo, *Illustrated Itinerary of the Ward of Bishopsgate in the City of London* (London, 1862) as having 'an imposing hall, magnificent staircase, well proportioned rooms, Louis Quatorze style cornices and doorcases etc.' The outline plan of the house

appears on the OS for 1875, but it was evidently demolished with the construction of Bishopsgate Station, which was completed in November of that year. Simeon also had addresses at Catherine Hall, Cambridge (which Soane noted surveying, *Journal*, iv) and St. John's, Isle of Wight.

4 He married Harriet Parry (daughter of a Director of the East India Company) on 14 June 1792 at St Mary's (*Reading Mercury*, 18 June 1792) and died, 'cut off prematurely with a peculiar and distressing malady' on 14 December 1812 at Fitzroy Farm, Middlesex ('a villa in Highgate'); he was buried in the family vault at St Giles on the 22nd (*Reading Mercury*, 28 December 1812). A portrait of him by Sir William Beesley was bequeathed to the Corporation of Reading in 1836, and is now in store at the Art Gallery there. It depicts him holding a paper with the just readable words 'Reading' and 'Lighting' on it.

5 The letter is quoted in full in the minutes for the meeting of 31 January 1804, Corporation Diary, (1786-1809), Berkshire Record Office.

A series of drawings concerning this project survives in the Soane Museum,[6] and they are of some interest in that they suggest the evolution of the design of this strange (and never very popular) monument from its beginnings in a relatively orthodox architectural concept through to the characteristically Soanian form in which it was eventually built, and which it retains to this day: one in which, as John Man (who is believed to be the author of *The Stranger* etc.) recognised, there is a fusion of motifs from many different periods in architectural history.

It is very likely that they may have been offered as alternative projects, but I believe that the drawings (all inscribed 'Edward Simeon Esq. 1804') can to some extent be considered as a sequence leading to a sheet with a plan and elevation of the monument almost exactly as executed. I think that the drawings can be put in a conjectural order of execution as each one in the group incorporates some motifs common to at least one of the others; the features which are omitted from any given drawing (if they are a sequence) are also omitted from the monument as built, whilst those features which appear to have been introduced are those retained in the drawings which are closest to the monument as realised. A process of assimilation and elimination seems to be recognisable.

By this reasoning, the first idea for the monument appears to have been a tall pier, square in plan, with fluted Ionic columns set at each corner, surmounted by a correct entablature supporting a segmentally curved pediment on each face; the whole is crowned by a little dome, on top of which stands a caduceus, or Mercury's staff, entwined with snakes (Fig 113a). Each pediment is decorated with a wreath tied with flying ribbons, and the wall space between the columns is of ashlar blocks with strongly recessed joints. The whole rests on a plinth decorated with a Greek fret, and this is in turn set on a vigorously rusticated base which has diagonally placed piers, each with recessed panels at the corner, and each bearing a glazed lantern standing on wrought-iron scrolls. Each face of the base has a rectangular panel in the centre, and the projecting piers are protected from damage by traffic in time-honoured fashion by hemispherical stones standing on extensions of the base plinth of the entire monument.

It is essentially a Palladian design, recalling the basic elements of parts of any number of works familiar to Soane, and which he is known to have admired, from, for example, a typical bay of Inigo Jones's Banqueting House (of which Soane made his well-known measured drawing) to the piers of Sandby's Bridge

6 They are in fo. 4 and in drawer 65, set 3. Soane kept day books recording the work on which he and each of his assistants was engaged: The day book for 1804, however, is missing, so it is not possible to cite the exact date when most of the drawings were executed, or who did them. I am very grateful to Susan Palmer, the Archivist of the Soane Museum, for her opinion that 65/3/12 (see n. 14) was almost certainly by Henry Hake Seward.

of Magnificence of 1760. For that matter, the bays of Sir Robert Taylor's façade of the Bank of England were similarly composed. Perhaps Edward Simeon asked the architect for something combining features of a building familiar to him as a Director. Taylor's Court Room at the Bank (where Simeon very regularly attended meetings, as the court minutes show) was prominently decorated with the caduceus, an attribute of Mercury as god of merchants and of commerce (words which have their root in Mercury's Roman name).[7]

In his lectures at the Royal Academy some years later, Soane urged students to consider the symbolism of decoration very carefully, and condemned the arbitrary use of antique motifs without understanding of their meaning.[8] It is possible, therefore, that he also had in mind the role of the caduceus as an attribute of Mercury-Hermes as a patron of travellers, and of the ancient practice of setting up a stone, a herm, as a public landmark.

It is not so easy to understand the symbolism of the beribboned wreaths in the pediments: Sir John Summerson has suggested that this motif was taken by Soane from the lid of a Roman cinerary urn and has pointed out that his first use of it was for topping his gateposts at Pitzhanger (which are also, in block form, not unlike the design referred to above) in 1800.[9] It was a motif Soane used with variations on other designs: on the Bosanquet Monument of 1806, for example, and the Pitt Cenotaph of 1818.

There are two more perspective drawings, one a rough sketch, the other more precisely executed. The latter (No. 11 in the set) includes a faint sketch of a couple of figures in order to give scale (Fig. 113b). Both drawings offer a fundamental change, in that the whole monument is triangular in plan.[10] Soane here related the design to accord with the shape of the market-place (as Mr Man supposed) and in so doing reduced the number of lanterns to three. (Simeon's first letter to the mayor stated that there would be four, another argument for the first design being the one square in plan). There is also a sheet with a plan and elevation corresponding in most respects to the more precise design.

The base is similar in style to the rectangular design, but the upper shaft is inevitably different. As he could hardly have placed two Ionic volutes meeting at the corner (each volute would have been at an oblique angle to the

7 Court Minutes Books: Y through to Z (15 Dec 1791-10 Sept. 1795) and Aa to Ga (11 April 1811-2 April 1812), in the Bank of England Archives. Simeon was a member of a number of committees over the years (to examine the state of discounts; to appoint clerks etc.); he was the captain of 450 men raised as a corps for the defence of the Bank (1798) and was appointed to receive tenders of service from volunteers in 1803 when it was decided that war was imminent.

8 Lecture XI.

9 John Summerson *The Unromantic Castle* (London, 1990), pp. 125-26, and ill. 112 p. 134.

10 An outline plan to scale of the market place which is in the collection (signed by J.W. Sanderson), with an indication of the site of the monument, may have arrived at a stage when it reminded Soane of the triangular shape of the market place.

entablature above it), Soane placed the volutes of the capitals across each corner, making the entablature into a six-sided figure, with three long and three short faces, surmounted by six curved pediments, three big ones and three little ones, each one of which is a segment of a circle.

The angle columns of a perfectly normal Ionic system always present something of an aesthetic problem, but Soane's uncertainty as to how he should treat the capitals of columns placed on a 60° acute-angled corner is perhaps revealed in the minor variations in the three drawings relating to this design: one of them suggests that a little over half the volute of a four-sided Ionic capital should emerge from the 'wall' surface on either side; the other two indicate a pulvinus on either side instead , similarly emerging in an inelegant fashion from the oblique surface of the masonry. Setting such a capital, which is related in design to its abacus and which has to be square in plan, at the angle of an equilateral triangle cannot really avoid exposing two of its sides in an unacceptable way.

The seating of the little cupola on top of all this also presents difficulties: The drawing in Fig. 113b suggests a shell-like fan motif filling the place where several surfaces meet rather awkwardly. A Greek fret appears down the sides of the little piers supporting the lanterns.

Another well-finished perspective drawing differs in that there are no small pediments at the angles, while the crowning feature is a cylindrical, serpentine-fluted cinerary urn topped by a pine cone or pineapple, as in the monument as it was built. Vertical joints appear in the masonry of the surface between the columns and the fret is applied to the front of the lantern supports as well as the sides. Another drawing (of a side elevation), similar in all other respects, experiments with omitting the curved pediments. Yet another variant (a perspective) replaces the Ionic columns with fasces, a decoration which appears on the finished monument, and omits the entablature altogether. (Fig. 113c)[11]

In his *Journal* Soane noted sending 'two different fair drawings of design for the monument at Reading' on 4 April 1804 (by inference to Edward Simeon) and on 27 April that he had sent a plan to the Mayor, Austwick.[12] It was approved at a meeting of the Corporation in Reading on 15 May, and the Mayor signed the plan to confirm this.[13] Which drawings these were cannot be determined, but the final design was certainly ready a month later.

---

11 A very unattractive variant on this design, omitting any shaft, having a gross version of the serpentine-fluted cylinder, topped with a fourth lamp, was proposed by Soane for Norwich Market. Pierre de la Ruffinière du Prey, *Sir John Soane: Architectural Drawings in the Victoria and Albert Museum* (1985), catalogue, no. 86.

12 *Journal*, iv, Soane Museum.

13 Corporation Diary (1786-1809). Berkshire Record Office.

A scale drawing dated 29 May 1804, with detailed measurements showing the plan, an elevation and some of the mouldings set out large (Fig. 113d),[14] and a small mahogany model in the Soane Museum[15], represent the monument as a whole almost exactly as it was built.

A radical transformation of the proposed monument had taken place, compared with the designs so far described. The base is taller and narrower in proportion, while the piers supporting the lanterns are rounded, each decorated with a bundle of fasces and with deep vertical flutes on the sides. The upper part is a tapering three-sided shaft with splayed angles: its broad faces have five vertical flutes and the narrow ones a fret. The whole is crowned with six curved pediments (the three larger ones slope backwards and are as if sliced from a cushion-shaped form on the drawing, but they are in a vertical plane on the model, cut into a hemisphere, as in the monument as realised). The serpentine-fluted cinerary urn and its pineapple (inscribed 'copper, bronze or gilt' on the drawing) are more slender in proportion on the model.

When the building of the monument began, Soane travelled to Reading and stayed three days in July (the 19th, 20th and 21st; J. Lovegrove, a bricklayer, was paid £26 15s. 8d. on 23 July, presumably for the core), and Soane 'surveyed the monument' on 3 September, evidently when it was finished, as John Neville was paid for the lamps and lamp irons to support them shortly afterwards.

However a sum of £20 9s. 7d. still due to Mr Neville remained unpaid after his death, and so it remained until his brother William threatened (18 August 1809) to have a plate measuring 12 x 16 inches engraved and fixed to the obelisk bearing the following inscription:

Edward Simeon Esq. of Salvadore House Accepted From William Neville of Fleet Street London £20 9s. 7d. as a small donation towards the expense of erecting his obelisk *in commemoration of his name* for the work and expenses attending the same performed by his late brother John Neville 416 Strand London.[16]

14 No. 12 in the Set; the total height is given as 29'3", although the cumulative measurements add up to 29'7". The pine-cone or pineapple is set out on the reverse side of the sheet, and dated 19 June 1804. Susan Palmer has indicated that some of the annotations on the sheet are in Soane's hand.

15 Illustrated in A.T. Bolton, *The Works of Sir John Soane, R.A. Architect* (London, 1924), p.xxx. It and a model of a variant for the plinth are listed as 98 and 99 respectively in John Wilton-Ely: 'The Architectural Models of Sir John Soane: A Catalogue', *Architectural History*, xii (1969), p. 37.

16 On being paid (half by Soane and half by Simeon), William Neville wrote to Soane (31 January 1810) returning both cheques, asking Soane to dispose of his (for £10 5s. 1d.) as he wished, and for the other one to be returned to Simeon, asking him to give it to the [Green] Girls School or to some other needy charity in Reading. He apologised to Soane, making it clear that 'if Mr Simeon had come forward in a handsome manner as it is the custom with him on public occasions', things would have been 'very different', *Letters*, box 6, bundle 21, (Soane Museum). The other accounts are in *Bill Book D*, Soane Museum. James Marshall, the mason, was paid for '12 Portland Posts' on 21 September, and Robert Spiller (1794-1817) was paid £310 (according to R. Gunnis, *Dictionary of British Sculptors*) for work on the monument. This was perhaps for the decorative carving. Soane mentions paying J. Spiller (17 August) an advance of £100, and Robert Spiller £32 8s. 9½ 'for men's time' on 23 September.

The monument still stands, a little weathered, but in reasonable condition, in the market-place in Reading, although the oil lamps are now missing (Fig. 114).[17]

A notable change from the preliminary drawings and the model (although the scale drawing is very close) can be seen in the decoration of the splayed facets of the shaft. As Mr Man observed, they are in the Egyptian style. In place of the Greek key or fret, Soane had evolved a decoration based on it, perhaps, but suggesting, as Mr Man evidently thought, a repeated Egyptian hieroglyph, Π , which has, as it happens the phonetic value in our script of 'S'.

It would be attractive to believe that this was intended to stand for 'Simeon', but in 1804 the full decipherment of hieroglyphs had not yet taken place,[18] so it must be assumed that Soane's ornament was purely fortuitous in its associations. He used something similar on a chimneypiece at Port Eliot, Cornwall, shortly afterwards.

Soane was familiar enough with the many obelisks of Rome, incongruously crowned with papal insignia, which, in silhouette, the Simeon monument vaguely recalls; but as there are no known Egyptian obelisks triangular in plan, the traditional term for the Simeon monument, used by Edward Simeon himself in his first letter of proposal, is not altogether correct. For that matter, it is not truly a monument (the term used by Soane in his *Journal*) as it does not really commemorate anything. In some of its basic essentials, as a shaft standing on a triangular base, it recalls a Roman candelabrum or lamp stand of stone, a common artefact in antiquity.

17 It is rather hemmed in ('insulted' as John Betjeman and John Piper put it in *Murray's Berkshire Architectural Guide*, 1949) by the dignified neo-classical public lavatories (also in Portland stone) built during the winter of 1933-34. The wrought-iron brackets, still extant, of a rather more graceful shape than those in the drawings, appear in a print of 1823 (PH280/A in Reading Municipal Library, Local Studies Collection) and so may well be original. The oil lamps, which Edward Simeon claimed, in a letter of 7 January 1805 (Corporation Diary, 1786-1809) would be together equal to twenty-seven of the existing town lamps, were replaced (presumably in 1883; see n. 2) with tall cast-iron lamp-posts standing on the ground but attached half-way up to the brackets, bearing gas lamps. Soane's neat railings with their anthemion motif were replaced at the same time with the (still surviving) vaguely Gothic ones. The supply of gas was discontinued in 1911 and the lamp standards have disappeared. In 1962, according to Mr Blandy (n. 2) the income from the stock had been accumulating in a repair fund which showed 'a considerable balance'. A sum of War Stock sufficient to produce £10 a year

was then transferred to the corporation for the care and maintenance of the monument, and the balance, together with the accumulated income to that date was invested for the benefit of the Alms House Charities. At the time of writing, Jennifer Barnes of Julian Harrap, Architects, is in charge of the restoration of the monument on behalf of the Soane Monuments Trust.

18 The arrival of the Rosetta Stone in London in 1802 aroused intense interest and precipitated an avalanche of speculation, of lectures and publications, but until Thomas Young's article 'Egypt' published in the *Supplement to the Fourth Edition of the Encyclopaedia Britannica* in 1819, the only progress that had been made was focused on the Demotic script on the stone. Soane's interest in and acquaintanceship with Egyptian art and architecture is well known, from the time of his frequenting the Caffè degl'Inglesi in Rome in 1778, which had been decorated by Piranesi in the Egyptian style a few years earlier. The visits he paid to Piranesi, and his familiarity with Piranesi's work as a whole could only contribute to this enthusiasm.

The dedication occupies one panel of the base; the arms of the Simeon family another and those of the borough of Reading the third, all in bronze. Bearing in mind Soane's remarks on the subject of the meaning of antique symbols, it is fair to ask if there is any meaning in the other decorations of the Simeon Monument. The fasces could refer either to the authority of the corporation or, as they were the emblem of higher Roman magistrates, to the fact that Edward's younger brother, Sir John Simeon (1756-1824), was Recorder for Reading from 1779 until 1807.[19] Soane quoted Plutarch on the subject of these insignia in his Royal Academy Lecture XI.

The cylindrical urn, with its serpentine fluting and its lid with a knob formed by a pine-cone, was a type of object well-known to Soane from his time in Italy (examples of which he eventually collected and which are now in his museum), and from publications. The title page to Volume II of Piranesi's *Le antichità romane* depicts a very striking illustration of one. A cinerary urn might possibly have been intended to recall the memory of the eldest Simeon brother, Richard, who had died in 1782. Perhaps the sinuous fluting stood in the architect's mind for the first letter of the name of the patron; Soane used the motif in the ironwork of the balconies on the façade and throughout his own house in Lincoln's Inn Fields, quite possibly for the reason that his own name began with a letter of that form. Perhaps even the triangular plan of the monument, with its three lanterns, might have been thought to symbolise the three Simeon brothers, each distinguished in his way: the third living brother, Charles, was incumbent of Holy Trinity, Cambridge and a leading Evangelical.[20]

Did anything more than simple affection prompt Edward Simeon to bestow this ornament to the town? According to John Man, he began to make 'very generous' donations to the poor in Reading in 1802, and continued to do so until his death.[21] 1802 was the year in which his brother John, a Tory, lost his

---

19 John Simeon had views which today would be considered to be reactionary. He was against the Poor Removal Bill (which aimed at making parishes support the casual poor instead of 'removing' them), *Parliamentary History*, xxxv (1800-1), p. 199; he opposed a petition on behalf of a young man imprisoned at the age of eighteen on a charge of treason, who had been languishing for three years without trial in Reading Gaol (p. 744); he spoke up in favour of informers (p. 1554) and expressed 'radical and fundamental objections' to the idea that the poor should be taught to write or to learn arithmetic. To be able to read was enough, he argued, and in any case, poor people needed children aged seven to fourteen for work in the fields, *Parliamentary History*, ix, p. 544.

20 For long, Charles Simeon experienced con-

siderable hostility in public in Cambridge for his views, and also in private from his family. John Simeon wrote to Charles on his ordination as deacon (August 1782) describing himself and his brother Edward as 'the two heretics of the family', and expressed their fear that their brother might lose his 'common sense'. When, according to Charles, in the October of that year Richard was dying, the two brothers strove to keep him away, 'lest I should disturb his mind . . . ' Later, however, he converted them, and received a legacy of £15,000 from Edward; see Charles Smyth, *Simeon and Church Order* (Cambridge, 1940), and the Rev. William Carus, *Memoires of the Life of the Rev. Charles Simeon M.A.* (London, 1848).

21 John Man, *The History and Antiquities of the Borough of Reading* (Reading, 1816).

seat as M.P. for Reading (which he had held since 1797), after what appears to have been a bitter campaign. Francis Amersley and Charles Shaw Lefevre, Whigs, were returned with 385 and 349 votes respectively; John Simeon received 231.[22] The charitable acts of Edward and the erection of the Simeon monument were subsequently regarded by unsympathetic contemporaries as no more than vote-catching strategies. Indeed the first critical response to Soane's monument to appear in print was directly related to a political squabble. At the Venison Dinner of Mr Shaw Lefevre, held in the town hall, one of the speakers, a Mr Monck, was reported in the *Reading Mercury* as having been:

> remarkably happy in his allusion to a certain newly erected monument by observing that some gentlemen endeavoured to ingratiate themselves with the electors, by raising monuments of stone and having their transitory names emblazoned on them in brass, but that his friend raised a more lasting monument, in the breasts and hearts of his constituents.[23]

This sparked off a correspondence on the subject which continued through September and into October. Mr Simeon and his brother were accused of 'an attempt to bias the heads of the Borough in his favour by setting up in the market-place a paltry gewgaw thing without use or name', of advertising for votes under the mask of conferring favours on his brother townsmen. Moreover, the rhetorical question was asked (by An Elector):

> Has he not sent circular letters to all the publicans, telling them that he could supply them with gin without the intervention of the middle men or dealers? Have not offers been made to supply one with deals and timber, another with iron, a third with sugar, a fourth with cloth, a fifth with logwood and so on with almost every article of merchandise?[24]

Even worse, 'A Real Elector' complained (using over three columns) that there was no explanation forthcoming from Mr Simeon as to:

> why he has opened a warehouse to supply the town with articles of merchandise without the middle-man's profit, to the great loss of the wholesale dealers? Nor why the Pretty Dears of Reading were taken to the races in Mr Simeon's carriage, and treated with a new invented little go? Nor why Mr E.S. imported a cargo of thimbles to be fitted on the fingers of the fair with his own hands, nor lastly why, the eighth wonder of the world, a three-cornered column was erected in the market place –

> 'On a spruce pedestal of Wedgwood Ware
> Where motley arms and tawdry emblems glare'[25]

22 Ibid., p. 242.
23 *Reading Mercury*, 10 September 1804.
24 Ibid., 24 September 1804.
25 Ibid., 8 October 1804.

Edward Simeon was rewarded the following year with the Freedom of the Borough of Reading. The year after that his brother John was returned to Parliament again. Reporting the funeral of Edward Simeon in 1812, the *Reading Mercury* closed its report with a little 'Elegy' by S.H.:

> When time has shook the sculptured column's base
> And slander failed true merit to deface
> His praise the teeming mother shall proclame
> Or tender infants, lisping, tell his name[26]

Today the teeming mother and her brood might have difficulty in squeezing past the more recent amenities provided by the corporation in order to read the dedication. The question of Soane's design procedure remains open, however; an approach which would have seemed very strange in a painter of the same period, had he prepared alternatives for a composition with a series of variations in the styles of Sir Joshua Reynolds, of Sir Thomas Lawrence and finally of William Blake.

26 Ibid., 28 December 1812.

21

Meyer or Myers?: St Joseph's Catholic Church, Avon Dassett

PETER MURRAY

Avon Dassett is a hamlet in Warwickshire, on the border with Oxfordshire and about seven miles from Banbury. In spite of its tiny population it has two churches; the medieval St John Baptist, the Anglican parish church, enlarged in 1868 and now closed and redundant, and the Catholic church of St Joseph, built in 1854 by Joseph Knight, a Fellow of the Horticultural Society, who had made his fortune in London and settled in Avon Dassett.

St Joseph's (Fig. 115) is a fine example of a small church built in the middle of the nineteenth century and entirely typical both of the Gothic Revival and of that 'Second Spring', the great upsurge of Catholicism in England which was the subject of one of Newman's most famous sermons, preached before the newly-established Hierarchy, at Oscott in 1852. It followed the repeal of the penal laws by the Catholic Relief Act of 1829, the conversion of Newman in 1845 and of Manning in 1851, as well as the restoration of the Hierarchy by Pope Pius IX in 1850, ill-advised as it seemed at the time. St Joseph's remained untouched until it was vandalised in the wake of the Second Vatican Council. Fortunately, we have documentary and photographic evidence (Fig. 116) for its original state, and there are three things about it which justify a brief note. First, it has been wrongly attributed to George Myers, Pugin's principal builder, ever since it was opened, although it was in fact designed by Thomas Meyer; second, it contains a quantity of stained glass by Hardman datable to 1854-55 and fully documented and third, it has a very large crucifix by the Austrian sculptor F.-X. Pendl, which may be the only work by him outside the German-speaking lands. (Fig. 117)

Joseph Knight, who died on 20 July 1855, sixteen days after the opening of the church he founded, was born in 1778, and is entered in the *Liber defunctorum* as being seventy-seven years old when he died. He was born in Brindle, near Preston in Lancashire, on 7 October, 1778, and was brought up as a gardener, entering the service of George Hibbert M.P., a well-known horticulturalist, in Clapham, London. Hibbert helped him to set up on his own as a nurseryman in King's Road, Chelsea, then still almost a village. In 1809 he published a book, dedicated to Hibbert, on the *proteacae* and his 'Royal Exotic

Nursery', later more prosaically Knight & Perry, became an extremely successful business, visited more than once by royalty. In 1820 he married Mary
Lorymer (1782-1845), who came from a grander social background. She was
the daughter of John Lorymer Esq., of Porthyre in Monmouth, and had been
educated in the English Augustinian convent in Bruges – it was usual for
recusant families to educate their daughters in French or Belgian convents.
Knight was then forty-two and she was thirty-eight. They lived in Chelsea and,
being childless, were generous donors to Catholic charities, including St
Mary's, Cadogan Gardens, where a stained-glass window and a plaque record
their pious benefactions.

By this time the firm had become Knight and Perry, and Thomas Aloysius
Perry (1820-1907) had married, in 1840, Helen Knight, Joseph's niece. Helen
was also born in Brindle, on 14 May 1816, and was Joseph's brother's child. She
died in 1875. In January 1845 Mary Knight died. Some years later, Joseph
decided to build Bitham House in Avon Dassett and live there with his niece
and her husband. They founded a mission there about 1848/52 (the dates
vary), but the choice of Avon Dassett was probably determined by the connection of the Perry family with Banbury. Perrys are recorded in 1806 among the
tiny Catholic population of Banbury – they were the grandparents of Thomas
Aloysius and are commemorated in the West window of St Joseph's. The Perrys
had extensive market gardens and became one of the largest businesses in
Banbury, employing about forty people in the 1850s and 1860s.

It is not known how Thomas Aloysius came to meet Joseph Knight, but it
seems probable that he was sent to London to learn horticulture under his now
famous co-religionist. Thomas himself became an established country gentleman, his youngest daughter living in Bitham Hall until her death at a great age
in 1941.

We are fortunate in having a very detailed description of the church at the
time of its consecration on 3 July 1855, and the solemn opening by Bishop
Ullathorne on the following day. This description was supplied to the *Royal
Leamington Spa Courier and Warwickshire Standard*, the *Banbury Guardian*, the
Tablet and the *Builder* almost certainly by a member of the family, and appeared
in variously abbreviated forms in July 1855. An account, based on the *Banbury
Guardian* and *Tablet* versions, reads:

> Avon Dassett is a small village beautifully situated a few miles north of Banbury . . .
> On the upland side of the village stands the mansion erected by Joseph Knight Esq.,
> formerly of King's road, Chelsea, for his own residence and that of his nephew and
> niece, Mr and Mrs Perry, commanding an expanded and beautiful prospect, a great
> part of which is their estate. In the village itself Mr Knight has built and endowed a
> goodly church, which was solemnly consecrated on Tuesday the third inst. by the
> Bishop of Birmingham, assisted by a number of clergy . . .

Fig. 115 St Joseph's, Avon Dassett, general view from the west (1991).

Fig. 116 St Joseph's, Avon Dassett, general view from the west in 1920s or 30s. (*Mrs Herbert, Avon Dassett*)

The church, which is dedicated to St Joseph, is a well-designed structure, uniting solidity with picturesqueness. It is in the style of the 11th [*sic*] century, and does credit to its architect, Mr Myers of London. It consists of a nave, chancel, Lady Chapel on the south of the chancel, a southern transept opening to the Lady Chapel and a music gallery opening over the sacristy into the transept, whilst the sacristy itself connects the church with the presbytery. On the south-west [*sic*] rises a tower, surmounted with a spire furnished with bell and clock. The lower portion of the tower forms an ample porch, by which the church is entered from the street. The appointments of the church are very complete. The altars are furnished with sculptured reredoses. The subjects carved in that of the high altar are the Nativity and Flight into Egypt, whilst that of the Lady Chapel consists of enriched panels. Within a carved arch, surmounted by a floriated canopy of stone above the High Altar, is a tabernacle of metal work with chased and enamelled doors. A stone pulpit projects from the north side chancel arch, and is approached by stairs in the chancel wall. The font, confessional, and piscinas, aumbries etc. exhibit an accurate attention to rubric with appropriateness of design. But the most beautiful ornamentation of the church consists of twelve stained glass windows, many of them gifts of the founder. They are amongst the very finest specimens of the artistical skill of Mr Hardman of Birmingham. In the centre lancet, over the High Altar, is represented the Eternal Father, crowned, coped, and seated on a rainbow in a *vesica*, the very atmosphere within which is made of ruby seraphs, whilst Angels hover over the rest of the lights. In the lancet on the right [*sic*] is the Blessed Virgin, in that on the left [*sic*] St Joseph. On the northern wall of the chancel is a double lancet, in which are represented SS Peter and Paul with their emblems. In the window over the pulpit is a very beautiful historical representation of St Charles Borromeo administering Communion to the plague-stricken people of Milan. The subjects which fill the two windows over the altar in the Lady Chapel are the Annunciation and the Assumption of the Blessed Virgin; whilst the window represents St Stephen, the protomartyr. But the crowning works of art in this church are the three detached lancets at the west end. In the centre light is a most exquisite and moving representation of Our Lord on the cross; at the foot of the cross kneel St Thomas of Canterbury on the one side, and St Anne on the other. In the other two lancets are the Blessed Virgin and St John in grief before their crucified Lord . . .'

The windows are all by John Hardman of Birmingham and are an integral part of the whole design, executed in two stages, most of them during the years 1854-55, while the church was being built and probably in consultation with the architect as well as with Joseph Knight and the Perrys, and the remainder between 1857 and 1877 to commemorate particular donors.

John Hardman (1811-67) was a member of an old Catholic family, originally button-makers, who set up in the new business of electro-plating, but in 1838, under the influence of Pugin, he set up a company of 'medieval metal-workers' using designs supplied by Pugin, and providing all kinds of ecclesiastical metalwork, often electro-plated, and other church furnishings. Later, he worked with Pugin on the fittings for the new Houses of Parliament. His partner,

Fig. 117 St Joseph's, Avon Dassett, detail of crucifix
by Franz-Xaver Pendl (1859).

William Powell, had a son, John Hardman Powell (1827-95), who was Pugin's
only pupil and who married Pugin's daughter. Gradually Hardman concentrated on stained glass and St Joseph's contains fine examples of his Puginesque
style, mostly in good condition. Some of the inscriptions are now almost
illegible and all the original brass plates which were designed to go with them
were wantonly removed some years ago. Fortunately, we know what they
contained, since the records of the Hardman firm are now in Birmingham
Public Library and many of the original designs for stained glass are in the Art
Gallery there. In the following account these documents have been used to
supply lost or damaged inscriptions.

We know from the report in the *Banbury Guardian* that there were twelve
windows in the church at the time of the opening ceremony; namely, the three
large lancets over the high altar, the corresponding three at the west end, the
two lancets over the Lady altar and the single window beside it, as well as the
two lancets on the left of the high altar and the single window near the pulpit.
As these were the original decorations they will be described first, with the
remaining windows in chronological order afterwards.

The large central window (Fig. 118a) above the high altar is identified in the
Banbury Guardian account as 'the Eternal Father, crowned, coped, and seated
on a rainbow in a *vesica*, the very atmosphere within which is made of ruby

a   b

Fig. 118 St Joseph's, Avon Dassett, stained glass.

(a) East window: the Virgin of the Annunciation, with donor portrait of Mary Knight; Christ in Majesty, with symbols of the Evangelists; St Joseph, with donor portrait of Joseph Knight. By John Hardman (*c.* 1854).

(b) Window in the nave: SS Thomas the Apostle, Helen and Aloysius, with the arms of Perry and Knight. By Hardman and Co. (*c.* 1877).

(c) Window in the nave: the death of St Joseph, with donor portrait of Joseph Knight. By John Hardman or his studio (*c.* 1856-57).

(d) Window over the altar of the Lady chapel: the Annunciation, with St Aloysius Gonzaga, and the Assumption with St Helen. (Aloysius and Helen were the name saints of T.A. Perry and his wife Helen). By John Hardman (*c.* 1854).

c

d

seraphs, whilst Angels hover over the rest of the lights'. It is more accurately described as a *Majestas Domini*, with the New Jerusalem below. The subject was popular until the thirteenth century and was revived in the nineteenth as part of the Gothic Revival. Below are the symbols of the Four Evangelists – the Angel (Matthew), the Winged Lion (Mark), the Ox (Luke) and the Eagle (John), with identifying inscriptions.

The smaller window to the left has an angel with a scroll above the figure of Our Lady, who holds a lily symbolising the Annunciation. Below her, in a roundel, is a kneeling figure inscribed 'Sancte Maria ora pro nobis': she is an idealised representation of Mary Knight and below her is an inscription 'Pray for the Soul of Mary Knight wife of Joseph Knight who founded this church in the year of Our Lord 1855. She deceased the 11th of January 1845'.

The corresponding window on the right has another angel with a scroll above the figure of St Joseph, who holds the flowering rod which, according to the Apocryphal Gospels, marked him as the successful suitor of Mary. Below him is another roundel with a kneeling figure inscribed 'Sancte Josephus ora pro nobis' – this is again an idealised donor portrait, and below it is 'Pray for the good estate of Joseph Knight who built this church in honour of his Holy patron St. Joseph and our Blessed Lady'.

At the opposite end of the church, on the west wall, there is a similar large triple lancet window, now badly weathered in parts, with the crucifixion as the central subject and Mary and St John the Evangelist on either side. At the foot of the cross kneel SS. Thomas of Canterbury and Anne: below them the inscriptions read 'Pray for the Souls of Thomas Perry and Ann his wife. The said Thomas deceased the 5th of December 1838 and Ann the 24th March 1838 – Their bodies lie buried in the church of St John at Banbury', 'This window was set up by Thomas and Stephen Perry, the sons of the said Thomas and Ann Perry and their grandson Thomas Aloysius Perry in memory of their parents and sister', 'Pray for the soul of Mary Theresa Perry a professed religious in the order of Our Lady of Mercy, who deceased in the Convent at Nottingham 13th of November 1852'.

Returning to the chancel, there is a double lancet on the left (north) wall, with figures of SS. Peter and Paul and half-length figures of angels with scrolls inscribed with their names and *Ora pro nobis*: the bill for these windows, dated May 1855, records the inscription below as: 'Of your charity pray for the good estate of Ellen France who set up these windows in honour of the glorious Apostles Sts Peter and Paul'.

In the Lady Chapel there are three windows (Fig 118d), two over the altar with the Annunciation and the Assumption as the major subjects, and small figures of St Aloysius Gonzaga, with crucifix, skull, rosary and lily, inscribed San A..ysius, and of St Helen, with the True Cross, inscribed 'Sancta Helena'. The inscriptions below are now almost illegible, but were recorded in 1854 as 'Pray for the good estate of Thomas Aloysius Perry, and of his wife Helen, niece to Joseph Knight Esqre Founder of this church. This window was set up at their expense in honour of the ever-blessed and Immaculate Mother of God'. (The dogma of the Immaculate Conception was officially promulgated on 8 December 1854). On the south wall of the Lady Chapel there is a single window representing St Stephen (now rather damaged), with a small donor figure below and the inscription: 'Of your charity pray for the good estate of Stephen Perry who caused this window to be set up'. The bill, for £13, was sent to Stephen Perry in London. He was presumably the Stephen, born in 1800, who was Thomas Aloysius's uncle.

The last of the windows recorded in the account of the opening of the church is the one near the pulpit, on the north wall of the nave. The rather unusual subject (outside Italy) represents S. Carlo Borromeo, bringing communion to the sick during the great plague in Milan in 1576. It is inscribed: 'This window was set up by Major Charles Stapleton in honour of his patron St Charles Borromeo. Pray for the good estate of the donor while living and for his soul when dead'. Below the main scene is an idealised portrait of the donor as a soldier, with his coat of arms and the inscription 'Sancte Carole ora pro me'. Nothing more is known of Major Stapleton.

The remaining windows in the nave were all executed after the opening of the church and with the possible exception of the 'Death of St Joseph', are probably not by John Hardman himself, since he died in 1867. His workshops continued to produce designs in the same style, and it would be difficult to distinguish between these and the earlier windows. The window next to the font (Fig. 118c) represents the death of St Joseph and was set up as a memorial to Joseph Knight, whose death occurred a few days after the opening of the church. There is a donor portrait below the main scene and a shield with what seems to be the monogram IK for Iosephus Knight. There are bills of 1856 and 1857, and one of these, for an inscribed brass plate, must refer to the plate formerly below the window

> Pray for the Soul of Joseph Knight Esq who died at the age of 77 on the 20th of July 1855, 16 days after the Solemn Consecration of this Church, which he erected to God's Honour, and the Salvation of Souls. This window was set up in grateful remembrance by his Niece Helen and her husband, Thomas Aloysius Perry. His body rests in front of the Chancel of this Church.

The tomb-slab is no longer visible, having been covered by the extension of the chancel into the nave to accommodate the second, new, altar.

The remaining four windows in the nave were all executed between 1872 and 1877. Next to the Knight memorial is one, much poorer in quality, of St George killing the dragon. Once again the brass plate is missing, but we know that it read: '+ Of your charity pray for the Soul of Georgina Mary the beloved Wife of The O'Conor Don M.P. who departed this life the 18th August 1872 at Clonalis, aged 25 years. Her body rests in the family place of burial at Castlerea Co. Roscommon.' Their coat of arms is below the figure of the saint, and an angel above holds a scroll inscribed 'Sanctus Georgius'.

Next to it, at the angle with the transept, is a memorial to Mrs Mary Perry and three of her daughters who were nuns: the subject is the rare one of St Anne teaching the Virgin to read, symbolic of a mother's care for her daughters. The coat of arms is that of the Perry family, the three golden pears being a pun on perry. The brass plate has again gone astray, but the inscription read:

> Pray for the Soul of Mrs Mary Ann Perry who died March 27, 1858 and whose body is interred near the Chancel of this church and of her daughters Mary Teresa, who died 13th Novr. 1852, Frances Elizabeth who died 17th May 1857, Matilda Veronica who died 20th Sept. 1866. All these were professed religious in the order of Our Lady of Mercy at Nottingham where their bodies are interred.

The remaining two windows are on the north wall of the nave and are both of about 1877. The central one (Fig. 118b) represents SS. Thomas the Apostle, Helen, and Aloysius and seems to be a replacement for one projected in 1855 as SS. Thomas, Stephen, and Aloysius, perhaps in memory of Thomas, Stephen and Thomas Aloysius Perry. The present one however, was paid for in 1877 and certainly represents St Thomas with the carpenter's square (as patron of architects and builders), identified by the inscription: 'My Lord and my God' (John 20:28). Below him is St Helen with the Cross and the inscription: 'No Salvation except through the Cross'; and, below her, St Aloysius with the inscription: 'What will it avail me for Eternity.' The arms at the bottom are Perry (on the left) and Knight.

The window next to the door is probably the latest of all, since it was set up to commemorate Miss Ellen France, who died on 4 September 1876, at the age of eighty-six. She had already given the two windows in the chancel, and this one was erected by T.A. Perry as her executor in 1877. She was the fifth child of Thomas Hayhurst who changed his name to France in order to inherit Bostock Hall, near Middlewich in Cheshire. She was born an Anglican and seems to have been received into the Catholic Church and came to live in Leamington in the early 1850s, where she contributed handsomely to the building of St Peter's (1861-64), by Henry Clutton, also a convert, to which she left a bequest big enough to allow of the building of the splendid tower. Nevertheless, she is buried in Avon Dassett in the Perry vault. The arms at the bottom of the window are hers, with the ancient royal arms of France – three gold fleurs-de-lis on a blue ground – at the top.

Apart from the glass, the most notable work of art in the church is undoubtedly the over life-size crucifix which now hangs from the chancel arch, but which was originally at ground level in front of the southern pier of the chancel. According to the diocesan directory for 1912 it is by Franz-Xaver Pendl and dated 1859: it is impossible to read a signature and date now, but there is every reason to believe it correct, since the cross was apparently cut down when it was moved to its present position. Franz-Xaver Pendl (1817-96) was one of a family of Austrian sculptors and woodcarvers from Meran in the Tyrol. According to Thieme-Becker, his father, Johann Baptist, specialised in crucifixes and was his first teacher. Franz was later trained in Vienna and in Munich (1838-41), where there is a *pietà* by him in the Capuchin church. He also made statues of the Evangelists for the Ursuline church in Innsbruck and for churches in and near Meran, including at least one crucifix. So far as is known, this is the only work by him in this country.

Virtually all the fittings were designed or supplied by Hardman from drawings originally made by Pugin for the firm (which was awarded a prize at the Great Exhibition of 1851). Fortunately, it is possible to gain some idea of the interior in the 1920s or 30s from a set of postcards which have survived.

There have been major changes in the chancel, where the original altar rails have been removed and a clumsy extension made into the nave to afford space for a second altar which obstructs the view towards the original high altar, of stone, but painted white, like the Lady altar and the font. The high altar still has the reliefs of the *Nativity* and *Flight into Egypt* and the canopy mentioned in the account of the opening of the church. The tabernacle is a particularly fine piece of chased and enamelled metalwork and, like the six candlesticks and the brass crucifix, can be attributed to Pugin. There were originally brackets at either side of the altar to carry the hangings which were traditionally placed at the sides of a high altar. The Lady Chapel has a stone altar decorated with lancets and trefoils and three roundels below, the centre one bearing the Marian monogram. On it is a statue of the Madonna and Child, almost life-size, of a vaguely French Gothic character and probably of French or Belgian workmanship of the mid nineteenth century. The original carved wooden altar rails have fortunately been preserved. The transept has been much altered by the suppression of the musicians' gallery above the sacristy and the removal of the stair up to it: however, the front of the gallery is still preserved, built into the wall, and the line of the stair is clearly visible on the west wall. At the junction of the nave and chancel there is a wall-plaque, dated 1854, commemorating the foundation of the church by Joseph Knight, but it is now almost obscured by the statue of St Joseph which was originally, and more appropriately, at the right of the Lady altar. On the opposite side is the pulpit, of stone with sunk quatrefoil panels. It seems that this was once painted, but it was cleaned many years ago and it is unlikely that the paint was original.

The walls of the nave have the remaining consecration crosses (all of which once had candle-brackets below them), and the fourteen Stations of the Cross in painted high relief. These are certainly of Belgian workmanship – Hardman is known to have had dealings with ecclesiastical suppliers in Belgium – but they may not be identical with those in a bill of 1855 for '14 Stations with frames' at £10 13s., which seems remarkably cheap. They are typical of the mid nineteenth century religious art of northern Europe.

In the south-west angle, railed in, is a stone font with an oak lid, the stone again painted white. A door in the corner leads to the small vestibule at the north-west angle under the tower.

Externally the church is a simple stone building with a slated roof and spire, exactly as shown in a watercolour drawing, now in the presbytery, which is signed and dated 'Tho Meyer Archt – Church-and-Presbytery-Avon Dasset – April 1854'. This is the 'Mr Myers of London' mentioned in the account of the opening of the church and given authority by repetition in *The Builder*, confusing Thomas Meyer with George Myers, who was Pugin's principal builder, but who is not known to have been an architect. Pevsner, in his Warwickshire volume, noted: 'according to GR [Goodhart-Rendel] by *Myers*. But is he the architect? He was Pugin's builder'. Thomas Meyer was also the architect of St Mary of the Angels, Bayswater, which was later the mother-church of Manning's Oblates of St Charles. It was, however, extensively rebuilt at that time by Francis Bentley. Meyer's work in Bayswater dates from 1852-57, exactly the period when St Joseph's was built. He is known to have been still active in 1868, but little else is known of him at present, although the name Meyer occurs in a Banbury parish census in 1864 and Thomas may therefore have been a member of a local family. The drawing shows the presbytery as well as the church, and it also is virtually unchanged. The buildings form a single unit, since the sacristy is really a passage linking the house with the transept of the church. The space above the sacristy, once the musicians' gallery, has been converted into a room. In the sacristy is a monstrance which may well be the one mentioned in a bill of 1855 (for £16 10s. 6d.), specified as electro-plated, which must be one of the earliest ever made, recalling Hardman's original business.

22

Conspicuous by their Absence:
Town Halls in Nineteenth-Century London

RICHARD HOLDER

Anyone looking in London for a Victorian equivalent to the great town halls of the north will hunt in vain; the capital of the Empire had nothing of such stature until the commencement of Ralph Knott's Edwardian County Hall. An explanation is to be found in London's nineteenth century local government which is the most surprising and complex of any area in the period, and in the pattern of landownership before and during the nineteenth century.

The City of London was administered by the City Corporation, whilst the surrounding area was run by a tangled web of authorities, overlapping and acting at cross purposes.[1] Until the establishment of the Metropolitan Board of Works in 1855, the only body to deal with the area of London outside the City as a whole was the Metropolitan Police (established in 1829). The outer London area was administered by a patchwork of open and closed (or select) vestries. Open vestries were open to all male ratepayers. Select vestries were restricted to a group of the 'principal inhabitants', who filled vacancies by nomination. The vestry system derived from church administration and took its name from the original meeting-place, the church vestry. This might have coped with London's problems if a vestry had been identical to a town council, but this was not the case. Vestries did not have ultimate control over all that happened in their area, and boundaries were not shared by other administrative bodies. The problems this led to were demonstrated in a speech given in Parliament by Sir Benjamin Hall in 1855 supporting the establishment of the Metropolitan Board of Works:

> the case of St Pancras was one of the greatest instances of abuses that had ever existed in a civilised country. In the year 1834 these parties came to Parliament through their vestry. They desired their vestry to expend money for the purpose of remedying these abuses. The bill was thrown out in the second reading. In 1837 a similar attempt was made with similar results, but at a heavy cost to the ratepayers. In the year 1851 they were more fortunate. A bill was introduced and was referred

---

1 Francis Sheppard, *London 1808-1870: The Infernal Wen* (London, 1971).

to a select committee. It passed through the committee, and was sent up to the House of Lords, where it was thrown out, and from that time to the present no step has been taken to remedy these abuses, because they spent £4,000 on the former occasion and the paving boards, over which they had no control, spent nearly £3,000 in defeating the ratepayers, which the ratepayers had likewise to pay.[2]

With problems like this hindering effective administration it is easy to see why London had many squalid areas in the nineteenth century.

However, there were some areas of London that were efficiently run. These were the estates of the major London landowners, who largely shaped the London of today. The vast incomes obtainable from successful estates ensured that they were a jealously husbanded resource. The Duke of Westminster's London estate, for example, yielded an income of over £250,000 per annum at the end of the century.[3] Most major landowners were scrupulous in maintaining their property, ensuring that it remained desirable and continued to produce a high income.

In these areas local government was effectively in the hands of landowners, their control deriving from their ownership, their ability to control the vestries (since in open vestries the larger the landholding the larger the vote, and in select vestries the major landowners were often the only people that qualified for nomination), and by the leases they imposed on their property. However, this situation was not universal. The major estates dealt with houses for the middle and upper classes, the high rents chargeable producing a high income per acre. Although certain estates provided artisan housing as a charitable measure, others were forced to do so because the estate's location was not good enough to draw the middle classes. Much of the artisan housing in London was too expensive for the class it intended to attract; there was always insufficient cheap property to satisfy the demand.

London's population growth and the need for more housing were recognised as early as 1829 in George Cruikshank's engraving of *London going out of Town: The March of Bricks and Mortar*, and in *The Builder's* report on the construction of Paddington Vestry Hall in 1853:

> Some idea of the increase of parochial business . . . may be gathered from the fact that upwards of 400 new houses are taken into rating annually. This prodigious increase is not a new feature in the parish, for during the last sixteen or eighteen years its meadows have been undergoing the brick and mortar transformation to such an extent that the turf-cutter has had to bustle in his work to get out of the way of the carpet-planner. Squares, streets, and crescents have sprung up as if by magic.[4]

2　G. Laurence Gomme, *London in the Reign of Queen Victoria, 1837-1897* (London, 1898), p. 52.

3　Gervas Huxley, *Victorian Duke, the Life of Hugh Lupus Grosvenor, First Duke of Westminster* (Oxford, 1967), p. 149.

4　*The Builder*, xi (1853), p. 753.

The vast expansion of London in the nineteenth century and the lack of effective planning controls meant that minor problems became major causes for concern. It is evident that overcrowding, lack of effective drainage, and dirty conditions led to the many attacks of cholera in nineteenth century London. The epidemic of typhus in 1837-38 led to two examinations of areas, which demonstrated how the lack of an effective system of local government was turning the capital into a breeding ground for disease. Arnott and Kays' report separated the causes of fever among the poor into two groups, those 'arising independently of their habits', and those 'originating to a considerable extent in their habits'.[5] The first, including the shortage of sewers and drains, unemptied cesspools and privies, inadequate ventilation in narrow courts and alleys, and accumulating refuse, could have been solved by effective local administration. Less than half of the 16,000 buildings in the City were connected to sewers, and there were 5,400 cess pools in the City's square mile. This produced horrifying results.

Arnott and Kay made several recommendations: the creation of a proper system of sewers and a good supply of clean water, efficient refuse collection, the paving of courts and alleys, and the control of the location and condition of such things as slaughter-houses and burial-grounds. The report suggested that the implementation of these recommendations should be supervised by the local Poor Law Boards of Guardians.

The two reports, commissioned by Edwin Chadwick, led him to produce his major, widely read report, *An Inquiry into the Sanitary Condition of the Labouring Population of Great Britain*, published in 1842. This, although dealing with the entire country, devoted a large amount of space to London's problems, particularly the administration of drainage.

The Metropolitan area was administered by eight independent Commissions of Sewers. Each built sewers to a different design; the junctions between the sewers of different commissions were often a source of trouble. Large sewers discharged into small ones, and sewers of different cross-section were joined with little regard for the effectiveness of the joints. Certain commissions did not deal with sewage, but solely with the disposal of surface water; in these areas cess-pools were the normal means of sewage disposal. This arrangement might have worked when London had a small population, but it was unable to cope with the demand for water and sewage disposal created by a rapid rise in the population and the growing use of water-closets. Chadwick related the consequent filth to the outbreaks of cholera and typhus, laying the blame for the illnesses and deaths on London's inefficient drainage system. Chadwick

5 Dr Neil Arnott and Dr James Kay, *On the Prevalence of Certain Physical Causes of Fever in the Metropolis, Which Might be Removed by Proper Sanitary Measures*, examined Wapping, Ratcliffe, and Stepney. The other report, by Dr Southwood Smith, *On Some of the Physical Causes of Sickness and Mortality to Which the Poor are Particularly Exposed, and Which are Capable of Removal by Sanitary Regulations*, examined Bethnal Green and Whitechapel.

proposed an arterial form of drainage, involving a large number of engineers and a new administrative machinery to supervise the work and raise the money.

Chadwick's report led to the establishment, in 1843, of a Royal Commission on *The State of Large Towns and Populous Places*. This reported in 1844 and 1845 and recommended that the 'local administrative body' was to direct 'the works required for sanitary purposes' in towns. London, however did not have such a body, save in the City, and the commission did not suggest how this difficulty might be overcome. The Government failed to act quickly. A Public Health Bill was put before Parliament in 1847, but London was not included in its bounds and the Bill was withdrawn. However with cholera again sweeping across Europe in 1847, Chadwick headed a Royal Commission to enquire into 'what special means may be requisite for the health of the Metropolis'. The threat of cholera provided Chadwick's proposals with the force they needed.

Chadwick proposed that for the duration of the epidemic the Crown Commissioners of Sewers in London should be replaced by a single body for the whole metropolitan area. The new Commissioners, twenty-three as opposed to the previous 1,000, began the process of flushing out the sewers to disperse the smells thought to cause cholera. Unfortunately cholera is water-borne, so the effect of this operation was to transmit it to other areas.

The cholera attack did, however, lead to a revolution, if temporary, in the administration of London's sewerage. The City's opposition to the creation of a Metropolitan Commission of Sewers was resolved by allowing its own commission to remain independent, while requiring it to send representatives whenever main drainage was discussed. This arrangement split the City from other opponents to the Bill and left the other opponents with no effective voice. A Metropolitan Commission of Sewers was thus created in 1848, with a General Board of Health. *The Builder* followed events with cynical interest and reported in 1852:

> Another Metropolitan Commission of Sewers has held its opening meeting at Greek Street, Soho. Our readers, however, will be sadly mistaken should they imagine that surely something therefore will now at last be done, after three botched commissions have been duly disposed of, and a fourth – attempt shall we say – made to carry out the one great object of all these appointments. The present commission, according to its own Chairman, Mr. Jebb, 'Is only provisional, being merely in a state of transition to a more satisfactory footing and a better basis'! The Chairman concluded his explanation by saying that, 'unless further powers be given by the Government and the Legislature, either by increasing the Commission's powers of rating or of obtaining money by loan or otherwise, it is absolutely impossible that you can carry out any great drainage works . . . let their urgency be ever so great'. Such is the hopeful state of our thrice new commission.[6]

6 *The Builder*, ix (1852), p. 504.

The reconstitution of the General Board of Health in 1854 was followed by the creation of the Metropolitan Board of Works by the Metropolis Management Act of 1855. This reorganised London's local government but beyond that proved remarkably ineffective. The reorganisation set up thirty-eight areas of metropolitan administration. The twenty-three largest parishes retained their vestries but in a different form. The vestrymen were elected for three years by all householders rated for the Poor Rate at £40, or £25 in some areas. The rest of the metropolitan area was divided into fifteen district boards, members being elected by the vestries in their area. Above these thirty-eight areas and the unaltered City, and elected by them, was the Metropolitan Board of Works. The Board was to construct a sewerage system that took London's sewage away from London, and did not pollute the Thames. Vestries and District Boards were to construct sewers under the Board's supervision.

The creation of the Board established democratic vestries and eliminated the great tangle of Sewage Commissions and Paving and Lighting Trusts. Yet it still had little power. The Board could not enforce its building bye-laws on the vestries and needed Parliament's permission to raise or spend large sums of money. As Simon Jenkins puts it:

> The years between 1855 and 1888 were ones of almost total legislative failure. Considering the weight of evidence submitted to public scrutiny and the often desperate efforts of social reformers, the reaction of Parliament to the state of London was phenomenally inept. The story of the Metropolitan Board of Works, which spans exactly these years, was one of constant meanness and lost opportunities, largely as a result of its circumscribed constitution. Parliament was still packed with the representatives of interests who saw their role as one of narrow self-defence. There was no doubt that many of the spokesmen for the City, the vestries, the railway and docks companies and other commercial interests viewed with delight the inability of legislative reform to live up to its promise.[7]

Although London had no central government during this period many vestries found their workload increasing. *The Builder* reported that Kensington Vestry had found,

> the continued growth of the parish, together with the increased work in the clerk's and surveyor's departments, . . . and the Vestry undertaking the extensive works of scavenging, dust removal, street watering, and street lighting by the average meter system, necessitated the appointment of additional officers, and rendered extra office accommodation still more requisite.[8]

7 Simon Jenkins, *Landlords to London: The Story of a Capital and its Growth* (London, 1975), pp. 188-89.

8 *The Builder*, xxxix (1880), p. 201.

In 1888 the government passed the County Councils Act which meant that London, except the City, became a county. In 1889 the first elections were held and the new London County Council met in the old Metropolitan Board of Works offices, in Spring Gardens, off Trafalgar Square. The L.C.C. was vociferous in its demands for changes in the laws relating to London and it was in an attempt to halt this drive for greater administrative power that the government passed an act in 1899 transforming the London vestries into municipal boroughs.[9] From 1899 there was a boom in the production of Town Halls for London.

It is easy to assume that because of London's long history of maladminist-ration in the nineteenth century there were few if any vestry halls built. This is not the case. Many were built and when the 1899 Act was passed most, for example those in Kensington, Chelsea and Battersea, simply changed their title and became town halls.

Few of the vestry halls had any great architectural distinction, being built mainly to satisfy the need for office space. Few vestries appear to have had the money or the inclination to produce anything noteworthy or redolent of civic pride. This lack of architectural excellence in London was recognised as early as 1853 in *The Builder's* comments on the Leeds Town Hall design:

> Sir Charles [Barry] having, according to the writer in your contemporary, 'spoken in the highest terms of the general design, and predicted that the new Town-hall would be the most perfect architectural gem out of London!' The last expression, which was perhaps uttered by Sir Charles himself, takes us somewhat aback, the 'architec-tural gems' in the metropolis being comparatively few, – not at all in proportion either to the opportunities afforded for producing them, or the countless sums that have been expended upon what, if we are to believe the public press, are little better than so many egregious yet costly failures, and an utter reproach to our taste as a nation. The metropolis has scarcely anything of the same kind and date that can view with St. George's Hall, alias the Assize Courts, at Liverpool, or with the façade and portico of the Fitzwilliam Museum, at Cambridge.[10]

Lack of merit is apparent in the words and phrases used by Pevsner to describe London's vestry and town halls: 'crushingly mean', 'little to recommend', 'very modest' and 'exceptionally uninteresting'.[11]

London during the Victorian period offers a contrast to other major English towns. It demonstrated the necessity for an effective local administration and the disasters that occurred if such was lacking. It is evident that although other towns may have shared some of London's problems – slums and poor drainage – they had the administrative machinery to deal with them; the great town halls

9 Alastair Service, *London 1900* (London, 1979), p. 219.
10 *The Builder*, xi (1853), p. 59.

11 Nikolaus Pevsner, *London except the Cities of London and Westminster* (Harmondsworth, 1974).

of Birmingham, Manchester and Leicester are evidence of this machinery. London's chaos provides perhaps even clearer indication of the need for, and power of, provincial town halls in the Victorian period than do such master-pieces as Cuthbert Brodrick's Leeds Town Hall.

23

The MARS Group and the Thirties

JOHN SUMMERSON

I should like to give you an impression of what architectural life was like in the late twenties and early thirties. It was pretty flat. There was a severe depression – the 'great slump' – between about 1928 and 1932, and this had a devastating effect on architectural practice; in fact, it killed the old style of practice. But that style was flat anyway – there was a sense of inertia. I worked in offices which were still perfectly Edwardian, if not Victorian – I remember that one of them didn't even have a typewriter. Success in architecture still meant success of an Edwardian kind. A rich uncle or a family friend was supposed to get you to design a cottage, with chauffeur's flat over. You started from something like that, rented an office, and went on either to country houses or city offices or, with luck, both and a church or two. (Well, of course, you didn't, because of the slump, but that remained to be seen.) What you did not do if you could possibly help it was to be a salaried architect – to work in a local authority office – housing, fire-stations and so on. That was only for hacks and second-raters. The work of such offices was described by, of all people, a president of the RIBA as 'stale chocolate', which shows pretty well where the RIBA stood in the matter of patronage.

The top English architect was, of course, Lutyens, building New Delhi. Giles Gilbert Scott, of Liverpool Cathedral, came second. But to people of my age, these splendid figures were remote and more or less irrelevant to our own prospective careers while the other traditionalists like Blomfield, Baker and Edwin Cooper we dismissed quite uncritically (and now, I think, perhaps wrongly) as utterly boring.

There was a huge generation gap. The war generation, which is to say men born between 1885-1900, was exhausted, throwing up no leaders – at least, not in architecture. The top men of the 30s were pre-war; we were post-war. When I say 'we' I am thinking of the relatively few young architects and writers who resented the boredom and inertia of the time and were looking for ways out of

* This essay is based on a radio talk originally prepared in 1974 for the Open University.

it or ways to bust it. Such ways were not discernible in England, but abroad they were. And so we travelled if we could – Stockholm, Berlin, Stuttgart, Hilversum – and we talked, endlessly, about the meaning of the word 'modern'.

What did 'modern' mean? In the early twenties any design with a square, frowning look would be said to have a 'modern' character. Exaggerated horizontals and exaggerated verticals were 'modern'. We looked mostly to the Germans for these notions until we caught sight of Le Corbusier. His book, *Vers une architecture*, appeared in 1923. Being in French, of course, it didn't have an immediate impact here. I picked up my own copy in a foreign news-shop in Charlotte Street where it had been lying about for years. But by 1927 quite a lot of people had read it or at least read about it, and Le Corbusier's name was on the lips of the sort of young men who wore black hats with rather wide brims; young men who had picked up a bit of Marx and a bit of Freud, had perhaps been to Russia, and thought of themselves as 'the intelligentsia'. Some of them (not many, I think) were architects. The situation is marvellously reflected in Evelyn Waugh's *Decline and Fall* (1928), where the progressive modern architect, Otto Silenus, is enthusiastically credited by a young man from Oxford with having got right away from Le Corbusier. You couldn't be more advanced than that.

By 1930 Le Corbusier, Gropius and Mendelsohn on the Continent and Frank Lloyd Wright in America were recognised by small groups in England as the really significant innovators. Moreover, they were recognised as having enough in common to be thought of as part of a movement – the 'modern movement'. Movements attract loyalties and the time was propitious for new loyalties, not only in architecture but in the arts generally. English artists like Ben Nicholson, Henry Moore and Barbara Hepworth were beginning to be heard of and were discovered to have aims and ideas entirely reconcilable with those of the new architecture. The publication of a volume of essays called *Circle* in 1937 underlined this. Rather oddly, we paid almost no attention to Wyndham Lewis, Vorticism and *Blast*. That movement seemed to belong to the pre-war and war years, and for us it had no momentum left, besides which, Lewis himself was becoming identified as 'reactionary'. Our 'modern movement' therefore began to grow out of experience of our own contemporaries, chiefly on the Continent.

I must emphasise here the absolute complacency and indifference of the public and, indeed, of most of the profession to the new ideas. If there had been no war the ideas which were stirring all over the Continent around 1910 might, I think, very well have developed as quickly in England as elsewhere. But war left behind it, in England, a massive psychological resistance to innovation, and this, in turn, produced a sense of militancy in protagonists of the 'modern'. Modern architecture became a 'cause'. And I rather think that when a group of young architects formed themselves into a society for modern architectural research they were not displeased to find that the initials of their enterprise, M.A.R.S. (Modern Architectural Research) nicely combined a sense of militancy with a vision of planetary exploration.

The MARS Group was founded early in 1933. It was affiliated to C.I.A.M. (the Congrès Internationaux d'Architecture Moderne), which was a propagandist study group centred in Switzerland, and supported by most of the pioneering figures. Who founded MARS? Well, I'm not really sure. I'm not sure that anybody is. P. Morton Shand, a very accomplished man of letters, an authority on wine, a good linguist, had a lot to do with it. So had H. de C. Hastings, the editor of the *Architectural Review*, the monthly illustrated magazine which had lately espoused the modern cause. The first chairman of the group, however, was the architect, Wells Coates. The other principal figures were Maxwell Fry, Serge Chermayeff, Raymond McGrath, A.D. Connell and Basil Ward. An interesting thing about this group is that only one, Maxwell Fry, was English by birth and training. Wells Coates, born in Hong Kong, arrived from Canada. Chermayeff, though educated in England, was born in the Caucasus, McGrath was from Australia, Connell and Ward both from New Zealand. We didn't think this important at the time, but one can see now that it was. These people had a detachment, sharper ambition, a fresher outlook than the average English architect. Also, of course, they hadn't got the Englishman's acute and sterilising sense of class.

Very soon the group was joined by architects from outside the English-speaking world. Berthold Lubetkin, the Soviet Russian architect who had practised in Paris was a challenging recruit, with more experience of building than most of us and a powerful critical intelligence.

Then with Nazism casting its shadow over Germany, came the famous emigrés. Erich Mendelsohn formed a partnership with Chermayeff, Walter Gropius with Maxwell Fry and Marcel Breuer with F.R.S. Yorke, another MARS member. The group did not consist entirely of architects. There was an engineer or two (notably Ove Arup), a quantity surveyor and some writers like J.M. Richards, myself and, rather unexpectedly perhaps, the poet and enthusiast for things Victorian, John Betjeman.

The aims of the group were, from the start, radical. Middle-class radical, of course, because, so far as I remember, all the MARS members had middle-class professional backgrounds. A working-class element in any group of qualified architects would have been a pretty unlikely thing in the thirties. Without adopting any specific political stand they were fairly well to the left. Architecture was to be firmly linked with social and technological considerations. Housing, a major problem in the thirties as it is now, was to be lifted out of its despised and pedestrian obscurity and put in the glow of imaginative enterprise. Materials and methods of construction were to be studied in relation to industrial production. Urban planning was thought of in terms of liberating

Fig. 119 The Isokon flats, Lawn Road, Hampstead (London), by Wells Coates (1933-34).

Fig. 120 Kensal House, Paddington (London), by Maxwell Fry (1936).

Fig. 121 Highpoint l, Highgate (London), by Lubetkin and Tecton (1936).

Fig. 122 Highpoint II, Highgate (London), by Lubetkin and Tecton (1938).

city centres by the creation of parkland and tower blocks. The influences, of course, were from Le Corbusier's writings and buildings, from Gropius and the Bauhaus and from the performances of such men as Bruno Taut and Ernst May under the Weimar Republic. The direction in which Europe was going seemed a good deal clearer then than it was to do a few years later.

The MARS Group started out with a fairly definite programme of work – there was, I think, to be a sort of manifesto, but I don't remember that it ever quite materialised. The reason for that was probably that from 1933 economic conditions improved and MARS members found themselves with real projects on their drawing-boards. The chairman, Wells Coates, built the Isokon flats in Lawn Road, Hampstead, in 1933-34 (Fig. 119). I do not think that it is exaggerating to say that this was the first English building in which both the programme and the design were seen imaginatively as 'modern'. The client was J.C. Pritchard, a young and enlightened industrialist. He proposed a block of small flats to suit people of moderate means, with a club and restaurant attached – just the sort of thing which young Hampstead intellectuals needed: decently equipped with no frills. Wells Coates interpreted this in a stark reinforced concrete building with cantilevered approach galleries connected at one end by dramatic zig-zag stairs. A direct solution which was, at the same time, a very striking three-dimensional object. Its qualities came out well in isometric projection – then perhaps the favourite way of illustrating a modern design, because such a projection eliminates the sense of *weight* – the building seems poised ready for siting – a delicate, aerial thing, not just a piled-up mass of materials. This is a rather subtle point in the presentation of 'modern' design in the 1930s. Anyway, the Isokon block was a real break-through. Coates never did anything else quite as good, perhaps because he never had another client who gave him such a clear 'modern' brief.

'Modern' programmes – that is, programmes with an acceptable social relationship, were what MARS members wanted. By this I mean a non-exploiting relationship. And, better than that, programmes aimed at some reasonable standard of life, education and work which could be seen as setting a standard in a socialist future.

Such programmes were few and far between. Maxwell Fry was in this respect more fortunate than most. The Kensal House flats at Paddington for the Gas Light and Coke Co. (Fig. 120) and the Impington Village College, in Cambridgeshire (designed with Gropius for Henry Morris, the innovating educationalist) were both commissioned by clients prepared to align progressive social ideas with the new architectural ideals of direct statement and of pattern obtained by the skilful disposition of the necessary elements of the structure – in a word, 'functionalism'.

Probably the most accomplished work of the thirties came from the office of Tecton, the firm founded by Lubetkin with some young MARS members as his partners. Their two blocks of flats in Highgate, Highpoint I and Highpoint II

(Figs. 121, 122), rank with some of the best continental work of the time. Highpoint I is rather severely diagrammatical, in the same spirit as Wells Coates's Isokon flats; Highpoint II, on the other hand, is more intriguing. It seems to suggest that the rhythms of the classical tradition cannot be entirely laid aside and may re-emerge quite naturally in new structural contexts. Another exciting work by Tecton was the penguin pool at the London Zoo, whose spiralling planes showed that reinforced concrete could be light, even gay.

And what else? Very little. And absolutely nothing which one could nominate as a uniquely British contribution to the modern movement. It was all derivative, trying very hard to belong to the movement, trying to breathe the new spirit – '*l'esprit nouveau*' -; trying not so much to be foreign as to be *international*. And succeeding, after all, in producing little that has stood the test of time.

The MARS Group was, nevertheless, important in English architecture. It provided a focus, a point of illumination, in a cultural scene which was confused and overcast. It was sufficiently exclusive to acquire and dispense prestige. It was noticed; and the attendance at its great exhibition in the New Burlington Galleries in 1938, to which Le Corbusier came, was quite startling.

The group went on meeting during the war and my last memories of it are of the blitz days and of informal discussion meetings in a London flat, with many new faces – students leaving the architectural schools and filling in time before the war machine got them. They were of the student generation which was to re-emerge in a modest cloud of glory in the 1951 Festival of Britain. More important still they were the generation which, with some of their elders, led the way in school building and in the making of the new towns, two fields of enterprise in which this country really did earn the interest and admiration of the world in the fifties and after. In this sense I see the MARS Group as a sort of link, or rather a bridge, carrying the hard militant minority thinking of the thirties over into the age of acceptance. After 1945, everything became 'modern', so that the very word, as applied to architecture, became an archaism.

The MARS Group continued in existence for some years after the war, but at midnight on 28 January 1957 it voluntarily extinguished itself. It had done its job and declined to grow old. A very proper attitude: very 'functional', very 'modern'.

24

Cyril A. Farey: A Personal Tribute to St Paul's Cathedral and the City of London, 1940-44

J.B. LINGARD

At least fourteen fine watercolour perspectives were drawn by the celebrated architectural draughtsman Cyril Farey (1888-1954) during the Second World War, between 1940 and 1944, that record historic buildings in the City of London and the St Paul's Cathedral precinct. Eleven watercolours have remained in one collection,[1] while a further three are known to have been dispersed. Alongside their many pictorial qualities the perspectives are interesting for several reasons. They depict certain historic London buildings, such as a number of City churches built by Wren, St Paul's Cathedral, buildings of the Inner Temple, the Record Office and Southwark Cathedral in the aftermath of the London Blitz and reveal a concern for the preservation of significant buildings at a time when so many proposals were being put forward for the redevelopment of London. The question as to how historic London buildings in an area of recognised beauty should be preserved, amidst the extensive rebuilding that was required to restore the City to working order, was crucial. A good many plans and recommendations were put forward in response to the situation both officially and unofficially, ranging from those presented by corporate bodies such as London County Council, the Royal Academy and the church to others put together by individual architects and surveyors from within the architectural profession. The future of the built environment in the City was a matter that greatly interested the general public, and was very much influenced by it, with suggestions appearing in both the national and building press: the debate that ensued was as keenly discussed during the 1940s as it has continued to be up to the present day.[2]

Farey is arguably the most renowned British architectural draughtsman of the twentieth century, whose skill in the casting and rendering of architectural

* I am most grateful to Mr and Mrs W. Hussey for their help and support.
1 Gallery Lingard, Walpole House, 35 Walpole Street, London SW3 4JQ.

2 The area around Ludgate Circus is under redevelopment. The future of the post-war development of Paternoster Square is again under review amidst lively debate.

perspectives has been acknowledged consistently by the architectural profession.[3] Cyril Arthur Farey was born in London in 1888 and studied architecture at the Architectural Association from 1909 to 1910 and the Royal
Academy School of Architecture. In 1909 he won a travelling scholarship at the
Architectural Association and in 1910 received an honourable mention from
the Royal Institute of British Architects for the drawings he submitted for the
Measured Drawings Prize.[4] Farey won the Royal Academy Schools bronze
medal in 1911 and proved himself to be one of the most brilliant scholars of his
time, going on in subsequent years to win the Tite Prize in 1913, the Soane
Medallion in 1914, the Royal Academy Gold Medal and the Edward Stott
Travelling Studentship in 1921 for architectural drawing. Farey served his
articles with Horace Field (1861-1948), with whom he entered many competi-
tions between 1911 and 1920. During the first war he served in the Royal Army
Corps attaining the rank of Captain. He worked subsequently as an assistant in
the office of Sir Ernest Newton (1856-1922), whose interests in the local
vernacular, traditional building methods and craft processes, drawn in large
part from his experience in the office of Norman Shaw, greatly influenced him.
A.G. Shoosmith, a friend of Farey, remembers the artist in these early years,
recalling that, 'it was on one or two bright little drawings for Sir Ernest Newton
hung in the summer of 1911 that I first met the name of Cyril Farey' and that at
the age of twenty-three Farey already had, 'a stream of commissions coming in
and worked incessantly upon them. No one could have been happier at work;
whistling snatches of a popular ragtime or of an aria from Puccini marked
relief from minutes of almost breathless concentration'.[5]

The period from 1900 to 1920 saw a flowering of the art of architectural
draughtsmanship: among Farey's contemporaries at this time, whose perspective work displays similar traits, were Robert Atkinson (1883-1953), Charles
Gascoyne (1871-1917), James Whitelaw (1856-1913) and Philip D. Hepworth
(1884-1963). Charles Reilly provides some idea of the life of a perspective artist
between 1900 and 1918:

> It was a merry life, with great rushes of work as the time for the Academy drew near.
> Atkinson, Gascoigne [*sic*] and Horsnell at one time or another each used to have
> some twenty drawings or so in the exhibition.[6]

Farey followed the same path and year after year the Royal Academy would
include perhaps a dozen or more of his perspectives:

3 The esteem in which he is held remains high:
   his perspective of Raffles College, Singapore
   appears on the cover of G. Stamp, *The Great
   Perspectivists* (London, 1982).
4 Farey prepared a set of survey drawings of

the Hotel Carnavalet, Paris.
5 A.G. Shoosmith, 'Obituary', *RIBA Journal*,
   3rd series, lxii (January 1955), p. 130.
6 G. Stamp, *The Great Perspectivists*, p. 101.

His services were always in great demand for he had the knack of making an indifferent design look pictorially attractive and to have your building drawn by Farey was almost a guarantee of hanging.[7]

At this time the architectural room at the Royal Academy featured so many perspectives by Farey that on one occasion Sir Edwin Lutyens was moved to make the memorable pun, 'What ho, the Farey Glen!'.[8] Farey worked for a great number of architects but in particular he favoured the work of Lutyens, Howitt, Maurice Webb, Albert Moore, Victor Heal & Partners, Guy Dawber and E. Vincent Harris. He enjoyed a lucrative career as a perspective artist, working assuredly and at a steady pace that would often produce two or three small drawings in a week or larger, more detailed drawings in two to three weeks.

Apart from his career as a perspective artist, and lending knowledge and experience to his draughting work for others, Farey also practised as an architect. He achieved some success in this field, winning in 1924, for example, the important competition for Raffles College, Singapore, with Graham Dawbarn. Dawbarn remembers watching:

a master craftsman at work. The confident way in which he chose his viewpoint, his delightful little preliminary sketches (which never saw the light of day) and the technique whereby he obtained that luminous background. Apart from William Walcot he had, at his best, few if any rivals.[9]

Further competition successes continued through the 1920s, 1930s and 1940s and, in 1947, Farey set up in partnership with his son Michael Farey and J.J. Adams. Farey experienced a long and varied career that took him to all parts of the world. His acclaim was further extended when he collaborated in 1931 on what many regard as the definitive book on this subject, *Architectural Drawing, Perspective and Rendering*.[10]

It is less well known that Farey also produced more informal images of buildings at home and abroad from his early student days forward.[11] These watercolour perspectives fall into the category of sketches, measured drawings, survey drawings and topographical works where personal preference for a building and its setting predetermined the choice of subject-matter. It was often the case that Farey would prefer to find previously unrecorded or little-known buildings to draw, finding a distinctive but unusual viewpoint, rather

7 *The Builder*, clxxxvii (17 December 1954), p. 976.
8 *The Builder*, clxxxvii (17 December 1954), p. 976.
9 G. Dawbarn, 'Obituary', *RIBA Journal*, 3rd series lxii (January 1955), p. 130.
10 C.A. Farey and A. Trystan Edwards, *Architectural Drawing, Perspective and Rendering* (1931; second edition 1949).
11 Cyril A. Farey, *An Exhibition of Watercolours and Drawings by Cyril Farey*, Gallery Lingard (1990).

than repeating an image already cast by others. A modest man of independent mind, he was quick to assess the merits or faults of a building and ready to choose his subject-matter by that measure early on in his career. The comments he noted in the diary he kept whilst a student on a sketching tour of Italy in 1910 reveal candid observations frankly recorded:

> On the whole I am very disappointed in Verona as a hunting ground for architects as beyond the Gran Guardia Vecchio and Porta Palio which have been measured time after time there is little else of any real merit in the Renaissance line.

In Florence he

> visited the Pitti Gallery again and much enjoyed the pictures . . . went . . . over the river to the Uffizi Gallery where I saw, principally, the sketches, mostly architectural by famous artists such as Peruzzi, Michelangelo, Bramante, Brunelleschi, Sangallo, Raphael etc. These are very interesting, for although very rough, they display great knowledge of design. In the afternoon there being nothing else to sketch I made a drawing of a facade opposite the Palazzo Vecchio. I find . . . Florence is a very much overated place for finding material for architects. Of course the work of Brunelleschi is very fine but all his best works have been illustrated and measured.

He noted in Vicenza that the town was:

> Very dull but fine architecturally. Was no more impressed by the Basilica by Palladio in reality than by the photographs. I much prefer the Palazzo Barbarano to all the others. Saw the Theatro Olimpico but did not very much care for it. The entrances on to the stage which were streets in perspective were very clever but hardly architecture. The Pal Valmarana very fine.[12]

For Farey even the most modest sketch should not be undertaken lightly. He devoted a chapter in his book to the subject of sketching, reminding the reader that, 'many architects are inveterate sketchers', and that while the sketches made by 'an architect on holiday and an architect bent upon adding to his own equipment as a designer' are not the same, it is vital to both that the draughtsman should have a distinct purpose in mind. He adds that:

> He must ascertain what benefit is likely to result, either to himself or others, from the particular sketch which he contemplates . . . It is not more practice that such draughtsmen need, for their industry is most commendable, but more thought, more analysis and more severe self-criticism.[13]

12 Diary kept by Farey on his tour of Italy, 10 April 1910, p. 47; 18 March 1910, pp. 35-36; 4 April 1910, p. 43 (Gallery Lingard). The misspellings are Farey's, written in haste.

13 C.A. Farey and A. Trystan Edwards, *Architectural Drawing, Perspective and Rendering* (London, 1931), p. 64.

Fig. 123 C.A. Farey, St Paul's Cathedral from Stationers' Hall (23 May 1942)

Fig. 124 C.A. Farey, St Paul's Cathedral from the south east with St Nicholas Cole Abbey (13 June 1942).

Fig. 125 C.A. Farey, St Paul's Cathedral from the north (11 July 1942).

Fig. 126 C.A. Farey, St Paul's Cathedral, interior from the crypt, north transept (2 July 1942).

Fig. 127 C.A. Farey, St Vedast-alias-Foster, Foster Lane (1942).

Fig. 128 C.A. Farey, St Paul's Cathedral from Bankside (June 1944).

Fig. 129 C.A. Farey, proposed western approach to St Paul's Cathedral from Ludgate (1942).

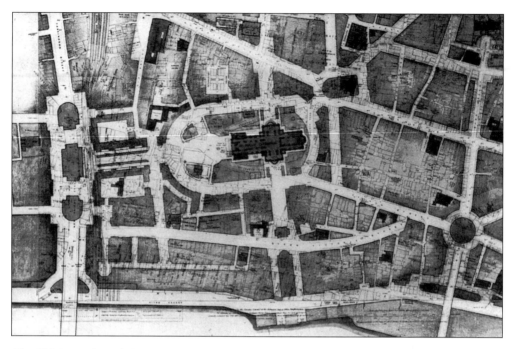

Fig. 130 New plan of the area around St Paul's Cathedral (1942). (*London Replanned*)

Fig. 131 J.D.M. Harvey, St Paul's Cathedral from the river. (*London Replanned*)

What purpose did Farey then have in mind for these fourteen highly finished perspectives of the City of London and what benefit did he hope would result? Were they commissioned works or undertaken for personal reasons? The perspectives are signed, inscribed and dated in almost every case and a list of them reads as follows:

1   St Paul's Cathedral from Stationers' Hall, 23 May 1942 (Fig. 123)
2   Blackfriars railway looking north across Ludgate Hill, 30 May 1942
3   St Paul's Cathedral from the south-east with St Nicholas Cole Abbey, 13 June 1942 (Fig. 124)
4   The Inner Temple Hall with a barrage-balloon, 20 June 1942
5   The Inner Temple Hall, 25 June 1942
6   The Record Office from the south, 25 June 1942
7   Interior of St Paul's Cathedral from the crypt, north transept, 2 July 1942 (Fig. 126)
8   St Paul's Cathedral from the north, 11 July 1942 (Fig. 125)
9   St Vedast-alias-Foster, Foster Lane, 1942 (Fig. 127)
10 Holborn Viaduct Station looking south to Ludgate and Blackfriars, 1942
11 Proposed western approach to St Paul's from Ludgate, 1942 (Fig. 129)
12 Southwark Cathedral, May 1944
13 St Paul's Cathedral from Bankside, June 1944 (Fig. 128)
14 Cannon Street Station from Bankside, 1944

At least six of the perspectives were hung at the Royal Academy between 1943 and 1949 and were clearly considered to be of the high standard associated with other perspective work by Farey.[14] The handling of the watercolour washes is smooth and sure over a precisely drawn pencil drawing rendered according to the strict rules of perspective. The 'wet-look' treatment that Farey adopted for the foreground of his perspectives is evident in many of these watercolours and adds to the highly finished quality of the composition. The perspective of the proposed western approach to St Paul's from Ludgate is alone in exhibiting a markedly more formal approach to the subject, in line with other perspective work commissioned from Farey by other members of the profession in order to project an envisaged architectural scheme prior to building.

Farey was no less busy during the 1940s in preparing perspectives of the designs of other architects and he also took employment in the draughting

14   (8) 'St Paul's Cathedral from the North', cat. no. 624 (1943).
(1) 'St Paul's Cathedral from Stationers' Hall', cat. no. 814 (1944).
(6) 'The Record Office from the South', cat. no. 741 (1946).
(3) 'St Paul's Cathedral from the South-East', cat. no. 885 (1948).
(13) 'St Paul's Cathedral from Bankside', cat. no. 1202 (1948).
(7) 'Interior of St Paul's Cathedral from the Crypt', cat. no. 803 (1949).

department of Handley Page.[15] In addition he volunteered as a member of the St Paul's Fire-Guard Watch in 1941 and it was this decision that placed him in a central position to witness the effects of the London Blitz and to execute these records of the damage it caused. The heavy bombardment of East London, along the dockland areas as well as the main rail links with the capital, had commenced some time before the air-raid attacks began to target sites in the City in the later part of 1940. This lapse of time had allowed fire-fighters in the City area to make provisional preparations to protect the buildings. The Dean and Chapter of St Paul's had prepared plans to safeguard the cathedral as early as April 1939, appointing Godfrey Allen in charge of the project.[16] By March 1940 Allen had formed the St Paul's Watch Committee, a small group of cathedral staff, who were joined by volunteers from the public.[17] Allen made two specific appeals to the Royal Institute of British Architects to enlist from their membership, as he knew that the ideal fire-fighters for his task-force needed to be men trained to follow the floor plans of the most complex buildings. Allen described the work of the Watch as being

> in itself interesting. It has been said that even a most eminent architect takes several months to master all the intricate passages and staircases as well as the working of the hydrants and fire-fighting appliances.[18]

Farey was recruited from the second appeal. Allen devised a rota system of duties for Watch members including keeping look-out, patrolling the passages of the cathedral and roofs at all levels, and also standing ready. There were two main H.Q. points, in the crypt and at Advanced H.Q. positioned at the top of the main stairs to the Whispering Gallery. The H.Q. points were vital, organising the patrols and keeping a log-book of events night by night. Coordination was maintained by means of the telephone link between the H.Q. points. Each member of the Watch wore a numbered helmet and carried an axe and torch. The result was a well-organised group of volunteers amongst whom a strong

15 The draughting department of Handley Page considered it an honour to have Farey among them and had been prepared to offer a salary of £20 per week for his services, double that of the other draughtsmen, but Farey declined to be treated differently and accepted £10 remuneration.

16 W. Godfrey Allen, Surveyor to the Fabric of St Paul's. The Dean and Chapter put Allen in charge of all practical precautions to protect the cathedral during the war and he commanded the St Paul's Fire-Guard Watch. 'He was qualified for the task not only by his unrivalled knowledge of the building but also by his intense love of it. Yet he was a volunteer

just as much as those who later rallied round him at his call.' *St Paul's in War and Peace, 1939-1958, The Times*, (London, 1960), p. 39.

17 'We had many distinguished architects, and they deserve to be mentioned first, because our first volunteers came from that profession. We had university professors, business men, civil servants, artists, members of foreign governments exiled among us, medical students, theological students, musical students, clerics and . . . friends from the Post Office', W.R. Matthews, *St Paul's Cathedral in Wartime, 1939-1945* (London, 1946), p. 69.

18 W.R. Matthews, *St Paul's Cathedral in Wartime, 1939-1945* (London, 1946), p. 24.

community spirit was fostered; in time they became thought of as 'the best club in London'. The Dean recalled

> the mess room as it was on one of our normal nights – between the alerts – I think I am trying to play chess amid the conversation . . . Two others, architects I suppose, are arguing about some building I have never heard of.[19]

Members might also deliver talks in the mess, such as that given by J.D.M. Harvey, a fellow architectural draughtsman, on the subject of 'Aluminium'. The Dean was full of gratitude to members of the Watch, yet it was felt by some that too few people at large knew of their contribution to saving St Paul's.[20] At a Thanksgiving service in honour of the St Paul's Fire-Guard Watch, held in the presence of the King and Queen, the Dean summed up the sense of purpose felt by members:

> it was not the thought of gratitude or praise from men that moved you to come here night after night and to endure the hardships and dangers of the Watch. You felt that something beautiful was threatened, you felt that something which stood for much that is noble and venerable in the life of England was threatened [and] . . . we remember too, how often the bombs, or the devouring flames, were so near that it seemed almost inconceivable St Paul's should escape becoming, like the buildings around it, a heap of stones.[21]

St Paul's was damaged by a total of sixty incendiary bombs and two 500lb high-explosive bombs between 1940 and 1942, yet it was little affected by comparison with the devastation around it. On 29 September 1940 many bombs fell around St Paul's, flattening parts of the churchyard, Amen Court, and much of the area south east of the cathedral. Further air attacks through to 29 December 1940 inflicted damage in the area to the north and east of St Paul's, including the destruction of the roof and much of the interior of Wren's church of St Vedast-alias-Foster,[22] the Chapter House, Dean's Verger's House and Minor Canons' House. An incendiary bomb had caused alarm when it had lodged on the outer shell of St Paul's dome but it fell into the Stone Gallery before the roof lead had melted to expose the vulnerable timber structure beneath. The air-strike during the night of 9 October 1940 had hit the cathedral choir roof leaving the high altar shattered and the interior damaged, but the incendiary attack on 16 April 1941 had caused greater damage when a high-explosive bomb hit the north transept, smashing through the roof and

19 Ibid., p. 71.
20 'We wish that the valiant work of the St Paul's Watch were more widely known . . . the devoted exertions of the St Paul's Watch under the inspiring leadership of Mr Godfrey Allen', 'Repairs at St Paul's', *The Builder*, clxxiii

(5 December 1947), p. 638.
21 W.R. Matthews, *St Paul's Cathedral in Wartime*, p. 68.
22 P. Jeffery, *The Church of St Vedast-alias-Foster*, (The Ecclesiological Society, 1989), p. 19.

bringing down the floor into the crypt, as well as shattering the north door and interior. Farey was on Watch duty, patrolling the dome that night as the log-book records

> 9.50pm: Siren. 9.53: Farey look out. 9.55: Dome patrol started, Mr Allen, Farey . . . 1.52: Cathedral roofs pelted with incendiary bombs, about twenty reported having been put out. 2.30: Bomb through North Transept. Blast terrific. Crypt H.Q. moved to shelter. 3.00: All people in Crypt ordered into shelter . . . 4.57: All Clear.[23]

On Saturday 10 May 1941 the Temple Church was completely burnt out and most of the buildings of the Temple and Gray's Inn were badly damaged in heavy bomb attacks, as were more buildings to the east of St Paul's.

Farey records the effects of many of the air attacks in this group of perspectives, particularly in the St Paul's precinct, Ludgate Hill area and the Temple and Gray's Inn sites. Taking the perspectives of St Paul's precinct together Farey has, in effect, walked all round the cathedral site and drawn the view in each case looking back to St Paul's with the dome towering above the foreground area. What appears is not the flurry and detail of destruction but the calm remaining masses, the buildings still standing rather than interior detailing. The same is true of the perspectives of the Inner Temple Hall, the Record Office and Ludgate Hill. Farey was not alone in recording bomb-damaged buildings in the City. The *Illustrated London News* had been quick to commission pictorial records of the area, publishing the drawings with head-lines such as, 'The City of London, 1942. The Pictorial Side of the Damaged Metropolis'.[24] They employed a number of draughtsmen, such as Dennis Flanders, throughout 1941 to document the Blitz week by week. The magazine published up-to-the-minute, illustrated news reports on historic buildings when damage occurred and included news on Stationers' Hall and the Temple buildings.[25] In particular they printed a series of features entitled, 'Bombed Wren City Churches', mostly illustrated by Flanders, including an interior sketch of St Vedast-alias-Foster on 14 June 1941 by Flanders.[26] A further drawing, published by the *Illustrated London News*, entitled, 'The City and St Paul's after the Raid on the Metropolis . . .', with the inscription, 'drawn on the spot', was executed by Sir Muirhead Bone (1876-1953),[27] a celebrated architectural draughtsman who, along with other draughtsmen such as Henry Rushbury (1889-1968), carried out many immediate views of blitzed London. The drawings prepared by Flanders, Muirhead Bone and Rushbury had a deliberately sketchy style, with hurried lines emphasising the immediacy of

---

23 W.R. Matthews, *St Paul's Cathedral in Wartime*, p. 52.

24 *Illustrated London News*, cc (16 May 1942), pp. 570-71.

25 Ibid., cxcviii (1 March 1941), p. 290; cxcviii (7 June 1941), pp. 734-35.

26 Ibid., cxcviii (14 June 1941), p. 783. Other features entitled, 'Bombed Wren City Churches', with illustrations by Flanders and photographs appeared on 7 June 1941, pp. 750-51; 21 June 1941; cxcix (30 August 1941), p. 283.

27 Ibid., cxcviii (14 June 1941), p. 781.

the task. Akin to the many photographs of damaged buildings in the City, printed in the press during the 1940s, these line drawings, with their attention to the small details of destruction, leave the reader with the feeling of seeing the masonry falling and the smell of smoke in the air. Not so Farey's water-colours where, by contrast, there is an air of quiet calm in areas where the dust has been left to settle around damaged buildings for some time.

While Farey was occupied in the St Paul's Watch he was in the best possible position to see the bomb-damage sites and reach them in advance of others, but he did not draw his perspectives until some time had elapsed. While artists like Flanders acted in haste to detail the immediate effects of the blitz, Farey delayed rendering his perspectives until sites had been cleared of rubble, stones set aside for reuse and cranes stood ready – with Londoners once again going about their business. With this approach in mind, along with the fact of the number of watercolours in hand, Farey's perspectives amount more to survey records of the area and, when this is set beside the careful choice of viewpoint, they ally themselves to the proposals put forward by the Royal Academy Planning Committee for the redevelopment of London. The report, *London Replanned*, was published in August 1942 and accompanied an exhibition of plans and drawings held at the Royal Academy.[28] The content of the Planning Committee's proposals was however known before this date, certainly by January 1942, when some ideas were printed in *Country Life*;[29] this would have provided Farey with time to prepare his perspectives from May through to August of that year. Indeed he is listed as one of the collaborators on the work alongside other architectural draughtsmen such as J.D.M. Harvey and W.F.C. Holden. Farey's involvement was not as central as that of P.D. Hepworth, listed as a committee member, but he had close links with the chairman Sir Edwin Lutyens and other committee members such as Godfrey Allen,[30] Patrick Abercrombie[31] and Louis de Soissons.[32] The report stated that the proposals were conceived as ideas:

> put forward more with the idea of stimulating the imagination of those who will be
> responsible for the work of reconstruction than of laying down any fixed or rigid

28 *London Replanned: A Nobler City*, Interim Report of the Royal Academy Planning Committee (August 1942), Country Life Ltd.

29 Sir G.G. Scott, 'Replanning the City', *Country Life*, xci (16 January 1942), pp. 110-11. The article was based on a recent Royal Academy discourse. As a committee member of the Royal Academy Planning Committee, Scott was aware of the forthcoming proposals and this piece was published in advance with the Planning Committee's consent. The article supports the recommendations put forward in August and exhibited at the Royal Academy in October so that the public were aware

of the Royal Academy proposals eight months earlier.

30 P.D. Hepworth, a fellow architectural draughtsman, executed many of the perspectives hung in the October exhibition at the Royal Academy. W.G. Allen knew Farey from the St Paul's Fire-Guard Watch.

31 Patrick Abercrombie worked on the County of London Plan (1943) and the Greater London Plan (1944). Michael Farey later married Deborah, Patrick Abercrombie's daughter.

32 For whom Farey worked as an architectural perspectivist.

solution . . . [that they were] not concerned with the design of buildings themselves, the plans having been prepared more to show the layout and grouping.[33]

The report advocated a sensitive use of land, recommending the careful setting aside of areas for industry, markets, offices, housing and open spaces, the positioning of mainline stations in the City, with special regard given to relocating railways away from these areas and where possible placing them underground. Approach roads to public buildings and monuments, bridges and areas of special interest were to be carefully studied with attention being paid to the height, back and sides of buildings as well as to the main façades. Clear recommendations were given for a new road structure in the St Paul's area. The cathedral was surrounded by an open garden space around which ran an encircling road which linked roads running into the precinct such as Cannon Street and Ludgate Hill. A new road running north to south from Newgate Street to the river, via the encircling road, ran on an axis with the north and south doors of the cathedral and created the opportunity for a wide open avenue between the river and St Paul's. From the river would be a marvellous view of Wren's cathedral which was drawn in perspective for the exhibition by Harvey. This perspective was much remarked upon in the press with its ceremonial steps rising up from the Thames adorned with details reminiscent of Canaletto's views of London (Fig. 131).[34] Christopher Hussey discussed *London Replanned* and commented on 9 October that 'It is safe to say that most people will be profoundly moved by the "perspective views" and marvellous superimposed map for the reshaping of familiar scenes now exhibited,' and he recommended the plans as being a 'considered, co-ordinated, inspiring but flexible blue-print for long-term reconstruction and development.[35]

Farey too felt moved to voice his suggestions for the site south of the cathedral in a letter entitled, 'Living in the City', published in the *Daily Telegraph* a month later:

Many people would like to live in the heart of the city of London at walking distance from their work, provided that the habitations were conveniently planned in healthy and pleasant surroundings. The devastation area around St Paul's provides a splendid site for the creation of a residential district, with shopping facilities and social services. By a system of squares leading off the main thoroughfares dignified blocks of flats could be built to a height of the level of the first cornice of the Cathedral and leading down to the river. These squares would be quiet and planned around gardens with trees. On those parts adjoining the main roads the ground

33 *London Replanned: A Nobler City*, Interim Report of the Royal Academy Planning Committee (August 1942), Country Life Ltd, p. 15.

34 J.D.M. Harvey, 'St Paul's from the River'. This

perspective was reproduced on the cover of *London Replanned*.

35 C. Hussey, 'A Vision of the New London', *Country Life*, xcii (9 October 1942), pp. 693-94.

floors could contain shops, offices, banks and restaurants. Standing high above the river and crowned by the Cathedral this site would, if well planned, make a pleasant residential district, in contrast to the former arrangement of dreary blocks of offices.[36]

The Royal Academy exhibition of these proposals prompted a considerable response from within the profession and from the public. A leader in *Country Life* for 11 December divided the response into two wide groups, firstly those who felt that the 'quaint pokey corners of dear old London' had been allowed to disappear and secondly others who believed the plans were too 'timid and nigglingly academic'.[37] Nikolaus Pevsner warned against taking either option too far when he pointed out the variety of architectural styles inherent in the traditional English architecture. Pevsner believed Wren too had come to this conclusion in his later work:

> Wren tried to impose a formal plan on the City of London. That plan would have broken away from the tradition of this country. Wren came to see this, and in his later work . . . built in a free and varied way. Forms of all kinds are to be found in his church spires, ranging from severe Classic to Gothic.[38]

Pevsner advocated a more informal planning for the City of London based on a system of independent yet interrelating squares taking their lead from Covent Garden and the Inns of Court. He felt the Royal Academy plans had paid too much attention to symmetry.

With a view to the perspectives prepared by Farey, however, the report included a 'New Plan of the Area round St Paul's Cathedral', which presents a sweeping new road layout (Fig. 130). A huge roundabout was recommended to the north east of the encircling cathedral road, linking Newgate Street with Cheapside, and the church of St Vedast-alias-Foster would have been incorporated as the key feature, offsetting the view to the cathedral from this point. Farey's perspective of the church takes precisely this viewpoint and strongly suggests prior knowledge of the Royal Academy plans. The same can be seen with the perspectives of St Paul's from the north, St Paul's from the south east and St Paul's from Stationers' Hall, each view taken by Farey being almost exactly on a line with a new road or vista recommended by the New Plan. In this way historic buildings would not be lost in redevelopment but singled out for

36 C.A. Farey, 'Living in the City', *Daily Telegraph* (19 November 1942).

37 'London's Future', *Country Life*, xcii (11 December 1942), pp. 1122. Among the criticisms was the feeling that the plans were too ideal, expensive and unrealisable. They would involve still more demolition than the war had created and few wanted further destruction. Several contrasting unrealised plans

for the post-Second World War development of London are discussed by F. Barker and R. Hyde, *London as it Might Have Been* (London, 1982), pp. 177-95.

38 N. Pevsner, 'Visual Planning and the City of London', talk delivered at the Architectural Association, *Architects' Journal* (13 December 1954), pp. 440-41.

attention. The treatment of St Vedast is exemplary; where *London Replanned* proposed to make the church a key feature of replanning, as endorsed by Farey's perspective, it is interesting to note the proposal put forward only five years later by Lord Holford in 1947 to enclose the church with office buildings leaving only a light-well on the east side.[39] A very useful feature of the New Plan is that the new ideas were superimposed over a survey of the existing area. The direction of the railway line from the river to Blackfriars and up to Holborn Viaduct Station is clearly visible and the two perspectives prepared by Farey of Holborn Viaduct Station looking south to Ludgate and of Blackfriars Railway looking north across Ludgate Hill clearly survey the existing conditions of the site with a view to redevelopment. Had the proposals set down in *London Replanned*, to remove Blackfriars Station with the railway running north to Holborn Viaduct, been implemented, the area would have been clear for the reconstruction of Ludgate Circus. It was planned to redirect Ludgate Hill on an axis with the east façade of St Paul's which would open up another wide vista to the cathedral, this time from the west. Ludgate Circus would change to become a tree-lined square providing a large open space. The new vista of the cathedral might have been one of the most magnificent views of St Paul's and Farey's 'Proposed western approach to St Paul's from Ludgate' illustrates this view of the envisaged redevelopment. It is the only perspective in the group where Farey has executed a view of the projected appearance of the plans and is more tightly drawn in comparison with the other survey perspectives.

South of the river, *London Replanned* suggested wide changes to the area around Southwark Cathedral, with a new traffic circus at the bridgehead and extensive road development which, like the north bank, included a low-level embankment that eliminated unsightly wharves. London Bridge Station would be moved and Southwark Cathedral made free of encroaching warehouses and provided with a 'proper "Close", approached from the Bridge by steps and from the lower level by suitable carriageways'.[40] The perspective of Southwark prepared by Farey in 1944 takes up the idea of providing a close; if the area immediately surrounding the building were widened then it might be more visible both from the Thames and the adjacent streets, where, at this time the streets allowed only a small glimpse at any one time.

The issue of unsightly river fronts and the recommendations that there should be no wharves built above Tower Bridge was a standard proposal of *London Replanned* and one that may be illustrated in Farey's two other perspectives executed in 1944, 'St Paul's from Bankside' and 'Cannon Street Station from Bankside'.[41] Both perspectives record the cluttered warehousing that

39 *The City of London: A Record of Destruction and Survival*, C.H. Holden and W.G. Holford for the Town Planning Committee, Corporation of London (1951), pp. 256-57.
40 *London Replanned: A Nobler City*, Interim Report of the Royal Academy Planning Committee (August 1942), Country Life Ltd., p. 24.
41 Ibid., p. 21.

ranged along the north bank obscuring the more interesting buildings behind them. The dome and towers of St Paul's stand high above the brick warehouses and an opening cut between them runs on an axis with the south door of the cathedral, so that the composition reads as if it were, yet again, a survey drawing of the site before the envisaged plans to create a wide central avenue. Interestingly, Farey includes in his perspective of Cannon Street Station a view up from the Thames by Cousin Lane stairs into Cousin Lane, alongside the train-shed, past St Stephen Walbrook to the white stone-faced elevation of the then new Midland Bank Head Office on Poultry.[42]

By 1944 many more plans for the redevelopment of London had emerged, and continued to do so in the years that followed. These included the *County of London Plan* in 1943,[43] H. Baily's 'Plan for the City of London'[44] and Lord Holford's plan.[45] The debate has continued until the present day. Lord Holford's plan was produced in 1947 and was published four years later. The title of the resulting document, *The City of London: a Record of Destruction and Survival*, gives an indication of the scope of the research and the recommendations put forward. An integral feature was the attention paid to the nature of the buildings in the City, the historical background to the different precincts and the thorough survey of the area. Each topic was treated as an individual section of the report and the whole was illustrated with reproductions of old drawings and contemporary photographs. In particular the report relied heavily on photographic records for the survey of the sites with architectural draughtsmen being employed to draw perspectives of the proposed redevelopment of the area rather than to survey it. The perspectives prepared by Farey are especially interesting since they provide a drawn survey of parts of the City of London at a time when the photograph was becoming more widely used for such depictions. They provide a valuable survey of those parts of the City that were considered for redevelopment by the Royal Academy Planning Committee in 1942 and offer a pictorial alternative to the many other surveys provided by photographic means.

42 Built to the designs of Gotch and Saunders and Sir Edwin Lutyens. Farey was commissioned to execute perspectives of the envisaged scheme as completed which were illustrated in the contemporary building press.

43 J.H. Forshaw and P. Abercrombie, *County of London Plan* (1943); P. Abercrombie, *Greater London Plan* (1944). Other proposals were put forward by the City (1944) and Westminster

(1948).

44 Harold Baily, 'A Plan for the City of London', *The Builder*, clxvi (31 March 1944), p. 256. A dry formalised plan that abolished obsolete buildings, including Wren City churches, if they obstructed a proposed new widened roads scheme. It is quoted here as an example of a privately proposed scheme.

45 *The City of London: A Record of Destruction and Survival*, as in n. 39.

Index

(The page numbers of illustrations are in italics at the end of the entries)

List of Subscribers

D. Abel Smith
David Adshead
M.R. Airs
Brian Allen
John Anthony
John Ashdown
George Atkinson
Bruce A Bailey
Dr Andrew Ballantyne
S.J. Balston
Ian S. Barcroft
A.H. Barker
Patrick Baty
L.K. Baxter
Peter Beacham
Dr Geoffrey Beard
Margaret S. Birney
Richard Bisson
Tye Blackshaw
Brian Blackwood
B.C. Blit
Andrew Boddington
John Bold
Jon Bolter
J.R.E. Bollon
N.E. Bridges
J.W. Briggs
Dr Steven Brindle
Allan Brodie
Dr W.A. Brogden
D.B. Brown
Michael Bullen
P.A.T. Burman
David Butcher
Lord Caldecote
Ian Campbell
Prof. David Cast
J.C.B. Catnach
Reginald Cave
Edward Chaney
Maaike Louise Chaney
Rebecca Child
Ian Chilvers

James Clare
E.D. Clarke
R.L. Cline
Robert Close
John Coales
Dr T.H. Cocke
T.P. Conner
Major R. Conningham
Dr R.T. Coope
Michael V. Cooper
Hugh P. Crallan
David Crellin
Stephen Croad
Prof. J. Mordaunt Crook
Peter Dietl
Nicholas Doggett
R.C. Donovan
P.M. Doran
J.G. Drake
Peter Draper
Patricia Drummond
H.M. Duckett
J.G. Dunbar
Thomas Duncan
John Dyson
Nancy Edwards
Cyril Eland
Dennis Farr
T.E. Faulkner
J. Feisenberger
Donald Findlay
David Firmin
Angus Fowler
Dr Terry Friedman
John Gadsden
Claire Gapper
A.G.H. Gibson
Lord Gibson
L.B. Ginsburg
W.D. Girvan
Alasdair Glass
Prof. A.H. Gomme
Dr I.H. Goodall

A. Green
Francis J. Green
Robert T. Gwynne
Dr Dennis Hadley
D.J. Hale
Nicholas J. Hale
Dr I. Hall
J. Harris
Martin Harrison
Elain Harwood
E.M. Hawes
L.M. Head
A. Heseltine
John Heward
Michael Hill
A.P. Hills
C.W. Hind
J.A. Hock
Keith Honess
G. Hood
St C.C. Hood
Dr Maurice Howard
Peter Howell
J.A. Howlett
J.A. Huber
Vernon Hughes
A.W. Huish
T.B. Hutton
Julia Ionides
Malcolm Jack
Gervace Jackson-Stops
Anthony Jaggard
Dr P.G. Jeffery
Dr S. Jeffery
Thornton J. Kay
Frank Kelsall
Pamela D. Kingsbury
N.W. Kingsley
James A.H. Kingswell
Laurence Kinney
George Knox
Dr Joan Lane
Brian H. Larkins

Dr Peter Leach
Terence R. Leach
Amanda Lester
Dr Nigel Llewellyn
David W. Lloyd
Stephen Lloyd
Jennifer Loach
Elisha Long
Dr John Lord
Isabel Loveland
Keith Lovell
Dr A.M. Maguire
J. Kenneth Major
Michael Manser
Stephen Marks
G.D. Martin
Prof. G.H. Martin
A.R. Martindale
Simone Mathews
Michael McCarthy
K.H. McIntosh
D.M. Meadows
Roger Mears
Dr H.A. Meek
Eric Mercer
N.A.D. Molyneux
F.A. Moody
Jennifer Moore
N.J. Moore
Dr T.W. Mowl
L. Murray
R. Nelson
Vic Nierop-Reading
B.F.J. Pardoe
John Peacock
Richard Pestell
B.D. Peters
Christopher Pickford

Michael Pickwoad
Van Pickwood
Clare Pillman
Christopher Pound
K. Powell
Alan Powers
Richard Prentis
Ruth L. Reed
Peter Reynolds
D.G. Richbell
Anne Riches
A. Ricketts
Richard Riddell
Prof. John Riely
C. Rimell
Dr David L. Roberts
Alan Robson
Alistair Rowan
Francis Russell
Lady Russell
Alicia Salter
John Sambrook
C. Saumarez-Smith
Andrew Saunders
Ann Saunders
Joshua J. Schwieso
Christina Scull
Roger Shaw
Dr Edwin Shearing
Derek Sherborn
M.R.C. Sherlock
A.D. Short
Andrew C. Skelton
Dr C.W.L. Smith
J.T. Smith
W. John Smith
Peter Smith

A.T.J. Stanford
Dr Christine Stevenson
David B. Stewart
Ian Sutton
Dr John Sweetman
Major A.R. Tavener
Dr Christopher Thacker
Peter Thomson
C. Tilbury
J.M. Tomlinson
Andrew Townsend
J.B. Trapp
G.H.B. Tregear
Michael Trinick
Dr T.J. Tuohy
P.S. Valois
Elliott Viney
Clive Wainwright
I.R. Watson
Prof W. Waugh
Ralph B. Weller
Andrew Wells
Juliet West
R.C. White
Richard J.S. Wilcock
D.F. Whitton
Richard Wildman
Gil Williams
Martin Williams
T.G. Williams
Elizabeth Williamson
Peter and Jenny Willis
J. Wisdom
P. Woodfield
G.A. Worsley
James D. Young
Anna Zaharova